INTELLIGENCE:
POLICY
AND PROCESS

Also of Interest

† *Nuclear Strategy, Arms Control, and the Future,* edited by P. Edward Haley, David M. Keithly, and Jack Merritt

† *International Security Yearbook 1984/85,* edited by Barry M. Blechman and Edward N. Luttwak

† *Defense Facts of Life: The Plans/Reality Mismatch,* Franklin C. Spinney, edited and with commentary by James Clay Thompson

Intelligence and Espionage: An Analytical Bibliography, George C. Constantinides

Estimating Intentions in Military and Political Intelligence, Frank J. Stech

Evaluating Intelligence Estimates of Soviet Naval Intentions, Frank J. Stech

The Military Intelligence Community, edited by Gerald W. Hopple and Bruce W. Watson

Bibliography on Soviet Intelligence and Security Services, Raymond Rocca and John Dziak

Military Intelligence and the Universities: A Study of an Ambivalent Relationship, edited by Bruce W. Watson and Peter M. Dunn

The Craft of Intelligence, Allen Dulles

The U.S. Intelligence Community, Lyman Kirkpatrick

† *The CIA and the U.S. Intelligence System,* by Scott D. Breckinridge

† Available in hardcover and paperback

About the Book and Editors

This book is the first comprehensive and multidimensional discussion of intelligence on all important levels: its domestic and international environments, its major actors, and the political, societal, military, and governmental structures to which it must relate. Consequently, it focuses on policy as well as process—how intelligence perceives the present and anticipates the future, how it integrates both factual evidence and psychological factors, and how it fits the results of research into a complex domestic environment and a constantly shifting international context. In particular, the authors consider the management of the intelligence community in terms of both external and internal controls, methods to improve the intelligence process, the problems of intelligence failures, the management of uncertainty, the anticipation of strategic surprise and deception, counterintelligence, propaganda, and the role of intelligence in the arms race and in arms control. Finally, in clarifying the distinction between intelligence as fundamentally a research activity and intelligence as a covert action, the authors consider the role of intelligence in a democratic society, including the importance of balancing the need for intelligence with the norms of an open society, the question of ethics in the use of intelligence, and the appropriate rules and procedures that enable the intelligence community to perform its functions without threatening the society it is charged to defend.

Major Alfred C. Maurer and Captain Marion D. Tunstall are assistant professors and Captain James M. Keagle is an associate professor of political science at the United States Air Force Academy.

INTELLIGENCE: POLICY AND PROCESS

edited by
Alfred C. Maurer
Marion D. Tunstall
and James M. Keagle

Westview Press / Boulder and London

Copyright © 1985 by Westview Press, Inc.
Chapter 11, "Congress, the Budget, and Intelligence" © 1985 by George Pickett

Published in 1985 in the United States of America by Westview Press, Inc.;
Frederick A. Praeger, Publisher; 5500 Central Avenue, Boulder, Colorado 80301

Library of Congress Cataloging in Publication Data
Intelligence—policy and process.
    Bibliography: p.
    Includes Index.
    1. Intelligence service—Addresses, essays, lectures.
I. Maurer, Alfred C.   II. Tunstall, Marion David.
III. Keagle, James M.
JF1525.I6I58   1985   327.1'2   85-5355
ISBN 0-8133-0029-0
ISBN 0-8133-0030-4 (pbk.)

Composition for this book was provided by the editors
Printed and bound in the United States of America

10   9   8   7   6   5   4   3   2   1

Contents

Part 2
Recurring Issues in Intelligence

Tables and Figures

Preface

This book is the culmination of an effort launched over a year and a half ago. It was born of a suggestion by Al Maurer that was subsequently developed, sharpened, and enriched by contributions from Dave Tunstall and Jim Keagle. In this final form it represents the end product of a substantive and editorial collective effort that included the planning and conduct of a major national conference, "Intelligence Policy and Process," held at the U.S. Air Force Academy in June 1984. As editors, we note with deep appreciation the contributions of the many academics and practitioners who attended our conference. Many of their papers are included herein for the focus and depth they bring to our conceptual framework. In addition, we have consciously attempted to include articles with a wide range of viewpoints about controversial topics. We do not agree with all of these views, but fairness demands that they be heard. We are confident that this text will serve not only as a beginning for learning about the relationship of intelligence and the policy process but, equally important, as a launching point for future research into this interesting and dynamic field.

The editors would like to thank all those who assisted them in the completion of this project. In particular, thanks are due to Nelson Drew and Mark Ewig, who were invaluable in helping to get the project off the ground. Our thanks also to the Department of Political Science at the Air Force Academy for the research time to complete the project and to the Dean of the Faculty and Air Force Intelligence for the financial backing that enabled us to hold the conference and type the book. The editors would also like to acknowledge the many individuals in the Department of Political Science, at NCR Corporation, and at Westview Press whose contributions to both the conference and the book helped make this project a reality.

We would like to acknowledge the professionalism and skill of Barbara Mikita, who typed the many drafts of the manuscript, and Kay Schneider, who typed the final version.

Finally, we would also like to thank our wives and children for their patience and understanding during the lengthy and arduous preparation of this text.

Alfred C. Maurer
Marion D. Tunstall
James M. Keagle

GENERAL INTRODUCTION: THE CONCEPTUAL FRAMEWORK

INTELLIGENCE: A DEFINITION AND APPROACH

We define intelligence as refined information desired or used by the state to further its national goals or policies. Intelligence concerns the means by which such information is collected, the translation of that raw information through interpretation or analysis based in both technical exploitation and a more subjective "expertise," and the possible utilization of that refined information—intelligence—by the policymaker. Intelligence may be collected overtly from a myriad of open sources. Success in this area is dependent on the "openness" of the society; yet it must also be noted that all societies will strive to protect essential elements of information deemed vital to their security. It is necessary, therefore, to collect information within closed societies or in contexts of denial and, as a consequence, to engage in clandestine activities to obtain the needed information. Although even aboveboard information must be interpreted and analyzed, we will focus more of our attention here on the less easily acquired "vital" information.

Intelligence also implies the protection of one's own information from acquisition by others. In counterintelligence procedures, collection, analysis, and action may be focused externally, but they also must have a significant internal focus. Although it is difficult to distinguish clearly between domestic and foreign activities in the task of counterintelligence, questions of acceptable behavior and legitimate activities often have answers that vary according to the side of the border on which they are conducted. As a result, the line between domestic and foreign intelligence can at times be blurred. It is not the purpose of this book to define that line exactly, but rather to note its existence and the possible problems that may arise therefrom.

Finally, we must acknowledge that intelligence also implies both functions and environment. That is, it is at once both a series of activities—tasking, collecting, analyzing, producing, and consuming—as well as a procedure that takes place within a framework of bureaucracies, personalities, and the larger governmental policy environment. Thus, to discuss intelligence in terms of success or failure, professionalism or amateur status, we must have a sense of how well it performs these functions and also of the impact of the individual, and of bureaucratic, societal, and other influences on performance.

In this light, we have chosen to address issues of intelligence both as a process and in relation to policy, utilizing a level of analysis model.[1] Ideally, we would place a high priority both on the accuracy of description associated with this model and on the completeness of the description. The model should also offer the explanatory power to discern interrelationships between its elements as well as an acceptable level of prediction.

Although we accept as valid the simplicity of the international/domestic distinction made by J. David Singer,[2] our primary focus is on the interactions within the "black box"; as a consequence, we must turn more to a specific and detailed examination of the domestic variables. We seek to learn more about the relationship between intelligence politics and policy, but we must move below the level of the state as rational actor to discover it. Our expected gain is a much fuller explanation of behavior, but the cost becomes that of dealing with the tangled web of interrelations between the subordinate levels. The state is a subsystem of the larger international system as well as a system unto itself; as such, its actions should be explainable in terms of the behavior shaped by its subsystems.

One problem immediately suggested by the adoption of the levels-of-analysis approach is the number of units needed to provide the desired adequacy of description, explanation, and prediction. As noted, Singer advocates two, whereas Kenneth Waltz argues for three, Robert North six, and James Rosenau five, although the latter seeks to explain domestic variables accounting for external behavior. At heart, the levels-of-analysis approach posits multiple causation and poses the questions of relative degree of importance and of the cost of increased complexity caused by adding another level to the framework. Certainly, no solution is without its cost either in terms of oversimplification or overcomplication. Acknowledging this difficulty, we have chosen to focus on the fuller, perhaps more complicated solution of six levels.

We are not engaged here in pretheorization as suggested by Rosenau.[3] On the contrary, our intention is to use the levels of analysis more as a means of approaching the problem of the relationship between intelligence politics and policy. Rather than endeavoring to assess the relative potency and completeness of explanation offered by each level, we are plowing what we see to be preliminary furrows. It is for the reader inspired by the problems suggested by this effort to launch into the subsequent effort to assign relative weight to the various levels of analysis. At present, we are capable only of talking in generalities that require much more research. We can but note the impact of an individual analyst or consumer, of the bureaucratic norms that influence what will sell. Concomitantly, there remains much to be done in evaluating the significant factors within each level—in examining the variables within as well as between. As Rosenau points out, with given levels one can suggest 120 different pretheories as preliminary fodder. Beyond this remain the problems of situational change and comparative analysis. The pretheory task of asserting causal priorities, then, is beyond the scope of this work effort. For now, we will direct our efforts to the United States, with an understanding of the intellectual distance yet to be traveled. Levels of analysis serve only as a crude frame of reference; hence we realize the need to develop shared concepts, to build pretheories, to accumulate materials, to challenge or prove those pretheories, and, in general, to move toward a greater possibility of theory building. The study of intelligence as more than a collection of anecdotes has only recently been born, yet preliminary faltering steps are being taken.

Our analysis begins with the international system as a first level. Acknowledging the realities of interdependent or penetrated systems, we nevertheless argue the utility of focusing on the international system both as an arena shaping options and influencing perceptions and as a stage upon which various parts are played. At this level the international system assumes an importance distinct from and beyond its composite parts. It is a context that encompasses various influences on foreign policy and intelligence goals and actions. In examining these influences, we tend to discuss the system in terms of the configuration of the relation of forces—or in terms of heterogeneity, or homogeneity—and in contrast with transnational activities.[4] More frequently, the international system is distinguished in terms of the former and, in particular, in terms of some hierarchy representing perceived distribution of power between states. In this connection, we are concerned with concepts of dominance: large and small state status, relative interests and influence, the hostilities and alliances that result from the configuration, and the degree of systemic stability. This level of analysis permits examination of international relations as a whole. At the same time, it contains a certain assumption of uniform behavior as well as a degree of determinism, whereby the actors are essentially black boxed.

Much of the conflict in the scholarly discussion of the level of analysis pertaining to the international system centers on the issues of (1) the degree to which the conduct of states must be described in terms other than the relation of forces (i.e., the nature of the states and their objectives), and (2) the proper explanations of the distribution of power. In this context, whether we describe the world as bipolar, multipolar, bimultipolar, or interdependent matters greatly. According to purists such as Waltz, power distribution results in a clear hierarchy of states within the system, and it becomes inaccurate and misleading to discuss power in terms of distribution across subunits or component measures as do the interdependence theorists. We contend that power is usefully discussed in terms of component elements and that relative distributions are important. Our perspective of the international system is one of bimultipolarity, in that we recognize the reality of two major blocs of actors but allow, to some extent in military, and particularly in other measures of power, a lesser concentration of power.

At the next level, we address the relations between states, cognizant of but apart from the concepts of the first level. It is a level at once concerned with the competition of the rival actors amidst the present currents of technological change and extension of the theater. It is the level of strategic and diplomatic conduct—the realm of machtpolitik for some and power moderated by principles, ideals, and morality for others. It is separated from the domestic by many scholars in terms of the actors and the relative stakes involved, and by others in terms of the absence of "authoritative allocations of values."[5] More recently it is a level marked by the admission of other nonstate actors, with all the concomitant problems of accommodation and the implications for theoretical arguments of sovereign integrity and penetrated systems. It is the level given to competition defined in terms of vital and essential national interests and, from time to time, in terms of survival. It is the level at which we must take note of the impact of ideology as well as strategic and diplomatic conduct. It is the level of a loose society which tolerates recourse to armed conflict. It is also the level of the chief competition or cooperation between the major international actions.

This competition or cooperation is in part a reflection of the relative configuration of forces defining the international system. It is also reflective of geopolitics and ideologies. Here or at this level the impact of state A upon B and of B on A must be considered. Impact may be measured not only in terms of raw force but of influence and perceptions. Rosenau defines this level in terms of any "non-human aspects of a society's external environment or any actions occurring abroad that condition or otherwise influence the choices made by its officials."[6] We must consider the asymmetries of power and its impact on the relations between states. The state, which is higher in Waltz's terms in the hierarchy of the international system, may define its interests and concerns in a more encompassing fashion. By the same token, at least in the abstract, the state found in the elevated position may be expected to have relatively greater means of effecting its wishes or realizing its goals. Accepting the impact of interdependence theorists and realities, we must note, however, that asymmetries should not be seen as cumulatively uniform and that assessments of relation and power, acknowledging the objections of Waltz, must take cognizance of the different capabilities that can be mobilized in defense of interests in varying situations. This is not to deny, but simply to moderate, the impact of large/small, powerful/weak arguments.

At this level, the decisionmakers evaluating the international system, the place of their state in it, and their interests and objectives recognize the true indeterminacy of the environment and the absolute need for information to enable them to better formulate, anticipate, and react. It must first be recognized that the definition of interests and assumptions of possible objectives are often structured by the position of the state in the hierarchy of the system. Thus the higher the state in the relative configuration of power, the more expansive the scope of its concern and the greater the information it may require. Even in the context of interdependence theory, with its asymmetries of dependence, there can be a recognition of a relative need for the state found less dependent to have greater information and, hence, better grounds to utilize the asymmetry to its advantage.

On the other hand, it may also be argued that the "less dependent" state or the state found higher on the hierarchy may be better able to collect the information deemed essential to its security and other crucial interests. It may have greater intelligence resources or more sophisticated technology to apply to the tasks. It may certainly be expected to collect more effectively the vital information on capabilities such as troop counts, weaponry, general economic or demographic data, and so forth. However, the facility of collection is a function as much of sophistication as of the openness of the society.

There should be little contention with the assertion that it is easier to collect in open societies such as our own than in closed societies such as the Soviet Union. Yet even in an open society only an approximation of perfect information is possible.

It is questionable that a relatively higher status or lesser dependence will always guarantee a better performance at the perhaps more vital intelligence tasks of gathering and analyzing information or intentions. Although higher status may be accompanied by greater educational or technical sophistication, giving the ability to put better-trained analysts on a problem or to apply computer technology for data bases or projections, it is still no guarantee of the ability to ascertain the "intent" of the mind or minds in charge of a targeted country or concern. It is in the realm of intentions that perhaps the greatest indeterminacy is to be found, for one can only make assumptions about the binding effect of roles, institutions, government, and society. Although we are not asserting the primacy of the individual, we are acknowledging the most indeterminate factor, that of the impact of the decisionmaker.

Our next level, the societal one, defines the nongovernmental aspects of a state that affect choices and behavior in the international realm. The societal level may be defined in terms as basic as the elements of capability—that is, geographic size, location, resource base, level of education, and industrialization. It may also be defined in more abstract terms, such as the degree of national unity, strength of national will, or quality of leadership. It is these accumulated factors that determine the place of the state in the system and, when mobilized in behalf of a policy interest or objective, may yield power in international relations. Such elements, in tandem, impact on the relative ability of a state both to afford and to implement the collection, analysis, and production of intelligence. Finally, and most important from our present perspective, this level may be defined in terms of the major value orientations and operational modes of the society.

Derived specifically from the perspective of Western democratic society are certain abstract norms of acceptable practice in the international environment and within the society. Part of the struggle in any democratic society is to balance these abstractions with political reality. The task of defining acceptable or tolerable compromises or trade-offs is a continuous one. In practice, democracies have yielded some principles more easily than others, particularly in the area of international relations. Still, there are limits, as the committee headed by Frank Church asserted, later executive orders stipulated, and the more recent flare-up over the psychological operations manual for the Nicaraguan Contras verified. Western democracies have been even more protective of principles in the domestic environment. However, even in this environment there are variations in the solution to the dilemma of national security versus acceptable measures to accomplish it—variations that may also reflect relative levels of perceived crisis. For a key example, one need only note the contrast between the Official Secrets Act of the United Kingdom and our own lack of such provisions. Certainly the principles of democratic society have a distinct influence on external objectives and action, but they are equally important in the assertions of the primary functions and proper relationships of the intelligence community within the domestic system.

At this still broad level of analysis, we may conclude, as Godson does,[7] that the acceptable practices and limits to intelligence within non-Western and totalitarian states are significantly different. He contends that the non-Western and totalitarian states direct most of their intelligence systems against their own societies first, and only then against external concerns. In addition, there is a greater freedom in the methods and fewer limitations on the ends for which intelligence may be employed. Furthermore, particularly in totalitarian states, a continually high level of emphasis on intelligence can be seen as vital to their survival in war and peace, though the Soviets draw a finer line between the two.

Why does a <u>democratic</u> state need intelligence? In an age that has experienced both a communications revolution and an information explosion, the idea that knowledge is power should not be hard to understand or justify. We believe that to be successful in its foreign policy, a nation—whether democratic, autocratic, or totalitarian—needs accurate political, economic, and military intelligence regarding its rivals, its competitors, its enemies, and—yes—even its friends. This gathering of intelligence, in and of itself, cannot be a moral anathema to a state merely because that state happens to be a democracy. There are, however, legitimate questions concerning how that intelligence is obtained. We have already pointed to the moral objection, with the answer that one cannot—or perhaps should not—hold the state to the same moral standard as that required of the individual. But is there a moral standard other than the law of necessity to which one can hold the state? Do Americans, like Hegel, believe that reason of state is reason enough or, like Machiavelli, that the state should at least appear to act in accord with high moral standards? Perhaps the letter of the Constitution, vague as it is, may be that standard. Certainly Americans who hold each of these views can be found, and at least part of the controversy in intelligence results from a lack of shared assumptions about the state and its morality. Clearly, reading the local newspapers in a friendly country to discover governmental intentions cannot raise much moral objection, but stealing state secrets for the same purpose could. Intelligence can be inappropriate for a state if means inappropriate to that state are used. Most people would agree, at an intuitive level at least, that inappropriate means have certainly been used by the U.S. intelligence community in the past, despite the inability of the United States to agree exactly about what is appropriate and what is not. In any case, do such inappropriate activities constitute just cause for dismantling the intelligence services, or are they the responsibility of those charged with controlling those services? Perhaps the real issue is not intelligence itself, after all, but rather the control and uses of intelligence.

Beyond the questions of propriety and embarrassment, intelligence services can be dangerous to their own governments in another, perhaps far more serious way. Through misinformation (whatever its source, be it deliberate effort or bureaucratic incompetence), conspiracy, or simply pursuit of their own institutional goals instead of the goals of the government as a whole, intelligence services can pose a real danger to the well-being of any political system. Accordingly, Herbert Scoville has argued that there is little value in the products

of military and economic intelligence, and some value in foreign political intelligence and that, on balance, when considering the risks involved, perhaps we could do with only a defensive counterintelligence function.

But that is not the view of the editors of this book. We have assumed, for the reasons just outlined, that a democratic state in the modern world, no less than any other type of state, needs an intelligence system. We recognize that there are potential dangers inherent in any such system, but that the gathering, processing, and production of intelligence is a vital function for any state.

At the governmental level, we focus on the structure of the government--on the organizations, institutions, procedures, and relationships between the various elements. In this connection, we step down one level from society and note, in the case of the United States, the workings of a "democratic" government within a broader democratic society. We are concerned specifically with those aspects of structure that may enhance or inhibit the actions of the state both internally and externally. We also note the impact of formally imposed (sometimes constitutional) restrictions as well as those that may rise informally. At this level, we note that electoral judgment, principles of accountability, and participation vary with the type of government. We also note the structural shadings that yield different end results within each type.

This level encompasses a number of concerns in the relationship between intelligence and policy. In a broad sense, the structural problem in the United States involves the putting together of forces that allow movement from the systemically preferred conservatism. In this process, intelligence becomes a source of information, a bureaucratic ally, and a subject of focus. At the level of government, we are at once concerned with the formal lines of authority running from the executive through the large bureaucracies that represent the community and with the reality of the <u>concept</u> of community. In the chapters that follow the mechanisms of executive control at this level are examined in addition to the structural impediments to that control. How specific is executive tasking, and what degree of flexibility do the community elements retain in determining what is important? It is at this level that the organization of the community becomes important. Here, too, we note the bureaucratic realities of organizational decentralization and of the ensuing rivalries over budgets, resources, manpower, and that most vital of bureaucratic assets--a focus for the decisionmaker's attention. We are concerned with the influence of this competition within the community in terms of its impact on both the quantity and quality of the intelligence produced. In what ways do the structural realities influence the gathering, processing, and production of intelligence? What is the impact of bureaucratic struggle on the intelligence product produced by any one bureaucracy? Are there organizational benefits derived from the dual-hatting of the director of the Central Intelligence Agency? Has the community become entangled in its own webs of protection, webs that impede good intelligence? Are the competitive analyses that arise from decentralization good or bad, and, concomitantly, are the attempts at compromising these analyses useful or harmful? What are the objectives and possibilities associated with the various executive plans for reorganization? Do any hold promise for better management and a more efficient process? The structures represent certain executive and bureaucratic realities that lie at the heart of the relationship between intelligence and policy.

It has been particularly clear since the 1970s that the structural realities include much more than just the executive branch. The sharing of power between executive and legislative branches is a constitutionally established structural feature of our government that has applied to the intelligence community since its national inception in 1947. More important, the relationship between the executive and legislative branches with regard to intelligence has undergone significant change since the Church and Pike committees met and reported their findings on intelligence. A previously limited legislative interest and involvement in intelligence has been replaced by an activist role representative of a broader change in executive-legislative relations in the post-Vietnam, post-Watergate era. This change has altered the structural realities of the intelligence process perhaps more significantly than any other since 1947. The battle has been pitched not only in terms of bureaucratic preserves, dollars, and other resources, but also in terms of control, appropriate activities, and executive-legislative turf battles. It is significant that this battle continues with no final resolution clearly in sight; moreover, from the perspective of constitutional checks and balances, a static resolution is not very likely.

At the next level of analysis, our focus turns to the roles occupied by the myriad members of the intelligence and policy community. Later in the book, we will consider the behavior of various actions generated by the place they occupy and likely to occur regardless of the occupant. We will also examine the institutional perspectives or concerns that constitute the context of any job--namely, the "socialization" that results from the occupancy of a given role and the equally important expectations and perceptions of others that frame the role. At this level we also take consideration of the small group that constitutes the immediate environment of the decisionmaker or actor and its influence on both the role and the occupant.

Perhaps Thomas Hughes best summed up this level of intelligence in his work The Fate of Facts in a World of Men. Noting that individuals will "react to facts and ideas according to their substantive responsibilities. . . " and in relation to "their rank and role. . . their place on the pyramid of specificity and generality,"[8] he discussed intelligence roles in terms of the butcher (as current analyst), the baker (as estimator), and intelligence maker (as the manager). To these examples we could easily add the people who set requirements, and those who collect information as well as the variety of consumers who round out the roles of interest in the relations of intelligence and policy. Each of these roles exists simultaneously within its own special preserve and the larger environments of the higher levels of analysis. Each is shaped by systemic governmental and institutional norms that not only guide behavior but also provide definitions of good intelligence, lay out "acceptable" mechanisms, establish reference points for job performance and success, define expertise and professionalism, and constrain the exercise of individualism. Roles are the boxes into which the system attempts to fit its members. Perspective and performance, expectations and constraints, vary both horizontally and vertically in any system, and although where one sits may not causally determine what one sees or says, it often is of extreme importance.

As we have noted, the intelligence "community" is a decentralized organization, and within each of its component parts are many roles to be filled. Thus, at one level one expects a difference between actors depending upon which "community" element provides employment. The Defense Intelligence Agency (DIA), the Central Intelligence Agency (CIA), the Intelligence and Research (INR) branch, and the others should be expected to have neither the same view of the proper distribution of resources or priorities nor the same end product. Similarly, those filling different functional roles within each of these agencies should not be expected to have the same perspective of the relative importance of their contributions as those in other functional tasks. We must also note at this level that these functional and institutional differences can result in cross pressures on the individuals who may share job perspectives with one set of actions and yet be divided by institutional rivalries. For example, it remains a vital question as to whether the director of the CIA can really be an objective director of the intelligence community and, hence, whether such a channel can provide the "best" intelligence for the executive. At the consumer level, we must be concerned with the number of filters, the number of different perspectives or interpretations, the structural battles, the elements of time and attention, and, most important, the role expectations and opportunities for leadership.

From this perspective we must realize that intelligence is a mass of information refined—and, in some cases, unrefined—flowing both throughout the community and toward the top of the system. It is not a single product; rather, it reflects the bureaucratic perspectives and interests of its producers. To some extent, our system loads the process in favor of the CIA, a fact that aggravates the rivalry. The structural factors may, however, be overcome by the realities of small-group relations, with one element gaining favor because of a personal relationship that benefits its position. The very disorganization of the "community" allows for the vagaries. At the same time, as Hughes notes,[9] intelligence reflects the perspectives of the current, estimative, and management tasks and therefore will be differently defined by each. Our system is biased in favor of the short, dramatic bursts of current intelligence benefiting the "butchers" over the estimators or "bakers" and imposing on the intelligence makers the task of trying to ensure quality intelligence and maximum utilization of the product, by brokering within and outside of the agency and community. The consumer, faced with a flood of information, must find a way to control the flow, to pick from the flood what is considered vital, and, at times, to chart his or her own path beyond the neat packages of intelligence information provided by the competing elements of the community or by the perspectives within each. A basic question concerns the extent to which the roles contribute to or impede the production and use of intelligence and help to determine that which is "good."

Our final level of analysis pertains to the individual. At this level we are concerned with the unique characteristics that individuals bring to their roles—that is, with the background, talents, expertise, and values of the requirement setters, collectors, analysts, managers, and consumers. Here, we are at the most disaggregated level, the level furthest removed from the external behavior of the state. We seek to examine the unique contributions or perceptions brought to intelligence and policy by the individual. Intelligence priorities are set, collections made, analysis conducted, reports produced, the process managed and the products consumed by people acting in roles, through bureaucracies and structures, within a society and in the context of a larger system. Information is received by individuals, and they interpret it in light of their own perspectives, values, and experience. The amount of information received and the relative prioritization of the information as well as the time spent on examining it also reflect the influence of the individual. Individual preferences and personal feelings regarding information and its sources are also important at this level. Neither the facts nor the process of interpretation, the reporting nor the usage, are conducted in a vacuum, and the individual level is the most basic point at which to begin an examination of the relationship between intelligence and policy.

Interesting personal-background values and preferences can also provide the context for other actions, and these may become even more important as we move higher within the structure in which a given actor is found. Actors may believe themselves to be more or less informed or more or less in need of information; they may be more or less willing to be content with the intelligence products received. Long years of experience may close the windows of receptivity to new or contrary information. A decisionmaker may demand consensus or welcome controversy, may desire information to guide or reinforce a particular decision. By the same token, the individual preference—particularly that of the executive—will have some influence on the what, how, and when of information presentation as well as on the manner in which the information is received. Henry Kissinger was well known in the community for insisting on raw rather than digested data, all the while contending, explicitly or not, that he was his own best analyst. Such factors raise important questions concerning not just the shaping of intelligence products to receive the best reception but, more seriously, of tailoring (rather than educating). More significant, they raise the issue of the extent to which the predispositions of the actor color receptivity—particularly at higher levels, where such predispositions result in the rejection of intelligence not in compliance with one's view of the "real" world. At this level we can understand "failures" in relation not only to the usual perception of the intelligence community's error but also to the refusal of the policymaker to be informed. Although policy failure often exhibits important bureaucratic, governmental, and other overtones, individual predispositions toward reconfirmation or tolerance for contrary information are also key. At issue is the extent to which it is proper or possible for intelligence to inform, educate, or persuade the decisionmaker.

INTELLIGENCE AND POLICY

The questions of the relationship of intelligence to the policy process are the foci of the rest of the book. We began this effort with a general definition and functional description. The levels of analysis challenge us to attempt a more complete examination. From the general and formal viewpoint, intelligence should gather and process information in an objective and somewhat mechanical fashion. It should be at once uninterested in policy options and capable of providing a completeness of information precluding surprise as often as possible. In its objectivity, intelligence should not only inform but also correct and educate the decisionmaker. The intelligence community can best serve the state through a policy neutrality and, in keeping with the U.S. perspective, would likely serve even more effectively if it were more coherently and centrally organized.

In light of the preceding questions suggested by the levels-of-analysis approach and the following examinations, the reality of the formal perspective must be called into question. The reality is more akin to that suggested by Hughes as "intelligence in search of some policy to influence and policy in search of some intelligence for support."[10] In the political world, the process of developing intelligence is not as objective and mechanical as the formal interpretation suggests—nor is the consumer as rational. The relationship is not unidirectional, and "good" intelligence is subject to many definitions.

From the beginning, the policymaker influences intelligence as he or she sets priorities, establishes interests, and defines receptivity most often in broad generalities form. Objectively speaking, although intelligence should inform in the fullest fashion and the generalized frameworks do leave some room for telling the policymaker what he or she should know, there are limitations stated, perceived, and acted upon that give some shape to intelligence. However vast the sea of intelligence, the policymaker still remains relatively free to be selective and to base decisions on other sources of information or even on "gut feeling" and to deny the intelligence community such information. The community becomes engaged in a struggle for success frequently measured in terms of favorable attention with relevance established by the decisionmaker. Reaching downward and reflecting structural realities, useful intelligence often becomes measured in terms of brevity, timeliness, and packaging. Contrary to the purely rational perspective, the decisionmaker may pay more attention to such information than to longer, perhaps more balanced, presentations of varying interpretations of facts and possible outcomes. As a consequence, the institutions involved become more attuned to such presentations, although internal battles may continue over the effort to reconcile the objective with the practical requirements. As one moves through the respective levels, it becomes equally obvious that personal relationships or perspectives may inflate the value of one interpretation over another. It remains a truism that facts may be variously interpreted, organized, and presented—that there is no simple truth, but rather many views from which one can be selected or from which a potentially less accurate compromise can be directed. As an aside it may be suggested that in such an environment, competitive interpretations may be as close to the objective norm as we can reach. The demands placed upon the intelligence community are great and the rewards are often uncertain.

The interrelationship between intelligence and policy is a complex web composed of several levels of human, group, governmental, and societal influences. The abstract concept of a complete separation of policy and intelligence is unrealistic. It is a question not of noninvolvement but of the proper balance of relations such that intelligence can still inform, educate, and provide information supporting but also contradicting policy. The relationship is not unidirectional, but it must be acknowledged that the degree and type of relationship are largely dependent upon the consumers. The decisionmaker cannot function without information but does remain able to be relatively selective in the refiners or refinements of it. Evaluated in such terms, success or failure cannot be laid solely at the doorsteps of the various intelligence producers but, rather, must take full cognizance of the uses and misuses of the products of intelligence and of the complicated interrelationships among its various levels.

The task of prioritizing or rank-ordering these levels and thereby beginning the development of a pretheory, including explanation of the intelligence/policy interface, is the challenge for future plowmen. Here, we attempt the first breaking of the soil.

PLAN OF THE BOOK

We have divided this book into two parts. The first four sections, in Part One, examine the nature of the intelligence community as viewed from the perspectives of the framework already defined. In the three sections of Part Two, we seek to explore three issues of the uses of intelligence in the United States. We analyze the uses to which policymakers put intelligence, in addition to certain of the specific tasks given to intelligence agencies that have caused problems in the recent past. Some activities, such as covert action, are considered by some to be outside the intelligence function altogether.

NOTES

1. J. David Singer, "The Levels of Analysis Problem in International Relations," in James N. Rosenau, International Politics and Foreign Policy (New York: Free Press, 1969), pp. 21-22.
2. Ibid., pp. 22-28
3. See James N. Rosenau, "Theories and Pretheories of Foreign Policy," in The Scientific Study of Foreign Policy, rev. ed. (New York: Nichols, 1980).
4. Ramon Aron, Peace and War: A Theory of International Relations (New York: Doubleday, 1966), pp. 94-111.
5. David Easton developed this widely accepted definition of politics in his The Political System (New York: Alfred A. Knopf, 1960).
6. Rosenau, The Scientific Study of Foreign Policy, p. 129.
7. Roy Godson, ed., Intelligence Requirements for the 1980's: Elements of Intelligence (Washington, D.C.: National Strategy Information Center, 1983), p. 5.
8. Thomas L. Hughes, The Fate of Facts in a World of Men, (New York: Foreign Policy Association, Headline Series No. 233, 1976), pp. 12-13.
9. Ibid., pp. 36-61.
10. Ibid., p. 6.

PART 1

Theory and Practice of Intelligence

INTERNATIONAL POLITICS AND THE
FUNCTION OF INTELLIGENCE

In this section we consider the nature of the international system and the intelligence requirements and capabilities of the states operating within it. The chapters contained herein mix two perspectives. First, there is the system defined in terms of a configuration of power, a reality shaping or influencing the perceived needs of the states and delimiting their abilities to accomplish their objectives. Second, there is the perspective of international relations, of the actions of state A and its ability to influence B, of the definition of state interests in an arena of conflict characterized by the lack of any authoritative allocator of values. We acknowledge, as do our authors, that perceptions of reality are equally important at these two levels and that intelligence must provide information as much on the "hard" countables as on the intangibles of intention and perceptions of other actors. At these levels, we must understand that factors and measures of power as well as the relations of states, while demonstrating consistency, remain mutable. The task of this section is to define the nature of the present system and the interactions of the states within it as they impact on the relationship of intelligence and policy, particularly from the perspective of the United States.

As previously noted, the editors of this text define the present international system as characterized by bimultipolarity. We recognize the reality of the two major blocs of actors defined in terms of systemic hierarchy, but we also acknowledge a wider distribution of relative power within that hierarchy defined in terms of concepts of "interdependence." At the state level, we may perceive the state as the actor described by Graham Allison's unitary, rational model. The state as the primary actor may be viewed as an abstraction, and its definition of interests, policy formulation, and intelligence processes defined not in terms of the interaction of component parts but within the framework of the state as decisionmaker. The state, as J. David Singer argues, becomes a "goal-seeking organism which exhibits purposive behavior."[1]

At the system level, we may discuss determinants of behavior with an assumption at the state level of cost-benefit analysis, an awareness of and influence from the external environment, and a choice between alternatives that the state then consciously strives to realize. To the extent that the state is considered an abstraction, one need not be concerned with what goes on inside.

However, the question arises as to the acceptability of this reification. Singer points out that a state may be seen as a "group of individuals operating within an institutional framework."[2] It is these individuals who are influenced by the externals, by their perceptions of the international system and the interaction of states. It is the actions of individuals within the structure of the state that define the interests and shape the policy by which intelligence tasks are assigned and finished products consumed. One may retain the perspective of a state as synergistic actor without moving completely to an organic concept of the entity. The model of the unitary actor may satisfy the need for simplification and be a starting point for explanation of continuity or consistency in the behavior of the states, ignoring the differences and stressing systemic "objective" influences. However, explanation may be equally served by an emphasis on the role of perception of those same factors and by an analysis that recognizes that collective internal behavior as well as the policy that results therefrom. The problem at these levels of analysis and others that may be posited involves the maintenance of discipline, for although the levels are related, they are not essentially additive and should not be freely interchanged.

Roger Hilsman launches our study with a paper that discusses the problem of intelligence from several perspectives. He begins with a definition of intelligence as both factual information and knowledge. By the former, he implies those more readily accessible and collectible bits of information as well as the means by which they are gathered. Intelligence as knowledge involves interpretation and "prediction"—in short, a recognition of the indeterminacy of the international environment and the possible conflicting interpretations that may result. Hilsman prefers to describe the international system not with respect to polarity but in terms of a focus on relative power, goals, and motivations. Although he recognizes systemic influences and the utility of the model of the state as rational-actor, Hilsman opts for an analytical view that stresses the importance of the internal political process in explaining the behavior of states and, in particular, the intelligence/policy relationship.

The remaining chapters in this section deal with the state from the perspective of a "group of individuals operating within an institutional framework." As such, they do not mesh with the definition of the state as a unitary actor. Neither do they mesh completely with one of the subunit levels of analysis. As Kenneth Waltz argues, the state is a container and these chapters are concerned both with the container and the contents therein.[3] We include these elements at this point because they are descriptive of intelligence and policy and their relationships at a more general level. Although they are not couched as comparative studies nor do they purport to provide general rules of state behavior, they do suggest important themes and questions that can stand as a guide to the study of the relationships between intelligence and politics in other states.

Harry Ransom sets out to explore the relationship between intelligence policy and partisan politics. Examining the development of the U.S. intelligence community from World War II on, Ransom discusses the concepts that gave rise to a standard of nonpartisanship, a corollary of the concept of separation of the intelligence and policy processes. He then traces the development of a breakdown in this standard--a recent breakdown wrought primarily by presidents--who came to view the leadership of the community as partisan staff and, as a consequence, voided the principle of independence. It is important to note that the presence or absence of some fundamental agreements about the role and independence of the intelligence actors will facilitate or inhibit the performance of an intelligence community as a source of information, education, advice, or support. For the United States and other states it is not a question of absolutes but one of conditions that maximize the relative independence and proper functioning of the intelligence arm.

Mark Lowenthal addresses the concept of "intelligence failure" from a case-study approach and concludes that the term is overused and misapplied. He asserts that the state wishes to avoid "surprise" and places responsibility for that avoidance upon the shoulders of its intelligence functionaries. Failure is not solely ascribed to the inability of the community to discover "all"; it is also deemed to result from the state's allocation of resources, from its level of technological development, and, fundamentally, from the clarity of (or lack of same in) its definition of national interests. Intelligence failure is costly for any state, but it must be understood as the occasional result of the indeterminacy of the environment and the imperfection of man. Even a major actor, such as the United States with its "global interests," cannot always dedicate equal attention to everything; in the process of prioritization, it may well miss some future problem. As Lowenthal concludes, intelligence will never be as effective as we might wish, for neither the states themselves nor their servants are omniscient.

Finally, Hans Heymann notes that in any society, it may be difficult to separate the intelligence function from that of policymaking. He takes contention with the assertion that to be of utility intelligence must be separated from and immune to policy currents; he also recognizes that the tension between the two is characteristic of many states. Arguing from the "state as individuals in institutional framework" perspective, Heymann concludes that the policymakers are neither unified and rational in perspective nor merely content with "objective" information. There remains a love-hate relationship in which intelligence may not be able—or perhaps should not try—to change.

Certainly it can be argued that states will strive to maximize the realization or protection of their national interests; that these interests are defined in terms of a careful calculation of potential costs and benefits; that the alternatives chosen in defining and attempting to realize or protect these interests are selected only after the fullest rational consideration based on maximum information inclusive of the reaction of the affected states has been given; that all states will attempt to deny others information deemed vital to their own interests or to the realization of that of others; and that all states behave similarly and in accordance with the freedoms allowed by their positions within the international system. It should be clear, however, that for most states it is a difficult exercise of limited utility to adhere to the discipline of this abstraction, particularly in relation to the realities of the intelligence/policy interface.

18

NOTES

1. J. David Singer, "The Levels of Analysis Problem in International Relations," in James N. Rosenau, ed., International Politics and Foreign Policy (New York: Free Press, 1969), p. 25.
2. Ibid., p. 27.
3. Kenneth N. Waltz, Man, the State and War (New York: Columbia University Press, 1959), pp. 80-81.

International Environment, the State, and Intelligence

Practitioners of the craft of intelligence since World War II have recognized that three factors, at least, interact to set the framework within which they must work—indeterminacy of international politics, the nature of the international environment, and the internal workings of the particular states. The first part of this chapter, which deals with indeterminacy, attempts to distinguish between intelligence as factual information on the one hand, and intelligence as interpretation and forecasting on the other. It concludes that the real problem of intelligence is one of interpretation and forecasting. The second part, concerning the nature of the international environment, disagrees with the traditional bipolar/multipolar thesis. The third part of the chapter addresses the internal workings of the various states.

Finally, as philosophers of science tell us that thinking is done in terms of conceptual models or theories, and if we are to improve not just our intelligence estimates but also our policies, it is to our conceptual models that we must look. Accordingly, the chapter concludes by examining two recent conceptual models of why states behave the way they do.

INTELLIGENCE AS FACTUAL INFORMATION

When intelligence is viewed as factual information, the most important sources are open documents, newspapers, radio broadcasts, and other media sources. The most vital factual information required for the invasion of North Africa in World War II, for example, concerned the nature of the harbors and beaches, the capacities of the road and rail networks, the loads the bridges could carry, the dimensions of the tunnels, and so on. Most of this information researchers obtained by working on old French engineering periodicals in the Library of Congress. If the criterion is factual information, it is probably no exaggeration to say that if the Kremlin was forced to choose between subverting the national security adviser to the president or taking a subscription to the New York Times, it would opt for the latter. The national security adviser deals with very high-level material, but the range of his knowledge is narrow. The Times does not contain as much high-level information, but the range of its coverage is enormous.

Other sources of intelligence as information are the "esoterics"--electronic intelligence, code-breaking, and reconnaissance vehicles such as the U-2. For certain kinds of information, the esoterics are fabulously effective. The U-2 is capable of distinguishing the two-inch white lines in a supermarket parking lot at an altitude of fifteen miles--a fantastic technical achievement.

On the other hand, many of the esoterics are not worth nearly so much as one might suppose. The United States broke the Japanese code in World War II with Magic, and the British broke the German code with Ultra. Now, the developments in computer technology make it easy for any nation taking routine precautions to prevent its codes from being broken at all. Even Magic prevented neither the United States from being surprised at Pearl Harbor nor the British--as we now know--from being surprised by the attack on Coventry. The information in the messages about Pearl Harbor and Coventry indicated that an attack was in the making, but it was not specific enough about either place or time.

Finally, intelligence as factual information consists of old-fashioned espionage, the stuff of spy-thriller fiction. In this area, experience shows that even though the "take" from a good espionage operation can sometimes be crucial, relatively little information is yielded through espionage and only rarely is it decisively important. The reasons are obvious: First, the placement and maintenance of agents in spots where they can gather decisive information are extraordinarily delicate and difficult tasks; second, communication with agents after they are in place without exposing them is an intricate and time-consuming process.[1]

A poignant example of the limited utility of espionage harks back to World War I. After years of unimaginably tense maneuvering, a French agent rose to the position, which he held throughout the war, of commissioner of field police in charge of the security of--a delicious irony--German General Headquarters. He had easy access to military information, but his continued existence was so precious to the French that they would risk his sending only information of paramount importance--mainly that concerning major offensives east or west. Contact was difficult, but even when the transmission was clear, his warnings of offensives arrived after the allies already knew, from air photos and interrogation of prisoners, all about the planned attack. In fact, only one offensive by either side in the entire war achieved surprise--Ludendorff's 1918 "soft-spot" offensive. In this case the allies did not learn of the attack from either air photos or prisoners--and the agent's warning arrived ten days after the offensive had begun.

Of course, espionage has had some successes. But these have been associated almost invariably with order-of-battle information on mass troop movements through occupied territory inhabited by "friendlies" or with technological developments. Rarely have espionage successes had to do with strategic or political information. An example of good espionage concerning order-of-battle information in World War I was the network of agents the British organized in Belgium to report on German military comings and goings. The casualty rate among the agents was horrendous, but the network did manage to get timely information back to England through the Netherlands; it should be added, however, that this would have been much, much more difficult if the Netherlands had not remained neutral.

INTELLIGENCE AS KNOWLEDGE

Intelligence as knowledge implies an interpretation and analysis of factual information and future prediction, including whether or not a particular policy is likely to accomplish the goal for which it is intended. High policy usually hinges on intelligence as knowledge. An example is U.S. policy toward Vietnam. In the Kennedy and Johnson administrations, two different views of the nature of the struggle in Vietnam were debated. One school of thought saw it as part of global communist expansionism. Although this analysis conceded that local, purely Vietnamese issues were also at work, it insisted that the Viet Cong movement was ultimately inspired by Moscow and Peking and that a communist victory would redound to their benefit strategically, economically, and politically. The policy implication flowing from this analysis was twofold. The first conclusion was that such an aggression could be met successfully only by military force. The second conclusion was that it must be met if the vital interests of the United States were to be preserved. Even failure, as Secretary of State Dean Rusk maintained, would at least teach the communist world that such aggression would be very costly.

The rival view did not deny that the leaders of the insurgency were bona fide communists and that Moscow and Peking gave it full support. They argued that the insurgency was more accurately described as an anticolonialist and essentially nationalist movement, feeding on social discontent in the south, whose leaders just happened to be members of the Communist party through an accident of history. This school asserted that the leaders were nationalists first and communists only second and conceded that a communist Vietnam would be politically troublesome to U.S. interests in Southeast Asia. Its proponents insisted that it would be no more than troublesome. The economic implications were minuscule. Strategically, Vietnam had little intrinsic importance. The Soviets would undoubtedly be given permission to use the port facilities as a base; however, as the proponents argued, Hanoi's demonstrated determination to remain independent of both Moscow and Peking ensured that the use would be limited. The policy that flowed from this analysis was fundamentally different. If the insurgency were a nationalist, anticolonialist movement, then sending foreign troops of any kind would be self-defeating. Foreign troops would recruit more peasants for the Viet Cong than they could possibly kill. As President Kennedy said, "In the final analysis, it is their war. They are the ones who have to win it or lose it. We can help them, we can give them equipment, we can send our men out there as advisors, but they have to win it, the people of South Vietnam."[2]

What is interesting and instructive in this example is that the debate took place not so much within the intelligence community as between two rival groups of policymakers. Intelligence as knowledge, in other words, is not the exclusive province of the intelligence community.

A similar debate continues over the central problem of our day--relations between the United States and the Soviet Union. It is a fact that the Soviet Union has been spending heavily on defense for the past fifteen years and that it has drawn even with the United States in most categories of defense and perhaps even ahead in others. The question remains: What is the reason that the Soviets have spent so much on defense? The secretary of defense, Caspar Weinberger, has publicly stated the reason: The Soviets have made this enormous effort because they are bent on "world domination." Marshal Shulman, senior Sovietologist to Cyrus Vance when he was secretary of state, has a different view. He concedes that there may be some Soviet leaders who still entertain such pipe dreams, but he argues that among the others there are a variety of motives including not only bureaucratic inertia but genuine fear. The policy that flows from Weinberger's analysis is a crash program of defense buildup. The policy that flows from Shulman's is a more modest effort in defense buildup combined with renewed political initiatives for arms control negotiations.

Let me stress, however, that these differences are not simple ones. Deciding who--Weinberger or Shulman--is the "good guy" and who is the "bad guy" is not really all that easy. If you have any doubt about this, consider the fact that even today a debate is going on as to the motive behind the Soviet deployment of nuclear missiles to Cuba.

So much, then, for the question of indeterminacy. My conclusion is that indeterminacy is caused not only by a lack of hard factual information, but, even more important, by the fact that the same set of facts can support quite different interpretations--and it is from interpretation that policy flows.

THE ENVIRONMENT

The nature of the international environment is the second factor setting the framework within which intelligence analysts must work. It is the interpretation that is key, and the same facts can support quite different interpretations. Since World War II, the starting point for most analyses of the international environment has been the concept of polarity. Is the international system bipolar, with the United States and the USSR at the two poles? Is it multipolar, with such middle powers as China, France, Germany, Great Britain, and Japan playing more important roles? Or is it some sort of mixture of these two, with some nonpolar elements to allow a role for the Third World?

I reject the concept of polarity, not because it fails to describe the power lineup with reasonable accuracy, but because it carries with it some deterministic baggage that confuses more than it helps. As an alternative, I would opt for a simple typology that focuses not just on relative power but also on goals and motivations. The types are (1) the United States/Soviet Union relationship, (2) the special case of China, (3) the industrialized nations who are largely allies, and (4) the countries of the Third World.

The United States/Soviet Union Relationship

Even though the world is no longer purely bipolar, the

relationship between the United States and the Soviet Union remains the single most important problem in international politics today. These two powers have the industrial strength, the population, and the skills to determine the world's fate. In 1831, Alexis de Tocqueville predicted that the Soviet Union and the United States would dominate the twentieth century—that "each of them seems marked by the will of Heaven to sway the destinies of half the globe." If Tocqueville could make that prediction in 1831, how much more confident can we be of such a prediction now that these two, and only these two, have the nuclear stockpiles and the delivery systems to destroy entire continents? No problem in international politics, no problem in U.S. foreign policy, no problem in intelligence is more important.

China

China is a special case. The differences that exist between China and the United States are similar to those between the United States and the Soviet Union—whether ideological, cultural, economic, or political. However, there are exactly these same differences between China and the Soviet Union. Further, although China has both nuclear and missile capabilities, they are not sufficient to threaten the heartland of either the United States or the Soviet Union. China understands these strategic facts, continually reminding the world that it is in fact an underdeveloped country. Accordingly, the threat it poses to each of the other two and its rivalry with them are regional, not global. It can project its power only in Asia, and its major motivation is to maintain both its independence and its influence in the Asian region.

The Allies

Like China, the industrialized middle powers of the world, largely allies of the United States, can exercise direct power in the pursuit of their interests only regionally. Their best hope of influencing the overall United States/Soviet Union strategic balance is by influencing one or the other of the superpowers. As a practical matter, this means influencing the United States. Their goal, first and foremost, is the avoidance of nuclear war while maintaining their independence. Once that goal seems secure, they will bend their efforts toward increasing their economic position, their regional influence, and finally their global influence by cultivating leverage against one or the other of the superpowers.

The Countries of the Third World

The dynamism that drives the Third World is neither socialism and the machinations of Moscow nor free enterprise and the machinations of the United States. It is the interaction of three forces: nationalism, modernization, and industrialization.

Probably the most striking thing that can be said about nationalism is how recent a phenomenon it is. If a careful and precise distinction is made between a sense of identity and the true phenomenon of nationalism, little evidence of nationalism can be found anywhere in the world earlier than two centuries ago, and some forms of nationalism are no older than two or three decades.

Nationalism, as we know it, began in the latter half of the eighteenth century in Western Europe. As good an estimate as any is 1789. A shared language and literature, shared history, culture, traditions, and religion, common territory and statehood—all these factors can facilitate the rise of nationalism, but they do not define it.

Exceptions can be found for each of these factors—Switzerland, for example. The mechanism by which nationalism develops in general has been most thoroughly described by Karl Deutsch.[3] It is sufficient to note here, that nationalism results from a process of communications in which political, economic, and social centers ("core areas," such as the Ile-de-France, in Deutsch's words) grow up and thereby serve various needs in the hinterlands, which in turn can benefit the centers. Both the leadership and the mass benefit; both share a stake in taking the process further.

The processes of reciprocal benefits and social communication link nationalism and the processes of modernization and industrialization. Historically, nationalism has gone hand in hand with the latter two. Its function has been to give precommercial, preindustrial peasant peoples a larger identity and to mobilize them for the tasks of industrialization. An incentive toward nationalism will become an incentive toward industrialization and modernization. The egalitarianism implicit in nationalism will lead nationalists to want to see the masses lifted from their poverty; the pride in the nation will lead them to want to see it strong and powerful. The nationalists will know—or will soon learn—that only industrialization can both give the nation strength and lift the people from poverty. In similar ways, an incentive toward industrialization will transform itself into an incentive toward nationalism.

The prospect for the Third World, then, is this: In each of the underdeveloped countries of the world, with only anachronistic exceptions, one or another leadership will eventually attempt to launch the country on a course of industrialization and modernization. In some cases, nationalism will be the major incentive for that effort. Where it is not, the leadership will sooner or later turn to nationalism as the handiest instrument available for mobilizing the populace for the industrialization effort. In some countries the traditional elites will be the ones to lead this march. Where they do not, they will be overthrown—by a middle class, by a communist revolution, or by a nationalist faction of the military, as has happened in so many countries of Asia, the Middle East, Africa, and Latin America. The leadership will need to industrialize to give their country the strength to take the place in the world that pride demands and to vindicate the humiliation of colonialism or of being so long left behind. They will need it to centralize sufficient power to make and carry out decisions in the name of the whole state. They will need it because the masses have seen or sensed the possibility of an end to poverty, sickness, degradation, and misery, and now demand the industrialization that brings about these dazzling gains, even though they may not understand the effort required. Where nationalism is not already vigorous and thriving, these leaders will inevitably be driven to create it. Nationalism is the instrument for accomplishing all the rest.

The implications of all this both for intelligence interpretation and for policy toward the Third World and the turbulence that will occur from these drives to nationalism and change are as profound as they are obvious.

THE INTERNAL WORKINGS OF STATES

Paradoxically, an examination of the internal workings of states permits better interpretation than an examination of the international environment or even the relations between states. It is in the internal workings of states that clues can be found to the motivations behind foreign policy action. It is interpretation that is key, and interpretation depends on the conceptual models used.

The question analysts ask is, Why do states behave the way they do? The conceptual model that most analysts have used has been a geopolitical, power-oriented, state model—what Graham Allison has termed the "Rational Unitary Actor" model.[4] The behavior of a state reflects purpose and intention. The action chosen is a calculated solution to a strategic problem. Explanation consists in showing what goal the government was pursuing when it acted and why the action was a reasonable choice. Policy consists in devising a counteraction that will alter the calculations of the adversary state so that it behaves in a way that is less harmful or threatening.

Although this classical, geopolitical, "Rational Unitary Actor" model is obviously a gross simplification of the real world, it has great utility. As Hans Morgenthau noted, it "provides for rational discipline in action and creates that astounding continuity in foreign policy which makes American, British, or Russian foreign policy appear as an intelligible, rational continuum . . . regardless of the different motives, preferences, and intellectual and moral qualities of successive statesmen." To the extent that the model works, you don't need to know anything about the leaders of a state. The czar of Russia will behave the same way as the chairman of the Communist Party of the Soviet Union. It doesn't really matter that one state was a monarchy and the other is a communist dictatorship—both behave the same way. Both sought a warm-water port, both tried to balance the powers of Europe, both tried to build a wall of buffer states between Russia and Europe.

The Political Process Model

In the last two decades, analysts asking why states behave the way they do have developed a different model—the political process model. Briefly stated, the political process model sees a number of different individuals and organizations involved in the policymaking process—that is, as rival power centers. Each of these power centers shares a commitment to state goals—power, prestige, survival—but the views of the exact nature of the goals and, even more often, the views about how to achieve them may vary widely among the centers. In addition, each power center also has goals of its own—the power and well-being of the organization and the success of the individual. The Air Force has Air Force goals as well as national goals. Secretary of State Alexander Haig had not only national goals but State Department goals and Alexander Haig goals as well.

Each power center also has power. Some centers have more power than others, and the power of each varies with the problem under consideration. The military has great power over weapons procurement; it has less but still considerable power with respect to questions of foreign policy that deal with national security, and it has very little power regarding questions of social welfare. The chief executive of most countries has more power than other power centers. Some of this power stems from constitutional prerogatives. But even more stems from political brokering: If he or she wishes, the chief executive can get involved in virtually any field of policy.

Different power centers attempt to build coalitions among like-minded power centers. They attempt to persuade each other; they bargain; they make mutual concessions; they logroll; they attempt to outmaneuver and to manipulate each other; and, at a certain point, they apply whatever naked power they can muster. Thus the result of a policy is often something that no power center really wanted, but a compromise that achieves a half a loaf for all. Neither is the resultant policy always completely logical or internally consistent.

Let me quote Graham Allison's description of the political process model, which he calls the "bureaucratic politics model":

> Government behavior can thus be understood . . . as outcomes of . . . bargaining games. In contrast with Model I [the Rational Actor Model] the bureaucratic politics model sees no unitary actor but rather many actors as players, who focus not on a single strategic issue but on many diverse intranational problems as well, in terms of no consistent set of strategic goals and objectives but rather various conceptions of national, organizational, and personal goals, making government decisions not by rational choice but by the pulling and hauling that is politics.
>
> Men share power. Men differ concerning what must be done. The differences matter. This milieu necessitates that policy be resolved by politics. What the nation does is sometimes the result of the triumph of one group committed to that course of action over other groups fighting for other alternatives, but more often the result of different groups pulling in different directions yielding an outcome distinct from what anyone intended. In either case, what moves the chess pieces is not simply the reasons which support a course of action, not the routines of organizations which enact an alternative, but the power and skill of proponents of the action in question.[5]

CONCLUSION

Intelligence is made necessary by the policy requirements of the state and the need for predictability. The effort to gain knowledge of the international environment and of the plans and activities of other actors is restricted not only by the complexities of the internal workings of the state but also by the condition of indeterminacy, which defines the international environment. States must decide not only what they must know but also how they will access such information. The answers to these questions will be determined largely by where the state finds itself placed in the hierarchy of power that defines the international system. As I have indicated, it may be most useful to focus on goals and motivations as well as relative power to develop a fuller appreciation of the definition of intelligence requirements. Relative power does not yield a sufficient understanding of why states behave as they do, nor does it reveal the motivations and objectives of the use of that power. The United States and other states must concern themselves not only with the relative power reflected in concepts of polarity, but also, and to an equal degree, with the motivations of other actors, their desires, and their objectives. It is only by taking such considerations into account that the interests, requirements, and resource allocations associated with intelligence can be properly managed.

NOTES

1. A fuller account, including sources, is given in my Strategic Intelligence and National Decisions (Glencoe, Ill.: Free Press, 1956, reprinted by the Greenwood Press in Westport, Conn., 1981).

2. Television interview with Walter Cronkite, September 2, 1963, in Hyannis Port, Mass.

3. Karl W. Deutsch, Nationalism and Social Communication: An Inquiry into the Foundations of Nationality (New York: MIT Press, 1953).

4. Graham T. Allison, Essence of Decision, Explaining the Cuban Missile Crisis (Boston: Little, Brown, 1971).

5. Ibid., pp. 144-45. See also Allison, The Politics of Policy Making in Defense and Foreign Affairs (New York: Harper & Row, 1971), pp. 14-15.

Intelligence and Partisan Politics

INTRODUCTION

The purpose of this chapter is to explore the relationship between intelligence policy (questions of intelligence organization, leadership, missions, functions, programs, and controls) and partisan politics in the United States. By partisan politics, I mean the process of interaction between the two major organized political groupings—Republicans and Democrats—as they contend with each other for power and policy determination.

Part of political reality is that the Central Intelligence Agency is an arm of the presidency that, in the American political culture, is normally a highly partisan office. Another part of the reality is the growing weakness of political parties that are approaching what Austin Ranney has termed a "no-party system." Nonetheless, knowledge is potential power—and, in politics, power is the central element. Accordingly, no way may exist to insulate the CIA from the impact of partisan politics. Yet, through most of its history since its founding in 1947, the CIA and its operations have been under a protective blanket of nonpartisanship. Indeed, bipartisanship has been the norm for intelligence policy most of the time. Some interesting questions thus arise: When does this nonpartisanship break down? Under what circumstances does a raison d'état principle protect the intelligence system from the slings and arrows of partisan conflict? What are the requisites for bipartisanship, and what incubates partisanship?

In seeking answers, my method will be a brief analytical summary of the historical experience since 1947 with regard to questions of intelligence leadership, policy, organization, and controls as they were addressed in the U.S. political and constitutional contexts.

What makes these questions so interesting and important? The primary answer is that intelligence may be an essential ingredient in making policy decisions. Furthermore, the covert-action arm is sometimes utilized for policy implementation. Therefore, it is important to understand the sources of leadership, policy, and organization of the intelligence system. We must be concerned with the relationship between perceived intelligence needs and "the internal workings of the state." We must be concerned also with the linkage of "external with internal policies." Put another way, presumably internal political—including <u>partisan</u>—realities affect the functions of intelligence just as much as do perceived external "realities." Our questions are, how and why?

THE BEGINNING YEARS

A proposal was made at the end of World War II that a central intelligence organization be created separate from the armed services and State Department. The proposal created a storm of bureaucratic controversy, but few signs of political partisanship were evident. Two years elapsed before a compromise truce settled an internecine bureaucratic war, and President Truman sent Congress his own proposal, which became the National Security Act of 1947. The larger issue at the time concerned armed forces "unification" and how much authority a secretary of defense should have. The proposed establishment of a central intelligence agency as part of this reorganization of the national security structure created little interparty conflict.

A few members of Congress expressed bipartisan concern about the possibility that the proposed central intelligence agency might become a domestic political police force (<u>Gestapo</u> was the term some used). This concern was met by the managers of the bill in the House and Senate, who stated explicitly that the proposed agency would operate overseas only, and would have no domestic security functions.

From 1947 to 1953, the formative years in the evolution of the new central intelligence system, at least the semblance of nonpartisanship prevailed because military professionals (Rear Admiral Roscoe Hillenkoetter and General Walter Bedell Smith) held these positions of intelligence leadership. Their appointments conveyed the impression that intelligence leadership and policy were above and beyond partisan politics. Intelligence was not a matter to be left to the politicians. Most important, however, was that a foreign policy consensus existed regarding the nature of the threat to national security and about the required response.

Very early in Dwight D. Eisenhower's first term as president, Allen W. Dulles became the first civilian to head the Central Intelligence Agency. Dulles was a Republican and had been the deputy director of the CIA since August 1951. His promotion at the beginning of the Eisenhower administration did not convey the impression of a party patronage handout. In 1947, Dulles had submitted testimony to Congress on the proposed central intelligence agency. He declared that "whoever takes the post of Director of Central Intelligence should make that his life's work." He strongly implied that a director should be completely removed from partisan politics—and prior armed service connections—and be expected, in his words, to " 'take the cloth' of the intelligence service." He may have had in mind something along the lines of the British model, whereby early heads of the British Secret Intelligence Service generally held long tenure.

During his tenure as director of Central Intelligence, Dulles had to deal with a Congress that much of the time was under Democratic party control. Although in those days Congress was anything but a vigorous intelligence watchdog, Dulles was required to practice a nonpartisan approach to intelligence policy and operations. This came naturally to him. When John F. Kennedy became president in 1961, he reluctantly asked Dulles to stay on as director. It took the disastrous Bay of Pigs in April 1961 to shake Kennedy's confidence in Dulles's leadership. Even then, Kennedy allowed some months to pass before replacing Dulles so as not to seem to be firing him.

In choosing a replacement for Dulles, President Kennedy selected John McCone, an active Republican, shipbuilder, and former chairman of the Atomic Energy Commission. While implicitly making a bipartisan gesture in the process, Kennedy was more interested in finding a tough-minded administrator than in making a symbolic statement of nonpartisanship. He may have been persuaded by talk that Dulles was all too casual an administrator and all too fascinated by the jiggery-pokery of covert action. The point is that political partisanship was clearly not a criterion for selection to the important position of director of Central Intelligence.

THE POST-ALLEN DULLES ERA

A small band of liberal Democrats led by Senator Eugene McCarthy opposed McCone's confirmation on the Senate floor, alleging that McCone was not an objective observer of the world scene. His record suggested to McCarthy and his allies that McCone was blindly anticommunist, intolerant of views dissenting from his own, and not the person best qualified to be the eyes and ears on world affairs for the president. The spirit of bipartisanship prevailed on the McCone nomination. Endorsed by the Democratic-controlled Senate Committee on Armed Services, McCone was confirmed as director of the CIA by a 71-12 vote. Ten Democrats cast negative votes. He served in the position until April 1965.

When Lyndon Johnson chose a director, he followed the Kennedy formula of seeking a person of demonstrated administrative skill rather than a sophisticated person knowledgeable about world affairs. Johnson had shown little interest in the intelligence apparatus up to this point. He nominated Vice-Admiral William F. Raborn, Jr., who had successfully managed the development of the Polaris sea-launched ballistic missile. His nomination was virtually uncontested; it had no partisan or policy implications, and he quickly gained Senate confirmation. Raborn served without distinction for a little more than a year. President Johnson nominated as his replacement a man whose qualifications were distinctly different from Raborn's. Notably, it was Richard Helms, also known as the "Man Who Kept the Secrets," who became the first professional intelligence person to be named to head the CIA. Arguably, Allen Dulles was to some degree an intelligence professional, but he was primarily a lawyer. Helms had spent most of his adult life as a CIA officer, and his appointment to the top position was certainly a symbol of nonpartisanship. When Richard M. Nixon became president, he was inclined to replace Helms, whom he associated with Georgetown liberals with whom Nixon felt ill at ease personally. So stated Henry Kissinger, who opposed Helms's removal because it "was dangerous to turn the CIA into a political plum whose Director would change with each new President."[1] Helms was the originator of the "honorable men" label that he wanted affixed to intelligence professionals. The idea was that one chooses as leaders persons one can trust, isolates them from the partisan struggles of the executive branch and Congress, and calls upon them for objective estimates of the situation and unquestioning obedience to orders from responsible political authority. As "honorable men" they would protect the secrets; serve constituted authority; keep careful watch on foreign adversaries; and participate when necessary in the "plausible denial" game, which protected politically accountable decisionmakers and required, on occasion, false or dissembling testimony, even to congressional committees. Helms could hold to this doctrine and try to practice its rules as long as the bipartisan spirit prevailed, but as director he often had to walk a political tightrope. When that spirit began to evaporate, he ultimately found himself in trouble, not in the partisan political arena but in the courts.[2] The rules and assumptions were changing in the late 1960s. The foundations of bipartisanship were eroding.

It may be that Richard Helms's nonpartisan stance eventually complicated his relationship with Richard Nixon. The president replaced him in February 1973 with James Schlesinger, whose ideological posture may have led Nixon to believe that this conservative former economics professor might prove to be more pliable, or at least more sympathetic. Schlesinger was skilled in the ways of Washington bureaucracy, having headed the Atomic Energy Commission. Later, he conducted a special study for the president on the organizational problems of the intelligence system. Schlesinger proved to be the most puritanical of CIA directors, ordering that an exhaustive confidential internal study be made of potential wrongdoing, past and present, including violations of the law or of the CIA's legislative charter. This study produced what came to be known as "The Family Jewels," a detailed report of a variety of irregular activities in which the agency had been engaged over the years. Schlesinger had served barely six months as director before he was named secretary of defense.

Nixon turned next to William E. Colby, another intelligence professional who, like Helms, had spent most of his adult life as a CIA officer—including service in Vietnam, where he headed the "Phoenix" program designed to destroy the Viet Cong substructure in South Vietnam. It was Colby's role in Vietnam that prompted thirteen senators to vote against his confirmation on August 1, 1973. But eighty-three voted in his favor. Colby bore the brunt of the furor that followed the leaking of major contents of the "Family Jewels" report to the New York Times in December 1974. He had been appointed by Nixon with no prior personal conversation with the president before assuming the directorship[3]—an appointment that might be categorized as the ultimate in nonpartisanship; alternatively, it could be seen as Nixon's symbolic disparagement of the importance of the CIA to him personally. When Nixon had tried to misuse the agency in his efforts to cover up the Watergate scandal, he was rebuffed. He may have unconsciously dismissed the agency as no longer useful or important to him.

THE YEARS OF EXPOSE AND DOUBT

Colby presided over the CIA during the major investigations of the agency by separate House and Senate committees and the special investigative commission headed by Vice-President Nelson Rockefeller. The latter limited its study to charges that the CIA had engaged in improper spying on Americans within the United States, a blatant violation of its legislative charter. Although a generally conservative group, the Rockefeller Commission approached its study in a nonpartisan manner. The abuses it was investigating carried back over several administrations, and it was not clear that either Republicans or Democrats could be blamed or could garner partisan advantage from disclosure of wrongdoing.

The same might also be said of the House and Senate Select Committees on Intelligence, which undertook comprehensive investigations in 1975-1976. The Senate Committee, chaired by Frank Church, centered heavily on misdeeds that occurred under Nixon, but its probe was by no means limited to past Republican administrations. The committee was set up to include a Republican as vice-chairman, thus symbolizing its bipartisan approach. The House Committee, chaired by Otis Pike, appeared somewhat more partisan; but in reality, its investigation, like that of the Senate, extended back into prior Democratic administrations. Neither committee's final report was characterized by partisanship. However, the House Committee became engaged in a bitter struggle over information with Secretary of State Henry Kissinger. At times, this conflict appeared to some to reveal an innate partisanship, but, for the most part, the issue remained one concerning the proper role and controls of a secret intelligence agency in a democracy and how accountability should be imposed on the political and intelligence leadership as well as the question of congressional intelligence oversight prerogatives. The conflicts in which the Pike Committee became embroiled turned out to have primarily an institutional focus (i.e., Congress versus the executive branch) rather than being a matter of partisan conflict. Partisanship did raise its head when it came to a vote in the House on whether or not to release the Pike Committee Report. The question was whether the House should release a report containing classified material until it "had been certified by the President as not containing information which would adversely affect the intelligence activities of the CIA." The vote on January 29, 1976, was 246-124 not to release the report. Of 121 Republicans voting, only 2 voted to release it. In this sense it was a partisan vote. In another sense it was a bipartisan action to withhold the Pike Report from public release.

President Gerald Ford eventually determined that Colby should be replaced as director. The administration felt that Colby had been overly cooperative with the democratically led members of Congress as they pursued their intelligence investigations. Earlier in his life, Colby had identified himself as a Democrat, and perhaps suspicions existed that he had been a bit too cozy with the majority party on Capitol Hill. Colby felt he was replaced because "I had not played the game during that turbulent year as a loyal member of the White House 'team.' "[4] In his memoirs, Gerald Ford denies this, saying that Colby had done a "splendid job" but that the agency, after all the turmoil, "needed a change at the top."[5] In this context, Colby's replacement had something of a partisan ring to it. George Bush, the newly nominated director, only a few years earlier had been chairman of the Republican National Committee, one of the most partisan jobs in the U.S. political system. In nominating Bush, President Ford apparently wanted to rebuild congressional confidence in the intelligence system and to establish better Capitol Hill/CIA relationships. In the furor over disclosures of CIA misdeeds, the agency had come close to losing its legitimacy, both within government and with the public. President Ford saw George Bush as a force for creating a new atmosphere. Certainly, the Ford administration did not want to be burdened with the CIA issue in the 1976 election; moreover, Colby was a symbol of the past CIA regimes. Bush's appointment contained partisan political overtones. No earlier director had quite so much partisan baggage nor had so outwardly displayed an ambition to be president.

IDEALISM TO THE FOREFRONT

President Jimmy Carter's election campaign in 1976 provides a benchmark for the injection of partisanship into the intelligence picture. In the first place, Carter campaigned on a "clean up the intelligence system" platform. Accordingly, covert action was to be permitted "only in the most compelling cases"; "assassination must be prohibited," "thorough Congressional oversight instituted," and "intelligence abuses corrected."[6] In a terse paragraph on intelligence, the Republican platform, somewhat defensively and ironically, pledged to "withstand partisan efforts to turn any part of our intelligence system into a political football. We will take every precaution to prevent the breakdown of security controls on sensitive intelligence information endangering the lives of officials abroad, or affecting the ability of the President to act expeditiously whenever legitimate foreign policy and defense needs require it."[7] President Ford had issued a revised executive order designed to prevent future intelligence abuses.[8] Carter implied that he would do even more to curb future intelligence abuses. As part of his larger strategy of running "against Washington," Carter also ran against the CIA. Carter rejected the notion that the United States had to choose between idealism and realism. "I was deeply troubled," Carter later wrote, "by the lies our people had been told . . . [and by] other embarrassing activities of our government, such as the CIA's role in plotting murder and other crimes."[9]

Carter became the first president to assume that the CIA directorship would change with the other top positions. Up to this point, the directorship of the CIA had not changed immediately with an incoming new administration. Carter treated the position in a manner similar to the Cabinet departments and, in effect, made a "political" nomination to replace Bush as CIA director. His choice was a politician, Theodore Sorensen, formerly a special assistant to President Kennedy and later heavily involved in New York state politics. Powerful conservative members of the Senate objected to the appointment for a variety of reasons. The apparent partisan nature of the appointment contributed to the provocation of major opposition. Carter, facing potential rejection of his nominee by the Senate, withdrew the nomination. He returned to the early practice of choosing as a replacement a professional armed service officer, Admiral Stansfield Turner, a distinguished career naval officer with little direct intelligence experience. The nomination of a naval officer carried the connotation of nonpartisanship, and Senate confirmation quickly followed. Carter subsequently issued an executive order[10] restricting the activities of the CIA in order to prevent past abuses, and he pushed unsuccessfully for a new legislative charter for the intelligence agencies. However, he attained no congressional consensus, and various charter efforts died aborning. As the Carter administration ended, Turner indicated that he might wish to continue in the position—but the Reagan administration had other ideas.

Carter had established the new precedent by immediately replacing CIA director Bush with Turner. President Reagan followed this precedent by making the most politically partisan nomination conceivable. For the post, he nominated the man who had been the Reagan-Bush national political campaign director for the 1980 election, William J. Casey. Casey was not without some intelligence experience. In World War II he had held an important position in the Office of Strategic Services in Europe. Later he had served on the President's Foreign Intelligence Advisory Board. However, the appointment's symbolism was unmistakable. Since intelligence had become a political issue, why not select an astute politician to manage it?

PARTISANSHIP AT ITS HEIGHT

Intelligence had become dramatically a partisan political issue in 1979, when the Republican National Committee condemned Democrats in Congress for weakening the intelligence system. Bill Brock, chairman of the Republican National Committee, indicted the Democrats for damaging the intelligence system, declaring that "the cumulative impact of these past few years has been harmful miscalculations, massive intelligence failures and setbacks in our foreign policy."[11] He disparaged as misguided President Carter's proposals for reorganizing intelligence, believing them likely to result in the politicization and bureaucratization of the intelligence community.

These partisan statements from the Republican National Committee chairman accompanied the release of a report by the Intelligence Subcommittee of the Republican National Committee Advisory Council on National Security and International Affairs. The implications of these statements and documents were that past attacks on the intelligence system had come primarily from Democrats and that such attacks had led to a serious deterioration of U.S. intelligence capabilities. The Republicans conceded that deterioration of the intelligence system had begun during the Nixon administration and had continued into the Ford administration. Even so, the subcommittee report argued, "it occurred primarily because of pressures and misguided initiatives of the Democratic-controlled Congress during those Administrations, and has continued and accelerated during the Carter Administration."[12] The report also stated that the intelligence community has been subjected to "debilitating political attacks which have harmed our national security."

In addition, the report catalogued the consequences of these alleged political attacks, for which the Democrats were held responsible:

- severe loss of morale in the intelligence agencies, made worse by wholesale firings under the Carter/Mondale administration;
- crippling of the intelligence community's effectiveness;
- confusion and uncertainty about the reliability of intelligence information;
- loss of public confidence in the intelligence system;
- reduced foreign confidence in the ability of U.S. intelligence to keep secrets;
- too much reliance on mechanized, technical processes and insufficient attention to human intelligence collection and analysis.

The consequences of these attacks, according to the report, had been " 'harmful' policy miscalculations, massive intelligence failures and setbacks in our foreign policy."[13]

This partisan document represents a landmark in the evolution of the U.S. intelligence system. Past policy and organizational disputes had been common. Here, for the first time, a national party committee had focused accountability for intelligence failure and poor administrative and policy judgment on the opposition party. Ironically, the Republican Intelligence Subcommittee preached the necessity both of structuring the U.S. intelligence system so as to separate it from "political influence" and of revising the leadership rules so that directors are appointed for fixed terms in order to guarantee their "political independence."[14] The further irony is that when the Republican candidate became president, his naming of William J. Casey as director of Central Intelligence was the most partisan appointment in the CIA's history.

The criticisms and reforms referred to earlier found their way into the 1980 Republican party platform, which contained an unprecedented nine paragraphs devoted to intelligence. These constituted a digest of the aforementioned Intelligence Subcommittee report. Passing reference was made to past intelligence agencies and promises were made to prevent future abuses, but the main emphasis was on rebuilding the intelligence system that allegedly had been damaged under the Democrats. The platform specifically asserted the need to repeal "ill-considered restrictions sponsored by the Democrats." The platform promised to remove these restrictions in order to have "the best intelligence capability in the world. Republicans pledge this for the United States."[15]

The Democrats shied away from the intelligence issue in their 1980 platform. In a general plank on national defense, the Democrats referred in one sentence to their intention to "further improve intelligence gathering and analysis,"[16] thereby clearly signaling that Democrats as well as Republicans perceived the public mood about intelligence to have changed in the five years since Watergate and the congressional investigations of intelligence. Ronald Reagan, as presidential candidate, was promising to "unleash" the CIA, and President Carter, in his 1980 State of the Union address, while endorsing the need for a comprehensive intelligence charter, was by then meekly speaking about the need to "tighten our controls on sensitive intelligence information [and] to remove unwarranted restraints on America's ability to collect intelligence."[17]

In sum, the Republicans in 1980 took an aggressively partisan stance; the Democrats retreated from their stridently reform position; and the independent party candidate, John Anderson, assumed the reform posture that the Democrats had held in 1976. Anderson's position was that intelligence activities should be sharply curtailed. He supported vigorous congressional oversight, insisted on prior notification of Congress on covert action, and took a dim view of the various versions of legislation resembling official secret legislation.

YEARS OF COUNTER-REFORM

In his first year in office, President Reagan was unable to build a consensus for most of his campaign promises about intelligence activities. The administration successfully sought sharp increases (estimated at 15-20 percent) in the CIA's budget, but it was less successful in amending the Freedom of Information Act to exempt the CIA, in obtaining some version of an official secrets act (protecting the identity of secret agents), and in removing some of the restrictions on domestic and foreign surveillance of American citizens. In June 1982, Reagan signed a bill making it a crime to disclose the name of a covert government intelligence agent, even if the information was obtained from published documents. This bill fulfilled one of Reagan's major campaign promises, but it was a measure adopted on June 10, 1982, with wide bipartisan support. The vote in the House was 315-32; in the Senate, 81-4.

Reagan's intelligence advisers spent much of their first year working on the draft of an executive order that would fulfill other aspects of his campaign promises with regard to easing the restrictions that Presidents Ford and Carter had placed on certain techniques of intelligence surveillance, particularly those related to domestic operations. Although the earliest drafts of new proposals remained confidential, leaks indicated that authority to use "intrusive techniques"--such as searches, physical surveillance, and infiltration of domestic organizations--was being considered. The balance between liberty and security was being rearranged as the Reagan administration responded to new perceptions of relations with the Soviet Union, new assessments of terrorist threats and the need for more vigorous control of the international narcotics trade, and a more alarmist view of pervasive efforts at espionage within the United States by the espionage services of unfriendly forces. Sharp and apparently bipartisan resistance to the radical removal of restrictions on intelligence operations emerged, and the original drafts were toned down in a number of respects.

Finally, on December 4, 1981, the president released his new executive order in its final form. This was Executive Order No. 12333, which broadened authority for intelligence agencies to collect data about certain Americans in this country and overseas. Civil libertarians protested the order but acknowledged that its toning down, forced apparently by the congressional intelligence committees, made it less objectionable than it would have been in its original form. Some conservatives suggested that the new order had been watered down too much and did not go far enough in "unleashing" the CIA. The main point, however, is that no clear partisan postures were visible on this issue. Republicans and Democrats could be found on both sides among those who supported the new rules or protested them. Clearly, the largest number of protesters were found among the Democrats. In issuing the new executive order, which represented the compromise version for "unleashing" the CIA, the president candidly admitted in a statement that the new rules were "consistent with my promise in the campaign [1980 election] to revitalize our nation's intelligence system."[18]

In sum, it is clear that various presidents have perceived the office of director of Central Intelligence in different ways. One can generalize two opposite "models" for the directorship:

1. a nonpartisan director who oversees the production of a politics-proof intelligence product and who conceives his office to be insulated from the political process, or

2. a director who views the world through ideologically tinted spectacles is subservient to the political leadership; and acts as an agent of the president in the conduct of covert action, including, if necessary, operations that violate domestic and international law.

CONCEPTUAL CONFUSION AND ORGANIZATIONAL DEFORMITIES

The record to date suggests that a lack of conceptual clarity about the structure and functions of intelligence has characterized the selection of directors of Central Intelligence. Perhaps the absence of a theory of intelligence has permitted the ill-advised marriage of intelligence collection-analysis-estimates with covert action, an issue of great controversy. This marriage has produced a structural confusion over roles, and it inevitably involved the directorship in policy and consequently in partisan politics. The director has performed as both "staff and line" simultaneously. A president who chooses to view the directorship as an office under his partisan control will normally be able to obtain Senate confirmation in keeping with the tradition that presidents are entitled to their choice. But such freedom of choice does not always happen, as shown in the case of President Carter's selection of Theodore Sorensen. The existing lack of conceptual clarity on the question of who should be director of Central Intelligence can threaten the legitimacy of the CIA.

It is perhaps naive to believe that the directorship, whatever its tenure, can be isolated from politics. Consider, in this connection, the following lengthy commentary from Thomas Powers, one of the most astute observers of the intelligence scene:

> [I]ntelligence is the most political of professions. In the United States, as in every other country, it is subject to endless attempts at meddling by every sort of special interest across the spectrum of domestic politics: by Republicans who want to blame the Democrats for "losing" China, Air Force generals who suspect CIA analysts are deliberately underestimating Russian bomber [or missile] production, liberals who think the CIA has a positive preference for right-wing military juntas, conservatives convinced that Castro never would have come to power if the

CIA weren't soft on Communism, State Department Arabists who think the Agency is blinded by the intimacy of its ties to Israel, Jewish organizations which are sure the CIA deliberately ignores a fundamental Arab intention to destroy Israel. The history of CIA can be written as a history of the attempts to politicize the Agency, some of them of appalling crudity, and more than a few successful.[19]

Powers is inaccurate in at least one respect: Intelligence in other nations is rarely subject to the degree of political harrassment that besets U.S. intelligence. Internal bureaucratic intelligence conflicts undoubtedly exist in other nations, shrouded by strict rules of secrecy that tend to protect the intelligence agencies from partisan or public interference in their operations. Official secrets legislation dampens media attention. Doubtless there are disadvantages as well as advantages associated with the agencies in other nations. Certainly their secrecy is more effectively guarded from media scrutiny. Furthermore, Powers may also have been wrong in saying that attempts to politicize the CIA were constant over its history, at least as far as partisan politics is concerned. For the most part, at least in the period between 1947 and 1968, a cold war consensus shielded the CIA from public and aggressive congressional scrutiny and provided the protective blanket of bipartisanship for intelligence operations.

Since 1968, questions of intelligence policy, leadership, and organization have been almost constantly a matter for public debate; hence CIA directors have lived in a political cauldron. The public and congressional mood has fluctuated in correlation with relations between the United States and the Soviet Union. At the height of détente, intelligence agencies were less favored in congressional, media, and public attitudes, and a substantial part of the secrecy protecting secret operations disappeared. This situation existed throughout most of the 1970s, which witnessed the winding down of the Vietnam War, the Watergate and intelligence scandals, and major efforts of intelligence reforms that placed new restrictions and oversight controls on intelligence. Then came the Soviet invasion of Afghanistan, the Iranian hostage crisis, the election of Ronald Reagan, and a renewed cold war posture.[20]

As earlier noted, the Republican party and Ronald Reagan made intelligence a major issue in 1980. This politicized the issue in a way that Jimmy Carter's campaign had not. The Republicans blamed the Democrats for weakening the intelligence system, and the appointment of William J. Casey as CIA director promised further politicization of the issue.

Such politicization has turned out to be the case. Casey's tenure as director has been embroiled in controversy from the start. His partisanship has barely been concealed. The president made him a member of the Cabinet, a move that seemed insensitive to concern over the policy/intelligence relationship. Under Casey's leadership, the CIA, instead of becoming the quiet, secret arm of government that was once its model, has been constantly in the headlines. Casey has appeared to be under almost constant investigation in connection with his private financial affairs. His relationship with the House and Senate intelligence oversight committees has been a stormy one. The fact that the Senate Intelligence Committee chairman was a fellow

Republican gave him little protection. That chairman, Senator Barry Goldwater, at one point called for Casey's resignation; at another point, he publicly chastised Casey for failing to keep the committee adequately informed.

U.S. policies and actions in Central America, particularly in the 1982-1984 period, provide the striking example of partisanship in action involving the Central Intelligence Agency and its leadership. The CIA had become an instrument of a policy for which no bipartisan consensus existed. In this circumstance, partisanship was inevitable; but it was partisanship American-style, meaning that the U.S. party system is one that commands less and less discipline from its affiliates, with most major policy decisions in Congress being made by coalitions combining like-minded members of both parties. Party discipline or not, the House Democratic leadership in 1982-1983 united in opposition to the Reagan administration's policy of giving secret aid to the Contras, a group of Nicaraguan rebels operating primarily from Honduras and attempting to overthrow the Nicaraguan left-wing Sandinista government. On two occasions in 1983, the House voted along party lines to suspend such aid. Perhaps the high point of party conflict in the House was the vote on the Boland-Zablocki amendment on October 20, 1983. Boland was chairman of the House Intelligence Committee, and Zablocki chaired the Foreign Affairs Committee. Their amendment prohibited the use of funds for the purpose of overthrowing the Nicaraguan government. The vote in favor of the amendment was 227-194, largely along party lines. In effect, the Democratic party members in the House were opposing covert operations in Central America, whereas the Republicans were favoring them. Only a handful in each party dissented from the official party position.

CONCLUSION

Looking back over the years since 1947, we must ask, How are we to answer the initial question of this chapter: To what extent has political partisanship been exhibited in intelligence policy? Several answers are possible. One is that partisanship determined by party affiliation has been subdued over much of the CIA's organizational lifetime. A strong foreign policy consensus, supporting cold war containment and all of the instruments assumed to be required, produced a bipartisan atmosphere with only an occasional exception concerning the CIA until the late 1960s. When the cold war consensus began to evaporate after 1968, intelligence policy and operations came under increasing scrutiny and criticism, but these remained for the most part bipartisan. In the process, however, the CIA lost its legitimacy, which can be sustained, perhaps, only in a period of strong foreign policy consensus. Efforts following the 1976 presidential election to reform the intelligence system so that it would conform to a more idealistic balance between security and liberty were only partly successful. The new cold war, declared by President Reagan after 1980, enjoyed only a limited foreign policy consensus. Meanwhile, Congress had claimed and gained a limited partnership role and now shared with the president the power to determine the nature and scope of covert actions conducted by the CIA. At the same time, William J. Casey, a Republican partisan, became the leader of the CIA during a period when bipartisanship was unlikely.

One major consequence was that in the fourth year of the Reagan administration, the mass media communicated an almost daily fare of disclosures and discussions of various "covert" operations, particularly with regard to such actions against the government of Nicaragua as CIA-directed mining of ports and territorial waters. In addition, the CIA and Congress were at odds about both "intelligence" policy and process. At times the conflict was partisan; at other times Congress was united in bipartisanship against the president. In protests that were symbolic because they were "non-binding," the Senate on April 10, 1984, and the House on April 12, adopted "sense of the Congress" resolutions prohibiting the use of U.S. funds to mine Nicaraguan harbors. The Senate vote was 84-12. Of the 12 no votes, only one was cast by a Democrat. The House vote was 281-111. Unlike their Senate Republican colleagues, the House GOP leadership fought the mining condemnation, which Minority Leader Robert H. Michel called a "non-binding media event."

All of which leads me to conclude that:

1. A prerequisite for the successful conduct of secret intelligence operations is a foreign policy on which the president, Congress, and the public are in substantial agreement.

2. The opposite conclusion is that covert action is not an efficacious instrument of foreign policy in the absence of foreign policy consensus--a conclusion that would seem to suggest, logically, that if the nation's vital interests are threatened in a region, say, Central America, the most effective action is the direct, open application of military force.

3. It seems clear that the system constructed in 1947 and evolving since then contains basic structural faults. A system that works reasonably well only when a strong foreign policy consensus exists is unsuitable for the U.S. constitutional framework. What are the possible remedies? They include the following.

4. The Central Intelligence Agency has had six directors in the past ten years. A fixed term for the director, such as ten years, seems wise and prudent, and it holds promise of insulating the position from partisan politics.

5. Also recommended is the establishment of the requirement that the director be a professional intelligence person, with an option of waiver of such requirement in special circumstances.

6. Radical organizational surgery that structurally removes the intelligence function from covert political action seems necessary to remove the CIA from politics.

7. Creation of a Joint Congressional Committee on Intelligence Oversight should replace the system of separate committees in the House and Senate.

EPILOGUE

The Central Intelligence Agency was born in an atmosphere of cold war, which generated a firm consensus on the nature of the threat to national security and the required response. Idealism yielded to the realism of power politics and the reality of 1947.

In such a crisis context, it was assumed that the executive

branch would dominate, that Congress would follow, and that intelligence oversight would be informal. "Trust in honorable men" and "plausible denial," as well as media cooperation in a high degree of secrecy for the secret instruments of policy, were the necessary compromises of an emergency situation.

This consensus and the accompanying bipartisanship persisted well into the 1960s. In 1961, President Kennedy proclaimed that no national security crisis in our history had been greater and no threat more imminent than the external capabilities and intentions of the Soviet Union. The prevailing consensus dampened partisanship with regard to the secret intelligence system.

Indeed, it would seem that the ethical standards of wartime had been adopted. Recall that in 1954 a Hoover Commission special task force on intelligence under General James Doolittle had declared:

It is now clear that we are facing an implacable enemy whose avowed objective is world domination by whatever means and at whatever cost. There are no rules in such a game. Hitherto accepted norms of human conduct do not apply. If the United States is to survive, long-standing concepts of "fair play" must be reconsidered. We must develop effective espionage and counterespionage services and must learn to subvert, sabotage and destroy our enemies by more clever, more sophisticated, and more effective methods than those used against us. It may become necessary that the American people be made acquainted with, understand, and support this fundamentally repugnant philosophy.[21]

However, the cold war consensus began to evaporate in the late 1960s, and such an amoral prescription came under serious questioning. A growing dissent manifested itself in partisanship. Most of the new foreign policy dissidents, demanding a return to idealism, were Democrats; but there was a handful of Republicans as well. In the process, the CIA began to lose its protective secrecy. Leaks and confessions abounded in published memoirs and books exposing past covert actions. The media abandoned their voluntarily accepted restraints. The legitimacy of the CIA came into question, particularly with respect to its clandestine operations.

Partisanship began to enter this realm of public policy, first under President Carter and subsequently under President Reagan. The partisanship can be attributed in large measure to the fact that the United States' foreign policy leaders were divided roughly evenly on important foreign policy issues. Surveying a sample of U.S. leaders, Holsti and Rosenau found in 1976, and in 1980, no consensus on the proposition that it is permissible to use the CIA to undermine hostile governments. By 1980, there was a 7-percent gain over 1976 in approval, but opinion remained sharply divided, with 56 percent approving and 43 percent disapproving of such use of the CIA.[22]

The existing structure, concepts, and practices of the CIA were established without adequate thought about how they would work when the foreign policy consensus disappeared. The history of U.S. foreign policy suggests that consensus is transitory. The readjustment of concepts and the reform of the structure in keeping with the proposals listed earlier constitute a sensible course of action.

In the final analysis, the efficacy and efficiency of a secret intelligence service will be greatly influenced by the degree of foreign policy consensus. Without a strong consensus, the U.S. constitutional and political process cannot adapt well to secret missions in an open society. Absent consensus, particularly in the context of structural deformities and intruding partisanship, the system will not work at all.

NOTES

1. Henry Kissinger, White House Years(Boston: Little, Brown, 1979), p. 36.
2. See Thomas Powers, The Man Who Kept the Secrets: Richard Helms and the CIA (New York: Alfred A. Knopf, 1979).
3. See William E. Colby, Honorable Men: My Life in the CIA, (New York: Simon and Schuster, 1973) p. 342-344.
4. Ibid., p. 14.
5. Gerald Ford, A Time to Heal (New York: Harper & Row, 1979), pp. 324-325.
6. Congressional Quarterly Almanac 1976, Washington, D.C., Congressional Quarterly Inc., p. 869.
7. Ibid., p. 915.
8. Executive Order No. 11905 (February 19, 1976).
9. Jimmy Carter, Keeping Faith: Memoirs of a President (New York: Bantam Books, 1982), p. 143.
10. Executive Order No. 12036 (January 26, 1978).
11. Republican National Committee, press release (August 6, 1979), p. 1.
12. Policy Paper of the Intelligence Subcommittee, Advisory Council on National Security and International Affairs, Republican National Committee (August 6, 1979), p. 1.
13. Ibid., p. 2.
14. Ibid., pp. 5-6.
15. See: Congressional Quarterly (July 19, 1980), p. 2051.
16. Congressional Quarterly (August 16, 1980), p. 2413.
17. Public Papers of the Presidents, Jimmy Carter: 1980-81 (Washington, D.C.: Government Printing Office, 1981), p. 198.
18. "Text of Reagan Statement on Order," New York Times (December 3, 1981), p. 11.
19. See Powers, The Man Who Kept the Secrets, pp. 57-58.
20. For a discussion of the relationship between domestic and foreign factors in intelligence policy, see Harry Howe Ransom, "Strategic Intelligence and Intermestic Politics," in Charles W. Kegley, Jr., and Eugene Wittkopf, Perspectives on American Foreign Policy: Selected Readings (New York: St. Martin's Press, 1983), pp. 299-319.
21. Final Report U.S. Senate Select Committee on Intelligence Activities, 94th Cong. 2 Sess., Book IV, April 23, 1976, pp. 52-53.
22. Ole R. Holsti and James N. Rosenau, American Leadership in World Affairs (Winchester, Mass.: Boston, Allen and Unwin, 1984), pp. 195-196.

3

MARK M. LOWENTHAL

The Burdensome Concept of Failure

INTRODUCTION

Napoleon died at St. Helena on May 5, 1821. Word of his death did not reach Paris until July. When it did, Talleyrand was at dinner with a friend. "What an event," she exclaimed. Talleyrand corrected her, saying, "It is no longer an event, Madame, it is news."[1]

Today such an occurrence would be more than an opportunity for a bon mot. Newspapers would cry out "intelligence failure," just as they did when intelligence reports of Soviet President Yuri Andropov's death failed to reach Washington until "more than nine hours . . . after tell-tale signs began appearing in Moscow."[2]

No other intelligence system operates as openly, or with as much legislative oversight, as does the U.S. intelligence community. Cries of "failure" appear again and again, often enough to lead the casual observer to believe that U.S. intelligence must be very poor indeed.   But can it really be that bad?   Would successive administrations and congressional overseers permit it?   Obviously not. Hence we are faced with an alternative conclusion, that the term intelligence failure is overused or at least misapplied.

It is the thesis of this chapter that the term has indeed become overused, and that it is actually a burden for the practitioners of intelligence analysis. The results can be far-reaching, insofar as this situation can undermine not only the confidence of intelligence consumers, overseers, and the public in intelligence but that of the producers as well. Part of the art of truly talented analysis is the ability to go beyond certain knowledge and to trust proven instincts. Occasionally, the analyst will be wrong. But a willingness to take such risks is undermined by fears of the accusation of "failure." No one wants intelligence that is brash and wrong; pusillanimous intelligence is not any better.

Intelligence failures are real; they have happened and they will happen again. We need to understand what constitutes a true intelligence failure, to understand the causes of these failures, to seek remedies for the causes, and to put the concept of intelligence failure in its proper perspective.

CASE STUDIES: THE ANATOMY OF INTELLIGENCE FAILURE

Government is theoretically an orderly process of handling the affairs of state. It requires planning and foresight. Buttressed by bureaucracies, it thrives on regularity and predictability. It stands to reason, therefore, that surprise is one of the great enemies of government—be it a sudden threat overseas or an unexpected drop in the economy. In the realm of national security affairs, we have created and tasked a wide array of intelligence agencies—some collectors, some analysts, some both—to bring their talents to bear on this very issue: eliminating surprise, especially that which can be most threatening to the security of the nation. This is an unenviable task, for, as Richard Betts has pointed out, surprise is inevitable.[3]

But is every case of successful surprise necessarily an intelligence failure? At a very basic level it is. But not every surprise will have equal ramifications. The attack on Pearl Harbor was a surprise of the most fundamental and threatening nature. The coup in Portugal in 1974, while a foreign policy problem for the United States, was obviously of a lesser magnitude.

What, then, constitutes an intelligence failure? To answer this question I have examined ten cases of so-called intelligence failure. Three of these involve surprise attack; one involves technological surprise. Most of the cases were suggested by the Final Report of the House Select Committee on Intelligence, 1975–1976 (also known as the Pike Committee), which exists only in its draft leaked version in the Village Voice.[4] The final case arises out of our greatest foreign policy trauma since Vietnam.

Several points are at issue in these cases: (1) What were the essential points of commonality and difference? (2) Where in the analytical or policy process did the failures occur? (3) How damaging were these failures? Is there significance in differences of magnitude?

Pearl Harbor, 1941

The Japanese attack on Pearl Harbor stands as a classic intelligence failure. What went wrong? Virtually everything.

Collection was the one bright spot. Not only had the Japanese diplomatic code been broken, but so had lesser codes. Other information came in from the U.S. Embassy in Tokyo, from Britain, and from public sources.[5] But this bountiful collection quickly went from asset to debit. There was too much information, a plethora of "noise" that drowned out the "signals." There was no central collection point at which the several strands could be put together; horizontal and vertical dissemination within the bureaucracy was irregular and haphazard. To this one must add analytical flaws, from the near-racist beliefs in Japanese inability to fly the kind of missions required to attack Pearl Harbor, to "mirror-imaging" at the policy level and below: Japan would never be so foolish as to precipitate a war with the United States.

Invasion of South Korea, 1950

In the case of the invasion of South Korea there appears to have been a significant gap between agreed national interests and contingencies of possible events. Although much was later made of Secretary of State Dean Acheson's speech of January 12, 1950, which excluded South Korea from the U.S. defense line in the Western Pacific as an unintentional signal to North Korea, this represented no change of policy. A year earlier General Douglas MacArthur had given a similar speech. In December 1949 President Harry Truman approved NSC 48/2, which, while allowing political, military, and economic aid to South Korea, again emphasized U.S. positions in Japan, the Ryukyus, and the Philippines.[6]

Nor were analysts or policymakers unaware of North Korean capabilities. It was clear that the North Koreans were capable of carrying out a successful invasion, but the likelihood of their doing so was uncertain or unlikely.[7]

U.S. intelligence did not appreciate that Kim Il Sung would change tactics in 1950. Thus, while reporting on capabilities was good, analysis of intentions was poor. But the two Koreas appeared to be an important intelligence target only after the fact. Until June 1950 there was widespread agreement in Washington as to South Korea's relatively low rank among U.S. interests. The very fact of invasion raised this priority, largely in keeping with the wider cause of avoiding a repetition of the 1930s (i.e., the Munich experience). Had someone assessing North Korean capabilities asked, "What if they do invade?" this gap would probably not have occurred.

Sputnik, 1957

The Soviet launching of Sputnik in October 1957 appeared as a major technological defeat for the United States. The Russians had stolen the march in an area where the United States was supposed to excel. What is interesting about the Sputnik case is that, in terms of intelligence, it was hardly a surprise. A National Intelligence Estimate (NIE) in 1956 predicted a Soviet capability to launch a satellite during 1957. In the spring of 1957 there was evidence of Soviet preparations for an ICBM launch. The Soviets claimed such a test in August 1957.[8]

Although in his memoirs President Dwight Eisenhower eschewed the concept of a "race" for space,[9] policymakers knew that the United States and the Soviet Union were proceeding on parallel courses in this area. Here was a case where the development of the capability actually signaled the intention. But U.S. policymakers failed to anticipate the tremendous public effect of a Soviet lead. Had they done so they would still have found themselves on the horns of an intelligence dilemma: Should the public be prepared for such an eventuality at the potential risk of exposing some intelligence sources and methods? In retrospect, one can imagine clear but not overly graphic statements that could have avoided the near-panic that Sputnik induced.

Cuba, 1962

The Cuban Missile Crisis is not commonly perceived as an intelligence failure. Indeed, it helped salvage the CIA after the debacle of the Bay of Pigs. However, as Wellington said of Waterloo, it was a close-run thing, such that the United States needed to act quickly before the Soviet missiles became operational.

Soviet strategic weapons began arriving in Cuba in July 1962, but the missiles were not discovered until October 14. The Soviets also mounted an apparently successful diplomatic deception campaign assuring U.S. policymakers, including President John Kennedy, that no offensive weapons would be placed in Cuba. U-2 flights in August and September did not pick up the missile sites. In the lead-up to the crisis, intelligence estimates consistently dismissed the likelihood that the Soviet Union would place missiles in Cuba. This action was seen as being too risky, even for the blustering Nikita Khrushchev, although Director of Central Intelligence (DCI) John McCone continually doubted these analyses. Moreover, there had been numerous reports of missiles in Cuba before 1962, all of them false.[10]

Additional reports from Cuba and renewed aerial photography then revealed the existence of the missile sites, leaving the United States sufficient time to secure their withdrawal before they became operational.

Roger Hilsman, director of the State Department's Bureau of Intelligence and Research during the crisis, argued in his memoirs that even accepting a failure in the imagination on the part of analysts of Soviet shipping, the missiles were probably found as soon as possible.[11] Technical collection difficulties notwithstanding, U.S. policymakers and analysts betrayed broader shortcomings.

Tet, 1968

Analyses of Tet inevitably drag one into the still murky order-of-battle controversy of late 1967.[12] But the inability to arrive at satisfactory estimates of enemy strength was not a cause of what went wrong; it was a symptom of a war that had already been overly quantified, and of a war whose popular support had waned significantly and needed buttressing. Indeed, it seems clear in retrospect that an enemy offensive was expected, although not necessarily one so widespread, so intense, or so militarily disastrous for the North Vietnamese and Viet Cong.[13]

Several factors appear to have been at work. First, the outcome of the intelligence analyses on the enemy order of battle did have political significance as a means of showing progress in the war. Although this may not have been a factor for all participants, or even one that changed the outcome, it did exist. Second, much like the Sputnik case, there appears to have been a choice between publicly acknowledging a likely event or waiting it out. In the Tet situation, waning government credibility may have been a factor militating against greater preoffensive acknowledgment, but it also served to heighten the sense of surprise. Third, as in Pearl Harbor, mirror-imaging took over. No U.S. commander would launch such a self-devastating offensive; why, then, would the enemy? The inability to see tremendous political gain even from a military defeat blinded analysts to enemy goals and decisions.

Czechoslovakia, 1968

As Soviet unease with the Dubcek reforms in Prague grew in 1968, it was apparent to U.S. policymakers that a Soviet invasion of Czechoslovakia was wholly within Soviet capabilities.[14] The only countervailing factor raised was that this Soviet action would risk the recently won agreement to open strategic arms control talks.[15]

Yet the actual execution of the invasion revealed intelligence problems for the United States. Certain Soviet combat units were "lost" by U.S. intelligence for two weeks in August. A "Rear Services Exercise," which allowed the Soviets to flesh out Class II and III divisions, was misinterpreted. Nor was there any advance warning of the invasion before President Lyndon Johnson was informed by the Soviet ambassador.[16]

To these must be added two other countervailing factors. First, beyond a general sympathy for the Dubcek government, the United States had neither precise national interest in Czechoslovakia nor any expectation that the Soviets would allow the reforms to proceed in what they felt to be dangerous directions. Second, as DCI Richard Helms informed his executive-branch overseers on the president's Foreign Intelligence Advisory Board, indications would have been better had the Soviet target been West Germany.[17] Under the self-protective shroud of the Warsaw Pact area, the Soviets enjoyed a certain operational freedom, especially in terms of U.S. intelligence, although significant questions remained about the United States' ability to see precursors of major Soviet military activity.

The Middle East War, 1973

The assumption that only military victory can achieve political aims returned to haunt policymakers in 1973. Analyses agreed that in any new war in the Middle East, Israel would win. Therefore, why would Egypt and Syria go to war?[18] Much that went wrong in the days before the Arab offensive resembles Pearl Harbor: false assumptions about the goals of other powers; excessive reliance on military capabilities as the mainspring of war and peace decisions; and a plethora of information that, again, drowned "signals" in "noise."[19] In retrospect, much seemed to turn on the surprising decisions of Anwar Sadat, whose subtlety and canniness were not yet appreciated in 1973. Even in a highly technological modern age, personality matters.

Portugal, 1974

One of the cases investigated by the Pike Committee was the coup in Portugal in 1974 that overthrew Marcelo Caetano, Antonio Salazar's successor, thereby ending a 48-year regime. The committee cited numerous indications of the growing alienation of the Portuguese military from the Caetano regime, as have other analysts.[20]

But aside from certain deep-rooted sociological causes stemming from the late 1950s, most of these indicators predated the coup by three or four months. Against that fact one must weigh DCI William Colby's statement that "Portugal had been such a backwater that in 1973 I suggested closing our station there."[21]

Three issues, at least, appear to have been crucial. First, there may have been deficiencies in collection by defense attachés in Lisbon, leading to insufficient information about the level of discontent in the Portuguese armed forces. But, here, the second factor intrudes. Lisbon was a backwater. Did perceptions of it, as such, lead to the posting of less aggressive intelligence officers? Such a self-inflicted reinforcement of initial weakness is not an impossibility. Third, intelligence agencies operate within resource constraints. Reasonable judgments as to priorities have to be made, and one's allies—or perhaps especially one's allies—are not likely to have as high a priority as hostile states or friendly states facing some sort of proximate threat. Portugal was simply not a high-priority intelligence target.

Cyprus, 1974

Based on the Pike Committee's summary of the events leading up to Greece's overthrow of the Makarios government on Cyprus and the subsequent Turkish invasion, it appears that most analysts were aware that the advent of General Demetrios Ioannides to power in Athens in November 1973 could lead to a confrontation over Cyprus. Policymakers and analysts appear to have been subject to repeated alarms between that time and the actual events of July 1974,[22] but the main flaws appear to have been the vigor with which U.S. warnings were passed to Ioannides and certain mixed signals from the United States, rather than inattention to a potential problem. Certain intelligence estimates did miss the imminence of the two key events--the Greek coup in Cyprus and the Turkish invasion--but U.S. intelligence had already categorized the first as possible and the second as likely, given the first.

There is a wide difference between knowing that something may happen and yet failing to prevent it, and not knowing it will happen at all. In the latter case, intelligence is seen to be a primary factor; in the former case, issues of policy decision and execution pertain.

Iran, 1978-1979

Given the foreign policy trauma in which they resulted, intelligence and events in Iran from the fall of the shah through the seizure of American hostages have already been extensively analyzed.[23] Collection was poor, but this was largely the result of imposed policy restrictions that forbade contact with opposition groups. At the same time, analysts seriously overstated support for the shah and underestimated the degree of dissatisfaction with his regime. Moreover, analyses that ran counter to a policy already reliant on Iran were not well received. Thus, the fall of the shah was not expected until his regime tottered to its conclusion.

These same problems exacerbated intelligence efforts during the Khomeini regime. Contacts obviously remained poor, despite the United States' efforts to improve them. The seizure of the U.S. Embassy on February 14, 1979, evidently failed to provide any sense of warning to policymakers. Nor did the policymakers themselves appreciate the inherent weakness of the Barzagan government, which now guaranteed the safety of Americans. Finally, the policymakers were aware that a second seizure of the embassy was possible should the ailing shah be allowed into the United States. But the size of the embassy staff remained large, and the shah was admitted.

It is difficult to extricate errors in intelligence from impeding policy factors in the case of Iran. Although the two areas necessarily overlap, in this case their interplay is too close to allow easy separation. Clearly, intelligence activities and performance were heavily influenced by policy preferences. But this fact does not serve to excuse intelligence: indeed, policy influence is something that intelligence managers and analysts should be able to avoid, or to protest loudly and vigorously.

ASSESSMENT

Table 3.1 offers a capsule summary of the ten cases discussed in this chapter. Certain points stand out as obvious and well known. Collection on capabilities is both an easier task and one that the United States does well; collection on intentions has always been more difficult. The mechanical aspects of intelligence, production, and dissemination have generally been successful since the inception of the modern intelligence community. Indeed, the only post-1947 case in which these standards may have been missed was Portugal, which had virtually no priority as an intelligence concern.

Certain points are less obvious:

1. Mirror-imaging was a factor in at least five cases (Pearl Harbor, Cuba, Tet, Czechoslovakia, and the Middle East War). Such mirror-imaging usually takes place at both the analytical and policy levels. Clearly there is an interplay here, but it is not possible to discern whether one level consistently leads the other in this. It does indicate the prevalence and pitfalls of "conventional wisdom."

2. Closely related to mirror-imaging, or perhaps a peculiarly American aspect of it, is the tendency to evaluate likely decisions by the probability of demonstrable military success, and the inability to appreciate that political aims can be achieved through unsuccessful military efforts (Tet, Middle East War). To a large degree, this reflects the traditional American bifurcation of peace and war into antithetical states rather than elements along the same continuum.

3. National interest matters. It helps determine intelligence priorities. In two cases (South Korea, Czechoslovakia), the United States had no agreed national interest, although in the case of South Korea this changed after the invasion. In a third case (Portugal), there did not appear to be any likelihood of a threat to U.S. interests, or alliance interests in this case, until a very short time before the events in question, thus giving Portugal a low intelligence priority.

4. Consumers (i.e., policymakers) matter. As noted, in five cases policymakers joined analysts in mirror-imaging. In the case of

TABLE 3.1: SUMMARY OF CASE STUDIES

Case	Collection	Evaluation/Analysis	Production	Dissemination	Effects of Policy	National Interest
Pearl Harbor	Fair to good, but decentralized	Poor. Underrating Japanese technical capabilities; mirror-imaging	Haphazard, uncoordinated	Poor	Mirror-imaging; no appreciation that deterrent is also a target	High. War and peace, effect on aid to Britain in Europe
South Korea	Good re North Korean capabilities; no certainty re likelihood	Limited, capabilities only; also a low priority	Standard	Standard	Absence of any sense of national interest beyond making South Korea self-sufficient	Evident only in reaction to invasion
Sputnik	Good re Soviet capabilities to launch ICBM, satellite	Good	Standard	Standard	Could public release of some intelligence have forestalled surprise?	Strategic threat to US; public competition with Soviets
Cuba	Poor up to mid-October; good thereafter	Poor to mid-October; mirror-imaging re Khrushchev; success of Soviet duplicity	Standard; good under pressure	Standard	Mirror-imaging, success of Soviet duplicity	Strategic threat to US
Tet	Fair to poor; large uncertainty re enemy order of battle	Better on likelihood of attack than on scope, intensity, etc. Mirror-imaging	Standard, but with controversy re enemy order of battle	Standard	Policy pressure to show progress in war. Could release of some intelligence have better prepared public vs. issue of credibility?	Domestic morale and support for war; readiness for enemy attack
Czechoslovakia	Poor; some Soviet units "lost" by US intelligence for two weeks	Limited; good on obvious Soviet capabilities; less capable re "if" or "when." Mirror-imaging re value of SALT to Soviets	Standard	Standard	Little, although some mirror-imaging re value of SALT to Soviets	None;
Mid East War	Technically good re troop movements	Poor re intentions; mirror-imaging re Sadat's willingness to risk losing war	Standard	Standard	Little, although some policymakers had interest in peace. Mirror-imaging	Interest in Israel; avoid U.S.—Soviet confrontation
Portugal	Poor	Poor; little done	Minimal	Minimal	Very low intelligence priority	Stability of ally; effects within NATO
Cyprus	Good	Good both on Ioannides' interest in Cyprus, and likely Turkish reaction	Adequate	Standard	Question of vigor of U.S. warnings to Greece and coordination of this effort	NATO solidarity
Iran	Poor; limited by policy	Poor, underrated opposition to Shah; influenced by policy preferences	Standard	Standard	Heavy influence re collection, re preferences	Friendly state, oil, regional stability

South Korea, also as noted, policymakers were responsible for not clarifying potential national interests in the event of a North Korean attack. In two cases (Sputnik, Tet), policymakers evidently had the option at least to deflate the effects of surprise by preparing the public for likely events, although always with some potential risk to sources and methods (Sputnik) or in the face of waning credibility (Tet). In one case (Cyprus), policymakers may not have acted with sufficient vigor after receiving warning. Finally, in another case (Iran), policy decisions very heavily affected intelligence collection and production. Thus, in nine of the ten cases policymakers played a significant role in the intelligence contribution or its net result.

Having said all that, I must now pose this question: Were these ten cases all intelligence failures? Pearl Harbor and the Middle East War certainly were; indeed, these two cases bear marked similarities. But Sputnik was not, although the public effect of the Soviet achievement could have been prevented. This was also true to a lesser extent in Tet, although here intelligence did miss the scope and magnitude of the enemy offensive. In South Korea and Portugal, and to some extent Czechoslovakia, priorities greatly affected performance. Although each of these latter cases exhibited intelligence shortcomings, none had large resources devoted to them. In Cuba, intelligence was late in detecting Soviet activity or intentions, but this problem was overcome with sufficient time to react successfully. Cyprus stands out more as a failure to clarify U.S. policy so as to forestall expected actions than as a failure to expect such eventualities. Finally, Iran appears to be a case in which policy decisions greatly and negatively affected intelligence utility and performance.

THE CONCEPT OF "INTELLIGENCE FAILURE"

We return again to the question: What constitutes an intelligence failure? The following definition is offered.

An intelligence failure is the inability of one or more parts of the intelligence process—collection, evaluation and analysis, production, dissemination—to produce timely, accurate intelligence on an issue or event of importance to national interests.

A number of variables are at play in this definition. First, the various parts of the intelligence process are interdependent. Poor collection undercuts evaluation and analysis, although there have been instances (such as McCone's continuing doubts about Cuba) in which intuitive judgments arose over and above poor collection or in the face of conventional wisdom.

Second, how timely? At best, soon enough to allow policymakers time to plan counteractions, if not to undertake them. In Cuba, and to some degree in Cyprus, the factor of timeliness ameliorated intelligence shortcomings.

Third, how accurate? But accuracy cannot be quantified. Intelligence should be accurate enough to lead to decisions that will preserve or advance national interests or the policies that stem from them. Accuracy, like timeliness, is also an important factor in building intelligence consumer confidence in the producers and their analyses.

Finally, are national interests clearly defined? Such clarity is unfortunately not always the case; in other instances, defined interests are not made clear either within the government or to other powers. This variable is often the most frustrating for intelligence producers because it is the one almost entirely out of their hands. Reluctant policymakers cannot be pushed to decide, nor can they always be relied upon to convey their decisions. None of these realizations will save intelligence producers, however, should policy be the victim of surprise. Finally, national interests may not be understood, or they may go unrealized until after something has gone awry, as was the case in South Korea. Samuel Johnson once said that the imminence of hanging tends to concentrate the mind. A threat, in other words, tends to clarify (and sometimes to exaggerate) one's interests.

The aforementioned variables notwithstanding, cases that do not meet these combined standards, or meet them for external reasons such as the role of policy, are not truly intelligence failures.

THE AMERICAN PREOCCUPATION WITH FAILURE

Defining what constitutes an intelligence failure and what does not still leaves open the issue as to why the United States seems to be preoccupied with this concept. I would argue that this American preoccupation has many causes. Some are governmental, some are geopolitical. Others lie deeper within the American psyche.

First, there is the inevitable tension within the intelligence producer/consumer relationship. As noted, when surprise occurs, the consumer feels that intelligence has let him or her down, even though in most cases the consumer probably played a role in the creation of the "failure."[24] One suggested solution would be a more rigorous typology (policy failure, analysis failure, technical warning failure) such that responsibility could be properly allocated. But, as conceded by Gerald W. Hopple, who made one such suggestion, this solution is not only simplistic but unrealistic as well.[25] No two analysts in a postmortem examination could be expected to agree entirely or to neatly pigeonhole each case. Indeed, the cases discussed earlier suggest that the interplay is so close as to make separation very difficult. Nonetheless, consumers expect to be warned and do not want to be surprised. When they are surprised, intelligence has "failed" them, regardless of the attention they devoted to the issue earlier or the priority they gave it in terms of tasking or resources. As Hopple points out, the very use of the term failure "implies that there is a culprit who should be punished."[26]

To some degree this perception on the part of consumers stems from a deeper American belief in perfection and perfectibility. Diverging slightly into psychology and sociology, I could refer to various examples of this preoccupation with perfection—the most obvious of which is the Preamble to the Constitution, which, in speaking of a "more perfect Union," fosters the belief that even perfection can be improved. I might also note the entire concept of a "New World" (i.e., one in which the mistakes of the Old World need not be repeated). Finally, I could point to our original national sport, baseball, which allows for the possibility of a "perfect" game. I know of no other team sport in which such "perfection" is possible; in all of the others, one can shut out the opposition, but one cannot reach perfection.

To these observations I must add that we are a problem-solving people. We are less interested in process than in results, and while a mistake might be tolerated, it best not be repeated.

When these attitudes are applied to intelligence, the effects can be dangerous. First, perfection in intelligence implies omniscience. Anything less constitutes a failure. Among the public at large, in the media, and among some consumers there exists an exaggerated view of what intelligence can know at any given time, or about any single event. No doubt this impression is deepened by the popular image of intelligence in fiction and movies—superspies, all-powerful agencies, fantastic technology, and mammoth computers. Second, the penchant for problem solving leads to a belief that ultimate truth or knowledge concerning human behavior is attainable, an idea prevalent in the social sciences in the 1950s but still a burden today.

The effects of these misperceptions are further fed by two other factors. In Marshall McLuhan's now hackneyed image of the global village, the ability to know "instantly" about events a world away feeds the impression that intelligence must be able to do the same, but in advance. The second factor is the scope of the United States' national interests. The United States is one of only two nations that must arguably have global intelligence collection and analysis because of its size, its power, its allies, its interests, its friends, and its enemies.[27] This requirement has nothing to do with imperialism or the idea of being a world policeman. But in an arena so large, priorities must be set to match resources, and, in so doing, some future troublespot could be overlooked. Without the expenditure of tremendous sums on intelligence, choices must be made; even with unlimited resources there might still be surprises.

Finally, part of the problem for U.S. intelligence lies in the history of intelligence since 1972. The attempt to use the CIA to stem Watergate, as well as the revelations of the intelligence investigations in 1975-1976, had a marked effect on the perception of intelligence. Intelligence not only got some things wrong; it also undertook some activities that undercut public support. To these contributors to negative perceptions of intelligence must be added two factors. The first concerns the hemorrhage of leaks that both benefits and plagues every administration and does little either to improve government or to help maintain public confidence. The second is the role of the media, given both its penchant for "investigative" reporting (a wonderful redundancy) and the normal simplification that is one of the media's necessities. In two minutes on the air, or in eight column inches, one would find it difficult to deal with the range of probable outcomes in an intelligence estimate. "Right or wrong" is a much simpler standard than "maybe" or "perhaps," although in fairness it must be noted that some intelligence consumers use the same standard.

For all of these reasons, then—intelligence producer/consumer tension, the belief in perfection and in problem solving, the belief in omniscience, the effect of global communications, the global scope of U.S. interests and responsibilities, the effects of intelligence investigations, the effect of government leaks, and the role played by the media—the concept of intelligence failure is overly large and overly burdensome.

CONCLUSIONS AND RECOMMENDATIONS

Each of the ten cases discussed in this chapter contain some aspects of intelligence failure, although it is difficult to characterize them all as failures per se, as we can Pearl Harbor or the Middle East War. Nonetheless, the legend of intelligence failure persists, and its effects can be harmful. How can this situation be remedied?

If we are to create a realistic standard for intelligence performance, much of the required change will be attitudinal in nature. Ironically, the very open nature of the U.S. government may be a key factor in effecting this change. Three groups can play a role in this process: the intelligence community and its policy masters, the overseers in Congress, and the media.

First, intelligence producers must be forthright about areas of uncertainty. Flagging such areas in advance can be critical—presuming that consumers understand the uncertainty, especially when capabilities are known but intentions are not. Consumers must appreciate the fact that uncertainty is inherent in intelligence. Producers would be very happy if they could speak with finality and certainty. The inability to do so is not a sign of failure.

Beyond this private adjustment, there is a public role to be played by the intelligence community, albeit a difficult one given that it will always appear self-serving—and, at some level, it is. Nevertheless, the intelligence community can be allowed occasionally to release data or analyses, as it sometimes does to Congress, to indicate areas of success. As Betts has pointed out, failures are glaring because they appear in isolation. Against the broader record they tend to shrink, although in the area of intelligence success often goes unnoticed because it isn't newsworthy as such.[28] I am not suggesting that the intelligence community release a report card or batting average at the end of each year ("We got 65 percent right, 35 percent wrong, up from 58-42 last year"). But the price of public support is evidence of success. I would argue that a few successes could be noted, without risk of sources and methods, and without necessarily going overboard.

The House and Senate committees that oversee intelligence can play a useful role in the reporting of success. Although they, too, have eschewed the notion of giving "report cards" to the intelligence community, the committees are perhaps in a better position than other actors to evaluate intelligence performance objectively, and to provide sound credit and criticism where it is due. Such feedback has been given in the past, as in the case of the Mariel refugees.[29] It could be done, as well, within the context of the committee's annual reports. The congressional committees have been supportive of the need for better intelligence. They are uniquely placed to help put failure (and success) in perspective without appearing to have become co-opted.

Finally, it would be useful if the media reported in a more realistic fashion about intelligence. Omniscience is an unrealistic standard. Intelligence rarely deals in absolutes or certainties. To ignore this fact when reporting on intelligence is either naive or intellectually dishonest.

Intelligence will never be as effective as we might wish, nor can all surprise be eliminated. Nor should we be willing to accept or overlook poor performances, avoidable errors, or repeated shortcomings.

But it is the very acceptance of the real limits of intelligence that would give both producers and consumers more confidence and put the concept of intelligence failure into its proper perspective.

NOTES

1. Jean Orieux, Talleyrand, translated by Patricia Wolf (New York: Alfred A. Knopf, 1974), pp. 533-534.

2. Michael Getler, "Intelligence Was Slow to Respond," Washington Post (February 11, 1984), p. Al.

3. Actually, Betts wrote that "intelligence failures are inevitable." In keeping with my own thesis, I have altered what I deem to be infelicitous phrasing on his part. See Richard K. Betts, "Analysis, War and Decision: Why Intelligence Failures are Inevitable," World Politics 31 (October 1978):61-84.

4. "The CIA Report the President Doesn't Want You to Read," Village Voice (February 16, 1976), pp. 76-81 [hereafter cited as Pike Committee Report, Village Voice].

5. The classic book on the multiple intelligence failures involved in Pearl Harbor is still Roberta Wohlstetter's Pearl Harbor: Warning and Decision (Stanford: Stanford University Press, 1962). The analysis that follows draws heavily on Wohlstetter.

6. Dean Acheson, Present at the Creation (New York: Norton, 1970), pp. 465-466; James F. Schnabel and Robert J. Watson, The History of the Joint Chiefs of Staff: The Joint Chiefs of Staff and National Policy, vol. 3: The Korean War (Part I) (Washington, D.C.: Historical Division, Joint Secretariat, Joint Chiefs of Staff, 1978), p. 36.

7. Ibid., pp. 49-53; Harry S. Truman, Memoirs, vol. 2: Years of Trial and Hope (Garden City, N.Y.: Doubleday, 1956), pp. 328-330.

8. John Prados, The Soviet Estimate (New York: Dial Press, 1982), pp. 62-63.

9. Dwight D. Eisenhower, Waging Peace (Garden City, N.Y.: Doubleday, 1965), pp. 208-209.

10. Prados, The Soviet Estimate, pp. 133-140; Roger Hilsman, To Move a Nation (Garden City, N.Y.: Doubleday, 1967), pp. 165-191.

11. Ibid., pp. 184-186.

12. Pike Committee Report, Village Voice, p. 76; see also the testimony of Samuel Adams et al. before the House Select Committee on Intelligence Hearings, 94th Congress, 1st session (1975), Part 2, U.S. Intelligence Agencies and Activities: The Performance of the Intelligence Community, pp. 683-719, and Part 5, Agencies and Activities: Risk and Control of Foreign Intelligence, pp. 1651-1727.

13. See the hearings cited in Note 12; see also Lyndon B. Johnson, The Vantage Point (New York: Holt Reinhart and Winston, 1971), pp. 380-381; William C. Westmoreland, A Soldier Reports (Garden City, N.Y.: Doubleday, 1976), pp. 312-316, 320-321.

14. Ibid., p. 486; James H. Polk, "Reflections on the Czechoslovakian Invasion, 1968," Strategic Review (Winter 1977):33.

15. Johnson, The Vantage Point, p. 487.

16. Pike Committee Report, Village Voice, p. 77; Thomas Powers, The Man Who Kept the Secrets: Richard Helms and the CIA (New York: Alfred A. Knopf, 1979), p. 353; Polk, "Reflections on the Czechoslovakian Invasion," p. 32.

4

Intelligence/Policy Relationships

> If we in intelligence were one day given three wishes, they
> would be to know everything, to be believed when we spoke,
> and in such a way to exercise an influence to the good in the
> matter of policy. But absent the Good Fairy, we sometimes get
> the order of our unarticulated wishes mixed. Often we feel the
> desire to influence policy and perhaps just stop wishing there.
> This is too bad, because to wish simply for influence can, and
> upon occasion does, get intelligence to the place where it can
> have no influence whatever. By striving too hard in this
> direction, intelligence may come to seem just another policy
> voice, and an unwanted one at that.
>
> —Sherman Kent[1]

In the catechism of the intelligence officer, the thesis that
intelligence is and should be strictly separate from policy is taken as
axiomatic. It is as hallowed in the theology of intelligence as the
doctrine of the separation of church and state is in the U.S.
Constitution. For much of our early history we tended, somewhat
self-righteously, to view intelligence as objective, disinterested, and
dispassionate and, somewhat disdainfully, to regard policy as slanted,
adulterated, and politicized. We strove mightily to maintain the
much-touted arm's-length relationship with policy, believing that
proximity to policy would corrupt the independence of our intelligence
judgments. Indeed, legend has it that members of the Board of
National Estimates of the 1950s and 1960s systematically discouraged
analysts and estimators from going downtown to have lunch with
policymakers, for fear that such exposure would make them policy
advocates and tempt them to serve power rather than truth.

Whatever the validity of this legend, such strictures were quite in
keeping with the traditional view of a proper intelligence/policy
relationship. By enforcing this kind of rigorous separation, the old
Board of National Estimates no doubt hoped to protect the policy
neutrality of intelligence; what it did was to impose a splendid
isolation upon intelligence that ensured its eventual policy irrelevance.
The vanishing applause for its product coming from the policy side
prompted intelligence to reexamine its assumptions, and a new,
unconventional wisdom came to be heard. Its message was that our
faith in the arm's-length relationship was misplaced, that no such

relationship really ever existed, and that close ties between intelligence and policy are not only inevitable but also essential if the policymakers' needs are to be served.

A new way of thinking about intelligence and policy emerged, in which the two communities were seen as awkwardly entangled and intertwined in what might be described as a competitive and often conflictual symbiotic relationship. Thomas Hughes put it most aptly when he spoke of the relationship "as a two-way search: of intelligence in search of some policy to influence and of policy in search of some intelligence for support."[2] Suddenly defunct is the comforting illusion that intelligence stands outside of and above the policy fray, that it can load analytic and estimative ammunition on its wagon and let the wagon roll down in the general direction of the battle without worrying where it will come to rest, whether the ammunition is of the right caliber, or how it will be used—to say nothing of whether someone might shoot it back. In place of that illusion is the less comfortable notion that if it is to be at all relevant to policy, intelligence must participate in the battle; it must be attuned to the strategy and tactics being pursued; and it is by no means invulnerable to being seesawed and whiplashed in the sociopolitical tug of war known as the policymaking process.

How this process unfolds in the real world and the intricate ways in which intelligence interacts with it have been the subject of some first-rate analytic writing. Within the past decade, three contributions to this literature on intelligence and foreign policy are particularly worthy of note:

1. First is the observation, vividly illustrated by Thomas Hughes,[3] that the intelligence community is no more a unitary actor than is the policy community, and that it should instead be seen as a Hydra-headed agglomeration of competing institutions often at odds with each other and not necessarily falling into predictable patterns. In studying the budgetary, organizational, and substantive struggles within this community, Hughes notes that

> the cross-cutting complexities were striking: position disputes within agencies, alliances shifting with issues, personal strayings from organizational loyalties, hierarchical differences between superiors and subordinates, horizontal rather than vertical affinities, and much ad hoc reaching for sustenance somewhere outside. Thus, while the struggles within the intelligence community sometimes mirrored simultaneous struggles in the larger policy community, they did so by no means invariably and never symmetrically.

It should not be astonishing, therefore, to find that policymakers view the intelligence process with as much ambivalence and suspicion as intelligence makers perceive the policy process, and that the interactions among them tend to be contentious and rivalrous. To quote again from Hughes:

> Viewed from above by the ranking policy-makers, the intelligence community often seemed cumbersome, expensive, loquacious, probing, querulous, and at times axe-grinding. Viewed from below by the intelligence experts, the policy community often seemed

determined to ignore evidence plainly before it—or (even worse) to mistake the intelligence managers for the experts. Viewed from in between at the intelligence-policy interface, it looked like controlled chaos—and not surprisingly—for here was where means and ends were brokered—jurisdictional rivalries compromised, contentious controversies delineated.[4]

2. Second is the thesis, persuasively argued by Richard Betts,[5] that so-called intelligence failures are more often than not policy failures; to put it more gently, it is usually impossible to disentangle intelligence failures from policy failures, since (intelligence) analysis and (policy) decisions are interactive rather than sequential processes. Betts sees the intelligence role as seeking "to extract certainty from uncertainty and to facilitate coherent decision in an incoherent environment." In seeking to reduce uncertainty, intelligence is often forced to extrapolate from evidence that is riddled with ambiguities. Inability to resolve these ambiguities leads to intelligence products that oversimplify reality and fail to alert the policy consumers of these products to the dangers that lurk within the ambiguities. Critical mistakes are consequently made by policymakers who, faced with ambiguities, will substitute wishful thinking and their own premises and preconceptions for the assessments of professional analysts. As Betts puts it, "Because it is the job of decision-makers to decide, they cannot react to ambiguity by deferring judgement . . . . When a welter of fragmentary evidence offers support to various interpretations, ambiguity is exploited by wishfulness. The greater the ambiguity, the greater the impact of preconceptions."[6]

3. A third example is the recent revelation, in a strikingly outspoken article by Yehoshafat Harkabi (Israeli scholar and former chief of Israeli Military Intelligence and adviser to the Israeli Prime Minister)[7] that the tense and ambivalent relationship between intelligence and policy is not a uniquely American phenomenon. Reacting sharply to the highly critical Kahan Commission report and its public indictment of the performance of the Israeli Defense Force's Intelligence chief of the Yom Kippur war, Harkabi argues that the greater fault lay with the policy side. His observations, made in an Israeli political setting, reveal some of the same peculiarities of the intelligence/policy relationship noted earlier by Hughes and Betts. To wit:

1. The selective rejection of intelligence by policy consumers: What they often look for is not so much data on the basis of which to shape policy, but rather support for preformed political and ideological conceptions.

2. The importance of preconceptions: Matters get worse the more ideologically motivated is the regime, for then policy is made more on the basis of ideological inputs than on the basis of intelligence reportings on reality which, to the extent that they contradict the ideology, may be discarded, and the intelligence service ends up frustrated.

3. Policy's resistance to change: Policy can be judged according to the extent of its "sensitivity" to intelligence. Will it change if a certain (intelligence) evaluation requires such a change? As a concrete example, what intelligence reporting could induce a change in Israel's present policy on Judea and Samaria? Does the rigidity of a

political position make it impervious to intelligence? In short, good intelligence is no guarantee of good policy, and vice versa.

4. The pros and cons of intelligence/policy intimacy at the top: Presumably it is good that the chief of the intelligence service be on close terms with the policymakers and have their trust. However, such bosom companionship also has its drawbacks. True, the more the policymaker is a part of the inner Byzantine court that develops as a matter of course around state chiefs, the greater is his or her influence; however, the policymaker then also loses perspective as well as independent critical vision, and gradually succumbs to the conceptions of the policymakers.

The dilemmas and foibles associated with the intelligence/policy interface are hardly novel or startling to seasoned intelligence practitioners, especially those senior officers charged with "brokering" the intelligence/policy relationship—the communicators and interactants who reside in the twilight zone between intelligence and policy. For them, this is familiar terrain. As managers and stimulators of intelligence production, they know with what difficulty a crisp, lucid analytic product is extracted from a dissentious community; as participants in the interagency policy process, they observe the ease with which that product can be selectively utilized, tendentiously summarized, or subtly denigrated. But for these privileged practitioners who move readily from the world of analysis to the world of action, familiarity with policy does not breed contempt. Rather, an appreciation of the murky and frenetic policy environment tends to evoke a certain sympathy for the policymakers' plight.

However, such knowledgeable, involved practitioners represent only a very small fraction of the intelligence population. The vast majority of that population—collectors, operators, and analysts—is essentially isolated from the hurly-burly of the policy process. The intelligence services at large, therefore, are often mystified and frustrated by the policymakers' perennial unhappiness with their product. Given this puzzlement, it seems worthwhile to try to delve a little more deeply into the reasons for such unhappiness.

THE VIEW FROM THE BRIDGE

Clearly, policy does not speak with a single voice. Policies have multiple authors. The numerous players who take part in policy formulation differ in temperament, education, and experience, as well as in personal and institutional loyalties. As a consequence, their attitudes toward intelligence and their propensity to accept or reject its assessments will also vary widely. Nevertheless, although generalizations are always hazardous, we can discern some common attributes and concerns of policymakers, especially the "national security principals"[8]—the key players at the highest levels of government—that predispose policymakers to react to intelligence offerings in predictable ways.

First, key decisionmakers are political leaders who have risen to their positions by being decisive, aggressive, and self-confident rather than reflective, introspective, and self-doubting. They attribute their success at least in part to their tried and proven ways of thinking, to the simplified models and paradigms that explain to them what makes the world go 'round. They often regard themselves as their own best analysts and hence tend to be distrustful of the untested and often counterintuitive judgments of the intelligence professionals.

Second, they have a strong vested interest in the success of their policies and will be disproportionately receptive to intelligence that "supports" these policies. They bear the burdens of great responsibility and find themselves perpetually embattled with a host of critics, competitors, and opponents, all eagerly looking for chinks in their armor. They thrive on optimists and boosters but encounter mostly alarmists and carping critics.

Festooned in this way, and operating in so hostile an environment, these highest-level consumers of intelligence can hardly be blamed for responding to its product with something less than boundless enthusiasm. In fact, it can be documented that every president since Eisenhower, and virtually every secretary of state since Acheson, has expressed dissatisfaction and irritation with intelligence analysis, either in his memoirs or in public or semipublic statements. The best-remembered and most widely quoted expostulation was reported to have been delivered by Lyndon Johnson to his director of Central Intelligence at a White House dinner: "Policy making is like milking a fat cow. You see the milk coming out, you press more and the milk bubbles and flows, and just as the bucket is full, the cow with its tail whips the bucket and all is spilled. That's what CIA does to policy making."[9]

Is intelligence at fault for creating this unhappiness? Should it alter its ways to court greater popularity? Or is the problem integral and endemic to the intelligence/policy relationship? The answers to these questions may become clearer as we look at some of the concrete ways in which the frictions arise.

WHY POLICY RESENTS INTELLIGENCE: FIVE WAYS TO BE UNPOPULAR

Presidents and their senior advisers will be unhappy with intelligence when it is not supportive of their policies. They will feel particularly frustrated under the following circumstances.

When Intelligence Fails to Reduce Uncertainty

Policymakers operate under a burden of pervasive uncertainty, much of it threatening to the viability of their policies. They are forever hopeful that someone will relieve them of some of this uncertainty, and so they look to intelligence for what common sense tells them should be reserved to augury and divination. Forecasting, to be sure, is the lifeblood of the intelligence estimator; but there is a world of difference between a forecast (an analytic judgment resting on carefully defined assumptions) and an oracular prophecy (secured by divine inspiration). Unfortunately, much of what is expected of intelligence by policymakers occupies this latter realm.

A good example is the perennial complaint that intelligence failed to predict a coup d'etat—that is, a coercive regime change or palace uprising; but, of course, a coup is typically a conspiratorial act that depends for its success on the preservation of secrecy. If intelligence gets wind of such an event, it means that secrecy has been compromised and that the coup is almost certain to fail.

Intelligence forecasting is actually done quite respectably by the community and can be of real value to the thoughtful policy analyst. When it stays within its legitimate bounds of identifying and illuminating alternative outcomes, assigning subjective probabilities to them, and exploring their possible implications for U.S. policy, the decisionmakers are well served; but the decisionmakers themselves will rarely think so. For such a forecast, far from narrowing uncertainty, will make them aware of the full range of uncertainty they face and render their calculations more difficult rather than easier. Indeed, much intelligence estimation is and must be of this nature. Precisely because it seeks to reflect complex reality, its product often makes for hardship in the lives of harassed decisionmakers.

When Intelligence Restricts Options

Every new administration comes into office with a national security agenda of its own, bent upon putting its mark on the nation's foreign policy. It believes that a significant shift in that policy is both desirable and possible. It will encounter a foreign policy bureaucracy (including intelligence) that believes it is neither. Intelligence professionals will greet the administration's new policy initiatives with cogent analyses, showing how vigorously allies will oppose these new policies, how resolutely neutrals will pervert them to their own ends, and how effectively adversaries will blunt them. At every step, it will appear to the policy leaders that intelligence fights them, seeks to fence them in, and, indeed, helps them fail.

The pattern persists. As the policy leaders face unexpected foreign challenges, their quick responses will often be met with more intelligence assessments that seem to be saying "it didn't work" or "it will almost certainly not succeed." The decisionmakers will conclude that intelligence not only constricts their room for maneuver but arms their political opponents as well. Worst of all, it constantly and annoyingly reminds them of their limited capacity to influence events. No matter how well the interaction may serve the interests of sound policy, there is no question that it builds tension between the two sides.

In these encounters, we should acknowledge that intelligence does not always "know better." There are times when intelligence is unaware that stated objectives are not real objectives of policy and will leave out of its analysis elements of the picture that may be important to the decisionmakers. Presidents paint upon a canvas far larger than the particular segments on which intelligence tends to focus. The assessments of intelligence, therefore, may be quite valid for those segments, but they may also miss broader considerations that presidents care about.

The Carter administration's proposal to impose sanctions—including a grain embargo—on the Soviet Union in response to their invasion of Afghanistan provides a vivid example. The stated objective was to penalize the offender by imposing political and economic costs on him. When intelligence was asked to assess the potential impact of the

17. Pike Committee Report, Village Voice, p. 77.

18. William Colby, Honorable Men: My Life in the CIA (New York: Simon and Schuster, 1978), p. 366; Henry Kissinger, Years of Upheaval (Boston: Little Brown, 1982), p. 459. See also Pike Committee Report, Village Voice, p. 78.

19. Kissinger's memoirs offer a concise summary of what went wrong; see his Years of Upheaval, pp. 459-467. The CIA postmortem can be found in House Select Committee on Intelligence Hearings, part 2, pp. 639-641.

20. Pike Committee Report, Village Voice, p. 79; Tad Szulc, "Lisbon and Washington: Behind the Portuguese Revolution," Foreign Policy (Winter 1975-1976):18-19, 22-23.

21. Colby, Honorable Men, p. 368.

22. Pike Committee Report, Village Voice, pp. 80-81.

23. The best critique is still House Permanent Select Committee on Intelligence, Iran: Evaluation of U.S. Intelligence Performance Prior to November 1978 (Staff Report, Subcommittee on Evaluation, 1979); see also Michael A. Ledeen and William H. Lewis, "Carter and the Fall of the Shah: The Inside Story," Washington Quarterly 3 (Spring 1980):1-40. An insightful view from within the Carter administration is Zbigniew Brzezinski, Power and Principle: Memoirs of the National Security Advisor, 1977-81 (New York: Farra Straus and Giroux, 1983), pp. 359-367.

24. See Betts, "Analysis, War and Decision," p. 61.

25. Gerald W. Hopple, "Intelligence and Warning Lessons," in Bruce W. Watson and Peter M. Dunn, eds., Military Lessons of the Falklands Island War: Views from the United States (Boulder, Colo.: Westview Press, 1984), p. 100.

26. Ibid., p. 100.

27. As the staff director of the committee in Israel's Knesset that oversees intelligence once pointed out to me, when you have four or five enemies and they are all on your borders, it is much easier to keep track. One might add that even then, as in 1973, intelligence failures can happen.

28. Betts, "Analysis, War and Decision," p. 62.

29. Margot Hornblower, "Aspin Says CIA Foretold Massive Influx of Cubans," Washington Post (June 2, 1980), p. A6.

sanctions package, it responded with a judgment, the thrust of which was that the sanctions package would not be an effective instrument. It was argued that without solid participation by our allies, sanctions would do no serious damage to the Soviet economy nor impair the leadership's objectives in any significant way. Not surprisingly, President Carter gave the assessment a rather frigid reception, and the assessment's negative judgments turned out to be a less than decisive factor in his calculus. From the president's perspective, the sanctions package was just right. He considered a highly visible response to Afghanistan to be imperative, but it also had to be low risk. A military undertaking was ruled out as far too hazardous. Inaction was ruled out because it would signal to the rest of the world the existence of U.S. irresolution and condonement. The sanctions, though unsatisfying in terms of direct effects, would convey a strong sense of disapprobation and censure, without engendering worrisome consequences. It would satisfy the popular need to express the nation's sense of outrage and would portray the president as willing to take the political heat of angering an important domestic constituency—the farmers—for the sake of a foreign issue of principle. Intelligence could not then, and can never, be expected to take such considerations into account.

When Intelligence Undercuts Policies

Administrations have often found that intelligence analyses appear at times and in various ways unhelpful to the pursuit of policies on which they had embarked. This can happen in two ways: (1) through a genuine and protracted divergence of intelligence judgments from publicly stated administration views of a given situation, and (2) through fortuity or inadvertence.

An example of the first phenomenon was provided by the stubborn independence displayed by the intelligence community in the early phases of the Vietnam escalation in 1964-1965, when its national intelligence estimates consistently offered up a far more pessimistic assessment of North Vietnamese staying power than was reflected in the Johnson administration's public assertions. Although this divergence between intelligence and policy did not become public knowledge until the infamous appearance of the Pentagon Papers in 1971, the intelligence performance of the mid-1960s evoked considerable disquiet and chagrin among policy insiders at the time.

The days of such protracted differences of view between intelligence and policy are probably over. In the intelligence/policy environment of the 1980s, it seems highly unlikely that a divergence of assessment could be sustained for very long. Congressional oversight and its intimate access to intelligence analysis would bring any significant disparities quickly to the surface and thus cause them to be resolved.

The other cause, policy undercutting by fortuity and inadvertence, is more likely to survive as it constitutes a matter of human frailty. Sometimes it is merely a question of miserable timing—as in the classic case of the intelligence reassessment of North Korean military forces that credited them with substantially greater capabilities than had been previously appreciated. The estimate was fine, but it just happened to "hit the street" within a week of President Carter's announcement of his controversial decision to begin withdrawal of U.S. forces from South Korea. A pure coincidence, but it caused understandable consternation.

At other times, this policy undercutting is a matter of inattention—as in the so-called discovery of the Soviet brigade in Cuba, which, it turned out later, had been there all along. Issues of this kind, seemingly unimportant, can suddenly escalate into heated public controversy and make life difficult for the policy leaders. However minor the transgression, they will regard intelligence less fondly thereafter.

When Intelligence Provokes Public Controversy

From time to time, routine differences within the community over how to interpret ambiguous intelligence evidence turns into heated, and perhaps even acrimonious, debate. When the competing interpretations clearly affect important policy issues, the internal controversy can easily spill over into the public arena. In the 1950s and 1960s, when what transpired in the world of intelligence remained largely opaque, such disputes could easily be contained within the executive branch. Now, with the progressive "opening up" of intelligence through Congress and the media, and through its more visible involvement with policy, a disputation within the community soon finds itself drawn into and exploited by the public debate, often in ways that make life more difficult for the national security policymakers.

Examples of policy-relevant debates that have been stimulated or intensified by intelligence controversy come quickly to mind: whether the Tupolev Backfire bomber is an intermediate-range or an intercontinental-capable bomber; whether extensive Soviet civil defense preparations add up to enhanced "survivability" for Soviet society; how significantly Western technology contributes to the growth of the Soviet economy and its military power; whether Western calculations of Soviet military spending adequately reflect the real size and burden of Soviet defense; and to what extent the Soviet natural gas pipeline will aggravate Western Europe's dependence on imported energy.

This brief sampling is sufficient to show that the issues in dispute often bear on strategic, budgetary, arms control, or economic policy decisions important to an administration's overall strategy. To the extent that intelligence controversy helps arm the opposition in such disputes, its contribution is not exactly appreciated.

When Intelligence Fails to Persuade

Ever since John F. Kennedy's _tour de force_ in unveiling photographic intelligence on the presence of Soviet missiles in Cuba to a hushed UN audience, successive administrations have sought to emulate that feat. Although the results have been mixed at best, hope springs eternal that a release of intelligence findings or a public display of exotic evidence will enlighten an uninformed or misinformed public, win over a cynical journalist, or convince a skeptical member of Congress. The intelligence product now finds its way into the public domain through more and more channels and in ever greater volume—most of it, of course, at the instigation and under the aegis of the policy community. It moves through such vehicles as press conferences, media briefings and backgrounders, testimony on the Hill, formal reports to Congress, and official glossy publications widely disseminated.

In a general way, this sea change in public access to intelligence has undoubtedly had its beneficial impact on public understanding of often complex and murky situations. Far more questionable, however, is whether intelligence can be used effectively as an instrument of public persuasion—whether the marshaling of intelligence evidence on one side or another of a sharply debated issue ever succeeds in gaining solid converts. In a tactical situation, when a heated debate moves toward a crucial vote, a well-focused, lucid intelligence briefing can often sway a wavering agnostic and stiffen an irresolute supporter. The record suggests, however, that the conversion will not stick, that the gnawing doubts will soon return.

The reasons for this phenomenon are not hard to find:

1. When public disclosure of intelligence was a rare and notable event that summoned up an aura of mystery and miracle, the product was endowed with uncommon authority. As disclosure became ever more routine, the gloss wore off and an inevitable "debasement of the currency" set in. Moreover, in today's world of global information overload and media hype, even the most striking intelligence "release" will find it heavy going to try to capture the attention of a perpetually distracted audience.

2. Intelligence assessments—when lifted out of their context, fuzzed, and diluted ("sanitized") to protect sources and methods--lose much of their authenticity. To the intelligence professional who has built his or her mosaic from a welter of carefully evaluated raw data, often accumulated over many years, the evidence may be totally compelling. To a public audience, coming to the issue cold and exposed only to the sanitized version, the evidence will often seem ambiguous and the judgments inadequately supported.

3. Intelligence evidence is brought into public play in situations of deep controversy, in which the contention usually occurs not over observable facts but over principle. The physical phenomena that intelligence is best at recording are often not much help in settling points of principle. Central America offers a good example: Divergent views of the threat implicit in that area revolve around the conceptual question of whether the revolutionary situation in El Salvador is fundamentally endogenous (i.e., rooted in and fueled by internal, historic forces) or exogenous (i.e., externally stimulated and sustained). This conceptual issue cannot be resolved by displays of intelligence evidence, however persuasive, that Soviet arms do indeed flow through Nicaraguan ports to Salvadoran rebels.

4. The impact that intelligence can have on public perceptions is further constrained by the understandable tendency of people to reject bad news—what social psychologists used to call "cognitive dissonance." A classic example is the case of "Yellow Rain," discovery of lethal toxins being used under Soviet tutelage in Southeast Asia and Afghanistan. In spite of the overwhelming weight of confirmatory evidence accumulated over eight years, the findings continue to be challenged and contested, sometimes with offerings of bizarre scientific

counterexplanations that utterly defy common sense. The extreme reluctance to accept the evidence at face value cannot be attributed simply to the fact that intelligence could never meet the rigorous laboratory standards for evidence. Rather, it must surely lie in the unpleasantness of the implications, insofar as they raise doubts about the viability of arms control agreements.

In sum, policy leaders are bound to develop a rather ambivalent view of the support they can hope to get from their intelligence community. Clearly the resulting "love-hate relationship" is endemic to the situation, and there is not much that intelligence can, or should, do to alter it. Indeed, a greater effort to "serve policy well" could lead to even greater ambivalence and discord on the part of those we seek to serve. Thus, we return to Sherman Kent's admonition in the leitmotiv at the beginning of this chapter: "By striving too hard in this direction, intelligence may come to seem just another policy voice, and an unwanted one at that."

NOTES

1. Sherman Kent, "Estimates and Influence," originally presented in London (September 1966) and subsequently published in Foreign Service Journal 46 (April 1969).

2. Thomas Hughes deserves great credit for being the first, and surely the most articulate, iconoclast toppling the old conventional wisdom. His two Farewell Lectures as departing director of the Bureau of Intelligence and Research of the Department of State in July 1969 contain the quoted passage. The lectures were subsequently reprinted in Thomas L. Hughes, The Fate of Facts in a World of Men (New York: Foreign Policy Association, Headline Series No. 233, 1976).

3. Thomas L. Hughes, "The Power to Speak and the Power to Listen," in Thomas M. Frank et al., eds., Secrecy and Foreign Policy (New York: Oxford University Press, 1974), p. 15.

4. Ibid., p. 19.

5. Richard K. Betts, "Analysis, War and Decision: Why Intelligence Failures Are Inevitable," World Politics 31 (October 1978).

6. Ibid., p. 70.

7. Yehoshafat Harkabi, "The Intelligence-Policymaker Tangle," Jerusalem Quarterly, no. 30 (Winter 1984), p. 125.

8. These principals include, at a minimum, the president, vice-president, national security adviser, secretary of state, and secretary of defense.

9. Henry Brandon, The Retreat of American Power (Garden City, N.Y.: Doubleday, 1973), p. 103.

INTELLIGENCE IN AN OPEN SOCIETY

The role of and restraints upon intelligence in a "democratic" state require an examination of such ongoing concerns as demands for openness, freedom of the press and information, protection of civil liberties, claims of executive privilege, requirements to safeguard information, and methods vital to national security. In addition, the ethics of operating within an intelligence system need to be examined.

Paul Lauren's chapter uses the examples of the attempt to assassinate Hitler and the prosecution of CIA Director Helms as a point of departure to explore the many conflicts generated by the interplay between ethics and intelligence. While Lauren sees no easy way out of these dilemmas, he argues that ethical issues must be neither avoided nor dismissed. Only by facing the issues directly will we be able to comprehend the crucial role that ethical standards do and must play in public policy.

Alfred Maurer's focus is the present balance in the United States between national security interests and the people's right to know, a focus clarified by his outline of the basis for official government secrecy and citizens' access to government documents. Not surprisingly, different actors within the U.S. system (for example, the press and the presidency) have remarkably different perspectives concerning where this balance should be struck. Maurer's investigation contrasts the U.S. system with that of Great Britain, in which the laws and courts place significantly greater restraints on both the press and those who "leak" classified information. He also examines particular actions and methods that government has claimed are essential safeguards of national security. Notable among these are electronic surveillance and warrantless searches, prepublication reviews, and polygraph testing.

Morton Halperin, in his chapter entitled "Intelligence and an Open Society," expands upon his previous writings in this field as he searches for a proper mix between the requirements of intelligence agencies and the norms and values of an open society. He concludes that both sets of demands are legitimate and that the legislative process leading to the enactment of laws (comprehensive charter legislation) can ensure a reasonable balance, thereby providing the United States an intelligence community with both the authority it needs to perform its vital missions and the appropriate rules and procedures under which it must act such that it poses no threat to the open society it is charged to defend.

All three chapters admit to legitimate claims for secrecy and openness in the conduct of intelligence business. Although they do not cover the entire spectrum of debate on these issues, they do suggest significant disagreement among those who are wrestling with the conflicting demands for secrecy and openness and searching for the means to achieve and maintain the right balance. Open debate can only help in this endeavor.

Ethics and Intelligence

> We [in the intelligence community] could not seem to free
> ourselves either at the top or bottom, could not free ourselves
> from that psychology. . . . Along came the Cold War. We
> pursued the same course in the Korean War, and the Cold War
> continued; then the Vietnam War. We never freed ourselves from
> that psychology that we were indoctrinated with, right after
> Pearl Harbor, you see. I think this accounts for the fact that
> nobody seemed to be concerned about raising the question, is this
> lawful, is this legal, is this ethical? It was just like a soldier in
> the battlefield. . . . We did what we were expected to do. It
> became a part of our thinking, a part of our personality.
> —William Sullivan[1]

ETHICS AND INTELLIGENCE

To some, ethics and intelligence in the same title may appear a
contradiction in terms. Many assume that intelligence community
activities, by choice or necessity, are devoid of ethical considerations.
But this assumption perpetuates a great disservice to those constantly
exposed to difficult ethical issues in intelligence and reinforces the
dangerous notion that it is normal and acceptable for public servants
to conduct policy in such a way that "nobody seemed to be concerned
about raising the question, . . . is this ethical?" Among all a state's
activities—particularly those of an open, democratic society—few rival
intelligence for raising serious ethical questions.

Two Cases and Many Conflicts

On July 20, 1944, in East Prussia, Adolf Hitler met with his
chief military advisers. The Normandy invasion just a few weeks
before now seriously jeopardized the western front while the Russian
advance from the east threatened the invasion of Germany itself.
Allied strategic air attacks pounded the country without relief. If
Germany ever needed the unified support of its best military and
intelligence officers, then now was surely the time. Nevertheless, into
this meeting came the brilliant staff officer, Colonel Claus
von Stauffenberg, who, with the active participation of several others,

including the legendary Admiral Wilhelm Canaris, chief of German intelligence, carried a bomb in his briefcase. Their purpose was to assassinate Germany's national leader and commander-in-chief, Adolf Hitler.

Such extreme action evolved over several years. Hitler's series of unparalleled diplomatic and military successes, combined with the initial appeasement and weakness of others, provided little support for those opposed to his policies but required to follow his orders. The torture and murder of dissidents, unrestrained exercise of state power, violations of international law, wars of aggression against others, and, especially, the unspeakable mass exterminations of defenseless human beings, all in the name of "national security," repulsed and horrified several officers who found these brutal policies contrary to their nation's interests and their own Christian convictions. They agonizingly concluded that only Hitler's death would end the brutality and horror. However, for military and intelligence officers who had sworn to defend their country and had pledged a personal loyalty oath to their leader, the decision to attempt assassination was reached only after excruciating wrestling with conscience and the wrenching agony of determining the relative value of competing ethical obligations. To murder Hitler they would have to break their loyalty oath, place their country's immediate security in danger, risk death as the worst possible kind of traitors, and violate their own religious commandment, "Thou shalt not kill." Each time they struggled with this terrible ethical dilemma, the same solution emerged. As one confessed to a friend: "We have examined ourselves before God and our consciences. It has to happen, for this man is Evil itself."[2]

For this reason, Stauffenberg carried a bomb into the staff headquarters. He started the ten-minute fuse before entering the room and then placed his briefcase not far from Hitler. He then unobtrusively excused himself—to place a telephone call to Berlin. Within minutes a powerful explosion shattered the building, killed several men, and wounded others; but the bomb failed in its true purpose, for Hitler escaped alive.

Hitler's revenge came swiftly. The Gestapo captured Stauffenberg the next day and shot him. Another of the army participants, General von Treschkow, wrote just before he died:

> I remain, now as before, of the firm conviction that we have done the right thing. I consider Hitler not only the arch-enemy of Germany, but also the arch-enemy of the world. When I stand before God's judgment seat in a few hours from now, to render an account of my actions and my omissions, then I believe I shall be able to answer with a clear conscience for what I have done in the fight against Hitler.[3]

Others faced trial, either in the notorious "People's Court" in Berlin or in special tribunals organized especially for the occasion. "The essential point," stated one of the defendants, "is . . . the claim by the state of total power over the citizen, with the elimination of his religious and moral obligations toward God."[4] "The points of discussion" during the trial, wrote another, "were questions of the practical and ethical claims of Christianity." "The decisive sentence" in the case, he concluded, was made when the judge shouted, "There is one thing Christianity and we National Socialists have in common, and only this one: We demand the whole human being!"[5] Canaris, as the former head of intelligence, echoed a similar theme and just before his execution declared, "I die for my country with a clear conscience."[6]

These courts and the government they represented condemned the conspirators to death for "high treason." Yet within months these accusers were either destroyed or had to stand trial for crimes against humanity. Today, the officers who attempted to assassinate Hitler are annually commemorated by the German government for their sacrifice and ethical courage.

This dramatic case certainly was not the first raising of difficult questions about ethics and intelligence—nor the last. Eight years before the attempt on his life, Adolf Hitler granted a rare interview to an American reporter. This young, aspiring journalist entered the newly established Office of Strategic Services (OSS) during World War II and eventually became the director of the Central Intelligence Agency. At the end of his thirty-five-year career working with the secrets of government, he too would be involved in a case drawing national and international attention to ethics and intelligence. His name: Richard Helms.

In 1977, a nervous Justice Department decided to prosecute Richard Helms. The evidence appeared overwhelming to support the contention that several years before he had lied to the Senate Foreign Relations Committee while under solemn oath by failing "to answer questions fully, completely, and accurately as required by law."[7] The CIA had carried out several covert operations in Chile to prevent the Marxist, Salvador Allende, from winning the 1970 presidential election. Helms provided evasive or deliberately misleading responses when questioned about these activities. The government wanted to prosecute to demonstrate that "no segment of the community was above the law" and that even intelligence officers did not have "a license to lie."[8] However, since a "trial of this case would involve tremendous costs to the United States and might jeopardize national secrets,"[9] a plea-bargain arrangement was reached. This provoked immediate criticism. "I thought there was to be an end to the double standard of justice for the big shots," declared one senator. "Apparently, Helms was too hot to handle."[10] Said another public figure in great frustration, "Rather than using a court trial to press for full disclosure . . . the administration has decided to contain the story and manage it under the tired excuse of national security."[11] Sympathetic with critics and highly suspicious of closed-door deals in open societies, presiding U.S. District Judge Barrington Parker quickly announced that his court would not be bound by any prearranged plea-bargain.

During the proceedings, Helms did not dispute the prosecution's version of the evidence. He admitted that he had deliberately misled the Senate and argued that he had been motivated by the special obligations and codes of his profession: "I found myself in a position of conflict. I had sworn my oath to protect certain secrets. I didn't want to lie. I didn't want to mislead the Senate. I was simply trying to find my way through a very difficult situation in which I found myself."[12] It was precisely this point, stated the <u>Washington Post</u>, that created "the dilemma that made this case genuinely agonizing to conscientious people."[13]

Judge Parker levied against Helms the maximum fine and a

suspended two-year jail sentence. He said he understood the dilemma that confronted the defendant but asked, "Were there no other alternatives open to him? He could have very easily stood back and considered very carefully the other alternatives." Then the judge sternly lectured both the agent and the agency:

> You considered yourself bound to protect the agency whose affairs you had administered and to dishonor your solemn oath to tell the truth before the committee. If public officials embark deliberately on a course to disobey and ignore the laws of our land because of some ill-conceived notion and belief that there are earlier commitments and considerations which they must first observe, the future of our country is in jeopardy.

Helms, whose arms had been at his side, then began to grip the lectern as the judge continued:

> There are those employed in the intelligence security community of this country . . . who feel that they have a license to operate freely outside the dictates of law and otherwise to orchestrate as they see fit. Public officials at every level, whatever their position, like any other person, must respect and honor the Constitution and the laws of the United States.[14]

These two cases provide a unique point of departure for exploring the many conflicts generated by the interplay between ethics and intelligence. Despite various differences, they together reveal the difficulty involved in confronting actual ethical dilemmas, the complexity of these problems, the frustration in finding simple answers to all situations, and the mistaken canard that ethics and intelligence are divorced from each other. Both defendants, as professional chiefs of large and powerful intelligence services, based their arguments upon some kind of ethical standard. Each maintained that his choice was not a crude or simplistic one between being "ethical" and "unethical." Instead, it involved a difficult, if not agonizing, choice between complex and competing ethical values ranging from intimate personal religious conviction, to the relatively narrow professional ethics of simply following orders and remaining loyal to one's colleagues, to the public ethics of respect for the values and institutions of one's society. Their dilemmas continue to be ours.

ETHICS AND DEMOCRACY

Every society, totalitarian or democratic, must confront ethical issues in its domestic and foreign policies. As Stanley Hoffmann wrote, "We must remember that states are led by human beings whose actions affect human beings within and outside: considerations of good and evil, right and wrong are therefore both inevitable and legitimate."[15] It is precisely this relationship between conduct and its effect upon the welfare of people that concerns ethics, for ethical considerations evaluate and judge human behavior according to standards of conduct based on moral principles. These standards, in turn, comprise two essential features. The first is that of limits, which restrict our actions. The second is that of <u>responsibilities</u>, which hold us accountable for our choices and resulting actions.

In a democratic society, open, pluralistic debates determine legal limits and responsibilities. Such a process is frequently complicated and cumbersome, as it attempts to balance competing interests and values. These include political principles, perceived threats, economic interests, historical traditions, individual consciences, and religious convictions. The ethical standards of conduct determined by this process are explicitly, but not exclusively, defined by laws, which delineate acceptable behavior within certain limits and with particular responsibilities. These laws apply to private citizens and servants of the state alike, including those in the intelligence community.

In democracies, however, the setting of ethical standards is a dynamic process involving constant testing, challenge, and reexamination. One of the most serious criticisms leveled by the special Senate Select Committee to Study Intelligence was that there had not been "significant rethinking of where boundaries ought to be drawn in a free society" after the intelligence community was established.[16] Debate and dialogue need to continue in light of unresolved problems, changing circumstances, different leaders, and the continual question of whether the nation's policies conform to its declared values. Public policy can easily be pursued "in the name of" such cherished values as justice, liberty, and democracy and yet have little to do with them in practice.[17] As the former inspector general of the Central Intelligence Agency, Lyman B. Kirkpatrick, observed, "The heart of the matter is that the American people will tolerate what must be done to protect the nation as long as it does not seem to destroy what it is protecting."[18]

Under these conditions, when the public or its representatives perceive that thresholds of ethical standards have been violated and trust betrayed, the results can be traumatic. The United States discovered how wrenching this experience can be when the Vietnam War, the Watergate scandal, and the revelation of abuses by over-zealous intelligence agents in the name of national security all combined to undermine an earlier consensus on policy and confidence in government. The nation examined itself more deeply than any democracy had ever done before. Senate Majority Leader Mike Mansfield declared that many must accept the blame for transgressions and abuse of ethical standards, and he called for action

> to foreclose any [further] demeaning of the basic premises of a free society. . . . The Senate must be satisfied that the intelligence community is doing the people's business, to the end that the Nation may be with assurance so advised. The Senate must be persuaded that what is being done in the name of national security under a cloak of obscurity is the people's business, as defined, not by employees of a Government agency, but the people's business as defined by the Constitution and the laws duly enacted thereunder. . . . It used to be fashionable for members of Congress to say that insofar as the intelligence agencies were concerned, the less they knew about such questions, the better. Well, in my judgment, it is about time that that attitude went out of fashion. It is time for the Senate to take the trouble and, yes, the risks of knowing more rather than

less.[19]

These risks are particularly serious and cannot be easily discounted with abstract moralizing. One of the most dangerous problems facing intelligence is that of a world in which adversaries sometimes observe few limits. Free people in open, democratic societies abhor secrecy and view it as a potential threat to their liberties; but what they tell themselves, they tell their foes. Wars, aggression, and subversion frequently dictate secrecy—a fact that has long tormented those who seek to apply democratic principles and ethical standards observed among individuals to public policy[20] and, even more difficult, to the specific arena of international politics.[21]

The well-documented activities of the Soviet Committee for State Security, or KGB, make the problem even worse.[22] As one expert has observed, Soviet commitment to clandestine operations of all kinds "is congenital, massive, and enduring."[23] This activity, when reinforced by that of others, creates an environment for intelligence described as "the back alleys of the world" and "the gray, shadowy world between war and peace."[24] To participate in such activity further contributes to deceit, intrigue, and suspicion in the world, thereby rendering peace and the very values it seeks to uphold more precarious. Not to participate imperils both the state and its values.

In the face of this problem, two extreme proposals have surfaced. The first is that a democratic society with any commitment to ethics should renounce all intelligence activities. Ethical conduct is a force of its own and nations can lead by example, so it is argued; hence the renunciation of intelligence would be an act of great moral courage with untold international benefits.[25] As one study phrased it, "Using secret intelligence to defend a constitutional republic is akin to the ancient medical practice of employing leeches to take blood from feverish patients. The intent is therapeutic, but in the long run, the cure is more deadly than the disease."[26] The second proposal takes exactly the opposite stance, claiming that the end justifies the means and that any intelligence activity serving the national interest should be allowed. This dictate applies with particular force when conducted overseas, where, in the recent words of one high-ranking intelligence officer, "we must lie, cheat, and steal."[27] The same point found even more direct expression several years ago when a top secret government report asserted that intelligence operations needed to become

> more effective, more unique, and if necessary, more ruthless than that employed by the enemy. No one should be permitted to stand in the way of the prompt, efficient, and secure accomplishment of this mission. . . . It is now clear that we are facing an implacable enemy whose avowed objective is world domination by whatever means and whatever cost. There are no rules in such a game. Hitherto acceptable norms of human conduct do not apply. If the U.S. is to survive, long-standing American concepts of "fair play" must be reconsidered. We must develop effective espionage and counter-espionage services. We must learn to subvert, sabotage, and destroy our enemies by more clever, more sophisticated, and more effective methods than those used against us [emphasis added].[28]

Dangers accompany extremes of any kind. Democracy itself is predicated on avoiding extremes—reaching a balance between contested public issues—and survival absolutely depends upon the ability to balance the requirements of both liberty and security. In this setting, observed one former CIA officer, the intelligence profession can no longer "afford to resist asking where its limits should be set." Intelligence, he writes, must clearly promote democratic values and international security, or the compromises that it makes "cannot and should not be stomached." To address this issue, he believes, we must ask these critical questions: "How can the intelligence function be carried out at the least risk to other values in our society? How can a professional intelligence service operate so that officials within it perform their roles in an ethical manner?"[29] Surely the place to begin searching for an answer is to recognize the ethical issues confronting those who serve in intelligence.

INTELLIGENCE AND ETHICS

Most intelligence operations are designed to provide information about the world. Leaders throughout history have attempted to secure knowledge and warning to avoid being forced to make uninformed decisions. For this reason, Moses sent out agents to "spy out the land of Canaan,"[30] and four hundred years before Christ the Chinese military strategist, Sun Tzu, wrote that the real test of statecraft was not in winning one hundred battles but rather in using intelligence to find security "without fighting."[31] In sixteenth-century England, Queen Elizabeth consciously developed an intelligence service to overcome the power deficiencies of her small country, as did Gustavus Adolphus in seventeenth-century Sweden. Early American leaders like George Washington, Benjamin Franklin, and members of the Committee of Secret Correspondence all agreed that "the necessity of procuring good Intelligence is apparent and need not be further urged."[32] Many others before and since have accepted this proposition and recognized that although the best intelligence cannot guarantee sound policy in a complex and dangerous world, decisions made without intelligence can succeed only by accident.

To provide accurate, timely, and continuous information, intelligence services seek to collect what they can. Collection of such information from open sources presents few, if any, ethical dilemmas. Acquisition of open source material requires no deception nor manipulation and violates no laws or ethical norms. More to the point, those who possess the information freely give it. Though often fruitful, open source collection alone is rarely sufficient, especially when it pertains to closed societies. Governments wish to keep some information from each other and sometimes from themselves, thus either consciously or unconsciously adhering to Cardinal de Richelieu's dictim that "secrecy is the first essential in affairs of the State."[33] To acquire such information, intelligence services rely on clandestine collection. Not surprisingly, this does raise ethical problems, for it fundamentally involves theft.

In this regard, the example of Henry L. Stimson is instructive. In 1929, Stimson became President Hoover's secretary of state. Upon assuming office he discovered an intelligence operation known as the

"Black Chamber," which intercepted, decoded, and then read the secret communications of twenty nations. Stimson's conflict arose from the fact that he desired the intelligence so obtained, but found the theft ethically repulsive. He terminated the operation, justifying his action by declaring, "Gentlemen do not read other people's mail."[34] One observer summarized Stimson's attitude as follows:

> He regarded it as a low, snooping activity, a sneaking, spying, key-hole peering kind of dirty business, a violation of principles of mutual trust upon which he conducted both his personal and his foreign policy. All of this it is and Stimson rejected the view that such means were justified even by patriotic ends. He held to the conviction that his country should do what is right.[35]

When World War II followed twelve years later, Stimson dramatically changed his mind. Although he remained uncomfortable about the idea of stealing, he came to believe that other ethical standards protecting human life had to be considered and that the United States could no longer afford to be without clandestinely collected information.

Today, the desire to obtain information has combined with high technology to revolutionize collection capabilities. Film and electro-optical instruments acquire photo intelligence (PHOTINT), while a staggering array of worldwide listening posts and satellites provide signals intelligence (SIGINT) by intercepting communications (COMINT) and electronic (ELINT) emissions. Although this new technology has facilitated clandestine collection, it has neither eased the ethical problem of theft nor reduced the possibility of abuse. More than fifty years ago, Supreme Court Justice Louis Brandeis openly warned that "the progress of science in furnishing the government with means of espionage" seriously threatened individual liberties in an open, democratic society.[36] As Senator Frank Church observed, the technological capacity that

> the intelligence community has given the government could enable it to impose total tyranny [upon the country, for with the means now available] . . . "there would be no place to hide. . . . I know the capacity that is there to make tyranny total in America, and we must see to it that this agency [the National Security Agency] and all agencies that possess this technology operate within the law and under proper supervision, so that we never cross over that abyss. That is the abyss from which there is no return."[37]

Ethical conflicts in intelligence collection are particularly acute when dealing with human sources (HUMINT). Agents are central to all clandestine activity because they alone are capable of collecting inside information about intentions that technological means cannot see or hear. As one intelligence officer testified in a recent espionage trial, "Agents around the world are our primary sources. Only from the minds of men can we find out what is going to happen in the world."[38] The purpose of agents can thus be easily presented and understood, but, by definition, such collection inevitably extracts from others information that their own governments may wish not to divulge. Stated more directly, collection of this sort requires another individual to betray the trust placed in him and to commit treason. Although defectors and "walk-ins" may occasionally volunteer their services,[39] they do not always suffice; the desired information in some cases can be acquired only through manipulation of unwilling sources. According to one former high-ranking official of the Central Intelligence Agency, it is this issue that creates the central ethical problem in human collection. The highest art in tradecraft

> is to develop a source that you "own lock, stock, and barrel." According to the clandestine ethos, a "controlled" source provides the most reliable intelligence. "Controlled" means, of course, bought or otherwise obligated. Traditionally it has been the aim of the professional in the clandestine service to weave a psychological web around any potentially fruitful contact and to tighten that web whenever possible. . . . The modus operandi required . . . is the very antithesis of ethical interpersonal relationships.[40]

Another feature of intelligence is that of analysis and estimates. Raw data, in and of itself, is generally meaningless. Information tends to be fragmentary and incomplete, occasionally ambiguous and contradictory, and sometimes deliberately misleading—as when an opponent engages in "disinformation." Accordingly, information is studied and evaluated to distinguish fact from fiction, to cull the important from the unimportant, and to provide interpretations of meaning. The analysis is then prepared in such a way that its products, or estimates, can be used by policymakers.[41]

Among the least controversial of intelligence activities, analysis and estimates nevertheless pose ethical problems. These arise over matters relating to what is reported in the estimates, when it is reported, and to whom it is reported. Here, various forms of distortion, evasion, concealment, and lying remain constant possibilities. Indeed, according to one authority on ethics in public policy, the "noble lie" on behalf of "national security" and "the public good" "in times of crisis" forms "the most dangerous body of deceit of all."[42] With the frequently legitimate need for secrecy and the necessity for restricted access to information, intelligence analysis and estimates are not subject to the open debate required by other branches of government in democratic societies. For this reason, analysis and estimates can easily be designed to please particular consumers, confirm ideological preconceptions, justify service bias, encourage increased appropriations, buttress political expediency, or hide embarrassing or illegal activities. The Defense Intelligence Agency, for example, must constantly seek to avoid accusations that it produces "intelligence to please" for the Joint Chiefs of Staff and Department of Defense while simultaneously being told, "Tell me what I'd love to hear."[43] Similarly, both the Johnson and Nixon administrations exerted enormous pressure on the Central Intelligence Agency to "prove" foreign control and funding of those who opposed U.S involvement in Vietnam.[44] Such pressures are difficult to resist.

The contrast between the motto and actions of Allen Dulles, former director of Central Intelligence, highlight more serious problems. Early in his long tenure, he proudly announced the slogan that was intended to guide the Central Intelligence Agency in its mission on behalf of a democratic society and is now etched into the south wall of its central lobby: "And ye shall know the truth and the truth shall make you free." This admirable motto makes practical as well as ethical sense, for truth telling is the very heart of intelligence analysis and estimates. Policymakers need a truthful depiction of a given situation. Anything else is not intelligence.[45] Yet Dulles himself was not always inclined to tell the truth—or at least the whole truth as he knew it—even when dealing with the democratically elected representatives entrusted with the nation's welfare. In a scene that anticipated the testimony of Richard Helms years later, Dulles faced serious questioning from the Senate Armed Services Committee about an operation gone wrong and likely to be highly embarrassing. He confided to his senior aides, "Well, I guess I'll have to fudge the truth a little." His eyes, according to the account by one of his chief assistants, twinkled at the word "fudge." "I'll tell the truth to Dick [Chairman Richard Russell]. I always do." Then, with a chuckle, he added, "That is, if Dick wants to know."[46]

This particular scene with Dulles in his office highlights one of the fundamental ethical problems in intelligence. The director was telling the truth to his assistants and they were telling the truth to him. An agent or a station chief or an official of the intelligence community who did not tell the truth, who departed in the slightest degree from a faithful account of what he knew or what he had done, was a serious danger to operations and to lives. "But the truth," wrote one of Dulles's former associates with years of experience in intelligence, "was reserved for the inside. To the outsider, CIA men learned to lie, to lie consciously and deliberately without the slighest twinge of guilt that most men feel when they tell a deliberate lie." He continued bluntly:

> The inside–outside syndrome is unavoidable in a secret intelligence agency. You bring a group of people together, bind them with an oath, test their loyalty periodically with machines, spy on them to make sure they're not meeting secretly with someone from the Czech Embassy, cushion them from the rest of the world with a false cover story, teach them to lie because lying is in the national interest, and they do not behave like other men.[47] Said Dulles himself, "I never had the slightest qualms about lying to an outsider."[48]

Protection of one's own activities from sabotage, espionage, and other forms of penetration requires <u>counterintelligence</u>. Passive measures may entail no more than preventative precautions against possible harm. Active counterintelligence involves more determined actions to detect, complicate, and disrupt the operations of spies, terrorists, and other agents seeking to bring harm. When directed specifically against others' activities, its basic defensive purpose is seen as necessary. Even critic Thomas Powers wrote that "if one elects to have an intelligence service, then inevitably the necessity for counter intelligence must also be accepted."[49] Nevertheless, even here, serious problems can emerge in open, democratic societies where there is strong distrust for any activity involving the surveillance of, and action against, the legitimate privacy and rights of individuals.

"Sensitive legal and ethical questions," stated the Senate Select

Committee to Study Intelligence, are raised in the pursuit of counterintelligence.[50] Indeed, their investigation revealed a series of nearly unrestrained activities designed to "disrupt" and "neutralize" private citizens perceived as dangerous enemies largely because they belonged to a racial minority or opposed the undeclared war in Vietnam. As William Sullivan, former assistant director for Domestic Intelligence of the Federal Bureau of Investigation, described it, "No holds were barred."[51] The results, concluded the Senate committee, were "illegal, improper, and unethical" counterintelligence operations conducted by agencies of the federal government.[52] These included Operation Chaos against dissidents; warrantless wiretaps and surreptitious entries against unsuspecting American citizens; interception of telephone calls and telegrams; opening of first-class mail; and the approval of and participation by the CIA, FBI, National Security Agency, and Defense Intelligence Agency in presidential assistant Tom Charles Houston's plan directed against those expressing opposition to the Vietnam War. When these activities became public and acquired the nom de scandale of the "Family Jewels," William Colby, as recently appointed Director of Central Intelligence, admitted under severe questioning that they constituted "excesses."[53] The difficulty in such situations, as the deputy director for operations testified, was to find a balance wherein the "U.S. counter intelligence program to be both effective and in line with traditional American freedoms must steer a middle course between blanket, illegal, frivolous, and unsubstantiated inquiries into the private lives of U.S. citizens and excessive restrictions which will render the Government's counter intelligence arms impotent to protect the nation from foreign penetration and covert manipulation."[54]

In intelligence, nothing provokes greater controversy and concern than covert action (or "special activities" as it is now known in the United States and "active measures" in the Soviet Union). Covert action is designed secretly to influence people, organizations, governments, and events within other countries in ways that cannot be attributed. It provides a middle range, or "third option," to implement policy, somewhere between a diplomatic protest on the one hand and a declaration of war on the other. Historically, the methods of covert action have varied enormously. At the low end of the spectrum one finds the provision of advice and counsel to leading decisionmakers, the presentation of subsidies or technical assistance, or the placement of articles in independent newspapers to influence opinion. Extreme covert actions include active involvement and intervention into the domestic affairs of another state in violation of treaties and international law; paramilitary operations, counterinsurgency, and terrorism to overthrow unfriendly governments; and attempts to assassinate political opponents.

It is hardly surprising that covert actions employing secrecy, deception, manipulation, and sometimes lethal force and murder should raise ethical questions of the first magnitude. Senate revelations of actual or alleged assassination plots against Jacobo Arbenz in Guatemala, Fidel Castro in Cuba, and Ngo Dinh Diem in South Vietnam; armed intervention during the Bay of Pigs invasion of Cuba and secret military missions in Laos; and "spoiling actions" against Salvador Allende in Chile, among other activities, opened serious public debate about covert action.[55] For some, these represented unsavory, but necessary, evils vital for preserving the security of democracy in a hostile world where Soviet "active measures" observe no limits.[56] For others, covert action is intrinsically unethical and contrary to the very political principles of freedom it claims to protect.[57] As former deputy assistant secretary of defense for international affairs Morton Halperin testified, covert actions, by avoiding open debate

> distort our democratic system [and the other] structures that normally govern the conduct of our officials. . . . One obvious area is lying to the public and the Congress. . . . The case against covert operations is really very simple. Such operations are incompatible with our democratic institutions, with Congressional and public control over foreign policy decisions, with our constitutional rights, and with the principles and ideals that this Republic stands for in the world.[58]

The members of the Senate Select Committee to Study Intelligence seriously considered proposing a ban on all forms of covert activity. After considerable debate, however, they decided that such actions might be justified in "extraordinary circumstances involving grave threats" but, even then, only within greatly restricted limits.[59] This did not include political assassination, which the committee condemned as violating "moral precepts fundamental to our way of life," prohibited as "a tool of foreign policy," and rejected as "incompatible with American principles, international order, and morality."[60] Yet even here the committee faced a persistent problem when someone raised the case with which this chapter began: the attempted assassination of Adolf Hitler. Would tyrannicide be ethically justified if it saved the lives of several million human beings? The committee found itself unable to resolve the difficult dilemma of this extreme case and did not address it in the final report; but Senator Barry Goldwater, one of the committee's members, wrote by way of a personal comment that the appalling atrocities committed by tyrants "raise a question which may be unanswerable but which needs to be carefully examined because the human carnage they created cries out for it."[61]

CONFRONTING ETHICAL DILEMMAS

The plea that certain ethical questions "need to be carefully examined" touches the crux of the problem. The difficult and complex ethical dilemmas posed by intelligence operations rarely receive careful examination. Individuals are generally either left to confront these issues by themselves or encouraged by others to ignore them completely. A few, of course, have responded by resigning in frustration and disgust, refusing to play any further part in intelligence.[62] Many others, however, have attempted to find some means of avoiding any thoughtful examination at all, usually by trying to wish or rationalize the ethical problems away.

One standard response has been to deny the existence of any serious dilemma by refusing to see any major conflict among one's individual conscience, the responsibilities of the intelligence profession, and the demands of one's state. Psychologically, this can be most comforting, for it denies the very idea of competition among different ethical standards and thereby legitimizes what is necessary for state policy under the "just war" theory.[63] The "position of conflict" experienced and expressed by Canaris and Helms, it argues, should never arise in the first place. Otto von Bismarck provided a classic example of this approach. In control of great power and secret funds to support numerous intelligence agents, Bismarck pursued a policy frequently regarded as ruthless and as the epitome of Machiavellian realpolitik. He nevertheless filled his correspondence with words like "duty," "justify," "service," and "right," and with declarations such as "I am God's soldier, and where he sends me there I must go." He convinced himself that serving the state was a divine duty, and that whatever the state required for its protection and advancement was divinely ordained. "I believe that I am obeying God when I serve my King," he said on one occasion.[64] As one critic observed, Bismarck fortunately "believes firmly and deeply in a God who has the remarkable faculty of always agreeing with him."[65]

Many dealing with intelligence minimize ethical conflicts by denying the validity of ethics in the international setting. They argue that ethics might be applicable among individuals at home, but that the vicious and uncertain world in which we live renders ethical considerations abroad unrealistic and unattainable at best and dangerous at worst. In the unrestrained arena of global politics, ethics is described as a "luxury" that cannot be afforded and likened to "a children's crusade against the powers of evil," of interest only to "dreamers and idealists."[66] Here, whether we like it or not, the best means of survival can be found only when "anything goes," when there are "no holds barred," and when "no limitations" and "no restrictions" confine behavior.[67] As declared in the top-secret report previously cited, "We must learn to subvert, sabotage, and destroy our enemies by more clever, more sophisticated, and more effective methods than those used against us."[68]

Another common response used to reduce the personal agony of confronting ethical dilemmas has been to shift responsibility to someone else, particularly in the process of following another's orders. One intelligence officer once highly praised a subordinate in his personnel assessment for exactly this trait by writing:

> He is indeed aware of the precepts of right and wrong, but if he is given an assignment which may be morally wrong in the eyes of the world, but necessary because his case officer ordered him to carry it out, then it is right, and he will dutifully undertake appropriate action for its execution without pangs of conscience. In a word, he can rationalize all actions [emphasis added].[69]

Although recognizing the importance of such behavior within the specific confines of any command and control structure, members of Congress investigating this case of intelligence concluded simply that "this rationalization is not in keeping with the ideals of our nation."[70] Even when Richard Helms argued during his trial that he had never acted without orders from the higher authority of the president of the United States himself, Judge Parker remained unpersuaded. "You can pick up any book on Western civilization and find this same defense. At the Nuremberg trials, we had that thread running through there, and more recently at the Watergate trials . . . [when people] frequently claimed that they were only doing their duty."[71]

The response of still others has been to avoid difficult ethical problems simply by ignoring the existence of ethics. This occurs when individuals become caught up in the immediate intelligence task at hand, asking only the how of efficiency rather than the why of purpose. During testimony, William Sullivan candidly remarked:

> During the ten years that I was on the U.S. Intelligence Board, a board that receives the cream of intelligence for this country from all over the world and inside the United States, never once did I hear anybody, including myself, raise the question: "Is this course of action which we have agreed upon lawful, is it legal, is it ethical or moral?" We never gave any thought to this line of reasoning, because we were just naturally pragmatists. The one thing we were concerned about was this: will this course of action work, will it get us what we want, will we reach the objective that we desire to reach?[72]

These different responses are easily understandable, especially in psychological terms. They all provide comfort by relieving the agony caused by confronting difficult issues that one would strongly prefer to avoid. They also are highly unsatisfactory, for through a variety of means they either dismiss or ignore the genuine ethical dilemmas posed by intelligence.

One of the greatest dangers in such responses is that individuals lose the habit of permitting an ethical component to enter their pattern of thinking. Gradually, standards of conduct are lowered and considerations of limits and larger responsibilities are reduced; ultimately, the entire realm of ethics becomes increasingly ignored in the formulation of public policy. This is precisely the problem singled out by E. Drexel Godfrey as his most serious criticism of the intelligence community. After spending many years as director of Current Intelligence and closely watching those within the CIA, he perceptively observed that "[f]oreign intelligence is not, by and large, conducted by people lacking the capacity to recognize ethical standards, but standards are lowered to accommodate the perceived national purpose. Once lowered, they can be more easily lowered a second time, or they can be lowered further and further as routine reduces ethical resistance to repugnant activities." Once this process is begun, he believed, the result among intelligence officers was a foregone conclusion: "Not immoral or even without ethical standards themselves, they had lost the habit of questioning where they should set limits on their official conduct" [emphasis added].[73]

Direct questioning and careful examination of the ethical dilemmas of intelligence are essential for the conduct of public policy in a democratic society. What distinguishes the genius of democracies from other governments is a willingness to take the risks involved in openly confronting issues, in asking questions from different points of view, in holding public servants responsible, and in setting limits on behavior.

Ethical dilemmas will confront us in the future, but with few quick answers or easy paths. Yet we must neither dismiss nor ignore ethics—nor can we be self-righteous and abstract moralizers who do not appreciate the practical exigencies of intelligence. In this respect, avoidance of ethical issues is no less excusable than ignorance of the "cruel realities" of world politics. We must move toward a more open, explicit, and articulate effort to understand the role that ethical standards of behavior do and must play in public policy.

ACKNOWLEDGMENT

I would like to acknowledge those current and former intelligence officers ranging from the director of Central Intelligence to the chiefs of station, case officers, and analysts who have been willing to discuss this topic of ethics and intelligence with me.

NOTES

1. William Sullivan, quoted in U.S., Senate, Select Committee to Study Governmental Operations with Respect to Intelligence Activities, 94th Congress, 2nd Session, Foreign and Military Intelligence: Final Report (Washington, D.C.: Government Printing Office, 1976), Book III, pp. 968-969 [hereafter cited as U.S., Select Committee to Study Intelligence, Final Report].

2. Claus von Stauffenberg, quoted in Bundeszentrale fur politische Bildung, Germans Against Hitler (Wiesbaden: Wiesbadener Graphische Betriebe, 1964), p. 222.

3. Von Treschkow, quoted in Germans Against Hitler, p. 292.

4. Graf Yorck von Wartenburg, quoted in Germans Against Hitler, p. 199.

5. Graf von Moltke, quoted in Germans Against Hitler, pp. 249-250.

6. Wilhelm Canaris, quoted in Karl Abshagen, Canaris: Patriot and Welburger (Stuttgart: Union Verlag, 1957), p. 393.

7. Statement filed by the U.S. Department of Justice, as reproduced in "Helms Failed to Answer," Washington Post (November 1, 1977).

8. "U.S. Defends Helms Deal," Washington Post (November 2, 1977).

9. Ibid.

10. Frank Church, quoted in "'No Contest' Plea Entered by Helms," Washington Post (November 1, 1977).

11. Laurence Birns, quoted in "'No Contest' Plea."

12. Richard Helms, quoted in "Helms Pleads 'No Contest' in Testimony Case," Washington Post (November 1, 1977).

13. "The Helms Bargain," Washington Post (November 2, 1977).

14. Barrington Parker, quoted in "Helms Fined," Washington Post (November 5, 1977).

15. Stanley Hoffmann, Duties Beyond Borders: On the Limits and Possibilities of Ethical International Politics (Syracuse, N.Y.: Syracuse University Press, 1981), p. xii.

16. U.S., Select Committee to Study Intelligence, Final Report, Book I, p. 188.

17. See the exchange, for example, between Ernest W. Lefever, "The Moral Case for Covert Action," Manchester Guardian Weekly (October 23, 1983) [originally published in Washington Post], and

Philip Hall, "The Immoral Case for Covert Action," Manchester Guardian Weekly (November 13, 1983).

18.   Lyman B. Kirkpatrick, Jr., The U.S. Intelligence Community (New York: Hill & Want, 1973), p. 187.

19.   Mike Mansfield, January 27, 1975, before the U.S. Senate, quoted in The Mansfield Papers. This speech set into motion the Senate Select Committee to Study Government Operations with Respect to Intelligence Activities. See also Harry Ransom, The Intelligence Establishment (Cambridge, Mass.: Harvard University Press, 1970), for background.

20.   See Joseph Monti, Ethics and Public Policy (Washington, D.C.: University Press of America, 1982); James Sellers, Public Ethics: American Morals and Manners (New York: Harper & Row, 1970); Robert Johansen, The National Interest and the Human Interest (Princeton, N.J.: Princeton University Press, 1980); John Rawls, A Theory of Justice (Cambridge, Mass.: Harvard University Press, 1971); William Sullivan, Reconstructing Public Philosophy (Berkeley: University of California Press, 1982); and Reinhold Niebuhr, Moral Man and Immoral Society (New York: Scribners, 1932).

21.   For more on this important subject, see Hoffmann, Duties Beyond Borders; Arnold Wolfers, Discord and Collaboration (Baltimore: Johns Hopkins University Press, 1962), especially "Statemanship and Moral Choice"; E. H. Carr, The Twenty Years Crisis (New York: Harper & Row, 1964), especially "Morality in International Politics"; Michael Walzer, Just and Unjust Wars (New York: Basic Books, 1977); Gordon A. Craig and Alexander L. George, Force and Statecraft (New York: Oxford University Press, 1983), especially "The Christian Stateman" and "The Problem of Ethical and Moral Constraints on the Use of Force in Foreign Policy"; Ernest W. Lefever, ed., Ethics and World Politics (Baltimore: Johns Hopkins University Press, 1972); and Thomas L. Pangle, "The Moral Basis of National Security," in Klaus Knorr, ed., Historical Dimensions of National Security Problems (Lawrence: University Press of Kansas, 1976), pp. 307-372.

22.   See "Espionage: Crackdown on Spies," Time (April 18, 1983). See also John Barron, The KGB (New York: Bantam, 1974); and Harry Rositzke, The KGB: The Eyes of Russia (New York: Doubleday, 1981), among others.

23.   John Barron, in Roy Godson, ed., Intelligence Requirements for the 1980s: Covert Action (Washington, D.C.: National Strategy Information Center, 1981), p. 185.

24.   U.S., Select Committee to Study Intelligence, Final Report, Book I, p. 9.

25.   This argument is summarized, but not with approval, in the excellent article by E. Drexel Godfrey, Jr., "Ethics and Intelligence," Foreign Affairs 56 (1978): 626.

26.   Morton Halperin et al., The Lawless State (New York: Penguin Books, 1976), p. 5.

27.   Personal interview (November 1983).

28.   A 1954 report on covert action prepared for the second Hoover Commission, in U.S., Select Committee to Study Intelligence, Final Report, Book I, p. 50.

29.   Godfrey, "Ethics and Intelligence," pp. 627-628. Another argument for balance is made by Scott D. Breckinridge, who served for sixteen years in the Office of Inspector General of the Central

Intelligence Agency, in his manuscript entitled "National Intelligence," which he kindly let me read.

30. Num. 13:1.

31. Sun Tzu, The Art of War, translated by Samuel Griffith (London: Oxford University Press, 1971), pp. 77, 144-149.

32. George Washington, quoted in Allen Dulles, The Craft of Intelligence (New York: Harper & Row, 1963), pp. 7-8.

33. Cardinal de Richelieu, quoted in an epigram by James Bamford, The Puzzle Palace (New York: Penguin, 1983).

34. Henry L. Stimson, On Active Service in Peace and War (New York: Harper & Brothers, 1947), p. 188.

35. David Kahn, The Code Breakers (New York: New American Library, 1973), pp. 178-179. See also Herbert Yardley, The American Black Chamber (London: Faber & Faber, 1931).

36. Louis Brandeis, in "Olmstead v. United States," U.S. Supreme Court Reports 277 (1927): 474-475.

37. Frank Church, quoted in Bamford, The Puzzle Palace, p. 477.

38. Leslie Dirks, quoted in Robert Lindsay, The Falcon and the Snowman (New York: Pocket Books, 1980), p. 345.

39. See the accounts, for example, in William Hood, Mole (New York: Norton, 1982); and Oleg Penkovskiy, The Penkovskiy Papers (Garden City: Doubleday, 1965).

40. Godfrey, "Ethics and Intelligence," p. 630. For a different opinion on the same subject, see John Langan, "Moral Damage and the Justification of Intelligence Collection from Human Sources," Studies in Intelligence 25 (Summer 1981): 57-64.

41. See Roy Godson, ed., Intelligence Requirements for the 1980s: Analysis and Estimates (Washington, D.C.: National Strategy Information Center, 1980); Sherman Kent, Strategic Intelligence for American World Power (Princeton, N.J.: Princeton University Press, 1949); and Ray Cline, The CIA Under Reagan, Bush, and Casey (Washington, D.C.: Acropolic, 1981).

42. Sissela Bok, Lying: Moral Choice in Public and Private Life (New York: Vintage, 1979), p. 175.

43. Patrick J. McGarvey, "DIA: Intelligence to Please," Washington Monthly 2 (July 1970): 68-75.

44. See Thomas Powers, The Man Who Kept the Secrets (New York: Pocket Books, 1979), pp. 267-270, 315-320.

45. Godfrey, "Ethics and Intelligence," pp. 625-626. See also Chester L. Cooper, "The CIA and Decision-Making," Foreign Affairs (January 1972): 223.

46. Allen Dulles, quoted by Tom Braden in U.S., Select Committee to Study Intelligence, Final Report, Book I, p. 547.

47. Ibid., pp. 549-550.

48. Ibid., p. 550.

49. Powers, The Man Who Kept the Secrets, p. viii. See also Roy Godson, ed., Intelligence Requirements for the 1980s: Counter Intelligence (Washington, D.C.: National Strategy Information Center, 1980).

50. U.S., Select Committee to Study Intelligence, Final Report, Book I, p. 165.

51. William Sullivan, quoted in U.S., Select Committee to Study Intelligence, Final Report, Book III, p. 9.

52. Ibid., p. 923.

53. See the account in Powers, The Man Who Kept the Secrets, pp. 367-371.

54. William Nelson, quoted in U.S., Select Committee to Study Intelligence, Final Report, Book I, p. 165.

55. U.S., Senate, Select Committee to Study Governmental Operations with Respect to Intelligence Activities, 94th Congress, 1st Session, Alleged Assassination Plots Involving Foreign Leaders, Report No. 94-465 (Washington, D.C.: Government Printing Office, 1975); Covert Action in Chile, 1963-1973 (Washington, D.C.: Government Printing Office, 1975); and Final Report, Book I, pp. 141-203.

56. See Ernest W. Lefever and Roy Godson, The CIA and the American Ethic (Washington, D.C.: Ethics and Public Policy Center, Georgetown University, 1979), pp. 17-18; Cord Meyer, Facing Reality (New York: Harper & Row, 1980); Theodore Shackley, The Third Option (New York: Reader's Digest Press and McGraw-Hill, 1981); Roy Godson, ed., Intelligence Requirements for the 1980s: Covert Action (Washington, D.C.: National Strategy Information Center, 1981); and Kermit Roosevelt, Countercoup (New York: McGraw-Hill, 1979).

57. See, among others, Victor Marchetti and John Marks, The CIA and the Cult of Intelligence (New York: Dell, 1980); Halperin et al., The Lawless State.

58. Morton Halperin, quoted in U.S., Select Committee to Study Intelligence, Final Report, Book I, pp. 520-521.

59. Ibid., pp. 446-448.

60. U.S., Select Committee to Study Intelligence, Alleged Assassination Plots, pp. 1, 257.

61. Barry Goldwater, quoted in U.S., Select Committee to Study Intelligence, Alleged Assassination Plots, p. 343.

62. See Marchetti and Marks, The CIA and the Cult of Intelligence; Philip Agee, Inside the Company: CIA Diary (New York: Bantam Books, 1981); Frank Snepp, Descent Interval (New York: Vintage, 1978); and John Stockwell, In Search of Enemies (New York: Norton, 1978).

63. For a thorough discussion of the "just war" theory, see Walzer, Just and Unjust Wars; for its specific application under particular conditions to intelligence operations, see Lefever and Godson, The CIA and the American Ethic, pp. 1-18, and Lefever, "The Moral Case for Covert Action." A response to the latter can be found in Hall, "The Immoral Case for Covert Action."

64. Otto von Bismarck, quoted in Craig and George, Force and Statecraft, "The Christian Statesman," pp. 257-258.

65. Ludwig Bamberger, quoted in Craig and George, Force and Statecraft, p. 259.

66. These words are from the novel by Morris West, The Ambassador (New York: Pocket Books, 1975), pp. 31, 203, 215, but the same point has been expressed in almost exactly the same words in personal interviews with a number of current and former intelligence officers (though certainly not all of them).

67. See the testimony in U.S., Select Committee to Study Intelligence, Alleged Assassination Plots, pp. 334-335.

68. See U.S., Select Committee to Study Intelligence, Final Report, Book I, p. 50.

69. See U.S., Select Committee to Study Intelligence, Alleged Assassination Plots, p. 259.

70. Ibid.

71. Barrington Parker, quoted in "$2,000 Helms Fine," Washington Post (November 6, 1977).

72. William Sullivan, quoted in U.S., Select Committee to Study Intelligence, Final Report, Book III, p. 968.

73. Godfrey, "Ethics and Intelligence," pp. 628, 632.

6

ALFRED C. MAURER

National Security and the Right to Know

INTRODUCTION

Success for the state in the international arena depends not only on accurate and timely intelligence, but also on protecting that intelligence from potential adversaries. National security is the reason given to protect such government secrets from unauthorized disclosure, although the phrase itself is sufficiently vague to cause concern in Congress, if not elsewhere. Because intelligence is often most valuable when potential adversaries are unaware of the extent of our knowledge, much intelligence is best gathered in as unobtrusive a means as possible. However, when such means are used within the borders of the United States, it becomes a matter not only of foreign intelligence collection but also of activities that may involve U.S. citizens in areas that are consitutionally protected by the Bill of Rights. A balance must then be achieved between these competing and equally valid interests. How this balance now stands, and what specific issues frame that balance, is the subject of this chapter.

THE BASIS FOR OFFICIAL SECRECY

The courts have long recognized the need to protect military, diplomatic, and sensitive security matters, a fact implied in as recent a case as that of <u>United States v. Nixon</u> (1974).[1] To protect information in these areas, presidents have established procedures for creating official secrets. These arrangements for restricting access to information began with nineteenth-century military orders and evolved into the present presidentially mandated security-classification system.[2] The first such mandate in recent times was Executive Order (EO) 8381, which was promulgated on March 22, 1940. It remained the principal directive on classification throughout World War II and it was primarily intended to guide the War and Navy Departments, as they were the agencies presumed to need to classify materials.

In 1950, President Truman issued EO 10104, which authorized the use of the present three classification labels—Top Secret, Secret, and Confidential—in addition to a "Restricted Data" category for atomic energy information. On September 24, 1951, coverage of the classification system was extended to nonmilitary agencies involved with national security matters by EO 10290. A controversial order, EO 10290 was rescinded by President Eisenhower in 1953 and replaced by EO 10501, "Safeguarding Official Information in the Interests of the Defense of the United States." This latter order remained in effect until 1972 with little modification. There was no provision for declassification until 1961, nor was there any penalty for mishandling or improperly disclosing classified material. There was also no review or sanction for overclassifying.[3]

In January 1971, following the publication of the "Pentagon Papers," President Nixon directed a review of security classification procedures by an interagency committee. The review eventually covered all aspects of information security. The result was EO 11652, "Classification and Declassification of National Security Information," released on March 8, 1972.[4] Congress's view of the newest executive order was that it did not improve on the weaknesses of the previous order; specifically, it lacked a clear definition of the term national defense and in fact broadened the range of materials that might be classified.[5] In response to this executive order, Congress, in 1974, passed certain amendments to strengthen the Freedom of Information Act. In 1976, President Carter enacted his own classification directive, EO 12065. In summary, the right to classify and withhold national security information from public access derives exclusively from presidential directive. Although the Congress and civil libertarians have called for a classification law to be enacted by Congress, and although they regard executive orders as something less than satisfactory, the Congress has yet to act.

SECRECY AND THE PRESS

As the situation now stands, then, there are review procedures in effect to ensure that only the information vital to the national security is classified and that declassification procedures are available to release information that has lost its sensitivity. There is still no penalty for disclosure of classified information aside from the possibility of being taken to court by the government to prevent publication (as were Marchetti and Marks in 1973.) If the information is given to a foreign agent, of course, the offender can be prosecuted under treason statutes.

In contrast to the development and state of classification laws in the United States, the laws and courts of Great Britain place much greater restraints both on the press and on those who disclose--or "leak"--classified information than do the laws and courts in the United States.[6] Moreover, the British Official Secrets Act protects the intelligence community and punishes those who violate its secrets. A recent British landmark case—Her Majesty's Secretary of State for Defense and Her Majesty's Attorney General v. Guardian Newspapers Limited[7]—dramatically highlights these differences.

A young lady named Sarah Tisdall mailed, unbidden, a secret memorandum between the secretary of state for defense and Prime Minister Thatcher to the editor of the Guardian newspaper. The memo gave the date of arrival of U.S. cruise missiles at RAF Greenham Common in addition to certain measures that Secretary Heseltine had planned to take to counteract negative publicity from protestors and to control expected mass demonstrations. The memorandum had no identifying data on it except some hieroglyphics that the editor did not comprehend. Following certain inquiries that satisfied him as to the authenticity of the document, the editor decided unilaterally that publication would not harm the national interests, and so he published it.

The next day the prime minister was embarrassed by questions in the House of Commons and gave orders to Scotland Yard to find the leak. The government's solicitor made a written demand to the editor to deliver the document. The editor replied that he was willing to comply but insisted that the hieroglyphics first be excised. The government found the terms for return unacceptable and brought suit to recover what it claimed was the property of the Crown. The trial judge ordered the return of the document intact, and both parties then appealed to the Supreme Court of Judicature, which heard the case the next day. (There are no delays in national security cases in Britain.)

The three judges of the Court of Appeal wrote separate opinions, but all agreed by various reasonings "that it is necessary in the interests of national security that the sources from which this document came should be identified."[8] The basis for the decision was perhaps best put by the Master of the Rolls, who, after stating that counsel for the Guardian had misunderstood the gravity of the secretary of state's complaint, continued:

> Whether or not the editor acted in the public interest in publishing this document is not the issue. The Secretary of State's concern is quite different. It is that a servant of the Crown who handles classified documents has decided for himself whether classified information should be disseminated to the public. If he can do it on this occasion, he may do it on others when the safety of the state will truly be imperilled. The editor will no doubt retort that in such circumstances he would not publish, but the responsibility for deciding what should and should not be published is that of the government of the day and not that of individual civil servants or editors. Furthermore—and this is the Secretary of State's case—friendly foreign states may well be prepared to entrust the government of the day with sensitive information if its security is in the hands of ministers, but will not be prepared to do so if it is in the hands of individual civil servants or editors.[9]

It seemed to the Master of the Rolls that identification of the leaker at the earliest possible moment and his or her removal from a position of trust were "blindingly obvious." Subsequently, Sarah Tisdall was identified, discharged from her job, brought to trial under the Official Secrets Act of 1911, and given six months in jail.

She was released after serving three months of that sentence.[10] More recently, Britain's commercial television channel aired a documentary entitled "MI5's Official Secrets," which alleged illegal wiretapping activity by that counterintelligence agency. The government decided against prosecuting anyone under the Official Secrets Act for appearing in that documentary, but a senior judge (Lord Bridge) also hurriedly exhonerated the government from charges of improperly authorized phone taps. Thus, while the Official Secrets Act is alive, it is not well: the Thatcher government is under attack by the opposition parties for its use of the act, and the act itself is increasingly under attack by civil libertarians in Britian who fear its use to hide abuses of power.[11]

The situation in the United States, however, is different. When Floyd Abrams, sometimes counsel for the New York Times, asked after hearing the facts of the Tisdall case how he would advise his newspaper with respect to return of the document, he stated:

> if they [the government] went to court seeking the identity of the source that no American court would say it is up to the government to decide what is published . . . I would protect the leaker in the sense that I would not disclose the leaker. . . . One way to describe a leaker is of course a leaker. Another way is a faithless employee. . . . But another way is a source of information to the public. And from a first amendment perspective, a situation like that [Tisdall] is a very good example. I don't think anyone would argue that the press has the right to that [secret] information. Once that information comes into its hands the government doesn't have the right to go to court and keep it from being published or to punish them [the press] in effect for having published it.[12]

What then, if any, is the responsibility of the press under U.S. law not to publish the secrets it acquires, whether legally or illegally? Very little, if one listens to the press.

Lyle Denniston of the Baltimore Sun stated in a seminar of the Columbia School of Journalism that, without qualms, he would break and enter the office of the secretary of defense and steal a top-secret document off the desk of the secretary of defense and then publish it. His explanation was this: "I have only one responsibility as a journalist and that is to get a story and print it. . . . the only thing I do in life is to sell information, hopefully for a profit."[13]

Dan Rather, in the same seminar, expressed similar sentiments: "My joy is to get the news and report it. If I determined this information is true and it's newsworthy, I'd run it. If this is or may be an illegal act, then I am prepared to take the consequences of having broken the law."[14]

In a panel on "The Media and Government Leaks" concerning Grenada, Stephen Rosenfeld of the Washington Post said with respect to the responsibility issue: "We don't have to be responsible. That isn't what the Constitution said, that they wanted a pussycat of the press. The Constitution had an entirely different theory. . . . Is the press responsible, is it all the time responsible, is it fully responsible? And the answer is, of course it's not."[15]

Later in the same seminar, Ford Rowan of NBC endorsed Rosenfeld's views in these words: "I agree with the idea that the first amendment doesn't mandate a responsible press. It's nice if the press corps acts responsibly. The question, of course, is who decided. And, emphatically, it is not the government that should decide under our system."[16]

THE RIGHT TO KNOW

The foregoing points to a widespread belief, in this country at least, that the government's right to secrecy is strictly limited by the people's right to know. The issues go beyond media attitudes regarding the acquisition and publishing of government secrets; the people's right to know is founded on a basic distrust of government. Openness is necessary for the people to hold their government in check. This theory abounds in the writings of our forefathers and was perhaps best expressed by James Madison: "A popular Government without popular information, or the means of acquiring it, is but a Prologue to a Farce or a Tragedy; or perhaps both . . . a people who mean to be their own Governors, must arm themselves with the power which knowledge gives."[17]

Improper Classification

The use of classification is necessary to protect government information from release, but it is potentially also a cloak to shield illegal government activity. The present executive-order guidelines carefully stipulate who may classify and what information qualifies for classification. A key test all classifiers must employ is the test of damage to national security if exposed. Proper classification establishes access to the restricted material and the degree of damage to national security should the information be compromised. The order also provides for monitoring of the system, for oversight, and for exemption from public disclosure under the Freedom of Information Act (FOIA). Nevertheless, access to government information is guaranteed by the First Amendment. The FOIA and its subsequent amendments presume the public's right to access to U.S. government records.

Freedom of Information Act

The Freedom of Information Act was enacted by Congress in 1966 to provide procedures whereby individual citizens could directly request a document from any executive branch agency. If access were denied, redress from the courts is available. Indeed, under this law, the government must prove why the information must be withheld; under previous practice, the individual would have had to prove a "need to know." The executive branch, from President Johnson forward, did not look favorably on the FOIA and took advantage of language in the act that could be misinterpreted or misunderstood in such a way as to largely ignore the FOIA.[18] As a result of the prevailing situation and President Nixon's order concerning security classification, the House Foreign Operations and Government Information Subcommittee held hearings on the FOIA in 1972.[19] As a consequence of the findings of those hearings, vigorous efforts were undertaken by the 93rd Congress to amend the act. Over presidential veto, the bill was enacted in November 1974.

Although no president has given his direct support to the FOIA, following the 1974 amendment to the act, the act has been scrupulously followed by the intelligence community. In testimony before the Senate Committee on Intelligence in 1983, the CIA detailed its efforts on behalf of the Freedom of Information and Privacy Acts since 1975. In 1975, the CIA alone received 6,609 cases and responded, in that same year, to 5,479 of them. The number of new cases has steadily declined to 1,010 in 1982. Nevertheless, a backlog of 2,739 cases remained in that year, and both man-hours and salary costs have increased over the eight-year period. Interestingly, however, more than half the cases—up to 84 percent in 1975—resulted in a finding of "no record" or were "canceled with reference." Especially in 1975, many requests were simply made by persons curious to see whether the CIA had a file on them. Other requests turn out to have come from former applicants or agency personnel, in addition to those requests from the media and academic researchers that the act was also designed to serve.[20]

Some damage to the national security has resulted from certain releases under FOIA, but in all fairness it should be noted that this damage resulted more from faulty processing of requests than from the act itself. Operational intelligence involving sensitive sources and methods is invariably highly classified and not releasable. Executive agencies must protect operational intelligence involving sensitive sources and methods.

Foreign Intelligence Surveillance Act

This act is concerned with electronic surveillance within the United States. It is part of a larger concern with so-called Fourth Amendment activities--namely, warrantless searches conducted by the intelligence community in support of foreign intelligence activities that would require warrants under the Fourth Amendment. The Foreign Intelligence Surveillance Act (FISA) of 1978 established the legal procedures by which foreign intelligence and counterintelligence could be collected in the United States. Such collection could be targeted against foreign agents in this country by proper approval of the appropriate executive branch agency and through review and approval by the Foreign Intelligence Surveillance Court, which was created by the act and consists of seven federal district judges.[21] The act intended to serve two often competing goals at the same time: the first of these was to provide the legislative authority to conduct wiretapping and other electronic surveillance when required by legitimate national security concerns. Previously, such activity had been carried out by executive order alone, and such a procedure had come under increasing criticism following Watergate in 1974. Furthermore, as a result of the questionable legality of such activity, federal officials were personally being sued in federal court. The second objective of the act was to protect the rights of Americans under the Fourth Amendment from warrantless search and seizure in the name of national security.[22]

Electronic surveillance covered by the act falls into four categories. Wiretapping is the unconsented acquisition of a wire communication and may involve telephone, teleprinter, telegraph, or other digital communication techniques. Radio intercepts are similar in nature except that the medium is radio communication. In both of these categories, the domestic nature of the surveillance is closely defined and depends on the physical location of the communication links as well as the standing of the parties to the communication. Monitoring devices constitute the third category, which includes not only "bugs" but also closed-circuit television and other similar techniques. The fourth category, "watch-listing," includes surveillance of wire or radio communications in which the recipient may be a protected U.S. person,[23] but the communication may have originated overseas and would thus be otherwise unprotected by the act.[24] The two principal agencies that conduct electronic surveillance under the act are the National Security Agency (in support of foreign intelligence) and the Federal Bureau of Investigation (in support of domestic counterintelligence), although other agencies of the executive branch have engaged in the activity as well.[25]

Has the act been successful in reaching its goals? The Senate Committee on Intelligence was required by the act to report annually on the effectiveness of the act for the first five years. In its final report, the committee concluded that the act had, indeed, assisted the intelligence community in the pursuit of intelligence information. The number of approved applications for surveillance has risen from 319 in 1980, to 431 in 1981, to 475 in 1982, and to 549 in 1983.[26] According to an official from the NSA, "the operaton of the approval process has been efficient and timely, and the security of the Foreign Intelligence Surveillance Court has been first-rate."[27] According to the FBI, "[We] have found them [the provisions of the statute] to permit necessary intelligence collection. We are convinced that it provides our personnel with the assurance that their activities today will withstand challenge in the future."[28]

The act has also protected the rights of American citizens, as well as those of foreign nationals located within the United States. Before a surveillance can occur, the executive agency involved reviews the proposal internally. It is then subject to review by the attorney general and the Surveillance Court before it can be implemented. Also in effect are minimization procedures that reduce the effect of the surveillance. For example, nonpertinent voice recordings are destroyed, and surveillance orders are for a limited time period and must be periodically renewed. The Senate Committee was convinced that the procedures of the act were adequate as they stood.[29]

Although not the subject of the FISA, the executive branch uses other techniques that are covered under the procedures of the Fourth Amendment. Such things as physical searches and mail openings have been and are covered under executive branch orders such as EO 12333 and its predecessor under the Carter administration, EO 12036. Under these procedures, the president and the attorney general authorize such activities without specific statutory authorization or court order, claiming general constitutional authority.[30] Such activities are approved under procedures very similar to those used under the FISA, however, and in many cases are more stringent than required in similar criminal investigation activities.[31]

Prepublication Review

A related issue concerns prepublication review and nondisclosure agreements. In an effort to protect classified information, many government agencies require employees and former employees to submit for review those publications or materials relating to sensitive intelligence matters to which they might have been exposed during the course of their employment. This is not a matter of censorship, however. The aim is not to review political writings or dissent, nor is it to squelch academic freedom. Often it isn't the intelligence producers who leak sensitive information but rather the users of the intelligence who may not be fully aware of the special sensitivity of the information or who for whatever reason believe that their purpose in releasing information should take precedence. This requirement for prepublication review does not mean everything dealing with politics or a senior official's view of history need be submitted, nor is a blind submission of everything they write required. That would be censorship. Instead, the concern is ensuring that valid national security secrets are protected. This review is not legally binding in the absence of an Official Secrets Act. If a given author chose not to follow the guidance given, the government would take the case to court on the basis of both the secrecy oath and any nondisclosure agreement the author may have signed while in government service.

Use of the Polygraph

A final issue involves the use of the polygraph, recently extended to almost everyone in the executive branch with access to classified information. Again, the aim is to stop leaks. On the other side of the issue is the concern for individual rights against self-incrimination and the veracity of the testing procedure itself. No document highlights the national security issue more clearly than the Report of the British Security Commission in the case of Geoffrey Arthur Prime, who for thirteen years leaked the secrets of Cheltenham (theirs and ours) to the Soviets.

The British Security Commission was appointed by Prime Minister Thatcher: "to investigate the circumstances in which breaches of security have or may have occurred arising out of the case of Geoffrey Arthur Prime, who was convicted on 10 November 1982 of Offenses under the Official Secrets Act of 1911; and to advise in the light of that investigation whether any change in security arrangements is necessary or desirable."[32]

A few facts about the Prime case are necessary to an understanding of the commission's task. For thirteen years, Prime, a Russian linguist, was employed in signals intelligence work at Cheltenham, the British counterpart of our National Security Agency. During that time he gave Cheltenham's sensitive secrets, and ours as well, to various Soviet controllers. For the Soviets the secrets passed by Prime were a gold mine of information; for Britain and the United States they constituted a disaster. In the words of the British Security Commission: "The extent to which his disclosures damaged the national interests of the United States and this country and impaired the effectiveness of the intelligence operations of the NSA and GCHQ [Government Communications Headquarters] can never be calculated with accuracy."[33]

The commission soon discovered massive failures of personnel and physical-premise security at Cheltenham as well as abysmal counterintelligence procedures. In fact, Prime was caught only because of his peculiar sexual activities, which led to the discovery of spying equipment in his house.

The entire thirteen-year hemorrhage of secrets may well have been avoided by the use of the polygraph. In his interrogation, Prime himself "stated that he would not have sought employment with G.C.H.Q. in 1968 if he had known that he would be required to undergo a polygraph examination."[34] Indeed, there could be no better endorsement of the use of the polygraph in screening tests for prospective employees.

Still, the British Security Commission was hard to convince. The civil liberties organization, the press, and the unions had a prejudice against the polygraph that made our own counterpart organizations' objections seem mild by comparison. Because American as well as British secrets had been leaked, two members of the commission (General Sir Hugh Beach and the chairman, Lord Bridge of Harwich) decided to examine the security procedures used by our CIA, NSA, and the Defense Department, including the use of the polygraph. They framed their conclusions in these words:

> The vivid demonstration which the Prime case affords of the great damage that can result from a single failure of personnel security to exclude a potential traitor from access to the most secret information or to detect his treachery at an early stage underlines the necessity for the adoption of the most effective practical safeguards which human ingenuity can devise.[35]

Sir Beach and Lord Bridge had departed England with typical British prejudice against the use of the polygraph. However, in their final report to the prime minister and Parliament, they stated:

> The most important conclusions we have reached in this inquiry have, we readily acknowledge, resulted from the visit of members of the Commission to Washington and the direct experience gained from this visit of the personnel security procedures adopted by the United States intelligence and security agencies. . . . Both the N.S.A. and the C.I.A. regard the polygraph as essentially an auxiliary aid to the ascertainment of the truth. . . . But most impressive of all is the patently sincere conviction of the very experienced senior staff responsible for personnel security in the N.S.A. and C.I.A. that the polygraph is their most effective safeguard against hostile penetration.[36]

On their return to England the two commission members recommended the use of the polygraph in personnel security matters and the training of operators in the United States. There was opposition by unions and in Parliament, but the prime minister simply abolished the unions at Cheltenham and ordered the training of operators and pilot use of the polygraph.

The U.S. Department of Defense recently published a pamphlet about the effectiveness of the polygraph as a tool in security investigations. The report states in part that

> The polygraph is extremely useful in intelligence and counter intelligence operations. There is positive evidence of the deterrent effect of screening examinations. Examples of espionage and attempted espionage cases detected by polygraph examinations are included in this study. Without the polygraph as an investigative tool, a number of espionage cases never would have been solved. Helmich, Kampiles, and Barnett probably would not have been successfully prosecuted without the skillful application of polygraph technique. In addition, there is definite evidence that some extremely sensitive U.S. intelligence operations would have been penetrated by hostile intelligence services if the polygraph had not been employed in screening for clearance and access. Examiners conducting screening cases have obtained confessions from applicants of their intention to commit espionage. In other cases they developed such significant admissions that penetration attempts by hostile intelligence were detected and neutralized. Screening has also kept our intelligence agencies from hiring some extremely undesirable people. Examiners in FY 82 obtained admissions from applicants of undetected crimes involving murder, attempted murder, arson, rape and numerous other felonies.[37]

CONCLUSION

Mutual trust and responsible actions can lead us toward the balance between the demand for secrecy and that for openness in our society. The polygraph and classification restrictions are invaluable tools in national security matters—matters that call for intelligence users who are fully aware of the special sensitivity of the information they are working with and that necessitate the means to identify those culpable, regardless of motivation, of acting against the legitimate national security interests of the United States.

We must all make up our own minds as to whether we have proper restraints on the press as well as on the intelligence community. Remember that national security and the national interests of our country and our allies are, or should be, a common cause. We cannot long survive, certainly not without rancor and distrust, if we do not guard each other's secrets as if they were our own. If we can develop mutual trust, if others act responsibly and if we act responsibly, the government can have the secrecy it needs and we can all enjoy our cherished civil rights.

NOTES

1. United States v. Nixon, 418 US 683, 706 (1974).
2. Harold C. Relyea, The Presidency and Information Policy (New York: Center for the Study of the Presidency, 1981), p. 9. See also

the discussion on pp. 9-18 of Relyea's text.

3.   See House Rept. 93-221, pp. 9-11.   Amendments to EO 10501 are listed in Relyea, The Presidency and Information Policy, p. 144, note 46.

4.   House Rept. 93-221, p. 31.

5.   Ibid.

6.   The Freedom of Information Act, including all its requirements, is scrupulously observed by the intelligence community.   It may be reasonable to exempt operational intelligence.

7.   Her Majesty's Secretary of State for Defense and Her Majesty's Attorney General v Guardian Newspapers, Ltd., Royal Courts of Justice (December 16, 1983). This account of the case is found in a paper delivered by William Mott to the intelligence conference at the USAF Academy, June 1984 [hereafter cited as Mott, 1984 conference], pp. 2-4.

8.   Mott, 1984 conference, p. 3.

9.   Ibid.

10.   Hunter R. Clark, "Challenging Government Secrets," Time, March 18, 1985, p. 37.

11.   Ibid., pp. 32, 37.

12.   Media and Government Leaks (Washington, D.C.: ABA Committee on Law and National Security, 1984).

13.   "The Constitution—That Delicate Balance," National Security and Freedom of the Press (New York: Columbia University School of Journalism, 1983).

14.   Ibid.

15.   Ibid.

16.   Ibid.

17.   James Madison, letter to W. T. Barry, August 4, 1822, in G. P. Hunt, ed., The Writings of James Madison, vol. 9 (New York: G. P. Putnam's Sons, 1910), p. 103.

18.   See Relyea, The Presidency and Information Policy, p. 31, who quotes several court cases.

19.   See   U.S., Congress, House Committee on Government Operations, U.S. Government Information Policies and Practices, parts 4-9, Hearings, 92nd Congress, 2nd session (Washington, D.C.: Government Printing Office, 1972).

20.   U.S., Congress, Senate, Hearings before the Senate Committee on Intelligence, 98th Congress, 1st session, on an Amendment to the National Security Act of 1947, June 21, 28 and October 4, 1983 (Washington, D.C.: Government Printing Office, 1983, pp. 18-42).   The hearings concerned the "Intelligence Information Act of 1983," an amendment to the FOIA to exempt the CIA and the intelligence community for operational intelligence.

21.   U.S., Congress, Senate, Committee on Intelligence, The Foreign Intelligence Surveillance Act of 1978: The First Five Years, 98th Congress, 2nd session (Washington, D.C.: Government Printing Office, 1984), p. 1.

22.   Ibid., passim.

23.   "U.S. person" is a legal term that includes U.S. citizens, permanent resident aliens,unincorporated associations composed of such persons or corporations incorporated in the United States.   For a fuller definition, see EO 12333.

24.   Ibid., p. 3.

25. Ibid., p. 4.
26. Ibid., p. 2.
27. Ibid., p. 4.
28. Ibid.
29. Ibid., pp. 5-10.
30. Ibid., p. 16.
31. Ibid., p. 17.
32. See Mott, 1984 conference, p. 6. The account of the Prime case is taken from pp. 7-9 of the same paper.
33. Ibid., p. 7.
34. Ibid.
35. Ibid., p. 8.
36. Ibid., p. 9.
37. Office of the Secretary of Defense, The Accuracy and Utility of Polygraph Testing (Washington, D.C.: Government Printing Office, 1984).

7

MORTON H. HALPERIN

Intelligence in an Open Society

The requirements of intelligence agencies and the norms of an open society pose the sharpest of apparent dilemmas for a democratic government. Intelligence agencies, by their nature, function in secret without being subject to the normal rules of the state. An open society, on the other hand, abhors secrecy and insists that all government agencies be fully responsive to the rule of law.

The need to find a proper balance between these norms is made all the greater by the fact that the failure to properly control intelligence agencies can have far more catastrophic consequences for a nation than most other policy failures. If the intelligence community fails to warn policymakers of impending threats to the nation, the result can be serious setbacks abroad and possible loss of areas of vital interest—even nuclear war. Alternatively, the failure to put effective controls on the operations of intelligence agencies, particularly as they relate to the rights of Americans, can lead to serious violations of civil liberties—violations that could threaten the very values that the intelligence community, as part of the national security establishment, is designed to protect.

The first step in reconciling these conflicting imperatives is to take both of them seriously. This means accepting the need for an effective intelligence community and recognizing the legitimacy of the concern that the intelligence community not be permitted to function in ways that undermine civil liberties. Too often in the past, analysts and those involved in the political process have focused on one set of imperatives or the other without recognizing and accepting the legitimacy of both. Those in the intelligence community, senior national security policymakers, and most scholarly analysts of intelligence have tended to ignore the dictates of civil liberties. Often they have simply been unaware of and unconcerned with such issues. When confronted with these issues, they have often viewed the demands underlying them as illegitimate because intelligence agencies, of necessity, must operate beyond the law, and because they did not accept the possibility that such agencies might operate in ways that threatened the values of an open society. They have tended to view such claims as disguised attempts to influence the direction of national security policy by those who objected to the policy on other grounds.

Approaching the problem from the opposite direction, we find that civil libertarians have tended to be skeptical of claims of national security.   Familiar with past abuses and the ways in which secret intelligence services in other countries have been used to subvert liberty, they have viewed the demands for special powers and exemptions for intelligence services as threats to liberty.   Often they have believed that such demands were put forward precisely to circumvent the limits on the ability of the government to conduct surveillance of its own people and to limit the participation of these people in the political process.

It is my thesis that if the United States avoids these extremes—if we accept the need for an effective intelligence service and the need to control it so that it does not become a threat to liberty—then we can find solutions that satisfy both sets of demands.

THE DEMANDS OF AN OPEN SOCIETY

The founders of this nation started out with a healthy skepticism about those in power.   They believed that a temptation existed for those in power to seek to maintain their authority by whatever means were put at their disposal.   Hence they saw the need to design within the government a system of checks and balances.   The potential tyranny of the legislature would be reined in by the power of the executive and of the courts.   The authority of the courts and of the Congress would check the president's power.   The power of both political branches, even when they sought to act together, would be checked by the courts, which would leave certain functions to the states, require certain open procedures, and, by means of a Bill of Rights, limit the powers of the government.   The framers clearly intended that these procedures and limits would apply even when the government was invoking what we now label its "national security" powers.   With James Madison, they shared the belief that "perhaps it is a universal truth that the loss of liberty at home is to be charged to provisions against dangers, real or pretended, from abroad."

That warning, contained in a letter from Madison to Jefferson, is the perspective from which those who drafted the Constitution and the Bill of Rights started and from which we should begin in taking civil liberties seriously with respect to intelligence issues.

The first and most basic principle is that the laws of the land, especially the Constitution and the Bill of Rights, must apply to the activities of the intelligence agencies just as they do to all other spheres of the government.   How they apply and what implications their application has for how these agencies may function is, as I will later discuss, a matter for careful analysis.   However, the starting point cannot be (as it was until the mid-1970s) the assertion that intelligence agencies are simply not subject to the dictates of the Constitution.

The second principle is that in a democratic society certain activities are simply ruled out.   These two principles are absolute because they violate fundamental norms of the society and pose too great a risk to the liberty of the citizens of that society and to the society's own perception of its moral worth.   A few examples will serve to illustrate this basic point.   U.S. intelligence services are not permitted to seize people on the streets of this land and torture them until they reveal whatever information of interest they have and then murder them and hide their bodies.   In all too many countries this practice is routine, but we rule it out not on short-run utilitarian grounds but as a matter of principle and as a means to protect our freedom.   Similarly, Americans would not accept or permit the temporary or permanent closing down of the press to keep it from reporting intelligence secrets.

That there are and must be such absolutes seems clear.   What falls within that category may from time to time be a matter of serious and intense debate.   In some cases when the debate spreads beyond the national security establishment and the intelligence community the accepted wisdom is altered.   For example, for many years the assassination of foreign leaders was considered to be an appropriate instrument of U.S. policy in certain circumstances.   When this fact became public in the mid-1970s, it produced a public outcry that has led every president since to include in his executive order on intelligence a flat prohibition against assassination.

A third principle stemming from civil liberties concerns is that in designing the rules for the conduct of intelligence agencies, one must consider not only what it is appropriate for them to do but also the possibility of abuse.   When the United States first established a set of peacetime intelligence agencies after World War II, this danger of abuse was simply ignored in all but a few cases.   When Congress debated the establishment of the CIA many members expressed concern about the creation of a "gestapo," but these fears quickly subsided.   It was assumed that U.S. intelligence agencies would not act in ways that threatened the liberties and rights of Americans.   Unfortunately this confidence—so antithetical to the skepticism about those in power that guided the founding of the nation—proved to be misguided.

At times, acting at the explicit direction of the president, and in some cases on their own, the intelligence agencies engaged in a series of actions that led a special Senate investigating committee to conclude as follows:

Too many people have been spied upon by too many Government agencies and too much information has been collected.   The Government has often undertaken the secret surveillance of citizens on the basis of their political beliefs, even when those beliefs posed no threat of violence or illegal acts on behalf of a hostile foreign power.   The Government, operating primarily through secret informants, but also using other intrusive techniques such as wiretaps, microphone "bugs," surreptitious mail opening, and break-ins, has swept in vast amounts of information about the personal lives, views, and associations of American citizens. Investigations of groups deemed potentially dangerous—and even of groups suspected of associating with potentially dangerous organizations—have continued for decades, despite the fact that those groups did not engage in unlawful activity.   Groups and individuals have been harassed and disrupted because of their political views and their lifestyles.   Investigations have been based upon vague standards whose breadth made excessive collection inevitable.   Unsavory and vicious tactics have been employed--including anonymous attempts to break up marriages, disrupt meetings, ostracize persons from their professions, and provoke target groups into rivalries that might result in deaths.

Intelligence agencies have served the political and personal objectives of presidents and other high officials. While the agencies often committed excesses in response to pressure from high officials in the Executive branch and Congress, they also occasionally initiated improper activities and then concealed them from officials whom they had a duty to inform. Government officials—including those whose principal duty is to enforce the law—have violated or ignored the law over long periods of time and have advocated and defended their right to break the law.[1]

The activities the committee had in mind included President Roosevelt's orders to the FBI to investigate those who sought to keep the United States out of the European war, Kennedy's orders for the FBI to spy on the sugar lobby, and those by Lyndon Johnson for the bureau to conduct surveillance of his critics at the 1964 Democratic convention as well as of various programs undertaken at the direction of President Nixon. The committee also was pointing to such agency-initiated programs as the FBI's counterintelligence program (COINTELPRO), the CIA's mail opening activities, and the NSA watchlist of Americans for other intelligence agencies.

Dispute abounds over whether the abuses of the intelligence agencies were as severe as their critics and the press seemed to suggest, and over how much harm the public investigations did to the intelligence agencies. However, there cannot be any serious dispute that many of the actions taken were simply unacceptable in a democratic society and hence justify—indeed require—rules and procedures that will guard against future abuses.

NATIONAL SECURITY PRINCIPLES

First, a vital need exists within an effective intelligence community for searching out information, analyzing it, and providing intelligence to senior policymakers. Second, some of this activity must be conducted in secret; some must be conducted in the United States and, at least in some circumstances, must be directed at gathering information from Americans. Finally, one must assume that those with responsibility in this area who seek increased authority do so out of a legitimate belief in its need. Their proposals must be judged on the merits and not dismissed on the basis of an assertion of bad faith.

RECONCILING THESE CONFLICTING DEMANDS

Beyond the injunction to take both sets of concerns seriously, there do not appear to be any general rules that might guide one to the appropriate solutions. However, a process does exist that is both appropriate and seemingly capable of producing a reasonable balance to the competing claims. That process, which is the normal way in which a democratic society makes rules, is the legislative process leading to the enactment of laws.

Until recently this procedure, common in all other aspects of American life, including the rest of the national security bureaucracy, was almost unknown to the intelligence community. The CIA, to be sure, was created as part of the omnibus National Security Act of 1947, but the act laid down only the most general rules for the conduct of the agency. The remainder were contained in a series of directives from the National Security Council and the director of Central Intelligence, whose very existence was, until the mid-1970s, considered a secret. Other agencies were created with even less reference to the Congress and with no public announcement of their existence or public description of their functions—much less with legislated rules for their activities. The National Security Agency (NSA) came into existence in this way. Today, almost no legislation affects it.

The Congress clearly has the formal legal authority within the U.S. system to establish the rules for the conduct of all government agencies, including those in the intelligence community. Moreover, the basic principles of constitutional democracy would seem to require that the members of the legislature, as the elected representatives of the people, function in this area. There are two other more pragmatic reasons for suggesting that the legislative process is the best mechanism for reconciling the demands of civil liberties with the requirements of the intelligence community. The first is that we now have evidence that it can work. The second is that it ensures that any changes in the system are subject to scrutiny, thus mandating that both sets of concerns will be fully considered.

Over the past few years, Congress has enacted several laws that illustrate the desirability of using this process to ensure an appropriate balance between the needs of the intelligence agencies and the requirements of an open society. In each case, prior to the enactment of the legislation, the intelligence agencies had operated under presidential direction without clear rules and with resulting conduct that many considered unacceptable. Many on both sides were skeptical of the utility of the legislative process. Intelligence agency officials were fearful of giving up the flexibility they had, and they were doubtful that legislation would permit them to operate effectively. Civil libertarians were concerned that the consequence of the process would be the legitimization of procedures they considered abusive, in the absence of effective rules or safeguards established by Congress.

The enactment by Congress of the Foreign Intelligence Surveillance Act (FISA) in 1978 well illustrates a process that balanced the two sets of interests. The law regulates the conduct of electronic surveillance for intelligence purposes within the United States. Before the law was passed, such activity was undertaken on the basis of the asserted "inherent" authority of the president. The Senate Intelligence Committee documented numerous cases of abuse proceeding both from agency initiative and at the direction of presidents. These disclosures generated support for legislation from most of the interested participants. Attorneys general had become reluctant to approve such surveillances, particularly when they were directed at Americans; the courts were generally giving sanction to such surveillances, but with reluctance; intelligence agency officials, subject to civil suits for their involvement in such activity, anxiously awaited assurances that what they were doing would not subject them to personal liability; and civil libertarians were interested in securing legislated restrictions on such activity before the memory of the abuses faded.

Despite such interest in providing legislation, the process was by no means easy. Many intelligence agency officials resisted from the start, fearing that they could not operate effectively with the court-ordered warrants that the legislation would have to require if it had any chance of enactment. Nevertheless, the Ford administration, under considerable prodding from then Attorney General Edward Levi, endorsed the principle of such legislation and the process began. Through four years of public congressional hearings, at which administration witnesses as well as outside groups testified, and after much debate in public and considerable private negotiation, the legislation evolved until it had very broad support in Congress and the endorsement of the intelligence community and many libertarians.

In 1984, the intelligence community continued to support the legislation and to assure Congress that it would not hamper the conduct of necessary foreign intelligence and counterintelligence operations. Many civil libertarians see the act as establishing reasonable guidelines and procedures that reduce the danger of abuse.

The debate in the early 1980s about the proper relationship between the intelligence community and the Freedom of Information Act (FOIA) also illustrates the critical role of the legislative process in ensuring a balance between the needs of the intelligence community and the requirements of an open society.

In 1976, Congress amended the FOIA in several ways, with the unanticipated consequence of requiring the CIA to respond to FOIA requests. The agency has had and continues to have the authority to prohibit the release of information that is either properly classified or capable of revealing intelligence sources and methods. Nonetheless, requiring the CIA to respond to FOIA requests was a traumatic experience: requests had to be officially answered, files had to be searched, and justifications had to be presented for why materials were withheld or why the agency could not even confirm or deny that it had the requested information.

After the initial trauma, the CIA discovered that much information in its files could be declassified and released following careful scrutiny. Agency officials began to tell the Congress that the FOIA had improved the operational effectiveness of the CIA. However, by the late 1970s, the agency's career officials, particularly those in the clandestine service, were persuaded that they needed substantial relief from the requirements of the FOIA. After exploring several alternatives, the Reagan administration came to the conclusion that the best option would simply be to exempt the entire intelligence community from the dictates of the FOIA.

This decision was, in my view, a classic case of looking at only one side of the equation. There is no doubt that from the point of view of intelligence operatives, it would be easier if the FOIA did not exist. However, the proposal to exempt the intelligence community failed to take account of the dictates of an open society and the need to seek a solution that would accommodate both sets of interests.

Since the FOIA is law, the executive branch could not act unilaterally. The CIA could get relief from the FOIA only if Congress acted. Congress made it clear that the argument for a total exemption was not persuasive and that, in any case, it would not act unless it was convinced that the requirements of an open society as well as those of the intelligence community were fully taken into account. By holding to this position, Congress forced a dialogue between the intelligence community and the civil liberties community as represented by the American Civil Liberties Union (ACLU). In May 1984, the CIA and the ACLU endorsed a bill that exempts certain of the CIA's operational files from the search and review requirements of the FOIA, but without altering the substantive standard for withholding material or changing the power of the federal courts to review CIA actions relating to FOIA requests. The CIA agrees that the bill gives it the relief it needs. With these changes the CIA has accepted the fact that the FOIA and a secret intelligence agency can coexist and that the agency can operate effectively while responding to requests in a timely fashion and releasing valuable information to the public. The ACLU has acknowledged that changes in the law that help the CIA can be supported if they are consistent with the requirements of an open society.

The most important area in which the principle of using legislation to strike the balance between the needs of intelligence and the requirements of an open society has not been met is that of legislated "charters" for the intelligence agencies. The Senate Intelligence Committee recommended charters that would set out the rules for the intelligence agencies, particularly with respect to their surveillance of the activities of Americans. The Carter administration endorsed such charters in principle, but a sufficient consensus did not develop to permit their enactment. The Reagan administration took the position that the mechanism of an executive order, which was then in place, was sufficient. Not needing the approval of Congress to change the order it had inherited from the Carter administration, the Reagan administration proceeded to consider possible revisions in secret and without public explanation or debate. However, an early and very controversial draft was leaked to the press. The public and congressional outcries forced the administration to withdraw some of the proposals. Nonetheless, important changes were made without full explanation and without careful balancing of the two sets of interests.

Embodied in the debates over the legislated charters and the executive orders are major issues affecting the rights of Americans as well as the effective conduct of the intelligence agencies. These include the following:

Use of Fourth Amendment Techniques. Under current procedures the attorney general can authorize the secret search of the home or office of an American if he finds that the target is an "agent of a foreign power."

Surveillance of Innocent Americans. The current executive order permits the secret surveillance of Americans not suspected of any crime or even of a clandestine connection with a foreign power in order to gather positive foreign intelligence information.

Surveillance of "Agents of a Foreign Power." Current procedures permit the clandestine surveillance of those believed to be working with or for a hostile foreign power, even if the connection is not illegal.

CIA Activity in the United States. The revised executive order permits the CIA to operate within the United States and even to conduct covert operations in this country with certain safeguards. The previous order prohibited covert operations in the United States and put more severe limits on other CIA activity in the country.

Electronic Surveillance of Americans Abroad.   When Congress enacted FISA, it stated that it would then turn its attention to regulating electronic surveillance by the U.S. intelligence agencies of Americans abroad, but it has not done so.

I raise these issues not to suggest solutions as such but, rather, to illustrate the range of issues that, in my judgment, have not yet been subjected to an appropriate balancing of the requirements of an effective intelligence service and an open society.

Only comprehensive charter legislation can ensure that balance and provide assurances to the American people over the long run that the United States has an intelligence community with the authority it needs to perform its vital missions and the capability of operating with appropriate rules and procedures such that it poses no threat to the open society it is charged to defend.

NOTES

1.   Senate Select Committee to Study Governmental Operations with respect to Intelligence Activity, Final Report, Book II, "Intelligence Activities and the Rights of Americans," 94th Congress, 2d session, 1976, S. Rept. 94-755, 5.

MANAGEMENT OF THE INTELLIGENCE COMMUNITY

In this section, we focus on the governmental level of analysis. The intelligence/policy relationship is examined not only in the context of the overall structure of government but also with respect to the realities of organization, institutional norms, and procedures. Our concern is with the impact of these various influences on the policy and intelligence functions within the state. We will examine both the formal lines of authority and the mechanisms for control over the bureaucracies that constitute the intelligence community. We will also consider the intricacies of bureaucratic power within the community and the impact of such power on executive/bureaucratic relations. As we have previously noted, it is quite clear that the structural concern of this level of analysis leads us to focus not only on the problems of effective executive administration but, most particularly, on the U.S. experience, on the interaction, and the more recent conflict, between the executive and legislative branches over guidance and control of the intelligence community. It is this latter element that has introduced perhaps the most important structural change in the intelligence/policy relationship since the creation of a centralizing core in 1947.

At its broadest, this level of analysis directs our attention to the formal and informal relationships that characterize the functioning of the government. Thus, in the case of the United States, we are concerned with separation of powers, checks and balances, and the formalities of constitutional limitations or grants while also focusing on the supposed hierarchy and control emanating from the chief executive over his branch. We are concerned with the centrality of direction, the clarity of tasking, and the lines of responsibility and accountability. Informally, our attention turns to the modifications of the "formal" picture, . . . to the bargaining, compromises, and coalition building that allow our normally conservative system to move forward.

From one perspective, we may contend that there is an intelligence community serving the common goal of informing or educating policymakers. As such, the community becomes part of the rational decisionmaking process underlying the unitary model. From another perspective, we recognize that the "community" is more accurately viewed as a collection of competing bureaucratic elements factionalized by their rivalries, jealousy, and competition for attention, dollars, and power. The fact that they are separate, that they serve different bureaucratic masters and interests, is also reflected in frequent disagreements about intelligence interpretation, analysis, and conclusions, which, in turn, raise the question of which intelligence will be chosen. These differences arise as much from the bureaucratic perspectives that frame the efforts as from the indeterminacy of the international environment that gives rise to the possibility of different interpretations.

Whether the state and executive are best served by the possible diversity of interpretation remains a fundamental question. The answer chosen reflects perhaps as much on executive preference as on the ability to locate a rationally motivated community that will arrive at the same conclusions. The executive retains the privilege to structure or restructure the community and to include or exclude its members from the policy process. This power and the inherent bureaucratic rivalries that result from the decentralized structure reflect a basic feature of the intelligence/policy interface. The executive branch cannot ignore the intelligence community, but it may be selective in determining which of the community's voices it will hear and, consequently, which of its members may reap the greatest rewards. Still, the diversity also works to inhibit effective executive control--as does the lack of executive expertise. The framework that evolved from 1947 favors certain elements of the community over others, thus establishing some consistencies, but it is far from providing clarity or consistency of results. In the end, the question may arise as to whether the concept of community is not also a reification of little practical utility.

Having perceived bureaucratic rivalries as a context for the intelligence/policy interface, one must also acknowledge the influences of the framework, organization, and procedures particular to each of the individual elements. Each community member functions in accordance with explicit and implicit norms. These norms have significant, though not unalterable, impact on the major aspects of the bureaucracy—from its hiring and promotions process, its prioritizations, its receptivity to executive control, and its preferred modes of analysis and reporting to its means of dealing with the surfeit of information confronting all of the elements. These norms create associations and condition perceptions and encourage divisions and loyalties; they are part of the concerns of the governmental level, and they provide the context within which individuals function. These concerns and realities only add to the difficulties of accurate interpretation posed by the indeterminate international environment. The chapters contained in this section address the community and its separate parts as they influence the intelligence/policy process.

First, Robert Jervis provides a description of the "perfect" system as a foil for analysis of the shortcomings of present intelligence structures. He contends that narrowness of analysis and selective recruitment must be overcome and a degree of specialization developed such that the findings of the generalist are enriched. Informally, the community must focus on competitive explanations, well-developed evidence, and presentations emphasizing completeness over eye-catching brevity. In essence, his ideal approach approximates that of good scholarship. Unfortunately, as Jervis argues, the U.S. community is inclined toward "error inducement," which is characterized by interlocking norms and habits that decrease the likelihood of the "ideal" analyses. In place of good analysis, the system encourages current reporting with few efforts to dig below the surface of any problem. The norms of the system neither encourage nor reward great depth and alternative explanations, and bureaucratic rivalries impede the exchange of views between analysts that might otherwise facilitate the development of a real community. Such problems may be amplified when crisis compresses the time continuum and, as a result, the intelligence analyst is omitted from the decisional loop. Finally, Jervis argues that good intelligence also depends on the perspective of the consumer and that the ideal system is one in which the work of the analyst is not made more difficult by the necessity of second-guessing his or her own policymakers.

Stafford Thomas also addresses the structural factors that influence the intelligence/policy relationship. Expanding on his valuable work entitled The U.S. Intelligence Community, Thomas argues that the intelligence community is characterized by norms reflecting a mixture of Graham Allison's three models of decisionmaking, including assumptions of national interest, unique operating procedures, and relationships between the unit and its environment. In the bureaucratic struggle, knowledge and sources become bases of power and success measured in size, share of the budget, and utilization of intelligence by the policymakers. In the midst of the diversity and rivalry, true coordination of intelligence becomes difficult and, as a process, is characterized by competition with and distrust of the ordained centralizer, the CIA. It is important to note that the consumers—including both community consumers (internal) and those without (external)—are equally diverse. The variety of consumers frames not only the producers but the products of the community as well, and their expertise and influences are important to the types of intelligence that emerge. All members of the community maintain checks on rivals, and all are engaged both in the competition for executive attention and by the current executive/legislative relationship. The structural realities provide freedoms for as well as limitations on the consumers, and these realities are core to intelligence/policy relations.

Glenn Hastedt delves even more deeply with his analysis of organizational influences on intelligence. He concentrates first on the artificial systems built around formal institutional relationships and the formal lines of authority structuring the organizations. The natural system derives from the artificial. It is internally oriented and concerned with the protection and survival of both the organization and its members. Derived from the natural system are a flexibility and a spontaneity that make the manager's task more difficult. From each system there is a set of benefits and costs that impact on the quality of intelligence products and the intelligence/policy interaction. In all intelligence there is the additional impact of secrecy on the interactions and functioning of organizations. Hastedt contributes a vital exposition of his organizational model as it applies to the CIA and offers keen insight into the interface between the agency and the executive branch, noting the conflicting logics between the intelligence and policymaking functions. Equally valuable is his clear conception of the relation of the governmental level to other levels of analysis.

George Pickett's chapter offers a unique and valuable explanation of the relationship between the intelligence community, the executive, and the Congress. He evaluates the changing nature of congressional involvement with the community through the medium of the budgetary process. He also offers an incisive perspective not only of the structural change resulting from increased congressional activity in intelligence oversight, but also of the change wrought by the increase within Congress itself. Congress has asserted the right to be much more involved in the allocation of intelligence resources and the approval of intelligence activities. It has assumed responsibility in a dynamic and conflictual arena and has been both student and teacher in the process. Pickett reminds us that the system is variable in spite of its consistencies, and he informs us of the problems and consequences of change in the operating environment and among the important actors in the intelligence/policy process. Most important, he also reminds us that such adjustments and changes are rarely unidirectional.

All of the chapters in this section suggest problems and concerns of importance not only to the United States but to the political systems of many individual states as well. Although there are differences between the operating environments and key actors, the problems of coordination of conflicting views and of competition among bureaucracies are present in many systems—as are the problems of reconciling the artificial and natural subsystems that emerge within any state structure. All such factors are important not only in terms of the questions regarding "community" and the implied corollaries of unity and rationality but also in terms of the definitions of good intelligence and the proper relationship between intelligence and the policy process.

Improving the Intelligence Process: Informal Norms and Incentives

Not only does the U.S. intelligence community keep getting taken by surprise by world events, but statesmen and outside analysts are often surprised when this occurs. We seem to expect that the intelligence community should be able to predict a great many of the nonroutine occurrences in world politics. Thus, when we are slow to detect a developing revolution in Iran, the growth of the peace movement in Europe, or the pressures leading to an Egyptian attack such as the one that occurred in 1973, people often look for blunderers if not villains. So it is perhaps advisable to begin our discussion of how the intelligence community might be structured by arguing that we should not be surprised at the frequent occurrence of surprises and errors. If we are keeping score, we should expect the success rate of intelligence to approximate a batting average more closely than a fielding percentage. In other words, there is no reason to expect a very high success rate—I suspect that if we were right something like one time out of three we would be doing quite well.

INHERENT LIMITS OF INTELLIGENCE

The impediments to understanding our world are so great that even without organizational deformities and politicization of the intelligence process, intelligence will often reach incorrect conclusions. The first intrinsic difficulty in intelligence is the most important and most obvious one: the world is not very predictable. Perhaps eventually our knowledge of human behavior will be much greater than it is today, but even those of us who have some faith in the progress of social science must retain humility about the levels of understanding that are possible in the foreseeable future. Indeed, even if our ability increased, we would still probably miss many important events.

A second reason for which even a growth in our knowledge would not lead to complete predictability is that many situations are interactive. That is, a state's behavior is determined in part by its leaders' predictions of how other states will behave. In international politics both the desire to increase one's bargaining position by seeming unpredictable and, more important, the need to take into account how the other expects you to behave in designing your own policy means that others' beliefs about what you know about them can influence their behavior in a way that causes intelligence predictions to be self-disconfirming.

Even if this were not a problem, an increase in general knowledge about human and state behavior would not lead to perfect intelligence because the latter usually requires a great deal of information about the specific factors involved in any particular case, some of which will exist only in the minds of one or two decisionmakers. Even in less extreme cases, it is hard to see how the United States could come by the necessary information.

A final problem that limits the extent to which intelligence could approach complete accuracy is the potential or actual use of deception. In many cases, we are trying to predict the actions of people who are, or may be, trying to mislead us. I will return to this topic later; suffice it to say here that the possibility of deception renders invalid any complete analogy between intelligence and social science, let alone physical science. Social scientists rarely have to worry about more than the danger that those they are studying are trying to conceal important facts from them; nations often actively try to mislead one another. The use of "turned" agents is only the most dramatic illustration of the problem. Indeed, if one country discovers what indices or aspects of its behavior the other is using to draw inferences, it may be able to manipulate them in order to project a desired, although often misleading, image.[1] Furthermore, the knowledge that the other may be attempting deception must lead intelligence analysts to discount various sources of information that in fact may be reliable.

In short, there are severe intrinsic limits on the effectiveness of intelligence. Even if the organizational problems and perceptual impediments limiting accurate perception were remedied or removed, we could not expect an enormous increase in our ability to predict events. Indeed, I think there is a danger in exaggerating the effectiveness of various reforms. We will mislead ourselves—and others—if we pretend that by changing the way we do business we can fully anticipate the behavior of others.

THE DESIGN OF AN IDEAL INTELLIGENCE SYSTEM

It may be a useful exercise to think a bit about what an ideal intelligence system would look like. I realize this is an "ivory tower" approach, and I will make little effort to deal with the enormous difficulties that stand in the way of implementing the system being described. I will also put aside two important topics: the current quality of intelligence personnel and the psychological factors that render accurate perception of other states very problematic. I have discussed the latter elsewhere,[2] and a treatment of the former would entail measures of individual quality that are simply unavailable. The essential premise of this chapter is that even if the quality of intelligence analysts is not as high as it should be, we are getting less out of these people than we might otherwise, simply given the nature of our intelligence system. A final introductory point is that only a few of my suggestions will deal with the formal structure and organization of intelligence production. Such questions as whether the CIA should be divided along regional or functional lines are important and have received a great deal of attention.[3] But at least equally important and much less commented on are the informal norms and incentives that exercise a great deal of influence on the quality of intelligence.

Formal Structure

Before dealing with informal norms and incentives, let me make three points about the more formal structure of a well-constructed intelligence system. First, one would expect that quite a bit of attention would be paid to a training program both for new recruits and for managers and analysts at higher levels. Perhaps this reflects an academic's bias in favor of courses and advanced degrees, but, without denying that much can be learned through apprenticeship, I will say that formal training programs are useful for conveying a great deal of information about the substance and methods of intelligence analysis as well as for countering the mystique that analysis is essentially intuitive. New recruits can be trained in the alternative methods of analyzing information about politics and can be taught some of the necessary tools of political science, history, and economics that they did not know when they came in. They can practice using the information available to the intelligence community and can benefit by having their analyses criticized by their peers and instructors. Similarly, midcareer analysts and managers can benefit from refresher courses, designed both to supply them with information about new ideas and techniques and to allow them the time and freedom to explore approaches and modes of argument that they do not have time to think about when they are fully engaged in pressing day-to-day work.

A second requirement for a good intelligence system is some degree of specialization. One simply cannot become an expert on a complex country or a difficult problem in a few months. Too rapid a rotation in position and excessive stress on the virtue of being a generalist will lead to an insufficient depth of knowledge. This is not to say that experts will necessarily get the right answers. Indeed, these people may become too wedded to their own point of view and get so caught up in the intricacies of "their" country that they are unable to provide the sorts of analyses that the government requires. On the other hand, there is probably a graver danger that those with insufficient expertise in a given area will be unable to detect and interpret important trends and developments. They will tend to impose on the information certain concepts, models, and beliefs derived from elsewhere. Although these concepts and beliefs may provide important insights, analysts frequently misinterpret the unfamiliar countries with which they are dealing because they see them in terms of other countries with which they are more familiar. Nonexpert analysts may even share the failings of less informed decisionmakers who see diverse countries in terms of implicit models derived from the Western experience.

More concretely, many issues in a country or region can be understood only against a background of historical developments that require detailed and often obscure information. Similarly, an interpretation of the behavior of a particular decisionmaker often requires a thorough knowledge of his or her background. National culture, largely derived from the country's history and social structure, is also often part of the explanation for the state's behavior and, as such, requires a significant degree of expertise to grasp. Understanding the behavior of another usually involves a grasp of their beliefs about their external environment in general and the actions of the United States in particular. Indeed, intelligence is often called upon to predict how a state will react to alternative U.S. policies, and this can be done only if one understands the images of the United States held by the other. A necessary condition for performing these tasks is intimate knowledge of the other country, its history, culture, economy, social structure, and leading figures. But this expertise cannot be developed quickly.

This is not to say that having experts on a particular region provides anything like a guarantee of accuracy. Experts are often wrong; the fact, for instance, that the senior CIA analyst on Iran had a fine command of that country's language, religion, culture, and politics did not prevent him from sharing the basic misconceptions held by people who know much less about that country. There is no perfect balance between the requirements of local knowledge and the need to avoid the dangers of "localism." Or, if there is a perfect balance, none of us knows how to find it. Nevertheless, when we look at the overall balance, we might wonder whether the intelligence community contains the necessary breadth and depth of expertise in many areas outside the Soviet Union and China. When it comes to less crucial but still "exotic" countries, it often seems that in the intelligence community, knowledge is very limited. (Indeed, in many areas there are few experts outside the government as well. How many specialists are there on Iraq, for example?)

To increase the level of expertise, we must not only supply adequate training and see that the analysts work on the same area for a considerable length of time but make certain, as well, that they get some firsthand exposure to the country they are dealing with. Obviously, this will not always be possible—experts on the PRC, both in and outside the government could not visit there before 1971. It is equally obvious that visits do not ensure correct judgments; indeed, the fact that information gathered firsthand has so much impact on one's beliefs may mean that such visits mislead rather than enlighten. In most cases it is probably difficult to gain a good understanding of a country without spending quite a bit of time there. The obvious question is whether the intelligence community permits or encourages this sort of exposure. Of course, the decision is not entirely up to the community.

Informal Norms and Incentives

Even more important than the factors discussed so far are the informal norms and incentives in the intelligence community. Three interrelated conditions are necessary for good intelligence. Analysts should present alternatives and competing explanations for events, develop the evidence for each of the alternatives, and present their arguments at a length necessary to do justice to the subject they are dealing with. This is not to imply, of course, that if these conditions are met the resulting analyses will always be excellent, but only that if they are not, the chances for a high-quality product are greatly reduced. Stansfield Turner has noted that both the CIA and the universities are creating and transmitting knowledge. I concur on this point; moreover, I believe that, while there are many important differences among the missions of these two institutions, the conditions that are effective in one setting are likely to prove fruitful in the other. Without arguing that universities are perfect, I will say that, at their best, their attributes of collegiality, peer review, and incentives for good work do in fact raise the level of scholarship.

Both intelligence analysts and scholars seek to understand and predict events. But there is a difference in emphasis here. Scholars are more concerned with understanding, analysts with predicting. This difference should not be exaggerated, however. One way to test a scholarly theory is to draw predictions from it, and predictions that are made without an understanding of the casual relationships are not likely to be satisfactory or accurate. Thus, although the nature of their work requires intelligence analysts to be deeply concerned about what will happen in the near future, the way they go about framing and answering their questions should not be enormously different from the outlook employed by scholars. It follows that good intelligence requires that the analysts undertake serious and careful investigation of why other states are acting as they are.

Although there is no agreed-upon "scientific method" in the social sciences, I think everyone would concur that, at a minimum, investigators must consider alternative explanations for the behavior they see and systematically marshal the evidence that is relevant to the alternative possibilities. Without full access to the products of the intelligence community, one cannot judge the extent to which these standards are met. But many commentators, starting with Roger Hilsman and his study in the late 1950s, argue that the intelligence community proceeds quite differently.[4]

Indeed, it seems that the informal norms and incentives of the intelligence community form what Charles Perrow has called "an error-inducing system."[5] That is, the interlocking and supporting habits of the community systematically decrease the likelihood that careful and penetrating intelligence analyses will be produced and therefore make errors extremely likely. The problems of each level reinforce each other, and changing one element without changing others is extremely difficult. For example, it would be hard to convince consumers that a different style of intelligence was needed unless one could first show them that the new style was more effective. But this would require that at least a part of the community produce analyses of the appropriate kind. To do this, however, would be almost impossible without making major changes in the community, changes that would require the support of the leadership of the community, or at least the support of the consumers themselves.

As it now stands, most political analysis would be better described as political reporting. That is, rather than analyzing developments, giving alternative explanations for the events, and presenting competing predictions that would follow from different beliefs, the political analyst is expected to summarize the recent reports from the field in a process known as "cable-gisting." This method produces good results when reports from the field are accurate and informative, but it cannot be expected to add much on its own. Such a process, of course, does not hold in all areas of the community's concern. Scientific and technical intelligence, coverage of Soviet and Chinese economies, and some of the discussion of politics in those two countries do not have these characteristics.

But politics in most countries is reported rather than analyzed. According to most accounts, the style of reporting is not an analytical one. By this I do not mean that the accoutrements and forms of scholarship are not followed—such an assertion would not be appropriate. Most important, there have been all too few attempts to dig much beneath the surface of events, to look beyond the next few weeks, to consider alternative explanations for the events, or to carefully marshal evidence that could support alternative views.

Requirements Imposed by the Appropriate Style

An appropriate style would impose a number of requirements. First, many analyses would have to be fairly long, say ten or twenty pages. Recent events can be reported in several hundred words, but complex events cannot be analyzed within the same constraint. It takes considerable time and space to develop several ideas and critique others; evidence cannot be presented and weighed in one or two pages. (An obvious consideration here is whether the intelligence community and the consumers are interested in reading such material, as I will touch on later.) A second requirement is the willingness to consider alternative explanations and alternative predictions. Of course, we are all familiar with arguments of the form: "on the one hand . . . on the other hand." But such arguments are not very useful. Much more helpful would be a clear exposition of possible explanations coupled with a presentation of the evidence that supports each view and the information that might be gathered that would point in one direction or the other. The development of alternative explanations can lead to better analysis by articulating the reasoning that leads certain outcomes to be expected and by exposing implicit assumptions to careful scrutiny. Such processes are also useful for helping to indicate what changes, unexpected events, or new evidence would, if present, alter the current predictions. Such an approach belongs only in the world of scholarship—what I am calling for describes the approach of the Crowe memorandum of 1907, which is a British analysis of German policy and intentions.[6]

A third requirement for good intelligence is the existence of a critical mass of analysts who can discuss and criticize other's views. This concerns both the number of available people and, more important, the style of "peer review," a process in which analysts pay attention to what others are saying and engage in constructive critical discussions. In other words, what we require is a real "intelligence community."

The need for functioning peer groups is related to a general characteristic of a well-designed intelligence system and an inherent tension created by the diverse pressures to which it is subjected. Part of the task of the intelligence community is to develop knowledge. For this task, the important structural elements of the organization should be horizontal. That is, knowledge is best produced through intensive interaction among individuals who are able to treat each other as intellectual equals. Ideas are developed, shared, criticized, and judged on their merits; people build on each other's work and learn from each other's errors. This is the ideal of a university, though one that is never reached, of course. But the intelligence community has to transmit as well as to generate knowledge. Furthermore, its audience is one not of peers, as in the case of a university, but one consisting of the superiors within the intelligence community and among the policymakers. This fact calls for a largely vertical structure, with analysts reporting to branch chiefs who report to office directors and so on up the line.

I do not see any way to determine the optimum balance between these two tasks. But it seems likely that within the intelligence community the latter task and latter structure predominate over the former. The result is that analysts are given more incentives for adequately conveying information to those who know relatively little about a problem than for developing their ideas with the degree of discipline and empirical support that would be required for the production of excellent analysis. Similarly, good analysts are generally rewarded for their labors, not by receiving greater pay and higher prestige for continuing to produce first-rate intelligence, but rather by being moved up the organizational ladder. It may be that they are not well suited for administrative positions, but the fact remains that in the implicit message conveyed what matters most is management, not the writing of excellent analyses of other countries. Of course, good management performs indispensable roles, but the primary work must be done by the individual analysts. Moreover, a reward structure should be congruent with this priority.

Most accounts concerning the CIA and other intelligence agencies suggest that just as most of the work in the political arena is a matter of reporting rather than analysis, these three requirements are not only unmet but discouraged as well. Papers and memoranda are usually quite short; alternative explanations are rarely suggested let alone rigorously analyzed. Although on some highly politicized questions the community is split in predictable ways, in most areas analysts rarely get the sort of careful criticism that constitutes peer review.

Of course, lengthy papers are occasionally produced. Under Turner, some National Intelligence Estimates (NIEs) were the equivalent of a short book. But again, excepting some of the NIEs on the Soviet military, these do not seem to have been the occasion for serious analysis. They were long not because important questions were analyzed in depth, but because the contributions of each agency had to be included. Furthermore, only rarely do they seem to have been taken seriously by consumers.

Most of the time, analysts sought to publish in the National Intelligence Daily (NID), and the NID, like the newspapers on which it is modeled, prints only brief accounts. By their nature, these can be little more than the "cable-gisting" referred to earlier. It is possible for analysts to write longer papers for other intelligence community publications, but the incentives for doing so are not great. The NID is more widely read because the articles are shorter and the analysts, therefore, receive more rewards for getting their reports into it.

Linked to the brevity of most reports is the absence of

alternative explanations for the events being reported. A necessary, though not sufficient, condition for this style is the ability to write at some length. But the space constraint is only one reason why alternatives are rarely presented. It appears that the presentation of competing explanations is viewed as likely to confuse the consumers, if not the analysts themselves. The job of intelligence is seen in terms of presenting the correct, or at least the most likely, version of events rather than as an attempt to clarify the issues by presenting alternative viewpoints. The informal norms of the community stress the presentation of facts, not speculation. Thus, when an explanation for events is given, it is likely to be put forth not as an explicit argument but rather as the only possible reason why events might be unfolding as they are. From this perspective, the idea of presenting several alternative explanations is a foreign one.

Greater contacts with outside experts including, but not limited to, academics would also be useful in this regard. The argument is not that these people are more likely to have the correct answers than are the intelligence analysts. Only occasionally will they have information and ideas that would not otherwise be available to the government. Rather, the advantage of the interaction is that the outsiders can often pose questions that the analysts need to consider and usually have disciplined patterns of thinking that are particularly useful. Outside experts are likely to be attuned to the possibility of alternative explanations for events and can help focus attention on what evidence could be mustered to support various views. It is these habits of mind, rather than—or at least in addition to—expertise on a specific country or problem that should help raise the quality of intelligence.

The third stylistic requirement necessary to support good political analysis also seems to be missing. Although we refer to the "intelligence community," this phrase does not seem to describe accurately the way the government works on most issues of political intelligence. There is an insufficient exchange of careful criticism of one another's work. Of course, extensive and often acrimonious debates tend to occur when institutional interests are at stake, and one sometimes finds long-term factions forming over such issues as internal Chinese politics before the death of Mao. (I do not mean to hold up these debates as a model. Because they often represent conflicts between well-entrenched positions, they are rarely very intellectually productive.) But on the day-to-day issues of politics in most countries, the number of analysts involved is quite low and the mechanisms for a real intellectual community are so weak that analysis is rarely disciplined by a high level of communication and critical assessment.

Personal relations are extremely important here. In some cases, analysts working on the same country in different parts of the government know and respect each other and often comment on each other's work. In other cases, someone, often from the State Department, will form an informal group composed of those concerned with a particular country. But it appears that in the majority of cases the intelligence analysts, expecially those in the CIA, work in intellectual isolation. Their connections with their counterparts in the rest of the government are tenuous, and they receive only scant critical and informed discussion of their views. The physical isolation of Langley plays a role here, as does the lack of readily available secure telephones in the State Department. But, again, informal norms are more important; the basic idea of peer review is not seen as a necessary part of the intelligence production process.

It should also be noted that the ability of analysts and policymakers to work well together in a crisis is increased by a high degree of communication in more routine situations. If people have not worked together before a crisis and have not developed a fairly good understanding of how each other thinks, their ability to listen and to cooperate in the much more pressured and politicized atmosphere of a crisis will be sharply reduced. This may be one reason why intelligence often plays only a small role once a crisis arises.

Deception

A good intelligence system must systematically consider the possibility of deception. This is especially true, of course, in dealings with adversaries. Although I think everyone would agree to this as a general principle, the practical difficulties are enormous. A deceiver wants to mimic the image that would be projected by the actor he or she is impersonating; any behavior that can be manipulated can be used for deception. Almost any evidence that at first seems convincing with respect to a given intention or image can be seen as just what a deceiver would want to do. Not only is there no way out of this conundrum, but there are obvious costs in being too concerned about it. Such an approach leads to endless cycles of "he thinks that I think that he thinks that I think. . . ." Alternatively, if one downgrades all information on the grounds that it might be deceptive, one would have little data from which to draw inferences. But if worrying too much about deception is not wise, this does not mean that we should put the possibility out of our minds entirely.

It seems that the intelligence community probably errs in the direction of underestimating rather than overestimating deception.[7] Although I cannot speak with confidence, it seems as though the community rarely worries that seemingly valuable evidence may have been planted. I think the main reason for this is not naiveté, but rather the understandable hesitancy on the part of the analyst to discard what few pieces of good information are available. It is difficult enough to try to draw inferences about others' behavior; it would complicate the task enormously to have to seriously confront the possibility of deception at every turn. Nevertheless, one can ask whether this behavior is in the interests of either the United States or the intelligence community as a whole. In the best of all possible worlds, the system would take account of the danger of deception without creating excessive paranoia.

Consumers' Attitudes

A final condition for the functioning of an effective intelligence system is that the consumers understand what should and can be done. The question of the reciprocal links between the policymakers and intelligence is fascinating but largely beyond the scope of this chapter.[8] I would just note that it is important to learn more about both the impact of policy on intelligence and the influence of intelligence on policy. It is frequently charged that intelligence on important issues is highly politicized and that the best way to predict what the intelligence community will say is to know the preferences of the policymakers, but we have remarkably little information that could actually confirm or disconfirm this view. Similarly, we cannot determine the impact of intelligence on policymaking. We usually assume that intelligence is important—and indeed the implicit assumption of this chapter is that if we increase the quality of intelligence, policy would benefit. In fact, however, we cannot be sure that changes in intelligence would have much influence. Indeed, it is hard to think of many U.S. decisions that have been significantly influenced by intelligence estimates.

Nevertheless, even if we think intelligence matters, it is important to recognize that the sorts of arrangements I have called for could not be fully implemented without support from the consumers. First, consumers should realize that no matter how effective an intelligence system is, it cannot predict all important events. Failures, then, do not automatically indicate general problems with the system. More important, decisionmakers should realize that it is dangerous to base their policies on the assumption that they can predict all aspects of the future. A policy that is too fine-tuned to expectations of how others behave is likely to fail. Both consumers and producers of intelligence need to pay closer attention to the question of what can be done with various kinds of warnings. The former need to appreciate the limits on the kinds of information and analyses they are likely to receive in order to be best prepared to act on the intelligence; the latter need to understand the links between what they can say and what policy can be in order to concentrate their energies most fruitfully.[9] Second, decisionmakers should not feel that the prime responsibility of intelligence is to beat the wire services in reporting riots and coups. Most presidents reportedly get angry when they learn about important events from the mass media rather than from intelligence. The latter should have more insightful things to say than the former, but it cannot always be faster in reporting sudden events. This is what the wire services specialize in. Their communications facilities are designed for speed, they have fewer layers of bureaucracy, and they need not be concerned with security. Third, decisionmakers should appreciate the importance of having an intelligence system that can raise the general quality of discussion in the government by systematically developing alternative explanations for events and marshaling relevant evidence. Quality intelligence also implies a willingness on the part of consumers to read documents that are more than one or two pages long.

Finally, consumers need to relax their understandable aversion to allowing intelligence analysts a detailed knowledge of U.S. policy. Standing rules prohibit the intelligence community from knowing much more about what the United States is doing than is printed in the newspapers. This seems to make sense; the job of intelligence is to predict what others will do, not to second-guess U.S. policymakers. But in many cases, one cannot understand what others have done or estimate what they will do in the future without knowing what they think the United States is doing to them. An important influence on their policy is their external environment, in which the United States usually looms large, and their behavior will be misinterpreted if U.S. actions are not taken into account. The most obvious examples are the cycles of mutual hostility previously noted, but other patterns are possible also—as when the other side grows bolder because it believes the United States to be weak. We must look at U.S. policy whether we are interested in our adversaries' general intentions or in the likelihood that they will take certain actions in the near future. Their image of the United States will usually play some role in setting their goals and in judging how they can achieve them; specific acts can be triggered by what the United States has just done or what they anticipate that it will do. To some extent, the relevant information about U.S. policy is public knowledge, but many aspects of this policy, such as covert actions, military maneuvers, and diplomatic communications, are not. Although access to these data is not a panacea, it is a necessary input if intelligence is to be accurate.

I grant that the chances for convincing consumers to change their ways are not great. Indeed, the reader might even question the premise of this chapter on the grounds that without such changes the kind of intelligence assessments I am calling for would not receive a favorable reception. Although there is something to this, perhaps the intelligence community has paid too much attention to the question of how to get the consumers to listen at the expense of considering how the community's internal structure might be improved so that intelligence would have more to say.

NOTES

1. Robert Jervis, The Logic of Images in International Relations (Princeton, N.J.: Princeton University Press, 1970), pp. 41-65.
2. Robert Jervis, Perception and Misperception in International Politics (Princeton, N.J.: Princeton University Press, 1976).
3. Sherman Kent, Strategic Intelligence for American World Policy (Princeton, N.J.: Princeton University Press, 1949), pp. 116-147. Relevant decuments can be found in Tyrus Fain et al., eds., The Intelligence Community: History, Organization and Issues (New York and London: Bowker, 1977).
4. Roger Hilsman, Strategic Intelligence and National Decisions (Glencoe, Ill.: Free Press, 1956).
5. Charles Perrow, Normal Accidents (New York: Basic Books, 1984).
6. Eyre Crowe, "Memorandum on the Present State of British Relations with France and Germany" (January 1, 1907), quoted in G. P. Gooch and Harold Temperley, eds., British Documents on the Origins of the War, 1889-1914, vol. 3, The Testing of Entente, 1904-6 (London: His Majesty's Stationery Office, 1928), pp. 397-431.
7. David Martin, Wilderness of Mirrors (New York: Ballantine Books, 1980); David Sullivan, "Evaluating U.S. Intelligence Estimates," in Roy Godson, ed., Intelligence Requirements for the 1980s: Analysis and Estimates (New Brunswick, N.J.: Transaction Books, 1980), pp. 49-73.
8. An excellent study of this subject in terms of British policy and intelligence in the 1930s is Wesley Wark, The Ultimate Enemy:

British Intelligence and Nazi Germany (Ithaca, N.Y.:   Cornell University Press, forthcoming).

9. For further discussions in this area, see Alexander George, "Problem-Oriented Forecasting," in Nazli Choucri and Thomas Robinson, eds., Forecasting in International Relations (San Francisco: W. H. Freeman, 1978), pp. 329-337 and Richard Betts, Surprise Attack (Washington, D.C.:   Brookings, 1982), pp. 286-295.

Intelligence Production and Consumption: A Framework of Analysis

INTRODUCTION

The purpose of this chapter is to present a framework of analysis for investigating the producer/consumer nexus. Such a framework will enable investigators of both national strategic intelligence and national security policymaking to address three important factors. It will assist in ordering the glut of data, thereby enabling us to use those data more productively. It will help to advance the scholarly investigation of intelligence phenomena by suggesting some future directions. It will indicate ways in which the intelligence community is related to its policymaking environment, thus helping us to better understand how and why policy is made. I do not intend to assess either intelligence "failures" or "successes" (although it is interesting and instructive to note that much is written of the former whereas intelligence "success" is not yet an established and common part of the lexicon). Rather, my objective is to provide some thoughts on how to conceptualize such assessments.

This chapter is concerned with intelligence analysis. The functions of clandestine and nonclandestine intelligence collection (including espionage), counterintelligence (and counterespionage), and covert action relate to intelligence analysis, and, indeed, all of these functions are mutually interrelated and interdependent. However, intelligence activities can be separated into discrete functions for the purpose of analysis. My focus is the analysis function, although some of the other functions will be discussed where they are relevant.

FRAMEWORK FACTORS

Producers

Nearly all of the bureaucratic elements that constitute the intelligence community are involved with making intelligence products. However, some of these entities are only marginally related to the majority of intelligence products dealing with national security. The major producers are the Central Intelligence Agency (CIA) and various Department of Defense elements, especially the Defense Intelligence Agency (DIA), Army Intelligence (G-2), Air Force Intelligence (S-2),

Naval Intelligence (ONI), and the semi-autonomous National Security Agency (NSA). Several key factors characterize this set of producers and should be included in any analytical framework that deals with intelligence production.

One of these factors concerns the diversity and variety of the intelligence community elements. Each of the units has a unique mission not only in national security and defense policy, but also in intelligence production.[1] Each also produces intelligence characterized by a mix of the three models of decisionmaking identified by Graham Allison: the rational actor, the organizational process, and bureaucratic politics.[2] That is, each community unit's products include the elements of assumptions and perceptions of the national interest (rational actor), the unique standard operating procedures by which the particular unit analyzes data (organizational process), and the relationship between the particular unit and both its community and policymaking environments (bureaucratic politics).

This combination of different actors producing intelligence according to a variety of imperatives constitutes a "community" in the sense that the actors share a common general goal, but it is characterized by a lack of coordination. The various actors are both functional and allocational rivals since they compete with each other for both resources and task assignments and preferences.

Functional competition is especially manifest in intelligence production, although it occurs in intelligence operations as well. For instance, the FBI is statutorily responsible for domestic counterintelligence (CI) operations, whereas the CIA has primary (but not exclusive) responsibility for foreign CI. This clear operational division is not maintained in practice and overlap inevitably occurs. At times this overlap has resulted in bureaucratic pique, as when J. Edgar Hoover forbade his field agents from cooperating with CIA officers, even though such cooperation was essential to successful CI operations.[3] Thus, rivalry characterizes all of the four intelligence functions, but it is especially pronounced in the production of analyses, estimates, and predictions.

The dictum "knowledge is power" explains the intensity of competition in the intelligence production function. Policymakers base their judgments on data, although other factors—individual backgrounds, experiences, and perceptions and political exigencies—obviously affect decisions.[4] Since data so greatly affect a policymaker's perception of the policy environment, each intelligence community unit wants to determine what data the policymaker will accept as the basis for his or her decision. And since different units produce different data sets, they must compete with each other to have their respective intelligence products considered.

This intramural struggle has several dimensions and takes place on different levels. The most important dimension from an analytical perspective is the civilian/military one. The more important intelligence products concern national security issues, since these constitute the raison d'être of the intelligence community. Throughout the United States' involvement in Vietnam, for example, CIA analyses and estimates were based on the notion that the war was primarily a sociopolitical struggle, whereas defense intelligence perceived it as a military problem.[5] This division over the essential nature of the war became transformed into a matter of defining the problem. The military prevailed in this case; the policymakers increasingly perceived the war in military terms, and the defense intelligence components became the prime suppliers of data to the policymakers.

Recalling the "knowledge is power" argument, in terms of defining the nature of the problem in Vietnam, the military version became the accepted definition. As a result, the military solutions took on greater validity with the policymakers, since those solutions were most appropriate to the perceived problem. Thus, whereas U.S. policy in Vietnam combined such diverse strategies as "winning hearts and minds" and "search and destroy," the military priorities dominated other factors, in large part because the military won the intelligence analysis "war" in Washington.[6]

This case suggests two factors that are important in assessing the civilian/military dimension of intelligence producers. One is the military advantage in terms of its preponderate size.[7] The second factor concerns the threat aspect of national security policymaking, which inclines policymakers to rely on the military in its role as the nation's guardian.[8]

This military advantage is potentially balanced by three other aspects of the producer side of intelligence. One concerns the internal divisions within the military intelligence sector. Although this factor is not as obvious as that characterizing the civilian/military dynamic, the notion of bureaucratic imperative means that military analyses and estimates will reflect allocational rivalry on a different level.[9]

The lack of consensus among the military branches is a function of the different national security missions to which each is assigned. This diversity results in differing needs and needs assessments, and is reflected in varying intelligence views of the branches. Former Secretary of Defense Robert McNamara described this problem of fragmentation in the following way: "We found that the three military departments had been establishing their requirements independently of each other. The results could be described as fairly chaotic: Army planning, for example, was based on a long war of attrition; Air Force planning was based, largely, on a short war of nuclear bombardment."[10] Clearly, such differences will be reflected in diverse intelligence analyses of national security threats.

A second aspect of the producer side of military intelligence concerns staffing procedures. Although the defense intelligence units employ civilian analysts, they also rely extensively on career military officers. The intelligence branches of the services have become more prestigious since the time they were staffed by officers undergoing career exile or punishment, but few careerists stay in intelligence and most regard it as a useful but only temporary duty assignment. The result is that "[because] of the frequent rotation of military personnel and a low civilian grade structure, these agencies have been unable to maintain continuity by attracting and retaining high-quality personnel. There are good and dedicated people in these agencies, but either they do not stay or they become frustrated and do not work up to their potential."[11]

A third element mitigating the apparent role of the military as the major intelligence producer is the salience of the CIA and its connection to the intelligence community via the director of Central Intelligence (DCI).[12] Despite the budgetary and personnel advantages of military intelligence, the CIA remains, for two main reasons, the most identifiable and single most important community component.

The CIA was the first major peacetime intelligence effort of the United States. It was established by the National Security Act of 1947, which also restructured our national defense machinery by detaching the Air Corps from the Army to create the Department of the Air Force, renaming the Department of War the Department of the Army, and combining the three major military services into the Department of Defense. Prior to 1947, U.S. intelligence concerns were focused on military concerns, and intelligence activities tended to be ad hoc; moreover, the intelligence bureaucracies manifested rapid personnel and functional increases followed by rapid decreases as the perception of the national security threat diminished. Even our most extensive and intensive civilian intelligence effort reflected these characteristics. The Office of Strategic Services (OSS), created as a response to the probable involvement of the United States in World War II, was primarily oriented toward wartime military exigencies, and was demobilized on October 1, 1945.[13]

The main justification for a central intelligence agency was to coordinate (i.e., centralize) what was to be known about international phenomena. Pearl Harbor indicated the need for such an agency, since various components of the government possessed information that, if centralized and integrated, would have left no doubt of the Japanese intentions and would have provided policymakers with adequate forewarning to repulse the attack.[14] Given the global nature of the U.S. commitments implied by the Truman Doctrine and the policy of containment, together with the pervasive, massive, and protracted threat to our national and international interests that the USSR then represented to policymakers, the need for an agency that could collate available intelligence and use that intelligence to provide policymakers with foreknowledge was obvious and critical.[15]

Consequently, the CIA became the primary structure of the U.S. intelligence community. Subsequent additions and modifications to the intelligence community have diluted its strength somewhat, but the CIA remains the intelligence unit that is statutorily responsible for coordinating the intelligence process and products. This means that even though it is neither the largest nor the single most expensive member of the community, it is in many ways the most important. In terms of the producer/consumer nexus, it is the most salient. Its original mandate has not been altered legally, and it continues to offset and counterbalance, if not always prevail over, military intelligence when there is a dispute between the two over intelligence products.

A second reason for which the CIA is able to continue as a major force in intelligence production concerns the dual responsibilities of the head of the agency. The director of Central Intelligence (DCI) is also the director of the Central Intelligence Agency (DCIA), which means that he is in charge of the entire intelligence community and the CIA simultaneously. This overlap produces inevitable role conflict, especially when a dispute over intelligence products occurs. Most DCIs attempt to compromise in these situations. One of the clearest examples of this role conflict occurred during the tenure of

Richard Helms as DCI/DCIA (1966-1973) and involved estimates of enemy troop strength in Vietnam.[16]

In estimating enemy troop strength, CIA and military analysts normally compromised, especially if the discrepancy between the two estimates was minor. However, in 1967 the CIA estimated enemy strength at 500,000 while military analysts set the number at 270,000. Such a large difference would mean very different policies, since the higher figure would indicate a lack of progress in pursuit of goals based on the strategy of attrition and would raise doubts about a policy of achieving military victory at acceptable levels of commitment, whereas the lower figure would justify a continuation of the then current policy. Compromise became impossible, and eventually Helms endorsed an estimate that was very close to that argued for by the military.

In most cases of civilian/military disputes, compromise is achieved without the direct and intense intervention of the DCI/DCIA. However, because a single individual holds both of these posts, the military intelligence components are often skeptical of his objectivity; CIA analysts often expect his role as DCIA to predominate in his decisions. Even though he may be a career military officer, his role as DCIA, together with the weight of the CIA, means that the CIA is often equal to, if not more significant than, the military as a producer of intelligence. Although they manifest disunity, dispute, and disagreement over intelligence products, the community also sometimes does agree or at least can achieve a consensual compromise. However, the divisions that constitute one of its basic characteristics are exacerbated by the relationships between the various producers and the various consumers.

Consumers

The consumers of intelligence vary even more than the producers. The set of consumers includes all of the producers plus the main nonintelligence national security policymakers as well as those who affect policymakers, such as Congress. This suggests two major foci in analyzing the producer/consumer nexus from the perspective of the consumer. One focus is directed to the units that comprise both producers and consumers; the other concerns those units that are not producers but which impact on the making of decisions in the areas of defense, national security, and foreign policies. This can be conceptualized in Figure 9.1.

Several factors characterize those community members who are both producers and consumers, referred to here as internal consumers. One such factor relates to the community cleavages mentioned previously and concerns the fact that most intelligence is produced for internal consumption by other members of the community. Even though each community unit has an area or several areas of primary responsibility, and despite the intramural rivalry that suggests conflict among the units, a degree of interdependence exists, in part because of the division of labor. For example, the collection of "raw" intelligence from "closed" sources (clandestine collection or, in common parlance, espionage) is a function that is performed by all the major units, including the CIA, the NSA, and the three military service

Figure 9.1
THE FLOW OF INTELLIGENCE PRODUCTS

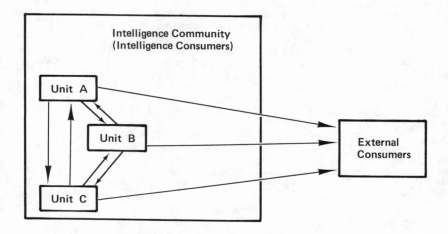

intelligence units. The data thus collected are "masked" in order to avoid revealing and compromising the source(s) and method(s) of collection and are then entered into the process of converting the raw intelligence into intelligence products.

The extent of the process varies according to several interrelated factors, including the significance of the intelligence, time constraints in processing, organizational considerations such as available manpower, standard operating procedures, predetermined responses, and the prevailing policy environment. However, except in the most extenuating cases, much of the raw intelligence is exchanged in some form among the various units. This cooperation within the intelligence community is necessary if intelligence "failures" are to be minimized, and it justifies the confederal structure of the intelligence community of the United States.

The process by which intelligence is converted into a product involves several phases that are conceptually distinct but which overlap in reality.[17] Moreover, the process rarely proceeds from one phase to another in the absence of reconsiderations and reevaluations about prior phases. Following its collection and masking, intelligence is evaluated for accuracy and authenticity, analyzed for content, integrated with other intelligence, and interpreted as a product.

Using established systems theory terminology, we can conceive of intelligence production as a system. (See Figure 9.2.) The inputs are the requirements for intelligence by the various consumers and the sources of intelligence available to the producers. The conversion activities of the system transform the raw intelligence, which begins the conversion process in a state more properly referred to as "information" than "intelligence," into a finished product or output. This output is then sent to consumers.

Figure 9.2
INTELLIGENCE PRODUCTION

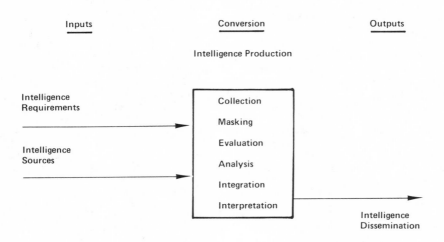

In order for this process to yield the most useful results, both the raw intelligence and the finished products must be shared among the producers. Consequently, the producers are also consumers. Even the masking of information transforms it into a raw intelligence product, and since the producers use these raw products to generate more finished products for external consumers, the community or internal producers consume most of the intelligence products.

This is also the case for the more finished products—namely, the reports and analyses that result from the intelligence process described earlier.[18]   Most are produced periodically, including several daily intelligence newspapers generated by different community members, and although the list of recipients includes external consumers such as the president, these finished intelligence products are also intended for members of the community.   The clientele for these intelligence products benefits from them since the compartmentation that is essential for secure intelligence operations sometimes precludes total knowledge of the activities of other areas of the community or even those of a single community member.   However, in terms of the national security policy process, the most important consumers are external to the intelligence community.

External consumers include both congressional and executive intelligence consumers.   The latter are the primary policymaking consumers, whereas Congress scrutinizes the intelligence community and thus is an important consumer of some finished intelligence products. The primary congressional consumers are the Senate and the House Permanent Select Intelligence Committees, including their respective professional staff members.   These units were created following the 1974 congressional investigations into intelligence community activities.

Their primary responsibility is to "oversee" the intelligence community, which means to apply the concept of checks and balances to intelligence.[19] Although the units are concerned primarily with covert action operations, they necessarily receive intelligence reports of a highly classified nature on a variety of subjects. The relationship between the producers and the congressional consumers is characterized by two factors. One is the security concern. Because these recipients are politicians and are subject to the impacts of their political environment, as contrasted with the policymaking context, the community is to some extent reluctant to provide them with what is sometimes extremely sensitive material that can be used for personal or partisan political profit. Offsetting this concern is the need for congressional support for the community.

The result of the 1975 congressional investigations of questionable activity by some community members was the so-called firestorm, characterized by a decrease in funding for intelligence activities of all sorts, a decline in the number and morale of community members, a reduction of intelligence activities and capabilities, greater scrutiny of the community by Congress, and legislative limitations that greatly restrained the intelligence community.[20] This has resulted in the need for a close and open relationship between the producers and the congressional consumers. Another aspect of the relationship that mitigates a reluctance to provide the congressional committees with sensitive data is the professionalism of the committee staffs. Consequently, for both legal and political reasons, the intelligence committees receive intelligence products and interaction is established that mutually benefits both producer and congressional consumer.[21]

A second factor characterizing the community's relationship with Congress is the lack of any other producer.[22] Although the bureaucratic rivalry discussed earlier may become manifest in congressional hearings and testimony, in most cases Congress has only a single source of national security intelligence. This situation puts the producer in a powerful but difficult role.

Congress must accept, ipso facto, the community's products, choose to ignore those products and conduct its role in the policy process on bases other than professional knowledge, or produce its own analyses and estimates.[23] Clearly, the first alternative is least costly in terms of resources and is therefore the most preferred option. The difficulty for the producer is that its products must be correct most of the time. Congress will rely on the producers only so long as their products are useful and relevant.[24]

A concomitant of this factor of product reliability is that if the products presented to Congress are unsatisfactory, congressional skepticism will shift from the products to the producers. Thus, the single-source position of the intelligence community vis-à-vis Congress includes both positive and negative aspects for both producer and consumer.

In general, the congressional oversight committees have been receptive to and supportive of the intelligence community, thereby reflecting a trend of congressional oversight since the inception of the community in the postwar era. Although the 1975 revelations produced a period of heightened skepticism and even antagonism, congressional security "leaks" appear to have been minimal and manageable and the consumers seem to have been satisfied with the quantity and quality of the product.[25] This satisfaction may be due either to an increasing concern over perceived international geopolitical threats to the United States in the late 1970s and the 1980s or to the recognition that Congress plays a secondary role in making and implementing national security policy. For although Congress is an important external consumer, it is the executive branch that constitutes the primary recipient of intelligence products.

A variety of executive branch units receive intelligence products, including units of the Department of the Treasury, Department of Commerce, and the Drug Enforcement Administration. However, the Defense Department, the State Department, and the National Security Council (NSC) consume the significant intelligence products. The relationship between these external executive branch consumers and the intelligence community is a symbiotic one. The consumers receive both periodic and ad hoc intelligence products from the community, and these analyses and estimates can result either from specific requests by the NSC for intelligence on a national security issue or from internally generated reports by the units that make up the community. In either case, the community engages in what is called "tasking"—that is, the assignment of specific product responsibilities to individual community units.

Products

The products received by this set of consumers are in many cases similar, if not identical, to those generated for internal use within the community. Thus there are daily, weekly, monthly, and other periodic intelligence reports intended to provide policymakers with an accurate assessment of the policy environment. Of particular note are the daily intelligence reports produced for the president.[26] These are the results of overnight compilations of events in actual and potential "trouble spots" and are generated by various community units. Although these reports are useful for planning, implementing, monitoring, and adjusting long-range policies and in dealing with crises, it is important to note the special case of the National Intelligence Estimate (NIE).[27]

Like most intelligence products, NIEs are produced both annually and on demand or in a crisis situation (as in the case of Special National Intelligence Estimates, or SNIEs). NIEs focus on various aspects of a wide range of concerns of particular importance to U.S. national security, such as the national assessment of Soviet strategic weapons strength and posture, global and regional reserves of and potentials for various national resources, economic and financial situations in key countries, and trends in terrorism.

NIEs are ultimately the responsibility of the CIA and especially of its Directorate of Intelligence. However, since they involve and represent the "collective wisdom" of the entire U.S. intelligence community, they manifest the dynamics of internal community politics. NIEs are also generated for a more limited clientele whose idiosyncratic perspectives are known to the producers. Finally, since NIEs attempt to predict a future state of affairs, many inevitably prove inaccurate. They are based on assumptions of how decisionmakers will act, but the vicissitudes of decisionmaking clearly cannot be consistently or reliably estimated or predicted. These three factors are important in understanding why NIEs are sometimes inaccurate, or, in other words, why "intelligence failures" are inevitable.[28]

Because they are the most salient linkage in the producer/consumer nexus, NIEs and SNIEs tend to be of critical importance to both the community units and their clients. One consequence of this attention is that all of the aspects that characterize the nexus tend to be exacerbated in the case of NIEs. The rivalry that sometimes characterizes the community tends to become more intense. Although each community unit may legitimately believe its estimate to be unbiased and objective, each may also be guilty of its own parochial form of what James Fallows calls "threat inflation."[29] Fallows used this term to refer to the military's overestimation of the enemy's capabilities, especially in order to obtain additional funding for more U.S. military ordnance. Regardless of the intent of threat inflation, the concept has relevance in the context of the intelligence producer/consumer nexus, given that estimates are clearly related to policymaking, which in turn is related to the future fortunes of the various producers. Thus different community members often reach different conclusions about NIEs, since they each emphasize different perspectives.[30] This lack of coordination is often reflected in the NIEs themselves, which include the conceptual equivalent of dissenting opinions.

When presented with conflicting estimates and advice, policymakers are forced to choose. While some executives are comfortable with choices, others have little expertise or knowledge of the dynamics of international affairs or the national security environment. In those cases, disparate advice is not considered a policymaking virtue; rather, it is viewed as a net liability whose only asset is the fact that if the resultant policy is unsuccessful the producer can be made to share the blame. Therefore, since many policymakers prefer concise, coordinated estimates that offer guidelines rather than divergent choices, those policymakers present the community with the task of producing consensual NIEs.

NIEs that reflect consensus are often more useful to policymakers, whose concerns frequently involve the politics and mechanics of public policy rather than rational decisionmaking from among several alternative policies. However, achieving consensus on an NIE involves compromise, and one result may be a product that is "highly qualified and tentative in both its rationale and conclusions."[31] NIEs that reflect this characteristic are the consequence of bargaining among those community units that have a germane interest in both the subject and the consequent policy of the particular NIE. Essentially, the bureaucratic-politics model of decisionmaking may be more useful than the rational-actor model to an understanding of how compromise is achieved and what that compromise really means.

Executive-branch consumers may prefer consensual NIEs that serve as guidelines for policy precisely because this type of estimate is often ambiguous. Such ambiguity permits policymakers to be flexible both in making policy based on the estimate and in implementing the resulting policy decision. Clear, definite, unambiguous estimates mean that the decisionmaker either has no options other than the extremes of rigid adherence to the guidelines suggested by the NIE or must reject those guidelines in favor of a set of ad hoc and, at least in the context of the NIE, arbitrary decisionmaking rules. Thus, the ambiguous nature of consensual NIEs may be viewed positively by certain consumers. This notion is reinforced by another factor that characterizes the producer/consumer nexus: the foreknowledge that producers have about the perspectives of the consumers.

Since the primary consumers of the NIEs are usually known to the producers, it is reasonable to posit that the producers will be affected by the known views that the consumers have about the NIE subject. Different from the "threat inflation" discussed earlier, this has been called "intelligence to please."[32] Certainly few if any NIEs are deliberately biased in order to be accepted by the consumer. The "culture" of intelligence analysts and the personality type commonly associated with them emphasize objectivity, analytical skills, and the application of established methodological and epistemological considerations to the raw intelligence data.[33] The issue is not so much the weakness of the producers as the strength of the consumers. If the estimates are inconsistent with the perspectives of the consumer, the latter are in a position to disregard the product, find alternative products, or replace the producers with analysts whose own perspectives are more closely aligned with that of the consumer.

Henry Kissinger chose to disregard his own State Department Bureau of Intelligence and Research (INR) in the 1973 Yom Kippur War. He failed to provide INR with critical information regarding Soviet responses to the military reverses of its client state, Egypt. Instead, he chose to act as his own intelligence analyst, when he had, in the words of his INR director at the time, "neither the technical knowledge nor the time to weigh all the evidence objectively."[34] A case of seeking an alternative product involved NIEs on Soviet strategic capabilities.[35] President Ford, in response to a suggestion from his President's Foreign Intelligence Advisory Board (PFIAB), authorized a group of analysts independent of the intelligence community to review the same data that the community used to produce its NIEs. The independent group, designated the B-Team, "concluded that the NIEs had been grossly underestimating Soviet developments and intentions. Despite loud wounded cries, the authors of the NIEs, unable to produce evidence to contradict the B-Team, changed their own views."[36] Finally, when confronted with estimates and analyses at variance with their perspective on the policy environment, consumers may replace the producers, as President Nixon and Henry Kissinger did by making James Schlesinger director of Central Intelligence with the mandate to deal with the " 'liberal' instincts of the CIA and ONE [Office of National Estimates, a part of the CIA]."[37] Schlesinger, who took the place of Richard Helms, also changed the estimating process so that it would conform to White House needs and style. These examples illustrate that the various factors characterizing the producers and the consumers also affect community products (especially the NIEs) and consumer needs.

CONCLUSION

An understanding of the intelligence producer/consumer nexus is complicated by many factors. The intelligence community performs a variety of functions, only one of which is the production of intelligence. Although this chapter has focused on the production function, it is important to recognize that the community is functionally diverse and, hence, that intelligence production may not always have the highest priority.

A second factor of importance is the structural diversity of the producers. Many of the disagreements over analyses and estimates among the producers are the result of bureaucratic and perceptual differences. The civilian-military dimension is one obvious taxonomy, but there are also classifications among the military producers as well as distinctions based on methodology and epistemology, as well as allocational and functional rivalries. Since the U.S. intelligence community is a confederation, its products reflect the "battles for bureaucratic self-interest and primacy."[38]

The intelligence consumers, too, are a diverse lot, including the producers as well as the congressional and other executive branch units. This diversity suggests two convenient categories of consumers--internal (to the community) and external, each with different dynamics and interests. Moreover, the relationships between the producers and the congressional consumers are different from those involving executive branch consumers.

The products themselves are the crux of the producer/consumer nexus. The majority of these products are routine and are intended for internal consumers. Analyses and estimates are produced both periodically and nonperiodically, and although the latter usually imply a crisis perception (by either producer or consumer) or situation, the former often have a more profound and extended impact on national security policy. The most important products are the National Intelligence Estimates.

It was the intent of this chapter to suggest how the intelligence producers and consumers are related and to offer an outline for further investigation of the relationship. By definition, national security policy concerns the most vital interests of the country. That policy necessarily demands the most knowledgeable and reasoned perceptions and assessments of the policy environment and its dynamics. Post facto reactions to "intelligence failures" are far less useful analytically and practically than an appreciation for the complexities of the producer/consumer nexus, thus suggesting the need for reasonable expectations of intelligence products.

NOTES

1. For a review of the various unique missions, see Stomley L. Falk and Theodore W. Bauer, The National Security Structure, rev. ed. (Washington, D.C.: Industrial College of the Armed Forces, 1972). For a more recent indication of specific duties and how the missions overlap, see Stafford Thomas, The U.S. Intelligence Community (Lanham, Md.: University Press of America, 1983), ch. 3.

2. Graham Allison, Essence of Decision: Explaining the Cuban Missile Crisis (Boston: Little, Brown, 1971).

3. See numerous references to the CIA/FBI rivalry, especially in

the 1960s, in Thomas Powers, The Man Who Kept the Secrets: Richard Helms and the CIA (New York: Alfred A. Knopf, 1979). See also Thomas F. Troy, Donovan and the CIA: a History of the Establishment of the Central Intelligence Agency (Washington, D.C.: Central Intelligence Agency, 1981).

4. This is an extrapolation of the basic argument that characterizes the work of John G. Stoessinger, Why Nations Go to War, 3rd ed. (New York: St Martin's Press, 1982), p. 209.

5. See Powers, The Man Who Kept the Secrets, ch. 11; and Sam Adams, "Cover-Up: Playing War with Numbers," Harpers (May 1975).

6. See Ray S. Cline, Secrets, Spies and Scholars: Blueprint of the Essential CIA (Washington, D.C.: Acropolis Books, 1976), p. 199. See also Larry Berman, Planning a Tragedy: The Americanization of the War in Vietnam (New York: W. W. Norton, 1982), especially ch. 4.

7. Thomas, U.S. Intelligence Community, ch. 3.

8. See Amos A. Jordan and William J. Taylor et al., American National Security: Policy and Process (Baltimore: Johns Hopkins Press, 1981).

9. The notion of how bureaucratic loyalties can affect intelligence analyses and estimates is based on a fundamental axiom of public administration. See Felix A. Nigro and Lloyd G. Nigro, Modern Public Administration, 4th ed. (New York: Harper & Row, 1977), p. 101.

10. Robert S. McNamara, The Essence of Security: Reflections in Office (New York: Harper & Row, 1968), p. 90.

11. Richard H. Giza, "The Problems of the Intelligence Consumer," in Roy Godson, ed., Intelligence Requirements for the 1980s: Analysis and Estimates (Washington, D.C.: National Strategy Information Center, 1980), p. 200.

12. The following discussion is based on Stafford Thomas, "On the Selection of Directors of Central Intelligence."

13. See Troy, Donovan and the CIA.

14. Roberta Wohlstetter, Pearl Harbor: Warning and Decision (Stanford, Calif.: Stanford University Press, 1962).

15. Four of the five statutory functions of the CIA, as outlined in the National Security Act of 1947, relate to intelligence production; the fifth function relates to covert action and is covered by the famous "elastic clause": "to perform other functions and duties relating to national security . . . as the National Security Council may direct" [emphasis added].

16. The following discussion of the troop strength issue is based on Powers, The Man Who Kept the Secrets, pp. 235-249, and Adams, "Cover-Up."

17. Discussions of these phases are provided in Harry Howe Ransom, The U.S. Intelligence Establishment (Cambridge, Mass.: Harvard University Press, 1970), and Lyman B. Kirkpatrick, The U.S. Intelligence Community: Foreign Policy and Domestic Activities (New York: Hill and Wang, 1973).

18. For a comprehensive classification of intelligence products, see Ransom, U.S. Intelligence Establishment, pp. 13-14, 45.

19. A review of congressional views on the oversight function from 1947 to the early 1970s is given in Ransom, U.S. Intelligence Establishment, ch. 7. Ransom also discusses the relationship between intelligence activities and domestic politics in "Strategic Intelligence

138

and Intermestic Politics," which was prepared for presentation to the 1982 American Political Science Association convention.

20. An especially useful account of the "firestorm" is provided in William E. Colby, Honorable Men: My Life in the CIA (New York: Simon and Schuster, 1978), chapters 11-14.

21. Thomas K. Lattimer, the staff director of the House Permanent Committee on Intelligence, concludes as much in "United States Intelligence Activities: The Role of Congress," in Robert L. Pfaltzgraff, Jr., Uri Ra'anan, and Warren Milbert, eds., Intelligence Policy and National Security (Hamden, Conn.: Archon Books, 1981), p. 273.

22. For discussion of both an attempt to use various producers and an experience with multi-advocacy, see U.S., Congress, Senate, Report of the Senate Select Committee on Collection, Production and Quality: The National Intelligence Estimates A-B Team Episode Concerning Soviet Strategic Capabilities and Objectives (Washington, D.C.: Government Printing Office, 1978).

23. Lattimer, "United States Intelligence Activities," pp. 279-286.

24. Ibid., p. 279.

25. U.S., Congress, Senate, Select Committee to Study Governmental Operations with Respect to Intelligence Activities, Final Report (Washington, D.C.: Government Printing Office, 1976). See also Lattimer, "United States Intelligence Activities," on the subject of congressional acceptance of and satisfaction with the community's products.

26. "Written products primarily include the Central Intelligence Agency's (CIA) 'National Intelligence Daily,' the Department of State's (Bureau of Intelligence and Research, INR) 'Morning Summary,' and the Defense Intelligence Agency's (DIA) 'Daily Intelligence Summary.' These are the intelligence community's top priority publications read daily at the White House and by others at the top in the foreign affairs and defense establishment." See Allen H. Kitchens, "Crisis and Intelligence—Two Case Studies" (pp. 1-2), a paper presented at the 1984 International Studies Association convention.

27. See Ransom, U.S. Intelligence Establishment, especially ch. 6.

28. Richard K. Betts makes the intriguing argument that "intelligence failures are not only inevitable, they are natural. Some are even benign (if a success would have changed policy)." See Richard K. Betts, "Analysis, War, and Decision: Why Intelligence Failures Are Inevitable," World Politics 31 (October 1978):88. This article posits three sources of intelligence failures—organizational paradoxes, operational pathologies, and consumer perspectives—and concludes that the latter are primarily responsible for intelligence failures.

29. National Defense.

30. Patrick J. McGarvey accuses the Defense Intelligence Agency of producing "intelligence to please" in order to support Pentagon arguments, especially in Congress. See Patrick J. McGarvey, CIA: The Myth and the Madness (Baltimore: Penguin Books, 1972).

31. Thomas, U.S. Intelligence Community, p. 69.

32. McGarvey, CIA.

33. Stafford Thomas, "CIA Functional Diversity and the National Security Policy Process."

34. Ray Cline, "Policy Without Intelligence," Foreign Policy 17

(Winter, 1974-1975):133.

35. See U.S., Congress, Senate, A-B Team Episode; and Daniel O. Graham, "Analysis and Estimates," in Roy Godson, ed., Intelligence Requirements for the 1980s: Elements of Intelligence (Washington, D.C.: National Strategy Information Center, 1979).

36. Allison, "Analysis and Estimates," p. 26.

37. Lawrence Freedman, U.S. Intelligence and the Soviet Strategic Threat (Boulder, Colo.: Westview Press, 1978), p. 53.

38. Angelo Codevilla, "Comparative Historical Experience of Doctrine and Organization," in Godson, ed., Analysis and Estimates, p. 30.

10

Organizational Foundations of Intelligence Failures

INTRODUCTION

Surprise is a fundamental reality of world politics—and few, if any, foreign policy and defense establishments can expect to escape its negative consequences. Four factors have been identified as contributing to the onset of an intelligence failure: perceptual bias, the nature of the intelligence estimating function, the attitudes and behavior of policymakers, and the organizational context within which the intelligence function takes place. Research has progressed furthest in examining the relationship between the first three of these factors and intelligence estimating. Studies of the organizational dimension of intelligence failures have not yet produced frameworks or insights comparable to those being developed in the areas of perceptual bias, the nature of the intelligence function and the problem of surprise, or the place of the policymaker in the intelligence process.[1] Studies of the organizational dimension have been content either to rely upon the bureaucratic politics perspective or simply to assert the marginal utility of altering organizational structures as a means of improving the quality of intelligence.

This chapter presents a framework for studying intelligence estimating that emphasizes the organizational dimension. Attaining a full understanding of intelligence estimating, and of intelligence failures in particular, requires the development of a framework in which explicit attention is paid to organizational variables. Without it, not only will the organizational dimension remain obscure, but our understanding of other contributing factors will also be impaired. This framework brings together the organization theory literature that deals with intelligence and the literature on the CIA, other U.S. intelligence bureaucracies, and foreign services.

ORGANIZATIONAL STRUCTURE AND INTELLIGENCE ESTIMATING

An organization-centered framework for studying intelligence estimating must integrate three lines of analysis: (1) the nature of the organization, (2) the sources of intelligence failures, and (3) the pattern of interaction between an organization and its environment. Neither of the two dominant approaches to the organizational dimension of intelligence failures noted earlier meets these requirements.

An organization-centered framework for studying intelligence estimating must divide an organization into artificial and natural subsystems. The artificial system is built around the formal lines of authority that structure an organization and consists of the formal set of institutional relationships that govern the behavior of organizational members. It is a goal-oriented system whose logic and coherence derive from the purposes or goals assigned to it by forces outside the organization.

The natural system springs up spontaneously around the artificial system. The logic of the two systems frequently collide. Where the artificial system is externally oriented, the natural system is internally oriented and concerned with the survival of organizational members. The natural system cannot, however, be viewed as dysfunctional. No artificial system can survive long without an effectively operating natural system. Mandators and organization managers cannot anticipate all of the contingencies with which an organization must deal if it is to prosper and grow.

The natural system introduces elements of flexibility and redundancy, which help to ensure an acceptable minimal level of performance. It also confronts mandators and managers with a challenge. As a spontaneous structure, it defies total control and planning. Attempts to manipulate it will fail. Likewise, alterations in the artificial system may produce an unwanted and counterproductive response in the natural system.

The Artificial System and Intelligence Failures

Sources of intelligence failures can be found in the artificial and natural systems. As argued by Harold Wilensky,[2] hierarchy, specialization, and centralization can be identified as the major sources of distortion in the artificial system. Hierarchy contributes to intelligence. It does so because rank in a hierarchy serves in part as a source of status and power. The interaction of hierarchy and information produces a situation in which only certain kinds of communications are facilitated. Subordinates resist transmitting to superiors information that could be used to disparage their performance or upset comfortable routines.

To Harold Wilensky, specialization is an even more powerful distorting force than is hierarchy. Specialization breeds parochialism as the lines on an organizational chart become lines of secrecy and loyalty. The inevitable result is rivalry and competition both between organizations and within them. Great benefits may result from such competition, and a competitive intelligence system is often argued for by reformers.[3] The normal tendency, however, is for rivalry to block the sharing of information, prevent penetrating analysis, and often result in the production of misleading or irrelevant information.

The third structural factor contributing to intelligence failures is centralization. The dilemma here is that if intelligence is lodged at the top of the organization, policymakers will be overburdened and too far removed from the source of the information; yet, if the intelligence estimating function is scattered throughout the organization, analysis will be carried out without the unifying presence of a common view of the problem.

The Natural System and Intelligence Failures

The natural system can serve as a source of intelligence failures in two ways: first, by interacting with the artificial system to further aggravate the three structural impediments to quality intelligence and, second, by being composed of norms, values, and mores that produce blockages of intelligence in their own right. These conditions are most prevalent in the organization's doctrine of intelligence, the shared assumptions underlying its analytical efforts, and the structure of its motivational system.

The most serious impediments to the production of high-quality intelligence are organizational doctrines of intelligence. These doctrines shape the way in which the intelligence-estimating function is defined and the manner in which intelligence and policy are joined in the policy process. The handling of the following three issues in an organization's doctrine of intelligence are especially important to the quality of intelligence produced. The resulting perspective may combine to produce an internally consistent outlook on the intelligence function or come together into a contradictory bundle of assertions. Whatever their makeup, doctrines of intelligence are highly resistant to change, and altering them is a difficult undertaking.

The most fundamental issue is whether intelligence is defined as raw data or as analyzed information. If the former view dominates, a tendency to inundate policymakers with "facts"—and especially the most current "facts"—will develop. Overwhelmed by this flow of information, policymakers will be able to indulge their whims and choose the "facts" most consistent with their policy predispositions. The latter view asserts that pure empiricism in intelligence estimating is impossible. Data must be interpreted, evaluated, and assessed with respect to a conceptual framework before it becomes intelligence.

A second issue is the extent to which a distinction is made between prediction and forecasting.[4] Involved here is the question of what is to be expected from intelligence. Forecasting involves judging contingencies and weighing the likelihood of alternative outcomes. Prediction involves making judgments about the outcome of a specific event or state of affairs in the future.

Forecasting and prediction entail different analytic undertakings and rely upon different methodologies.[5] In making forecasts, probabilities are used in presenting conclusions, whereas in making predictions they are dispensed with in favor of yes/no answers. The inability to distinguish between situations calling for forecasts and those appropriate for predictions contributes to intelligence failures by failing to alert the policymaker to the true nature of problems and may lead to the selection of an inappropriate response.

A third component to an organization's intelligence doctrine is the emphasis placed on secrecy, which confronts intelligence estimating with a serious dilemma. Secrecy is essential to the successful functioning of a national security system. Sources must be protected; information must be verified and kept secure; analysis must be kept free from deliberate distortion; and the organization must be kept free from infiltrators.

Yet secrecy threatens intelligence estimating through its ability to distort the decisionmaking process.[6] The most common distortions are (1) arbitrary limitation analysis, and (2) promotion of an unfounded and excessive preference for secret sources of information over that obtained from open sources. In addition, secrecy can serve as an instrument of power both for organizations and for individuals. It becomes a means of obtaining leverage over others and for circumventing accountability and oversight procedures.

In a recent review of forecasting efforts in such diverse fields as transportation, technology, energy, economic performance, and population growth, W. Ascher concluded that variations in the accuracy of forecasts are due not to methodological considerations but to differences in organizational biases affecting the nature of the object being studied.[7] Intelligence estimating appears to be no different. Israeli intelligence fell victim to a false and closed set of concepts in 1973.[8] The CIA's holding of unwarranted assumptions was central to the B-team's critique of CIA estimates of Soviet military capabilities.[9] In a somewhat different vein, Richard Pipes argues that the very use of social science models contributes to intelligence failures.[10] He argues that the methodology of the historian is most congenial to the production of quality intelligence.

The motivation system is a final aspect of the natural system requiring special mention. The issue here is how to motivate high-quality performance in the production of intelligence. More is involved than just selecting sanctions and incentives, though even this is no easy task. The problem is inseparable from that of choosing a mechanism for the evaluation of intelligence estimates. Attempts to address it quickly confront the spontaneity of the natural system and the difficulty of engineering changes within it.

The most intuitive evaluation standard is accuracy. However, if accuracy is chosen as the sole instrument of judgment, the intelligence system may overproduce estimates that have a short time frame, are vague or hedged, or focus on safe topics. How would one evaluate an estimate that will turn sensitized policymakers in a new or potentially dangerous direction? Should the same standards of accuracy be applied to forecasts and predictions?

Flexibility in evaluation standards thus appears desirable. But it, too, creates problems. How does one weigh the multiple measures of success being employed? Moreover, how does one prevent estimates from being written to fit this weighting system? Too much flexibility will be resisted because it brings an unwanted element of subjectivity and arbitrariness into the organization, thereby threatening the predictability and continuity of career opportunities. A concern for survival demands that this uncertainty be managed even if it comes at the expense of organizational goals.

The organizational sources of intelligence failures are thus deeply rooted in the nature of organizations. Hierarchy, specialization, and centralization are inescapable features of modern bureaucratic organization. The natural system spontaneously grows up around these features and defies attempts to control and direct it. Bureaucracy, however, while referring to a type of organization, permits variation in structural detail and operating procedures. The question becomes to what extent the CIA as a bureaucratic organization gives rise to and accentuates those organizational characteristics that serve as a source of intelligence failures. Answering this question involves examining in detail the characteristics of the CIA's artificial and natural systems for their impact on intelligence failures.

THE CIA's ARTIFICIAL SYSTEM

A key source of variation in the artificial system of organizations lies in the necessity of operating in an environment whose makeup is largely beyond its control. For the national security bureaucracies the fundamental reality is the same, although variations in detail do exist. For all the secrecy surrounding their daily work, they operate in a political and public setting. A number of consequences follow from this public character, which separates public bureaucracies from private-sector ones.

First, goals are more difficult to measure for public bureaucracies than for private-sector bureaucracies. Criteria include not only profit and efficiency, but also concerns for the common good and for national defense. Likewise, organizational health is more difficult to gauge. Profit statements, number of product lines, and personnel employed must give way to concerns for access, autonomy, and missions. Finally, public bureaucracies must also serve a more diverse set of masters than do private-sector bureaucracies. In his analysis of the State Department as a public bureaucracy, D. Warwick identified two sets of external forces that are especially relevant to organizational structure and performance—namely, its power setting and its operating environment.[11] Both will be examined for their impact on the degree of hierarchy, specialization, and centralization in the CIA as revealed in the literature on the CIA and other intelligence bureaucracies.

The Power Setting

The power setting refers to those actors who are in a position to exert an immediate influence on an organization's behavior. These people are referred to as mandators.[12] Mandators are distinct from other forces external to the organization who are affected by its actions and have an interest in shaping its goals but lack either the statutory authority or the resources to do so. With repsect to the CIA, four sets of actors occupy such a position: other members of the intelligence community, the presidency, Congress, and interest groups that monitor and evaluate the performance of the intelligence community.

From its very conception, the CIA has been unable to monopolize the field of national security intelligence. It has always been forced to operate as one member of an intelligence community. The concept of community implies a high degree of similarity and likeness, with members sharing common concerns and values. The U.S. intelligence community does not fare well by such standards. The ties that bind are at best loose ones. The intelligence community is more a federation of unequals in which members vary according to their degree of institutional autonomy, the nature of their contribution to the intelligence function, and their political clout.

The imbalance in the distribution of power within the intelligence community as well as the presence of competition between members mean that management by committee rather than by command characterizes the decisionmaking process. A committee approach increases the amount of interagency communication needed in order to arrive at a decision, thus producing pressures for greater centralization and coordination within each agency. The result is an increase in the flow of messages to the top of the organizational hierarchy that threatens the hierarchy with communication overload. The standard response to this threat is to build additional amounts of hierarchy and specialization into the organization.

A committee approach to decisionmaking also brings about, or at least reinforces, the demand for "legitimized" facts. At some point in any decision process, certain information must be accepted as true for action to be undertaken. Within the CIA such facts are established through a coding scheme designed to identify the reliability and accuracy of the information.[13] In deliberations with other organizations, these facts are often bargained into existence.[14] The ability of decisionmakers to decipher the dimensions of bargains struck decreases with the amount of hierarchy, centralization, and specialization. These factors combine to place the decisionmaker in a position far removed from the point at which uncertainty is absorbed and facts are created.

The central actor in the CIA's power setting is the president. The first duty of the DCI is to win the trust, confidence, and ear of the president. Helms took this one step further by commenting that as DCI he served the president—one president at a time.[15] In spite of this role orientation, neither presidents nor the CIA have found the other particularly easy to deal with in the area of intelligence estimating.

Presidents, upset with what they perceive to be the nonresponsiveness or policy irrelevance of many intelligence estimates, have often resorted to a crisis-manager orientation in the search for useful information. This solution, however, is not without its drawbacks. One likely result is to increase pressures for centralization. The superior being bypassed will want to be kept fully informed about the nature of these communications and will institute procedures for monitoring them. The superior will also want to have all of the information that his or her subordinates have so as not to be caught off guard or embarrassed by a presidential intervention. Lower-level officials will attempt to get as much raw data as possible in anticipation of such interventions. The combined result is communication overload, which, in turn, generates pressures for even more hierarchy and specialization to make the flow of communication more manageable.

To be effective, a crisis-manager approach must be used sparingly. When used regularly it is self-defeating. Organizational routines and standard operating procedures get created in anticipation of the next intervention and thereby negate the organization's potential for extracting high-quality intelligence. Overuse of the crisis-manager approach, however, is the norm. Having found a communications network that "works," policymakers tend to return to it in an indiscriminate fashion.[16]

Another way in which the crisis-manager approach serves as an irritant in the relationship between the CIA and the president is by failing to provide the analyst with any guidance about the concerns and priorities of the policymaker. All it does is create uncertainty. A crisis-manager approach provides no ready insight into the ongoing concerns and priorities of policymakers. It involves a constantly shifting set of issues. Guidance requires continuity of attention, which can serve to direct the analysis process. In the absence of guidance from the policymaker, analysts must establish their own points of reference; yet, in the process, they may run the risk of producing intelligence that the policymaker finds less than helpful, thereby setting off a new cycle of policymaker intervention within the estimating process.

The root causes for the lack of effective policymaker guidance in intelligence estimating lie deeper than the adoption of a crisis-manager approach by presidents. Most policies have multiple authors, and the requirements of coalition building have a negative impact on the clarity with which goals and problems are identified and communicated. Further undermining the clarity with which values and priorities can be expressed is the fact that policymakers do not face a single problem; instead, they confront multiple and interacting problems.

A final source of frustration in the relationship between the CIA and the presidency is one that grows out of the conflicting logics of intelligence estimating and policymaking.[17] The logic of intelligence estimating is to reduce the number of policy options by clarifying the issues, assumptions, and consequences behind various courses of action. The logic of policymaking is to keep options open for as long as possible. One way to do this is to keep secrets from intelligence agencies. Another, practiced by Kissinger, is to use unhappiness over the quality of estimates as a means of control. In both cases, the intelligence agency is placed in a reactive position. It is forced to expend resources on discovering the policymakers' values rather than on being able to take them as a given. The end result is greater freedom of manuever for the policymaker.

Though an actor of long standing in the CIA's power setting, Congress as an institution has only recently come to be a significant presence in it. For the majority of its history, the CIA has had little reason to fear Congress or to expend a great deal of energy trying to anticipate its concerns.

The House and Senate have now established permanent oversight committees that the CIA has not easily controlled. The relative newness of Congress as an important force in the CIA's power setting makes it difficult to speak with certainty of the impact this altered state of affairs will have on the CIA's structure.

Warwick asserts that the possibility of investigation serves to limit the discretion of lower-level officials.[18] Discretion is limited by the necessity of seeking clearances from higher-level officials who will be held accountable by Congress for the actions or statements of lower-level officials. The result is an increase in the communication flow and a slowing down of the decision process.

When the issue is covert action, a slowing down of the decision process along with added centralization may be highly desirable. A major criticism of U.S. covert action programs has been their disjointed and fragmented nature.[19] There tends to be a lack of coordination between efforts, with the result that no cumulative impact is achieved.

These same characteristics, however, may not be as beneficial in intelligence estimating. Speed and creativity are often essential in producing quality intelligence. Both are adversely affected by the institution of rules and procedures that attempt to meet the possible questions of outside monitors.

The newest set of actors in the CIA's power setting are interest groups. The once closed world of intelligence no longer exists, and the actions of the intelligence community have become the focal point for a great deal of interest group activity.[20] Three types of groups exist. All are knowledgeable in the field of intelligence; all can count ex-intelligence officers in their ranks; and all seek to mobilize support for their positions.

These interest groups exercise their power indirectly. They direct their activities not so much at the CIA as at Congress and the presidency. Their ability to exert influence varies with the general climate of political opinion. At the height of congressional charter writing efforts, the anti-CIA forces displayed a great deal of political clout in their ability to influence Congress. As these efforts began to wane and the political climate became more conservative, their influence has become more tenuous and more readily countered by the other two types of groups.

The Operating Environment

The operating environment refers to the set of conditions immediately impinging on the organization's daily work. The primary realities of the CIA's operating environment are similar in nature to those facing the State Department and Defense Department: high threat, high uncertainty, and high complexity. The CIA also shares with these organizations the need to undertake widely dispersed operations. An added complicating factor for the CIA is the high degree of secrecy surrounding its efforts. Taken together, these features produce pressures for hierarchy, specialization, and centralization.

Specialization is needed to cope adequately with the ever-increasing range of questions being examined and the wide variety of information being collected and analyzed. No longer do political and military estimates dominate the estimating effort. Economics, religion, and technological topics have also become crucial areas of expertise and investigation. Added hierarchy and centralization are needed to cope with the high message flow that must be analyzed and distributed throughout the intelligence community.

A second feature of the operating environment having an impact on the ability to produce quality intelligence is the nature of the decisionmaking situation.[21] High levels of tension and secrecy and severe time constraints are typically present, and the demand for quick responses to questions is not uncommon. Wilensky notes that theoretically such conditions are conducive to the production of high-quality intelligence, but the more fundamental political reality is that it is also on these types of issues that the analyst is most likely to be locked out of the decisionmaking process by the crisis-manager approach;[22] such is the case, too, with the tendency of policymakers to introduce their own biases into the estimating process, thereby arbitrarily resolving the inherent ambiguity of the available evidence.

The decisionmaking situation also creates pressures in the direction of redundancy. Intelligence failures are potentially expensive for U.S. national security interests, organizational survival, and individual career aspirations. To minimize this likelihood, steps are taken to ensure that every piece of information is collected, analyzed, and transmitted through channels. Multiple-collection, analytic, and reporting channels help ensure that this, in fact, will occur. Such redundancy, however, also requires added centralization and control mechanisms if it is to function as planned and not end up frustrating the intelligence effort. Unfortunately, often the worst of both worlds is achieved. Frank Snepp's account of Vietnam and John Stockwell's discussion of Angola both suggest that such communication blockages have reached disturbing proportions.[23]

A third feature of the operating environment that has a major impact on the intelligence function is the prevailing social and political climate.[24] This climate has an impact on attitudes toward events and variables adopted by members of the intelligence community. The desire to be involved in the policy process, to have one's work considered relevant, will lead many analysts, often unconsciously, to adopt the prevailing societal and political definitions of threats to national security.

The Israeli surprise in 1973 was in part attributable to such a sharing of values. To be sure, not all analysts will succumb to pressures of this sort. However, when shared values are placed in conjunction with the nature of the decisionmaking process, the probability increases that policymakers will be able to avoid having to confront reality on unpleasant terms. They will be able to find "intelligence" consistent with their interpretation of events. Measures for controlling this ability to pick and choose from among competing estimates do not easily--if ever--succeed.[25] Policymakers simply cannot be forced to accept intelligence estimates they do not want.

The CIA's Response to Environmental Challenges

Pressures for high levels of specialization, hierarchy, and centralization within the CIA are clearly discernible in its power setting and operating environment. The question that remains is whether the CIA's response pattern is a pathological organizational response or a rational one. One way to approach this question is to examine the manner in which the CIA has sought to buffer its core technologies from uncertainty. Under norms of organizational rationality, such an effort is necessary in order to protect the legitimacy of the core technologies, to promote the organization's effectiveness, and to ensure a favorable evaluation of it by outside monitors.[26]

Prestige is the cheapest way of accomplishing these ends. Co-optation and the employment of public relations and briefing units as buffers are also standard remedies.[27] Allen Dulles's attempts to create a James Bond image for the CIA and to spellbind congressional overseers with displays of gadgetry are not simply the product of a unique personality. Likewise, the employment of personnel solely for the purpose of briefing policymakers is not just a case of bureaucratic excess. Both constitute part of a rational response to possible challenges to its operational autonomy—challenges that grow out of the complexity and uncertainty of its environment.

More specific strategies exist, depending on the nature of the technology employed. Organizations employing a mediating technology, one that is required to operate in standard ways with multiple clients, seek to increase the size of the audience they serve. An organization employing an intensive technology, one in which various techniques are used to bring about a change in a specific object, seeks to incorporate that object into its own organizational structure. Here, too, CIA actions take on new meanings.

Intelligence estimating employs a mediating technology. It requires standardized operating procedures so that its output will be useful to many different customers. Although technically only the CIA is mandated to present intelligence estimates to the president, in reality all members of the intelligence community make their views known. This represents a challenge to the CIA. The predicted response is an attempt to increase one's audience. Clearly, this is what the CIA and the other intelligence agencies have sought to do by issuing a virtual flood of daily and weekly reports carrying a variety of security classifications.

Covert action employs intensive technology. It requires a bringing together of diverse skills and techniques to change a policymaker's position, a government policy, or the general climate of public opinion. The rational response is to incorporate the object into one's own structure in order to better control it. From this perspective, the CIA has repeatedly acted with a great deal of organizational rationality. Infiltrators are first placed in an organization and are then urged to seek and assume positions of power and influence. The process of career advancement not only supplies the CIA with more information than had the individual simply remained a member, but it also brings that organization more directly under its control.

Norms of organizational rationality also extend to evaluating the effectiveness of an organization. The two central measures for making such evaluations—agreement on causation and clear standards of desirability[28]—are not applicable to the CIA's intelligence-estimating function. The inherent ambiguity of the data frustrates agreement on causation. The distinction between forecasting and prediction complicates the clear definition of acceptable standards of performance.

Confronted with a stituation such as this, an organization will seek to mold criteria to suit its own needs. Commonly used tactics include making favorable comparisons with other organizations and demonstrating historical improvement. Visibility and importance to outside monitors are the key considerations in the organization's selection of criteria. To be effective, key officials in the policy process must take intelligence seriously. This means that intelligence must be readily available to them and must meet their needs. These needs are often political. Two of the most frequently posed evaluative questions by policymakers are (1) How will it effect my ability to mobilize support for my policies? (2) How will my constituency react?[29]

Intelligence is no more immune from this politically oriented evaluative process than is any other policy sector. Commenting on his experience at the State Department's Bureau of Intelligence and Research, Thomas Hughes stated that policymakers were most eager to get information that would help them convince Congress or the public about the merits of a policy.[30] They were most frustrated with information that was politically impossible to use and generally skeptical about the incremental value of added information for policymaking purposes.

THE CIA's NATURAL SYSTEM

Doctrines of Intelligence

As noted earlier, doctrines of intelligence are the ways in which people inside an organization think about intelligence. They form part of the natural system that both evolves in response to the structures and demands of the artificial system and is concerned with providing for the survival of organizational members. The primary reference points for an organization's doctrines of intelligence are the consumers' attitudes toward intelligence. It is their demands to which the organization and the individual must respond if intelligence is going to prosper and survive.

Regardless of their formal position in the policy hierarchy, consumers of intelligence tend to hold similar attitudes about intelligence.[31] First, there is the conviction that analysts should furnish information and nothing more. Analysts are not expected to explore alternatives or come to conclusions. That is the responsibility of the policymaker. The underlying assumptions are that facts contain self-evident implications and that if all of the facts are known, any question can be answered.

A second shared attitude holds that experience—first-hand participation—is critical to high-quality intelligence work. Insights produced by the application of analytical skills tend to be depreciated. As a consequence, a sense of anti-intellectualism is injected into the analyst/policymaker relationship. Closely related to these two attitudes is a third: an emphasis on current events. The perceived need is for up-to-the-minute information to solve ongoing problems. Long-range planning is too academic an exercise and too far removed from the policymaker's most immediate concerns to be highly valued. Likewise, the warning function is slighted. The inherent ambiguity of the intelligence function negates the possibility of developing clear-cut warning indicators. Preferable from the policymaker's view is obtaining all of the facts.

A final shared attitude toward intelligence is the tendency to treat intelligence estimates as a free good. Intelligence is seen as something always on call. Information demands are placed on intelligence services with little regard for the costs involved. Differences between prediction and forecasting become blurred in the rush to acquire the latest information on the current trouble spot. When demand exceeds supply, resources must be shifted. For instance, events in Cyprus and Portugal surprised the United States in the early 1970s because resources were shifted to meet the huge information demand created by the involvement in Vietnam.

While sharing a common point of departure, the doctrines of intelligence existing within the U.S. intelligence community are far from uniform. The variations that exist both between and within organizations reflect different individual and institutional experiences in responding to the demands of consumers for intelligence.

The most pronounced differences are found among members of different organizations. For example, whereas "intelligence to please" is a phenomenon common to all intelligence services as a doctrine of intelligence, it appears in a more pronounced form in the Defense Intelligence Agency (DIA) than in the CIA.[32] Within the CIA, noticeable differences can be found among the various directorates. Victor Marchetti and John Marks employ the term <u>clandestine mentality</u> to describe the mind-set of intelligence professionals who emphasize a sense of higher loyalty promoting secrecy, deception, and amorality.[33] The varied reactions within the CIA to the 1970 U.S. invasion of Cambodia suggest that clandestine morality is most prevalent in clandestine services. In 1970, CIA members remained silent while a few hundred employees from the Intelligence and Science and Technology Directorates signed a petition objecting to U.S. policy in Indochina.

With such considerations in mind, it is possible to identify four tendencies in the doctrines of intelligence adopted by members of the intelligence community. One tendency is to be current events oriented. This perspective appears to have been adopted only grudgingly by analysts out of a desire to participate in the policy process. Analysts see their most important role as one of giving warning. Recall, however, that the warning function is depreciated by policymakers. To adhere to this role orientation in the face of policymaker disinterest would be to resign oneself to a position on the margins of the policy process.

A tension is thus created for the analyst. His or her only options are to leave intelligence work or to alter role orientations. Many of those who have opted to leave are reported to be among the most qualified departing the intelligence-estimating field, which is heavily staffed by individuals either content to accept the policymakers' definition of their role or solely concerned with survival.[34] A vicious cycle is in operation. Policymakers emphasize current events which injects an element of anti-intellectualism into the intelligence-estimating process. In frustration, qualified people resign. The quality of work then declines, reinforcing the desire of policymakers for raw data as opposed to evaluated information.

A second tendency is for analysts to adopt the "jigsaw theory" of intelligence. The main premise of this theory is that a missing piece of information does exist and that if the piece is found the problem will be solved. Everything and anything is sought, classified, and stored on the assumption that at some point it may be crucial to answering a question. This role orientation is consistent with policymakers' notions of intelligence as a free good as well as with their belief that the ambiguity of data can be overcome by collecting more data. The combined effect of these views is to establish a flow of information that creates pressure from hierarchy, specialization, and centralization.

A third observable tendency is the production of "intelligence to please" or "backstopping." When consumers adopt an orientation that stresses current data and combines this with known policy preferences, the analyst faces yet another dilemma. Efforts directed at providing anything but supportive evidence will be ignored. Pressures for survival push career individuals into producing "intelligence to please." Decisions on troop strength in Vietnam and target selection for bombing and rescue raids are examples that reveal the extent to which such pressures can be felt and the detrimental impact they can have on the intelligence function.[35]

There is one final role orientation—the intelligence maker who acts as an organizational broker forging a consensus on the issues at hand. A consensus is needed for action, making this role orientation a valuable one. However, the consensus need not be based on an accurate reading of events. Facts bargained into existence provide an equally suitable basis for consensus.[36]

The existence of these variations in the intelligence community's doctrines of intelligence is both a benefit and a drawback to the intelligence-estimating function. It is beneficial because the variations, which build a degree of redundancy into the organization, lessen the likelihood that important information will go unnoticed. But the variations also serve as a handicap when they frustrate the establishment of common values around which the intelligence function can organize. In the absence of agreed-on starting premises, the redundancy produced is more likely to yield waste than an added dimension of security.[37]

The Motivation System

Doctrines of intelligence tend to arise in response to consumer attitudes toward intelligence, but they are reinforced by the mix of rewards, incentives, and sanctions that an organization uses to judge and motivate high-quality performance by its members. Our concern must be with how these rewards and sanctions are viewed by members of the organization and not with official statements concerning their nature. The effective as opposed to the official motivational inducements are most clearly revealed in two areas. The first concerns the nature of the training program. The second involves the skills, roles, and career paths being emphasized by the organization in its promotion decisions. In observing the CIA, one finds that high-quality intelligence is not being heavily emphasized in either area.

The CIA training process discriminates against the development of skills necessary for intelligence estimating. Although memoirs make it clear that there has been no single training program,[38] for this purpose they also make clear the fact that intelligence analysis was not typically stressed. Emphasis has been placed on clandestine operations. Midcareer training appears to be limited, with the most substantial effort taking place outside the CIA. Moreover, much of it appears to be directed at the acquisition of managerial skills.

The pattern continues today. Young operators are given special intensive-training courses, whereas newly hired analysts are "put down at a desk with an 'in box' full of paper and are just told to start working."[39] The consequences of this neglect are considerable. William Colby observed that the training process is directly related to the organizational and conceptual role of the analyst.[40] The CIA's training process establishes a twofold subordination for the analysts. First, they are made subordinate to policymakers who want facts. Second, they are made subordinate to operators by the pattern of organizational spending in their respective training programs.

This discriminatory pattern is further reflected in the skills, background, and role orientations of those occupying the senior-most posts in the CIA. In combination with the pressures generated from mandators and by the power setting, attitudes set the tenor for organizational behavior. Changes in the operating styles and attitudes of these people will often have a bigger impact than will structural changes.

Hilsman identified three role orientations held by DCIs: managerial, covert operations, and estimating.[41] For the majority of its history, the CIA has been run by men with concerns other than intelligence estimating. Dulles and Richard Helms, the two men who have headed the CIA longer than any others, stressed the agency's covert-action mission. Since James Schlesinger replaced Helms, all DCIs have had managerial orientation, which has emphasized the strengthening of White House control over the CIA. Only John McCone gave primacy to the intelligence-estimating role, and he was largely an outsider to the intelligence process before his appointment.

Evidence of bias in the motivation system working against the production of quality intelligence is also evident in the types of career paths emerging within the CIA. The "ticket-punching" phenomenon and a rating system long criticized for producing Foreign Service officer look-alikes have been observed operating in the CIA. The rating system produces a situation in which everyone gets excellent ratings but not everyone gets promoted.[42] "Ticket punching" results in generalists overtaking experts to the extent that the organization's capacity to analyze specialized information is hampered. There comes to exist a disincentive to being an expert because expertise could actually limit one's promotion opportunities.

The key to success in such a system is to avoid risks: one must report everything, even if it results in a crippling flow of information; must document the fact that the information was reported, even if it means dangerously slowing down the estimating process; and then must get the information there as fast as possible, even if it means turning the Warning and Indicator Network System into the predominant reporting channel as opposed to one restricted to fast-breaking crucial information.[43]

CONCLUSION

What is needed now are comparative case studies drawn from primary sources and centered on organizational variables. Carefully constructed case studies of intelligence failures will fill the gaps in our factual knowledge about intelligence failures and permit a refinement of an organizationally based approach to such failures. The possible directions that such refinements might pursue include an examination of the influence of organizational variables at the different functional stages in the intelligence-estimating process identified by Ransom in 1970[44] and an evaluation of their impact at

18. Warwick, Theory of Public Bureaucracy, pp. 73-75.

19. Paul Blackstock, The Strategy of Subversion (Chicago: Quadrangle Books, 1964), pp. 305-306.

20. Roy Godson, "Interest Groups," in E. Lefever and R. Godson, eds., The CIA and the American Ethic (Washington, D.C.: Ethics and Public Policy Center, 1980), pp. 67-95.

21. C. Cooper, "Micawber Versus De Joueuenel: Planning and Forecasting in the Real World of Washington," in N. Choucri and T. Robinson, eds., Forecasting in International Relations (San Francisco: Freeman, 1978), p. 338.

22. Wilensky, Organizational Intelligence, p. 81.

23. See Frank Snepp, Decent Interval (New York: Vintage, 1977); and J. Stockwell, In Search of Enemies (New York: Norton, 1978).

24. A. Shlaim, "Failure in National Intelligence Estimates," World Politics 28 (April 1976): 361.

25. Richard Betts, "Analysis, War, and Decision," pp. 73-84.

26. J. Thompson, Organizations in Action (New York: McGraw-Hill, 1967), pp. 14-24.

27. Ibid., pp. 33-36.

28. Ibid., p. 134.

29. R. Nakamura and F. Smallwood, The Politics of Policy Implementation (New York: St. Martin's, 1980), pp. 68-70.

30. Thomas Hughes, "The Power to Speak and the Power to Listen," in T. Frank and E. Weisband, eds., Secrecy and Foreign Policy (New York: Oxford University Press, 1974), p. 18.

31. See Roger Hilsman, Strategic Intelligence and National Decisions (Glencoe, Ill.: Free Press, 1956).

32. P. McGarvey, CIA: The Myth and the Madness (Baltimore: Penguin, 1973), pp. 7-15. It should be noted that McGarvey is an ex-CIA officer.

33. Victor Marchetti and John Marks, The CIA and the Cult of Intelligence (New York: Dell, 1974), pp. 235-277.

34. McGarvey, CIA: The Myth and the Madness, pp. 7-15.

35. Adams, "Vietnam Cover-up," pp. 48-73; McGarvey, CIA: The Myth and the Madness, pp. 148-151.

36. Adams, "Vietnam Cover-Up," pp. 46-73.

37. D. Felsenthal, "Applying the Redundancy Concept to Administrative Organizations," Public Administration Review (May 1980): 247-252.

38. See Philip Agee, Inside the Company: CIA Diary (New York: Bantam, 1975); and D. Phillips, The Night Watch (New York: Antheneum, 1977).

39. Thomas K. Latimer, "Comment," in R. Godson, ed., Intelligence Requirements for the 1980s: Analysis and Estimates (Washington, D.C.: National Strategy Information Center, 1980).

40. William Colby, "Paper," in R. Godson, ed., Intelligence Requirements for the 1980s: Analysis and Estimates (Washington, D.C.: National Strategy Information Center, 1980): 187.

41. See Hilsman, Strategic Intelligence and National Decisions.

42. J. Smith, Portrait of a Cold Warrior (New York: G. P. Putnam, 1976), pp. 12-13

43. McGarvey, CIA: The Myth and the Madness, pp. 69-72.

44. See Ransom, Intelligence Establishment, pp. 15-16.

156

45. Anthony Downs, *Inside Bureaucracy* (Boston: Little Brown, 1967), pp. 158-166.

11

Congress, the Budget, and Intelligence

INTRODUCTION

The changes in congressional oversight of intelligence funding in the 1970s may have presented a unique example of public-sector resource management. In those years, the Congress—a highly political, decentralized public institution, with strong senses for law and the Constitution—encountered a highly complex, administrative, and (justifiably) secretive set of agencies. Members of Congress were introduced in depth to new arenas of technologies, systems, and organizations, and were challenged to analyze the allocation of resources among these. Although the Constitution gave them the right to examine intelligence funding and to obtain reasonable cooperation from the executive branch, they had to modify their own rules and practices. A study of this period, therefore, is a case study of the immense difficulty involved in exercising complex management functions (e.g., resource planning, allocation, and control) in a political setting.

THE EARLY YEARS

Congress made several attempts to oversee intelligence before 1970, only to have them collapse in divisions of opinion among its members. In 1955 Senator Mike Mansfield introduced Senate Congressional Resolution 2 calling for a twelve-man Joint Committee on Central Intelligence, but it failed to pass. Ten years later the Senate Foreign Relations Committee approved Senate Resolution 283 to establish a Committee on Intelligence Operations. In a move that is common to congressional behavior, a jurisdictional struggle erupted. The Senate Armed Services Committee claimed principal responsibility over intelligence and defeated the resolution on the floor. However, three members of Foreign Relations were invited to attend meetings of the CIA Subcommittee of the Senate Armed Services. Few meetings occurred and interest waned.[1]

In the early 1970s, the intelligence budget was reviewed by a few senior members of Congress in brief meetings with senior administration officials. Special subcommittees of the House and Senate Appropriations Committees were presented the CIA budget in closed session. Senate oversight of the CIA was provided for through an informal agreement among its bipartisan leadership, involving shared jurisdiction between the armed services and the appropriations committees.[2] Through 1975, "neither the Senate Appropriations Committee as a whole, nor the whole Senate [was] informed, even in secret sessions, of the budget figures for the CIA, NSA, or certain other intelligence units."[3]

The stirrings of deep congressional involvement in the intelligence budget began in 1974-1975 in the House Appropriations Committee. Reflecting both the energy of its staff and the concern of its leadership, the committee began the more traditional actions of budget review—hearings, questions for the record, and staff visits to agencies. In 1975 the entire Defense Appropriations Subcommittee met to oversee the CIA intelligence budget.[4]

THE INVESTIGATIONS

The key events in congressional oversight of intelligence were the investigations by both the House and Senate during 1975 and 1976. Before the Church and Pike Committees came into being, the reviews of intelligence activities and budgets had often been uncritical analyses conducted by a few whose opinions and sentiments coincided closely with the members of the executive branch with whom they met. Afterwards, intelligence programs and budget would come under the direct scrutiny of more than thirty members of Congress and twice as many staffers, and their points of view, particular interests, and capacity for investigative inquiry would open the intelligence agencies to a depth of outside study not encountered before.

The Senate Select Committee to Study Governmental Operations with Respect to Intelligence Activities—commonly referred to as the Church Committee—was established in January 1975. For fifteen months the committee probed the activities of the intelligence community, seeking information on "allegations of abuses and improper activities" and attempting to respond to "great concern that the Congress take action to bring the intelligence agencies under the constitutional framework."[5]

The precipitating events leading to the Church Committee's formation were not principally those involving the budget. The investigation was prompted by a report in the New York Times that the CIA was engaging in domestic intelligence operations and other activities.[6] The committee's major interest seemed to be directed to whether and how intelligence was being used against U.S. citizens. Its staff and members studied whether the executive branch was violating federal or state laws through "surreptitious entries, surveillance, wiretaps, or eavesdropping, illegal opening of the United States mail, or the monitoring of the United States mail."[7] It examined CIA and FBI domestic intelligence and counterintelligence operations, and studied the so-called Huston Plan to use U.S. intelligence capabilities against individuals or organizations in the United States.[8] Included in these subject areas were questions such as whether the National Security Agency was intercepting domestic communications, whether drug testing had occurred "on unwitting Americans," and whether civil rights leaders had been blackmailed.[9]

The committee also focused on the more traditional and

well-known areas of intelligence activity. It gave particular attention to human intelligence and to covert action (clandestine activities to influence foreign states). The committee's members also probed such subjects as the quality of analysis, the power of the director of Central Intelligence (DCI), and the organization and management of the agencies.[10]

The concerns of the Church Committee were mirrored in a similar investigative effort by the House of Representatives. The House Select Committee—named the Pike Committee after its chairman--probed the operations of the intelligence agencies in the same areas as did the Church Committee. It did appear to give more attention to the quality of intelligence support to decisionmakers, a less exciting topic for investigation but the subject of frequent internal government study since the early 1960s. The Pike Committee studied "intelligence failures" such as the absence of adequate warning of the Tet Offensive, the Soviet invasion of Czechoslovakia, the 1973 Middle East War, and the India Nuclear Test program. The results of the Pike Committee were formally released, but not until after disclosure of the committee's work by the Village Voice.[11]

Both the investigative committees studied the intelligence budgets and the resource-allocation process in the executive branch. Their key concerns were directed to three areas: whether to publish the costs of intelligence, whether funds were appropriately accounted for, and whether resources were being efficiently used.

The committees' concern over publishing the budget and accounting for expenditures lay in strong congressional feelings regarding the duty of the Congress to uphold the Constitution. Article I, Section 9 states that "no money shall be drawn from the Treasury but in consequence of appropriations made by law; and a regular statement and account of the receipts and expenditures of all public money shall be published from time to time."[12] In applying that article to the intelligence agencies, many members (though not all) were concerned that Congress was not fulfilling its responsibilities when very few members were aware of the costs of intelligence, and when intelligence funding (particularly for the CIA) was hidden in other budgets. This practice of hiding intelligence budgets could hamper not only the oversight of intelligence, but also the oversight of other government activities.[13] For example, if 25 percent of the budget of the Agency for International Development (AID) were actually earmarked for the CIA, the committees overseeing AID would have a misleading impression of AID's size. More seriously, they would have an inaccurate perception of the nature of U.S. foreign policy commitments. Although both committees eventually concluded that some figures for the intelligence budget should be made public, the Congress as a whole could not reach agreement on this recommendation. The issue was passed to the new intelligence committees for resolution.

The committees were also concerned that the practice of hiding funding and the lack of visible accountability would lead to abuses or inefficiencies in the use of public moneys. The Pike Committee questioned the use of funds by CIA's privately controlled companies for the purchase of items such as televisions, home furnishings, and watches. It also noted that more than 80 percent of CIA's research contracts were of the sole-source type; competition seemed to be unusually limited. Probing the quality of accounting controls, it was greatly concerned that the GAO appeared to have less access to reviews of CIA's accounting than did (in one identified instance) a big eight accounting firm.[14]

The Church and Pike Committees both criticized the lack of a better coordinated and managed intelligence budget. The Church Committee noted that the DCI controlled less than "10 percent of the combined national and tactical intelligence efforts." In reviewing the national intelligence programs, it pointed out that the NSA had the largest single program, followed closely by the U.S. Air Force, which managed "certain reconnaissance programs." The General Defense Intelligence Program (GDIP), while drawing only a "fraction of the DIRNSA's budget," was in fact managed by the assistant secretary of defense for intelligence. In the Executive Committee (Ex Com), which was to coordinate reconnaissance programs under the DCI's chairmanship, the real authority for four-fifths of the total resources was in the hands of the secretary of defense. The committee reported that six major studies in the previous ten years had agreed that intelligence had "performed neither as effectively nor as efficiently as possible, due largely to its fragmented organization." Therefore, in the final report, the Church Committee recommended that the DCI be given more power to prepare a national intelligence budget.[15]

FORMATION OF THE COMMITTEES

As a result of the Church Committee investigation, the Senate established in early 1976 the Senate Select Committee on Intelligence (SSCI). The implementing Senate Resolution (SRES) 400, dated May 19, 1976, provided for a body of fifteen senators, organized with two distinct characteristics. First, as reflected in SRES 400, the members were drawn almost equally from the two parties in an attempt to demonstrate a nonpolitical orientation in overseeing intelligence. Second, seven senators came from the Senate at large, and two each were also members of the Armed Services, Foreign Relations, Judiciary, and Appropriations Committees. This dual appointment provided for coordination between the new committee and other committees having jurisdiction over organizations in intelligence (e.g., the Senate Foreign Relations Committee oversees the activities of the State Department's Bureau of Intelligence and Research). It has also helped to alleviate concerns that the presence of the Select Committee might reduce the ability of other committees to obtain the intelligence necessary to appraise executive-branch activities in foreign policy, defense programs, law enforcement, and so on. Substance and jurisdiction were integral to the decision for cross membership.[16]

The new committee was charged with a number of responsibilities, one of the most important being budget oversight. Under SRES 400, the Senate agreed that after September 30, 1976 (i.e., beginning with the FY 1977 government budget), "no funds would be appropriated for agencies such as CIA, NSA, DIA, INR, the FBI's Intelligence Division, and other DoD intelligence activities unless such funds were authorized by a bill or joint resolution passed by the Senate." For the first time, therefore, at least one house of Congress would group together a number of intelligence activities and authorize their funding. The

154

different points in an organization's history.[45] In the final analysis, careful research on the influence of organizational variables must replace conventional wisdom if a complete understanding of intelligence estimating and intelligence failure is to be achieved.

NOTES

1.   Richard J. Heuer, Jr., ed., Quantitative Approaches to Political Intelligence: The CIA Experience (Boulder, Colo.: Westview Press, 1978), pp. 294-327; Robert Jervis, Perception and Misperception in International Politics (Princeton: Princeton University Press, 1976); Michael Handel, The Diplomacy of Surprise (Cambridge, Mass.: Harvard University Press, 1981); R. Axelrod, "The Rational Timing of Surprise," World Politics 31 (January): 228-247; Richard Betts, "Analysis, War, and Decision," World Politics 31 (October 1978): 61-89.
2.   Harold Wilensky, Organizational Intelligence (New York: Basic Books, 1967), pp. 41-62.
3.   P. Szanton and G. Allison, "Intelligence: Seizing the Opportunity," Foreign Policy 22 (Spring, 1976): 206-214.
4.   "Key Issues in International Relations Forecasting," in N. Choucri and T. Robinson, eds., Forecasting in International Relations (San Francisco: Freeman, 1978), p. 4.
5.   Ibid., pp. 7-9.
6.   Morton Halperin, "Covert Operations: Effects of Secrecy on Decision Making," in R. Borosage and J. Marks, eds., The CIA File (New York: Grossman, 1974), pp. 147-177.
7.   See W. Ascher, Forecasting (Baltimore: Johns Hopkins University Press, 1978).
8.   J. Stein, "Intelligence and Stupidity Reconsidered," Journal of Strategic Studies 3 (September 1980): 147-177.
9.   See W. Lee, Understanding the Soviet Military Threat: How CIA Estimates Went Astray (New York: National Strategy Information Center, 1977).
10.   Richard Pipes, "American Perceptions and Misperceptions of Soviet Military Intentions and Capabilities," in R. Pfaltzgraff, U. Ra'anan, and U. Milbert, eds., Intelligence Policy and National Security (Hamden, Conn.: Anchon, 1981), pp. 76-77.
11.   D. Warwick, A Theory of Public Bureaucracy (Cambridge, Mass.: Harvard University Press, 1975), p. 61.
12.   B. Abrahamsson, Bureaucracy or Participation (Beverly Hills, Calif.: Sage, 1977), pp. 26-30.
13.   Harry Ransom, The Intelligence Establishment (Cambridge, Mass.: Harvard University Press, 1970), p. 40.
14.   Sam Adams, "Vietnam Cover-up: Playing War with Numbers," Harpers 251 (May 1975): 46-73; see W. Eveland, Ropes of Sand (New York: Norton, 1980).
15.   Thomas Powers, The Man Who Kept the Secrets: Richard Helms and the CIA (New York: Alfred A. Knopf, 1979), p. 327.
16.   J. March and H. Simon, Organizations (New York: Wiley, 1958), p. 167.
17.   Thomas Hughes, The Fate of Facts in a World of Men (New York: Foreign Policy Association, Headline Series No. 233, 1976), p. 247.

Select Committee was given exclusive control over the authorization of the budgets for the CIA and for the Intelligence Community Staff (IC Staff); it shared with other committees the jurisdiction over the budgets of such agencies as the NSA, the military services, and the FBI. Seemingly excluded from the Select Committee were budgets for tactical intelligence activities. SRES 400 stated that "funds" included "intelligence activities of . . . subdivisions of the Department of Defense" but also that "intelligence activities . . . did not include tactical foreign military intelligence serving no national policy making function." These clarifications reflected substantial concerns about jurisdiction that had surfaced in hearings on the resolution, and presaged a similar controversy that would erupt in 1977-1978.[17]

For budget oversight, the Select Committee was required by SRES 400 to comply with the Congressional Budget Act of 1974. It was to provide estimates of overall intelligence expenditures to the newly formed Senate Budget Committee, which would then prepare resolutions on total government receipts and expenditures. It also had to produce an authorization bill for intelligence in sufficient time to allow other committees (e.g., Senate Armed Services, Senate Foreign Relations) to have thirty days to review and propose changes before passage by the full Senate. To conduct the analysis of the intelligence budgets, the Senate Budget Committee formed a budget subcommittee whose membership was balanced between the majority and minority parties.[18]

A year and a half after the passage of SRES 400, the House of Representatives passed House Resolution (HRES) 658, which established the House Permanent Select Committee on Intelligence (HPSCI). Drawing upon the first year's experience of the Senate Committee, the resolution (dated July 14, 1977) emulated much of the language and instructions of SRES 400. However, at least two initiatives—one symbolic in nature and the other real—marked differences between the new House and the slightly older Senate counterparts. The House Committee inserted the word "Permanent" in its title, apparently to give it more stature among the standing committees of the Congress (e.g., Armed Services Committee). Second, in giving the committee authority over the budget, the resolution prominently mentioned "intelligence related activities" and did not define the HPSCI's role as excluding tactical military intelligence. A stronger role over the military services was thus established.[19]

The House Select Committee was to consist of thirteen members (vice fifteen in the Senate). Of these, one member each (vice two in the Senate) was to be simultaneously a member of the Armed Services, International Relations, Judiciary, and Appropriations committees. Unlike the Senate, there was no provision for a bipartisan balance among the members of the Select Committee, and the mix of Republicans and Democrats was to reflect the overall distribution of membership in the House of Representatives. Similar to the Senate, however, HRES 658 established that "no funds shall be appropriated for any fiscal year beginning after September 30, 1978—unless such funds shall have been previously authorized by a bill or joint resolution passed by the House." Thus FY 1979 became the first year in which both committees would act, and the president would sign the first authorization bill for intelligence.[20]

MASTERING THE BUDGET PROCESS: 1976-1980

Establishing Budgetary Control

The first years of oversight by the SSCI and HPSCI were marked by substantial changes in the management of budgets in the executive branch as well as the Congress. In 1976, a presidential executive order gave the DCI full authority over the National Foreign Intelligence Program (NFIP), and subsequent years were marked by the efforts of the DCI, others in the executive branch, and the Congress to organize control of the budget under the DCI's leadership. The Carter administration introduced zero-based budgeting (ZBB), and Congress increased its demands for information on programs, which were provided in lengthy Congressional Justification Books (CJBs). The DCI's implementation of ZBB and his direction of the agencies in completing the CJBs became two influential tools in the cementing of his control over the NFIP.

The Congress also pressured the executive branch to expand and organize Intelligence Related Activities (IRA). The creation of IRA could be traced to the frustrations of the House Appropriations Committee (HAC) in the mid-1970s in attempting to get the Department of Defense (DoD) to provide data on intelligence systems operated by the military services but not reported in an intelligence budget. These systems included, for example, the SR-71 high-altitude reconnaissance aircraft, which had originally been funded in intelligence but was transferred out of that part of the DoD budget.[21] Also included were the navy's surveillance systems, which tracked submarines, and the warning systems used by the Defense Department to monitor bombers, missiles, and satellites. In the 1974-1976 period, the HAC had created a budget category called IRA into which these and similar systems were placed. The four years through 1980 were marked by the addition of still more systems, requisitioned initially by the Congress and later by both the Congress and the DoD. By 1980, the DoD had actively embraced IRA as a management tool to coordinate and control a wide range of service intelligence activities.[22]

Mastering the Mechanics

The oversight committees stepped into a complex set of budgetary activities in which the mastery of administrative mechanisms could be considered almost as important as resource or program analysis. There were, in fact, multiple budgets with which the oversight committees had to deal:

- The NFIP, which was assembled by the DCI and contained activities of several cabinet-level departments.
- Agency budgets, such as those for the DIA, which could have funds in the NFIP, IRA, and other DoD budgets.
- The budgets, of the department (e.g., DoD, Justice, Treasury, State) that integrated intelligence with many other programs.

Projects and their funding levels in these budgets could be

presented in several forms, many of which overlapped in sometimes obscure ways:

Decision Units. The Carter administration's use of ZBB required that intelligence activities be divided into specific units. For example, all the manpower, administrative, and other operating costs of a 200-man analysis group could be in one unit; a major computer for the group could be in another unit. These units were then ranked in priority order. When the president decided on the total budget, the units were funded in priority order until the budget was committed. The remaining units (and, therefore, their activities) were dropped. Although the DCI grouped NFIP activities into small units focused on intelligence, the DoD included its IRA projects in very large units that also contained nonintelligence activities.[23]

Program Elements (PEs). DoD intelligence activities constituted the largest portion of the NFIP and made up all of IRA. Each of these activities was also accounted for in the ten major programs of the DoD budgeting system. At least four programs contained NFIP or IRA projects--Program 1 (Strategic Forces), Program 2 (General Purpose Forces), Program 3 (Communications and Intelligence), and Program 6 (Research and Development). Within each program an intelligence activity has a numeric identifier called a "program element" (PE). DoD often discussed its projects as PEs.

Justification Book Categories. The DCI and secretary of defense annually submitted several thousand-page descriptions of intelligence programs in the NFIP and IRA. In the former, the descriptions were often presented in the same decision units assembled by the DCI under ZBB. In IRA, however, the grouping of programs could follow ZBB, program elements, or some other format.

Appropriation Accounts. Although the intelligence committees could oversee projects or programs as decision units, program elements, justification book categories, etc., they had to translate these into appropriations in order to formulate the authorization bill. Although Congress does authorize programs (e.g., the SR-71), it actually appropriates funds to be spent for accounts such as procurement, research and development, military construction, military pay, and operations and maintenance. The translation from programs to appropriation accounts was essential to completing the authorization process.

For the committees, (particularly their staffs), analysis of the programs involved an understanding of the complex relationships among these different budgets and presentation forms. For example, a DoD project could be funded in part by the DCI in the NFIP and presented as a decision unit. Part of it could also be funded by the secretary of defense in IRA and presented in some descriptive form in the IRA CJBs. To gather information, the Congress might have to meet with DCI personnel (who talked about the decision unit), OSD personnel (who discussed IRA categories), military service personnel (who might discuss PEs), and agency personnel (who talked about the program from an agency perspective). The latter three could also further discuss the program by appropriation categories (e.g., Procurement, Research and Development, and Military Construction).

Within Congress the two committees also had to deal with three separate budget mechanisms—the budget resolution, authorization, and appropriation. Under the Congressional Budget and Control Act of 1974, the Congress established a budget committee in each house to develop overall targets for revenues and expenditures in the coming years. By March of each year, the intelligence committees had to provide to the budget committees an estimate of the overall intelligence budget for the next fiscal year (beginning October 1). The budget committees incorporated these into totals for the executive branch and submitted resolutions to their respective houses that established overall targets for revenues and expenditures in the government. When both houses agreed on the same targets, any programs that exceeded those targets could be challenged on the floor of the Senate or House. For the intelligence committees, meeting the March deadline required a rapid assessment of a multibillion-dollar budget in less than a month and a half as well as the submission of estimates that maintained the secrecy of overall funding levels while still meeting budget committee needs for information.

Authorization was the key role of the intelligence committees. Begun after World War II, it was the vehicle by which committees with a functional focus (e.g., Armed Services, Foreign Relations) limited the power of the appropriations committees to direct the government in their areas of special expertise and interest. Authorization bills often set ceilings on the amounts that could be expended for specific projects or programs, and provided specific · guidance. The appropriations committees, in turn, could allocate less for projects, but not more, and in general were expected not to deal with such designated projects too freely without consulting the functional committee. By 1970, for example, the armed services committees were authorizing—that is, setting ceilings on overall expenditures and projects—for procurement, research and development, military construction, and overall manpower strength (but not funding for personnel). Absent were the categories of other procurement and operations and maintenance, over which the appropriations committees had major influence.

The intelligence committees had to define what portions of the intelligence budgets they wanted to authorize (e.g., research, procurement, all funds, etc.) and then coordinate with other committees to accomplish this. They chose to authorize all appropriations, although this action led to some difficulties in relations with the armed services committees, which did not authorize appropriations for several types of funds but had concurrent authority over DoD intelligence. The authorization process thus required the intelligence committees to establish their presence among a set of sister committees while mastering the process and substance of the budget and its projects.

Whereas authorization set the ceiling on funds and specific projects, appropriations determined the exact funds to be made available. These funds were established by the House and Senate appropriations committees, based on their review of intelligence and on the instructions provided in the authorization bills of the intelligence committees. The appropriations committees began hearings on the intelligence budget several months after the intelligence committees began theirs. The appropriations bills were to appear in the late summer or early fall before the beginning of the new fiscal year, and delays would lead to the passage of a continuing resolution that allowed the government to function at a funding level equivalent to that of the previous year, but without any new initiatives. To support the appropriations process, the intelligence committees had to finish their hearings, reports, and authorization bills before the early summer, an action seldom accomplished. Moreover, these committees occasionally found themselves in consultation or conflict with the appropriations committees, which had expertise in intelligence programs, occasionally a different view on the long-term direction of intelligence, and significant power over the amount of funds to be provided.

Finally, at any one time there were three separate budgets for the intelligence committees to influence—the one being reviewed by the Congress for the next fiscal year, the one being executed for the current fiscal year, and the one being prepared by the executive branch for the subsequent years. For example, in March 1978 the intelligence committees were holding hearings on the budgets for the fiscal year beginning in October 1978 (FY 1979). The members were also reviewing specific expenditures for the year in progress (FY 1978)—for example, reprogramming of funds from one project to another. And finally, the executive branch was preparing the budget for 1980 and seeking informally to understand congressional attitudes toward new initiatives.

The committees thus became part of a complex set of administrative mechanisms—in both the executive branch and the Congress—for reviewing the funds being spent for intelligence. A typical budget cycle would begin in late January with the president's submission of the NFIP and IRA budgets for the fiscal year to begin in nine months (October 1). Official OMB notice of funding levels would be followed by Congressional Justification Books explaining specific projects and overall programs. The committees would begin hearings in February or March and continue into May. By March 15, a letter would be sent to the budget committees that estimated the total funds the committees might authorize. Each committee reached its conclusions on the budget in the early summer and submitted authorization bills to their respective houses. Other committees (e.g., the Armed Services) could request a thirty-day referral of the bills, and the two committees would attempt to resolve differences informally or on the floor of the House or Senate. An authorization bill would finally be passed by each house in midsummer, and the intelligence committees would then go into conference to resolve the differences between the two houses. The compromise bill would be approved by both houses, signed by the president, and become the authorizing legislation to guide the appropriations process.

Sophistication in using these mechanisms was important to the exercise of effective oversight. To understand the overall activities of the intelligence community, the committees had to recognize which projects were being funded. To understand how efficiently those resources were being used, the committees had to analyze the projects. Both actions required a more than passing acquaintance with budgetary systems. Moreover, in order for the committees to enforce their own rulings, they had to understand not only the formal procedures of which they were a part (e.g., authorization) but also the subtle ways in which their views could be enforced or deflected. A budget for the

coming year is an estimate of expected expenditures. Actual use of
the moneys could vary widely from the original plan and still be within
the law. Specific and almost undetectable (at the congressional level)
manipulation of budgeted funds could easily be used to bypass broad
congressional mandates. Knowledge of the intricacies of government
budgets was consequently important to the detection of even a minor
percentage of such manipulations.

Resolving Jurisdictional Difficulties

A major challenge facing the two committees in the first four
years involved jurisdiction. The establishing resolutions had given the
HPSCI and SSCI significantly different oversight powers. For the
Senate Intelligence Committee, jurisdiction had been a major issue in
the development of its implementing charter, and had resulted in such
key provisions as "nothing in this resolution shall be construed as . . .
restricting the authority of any other committee to study and review
any intelligence activity" affecting a matter within its jurisdiction.[24]
The SSCI had been given exclusive authority over the DCI's budget,
but this in essence meant only the DCI's Intelligence Community Staff
(ICS) and the CIA. Oversight of the other components of the
NFIP—for example, the Consolidated Cryptologic Program (CCP), the
General Defense Intelligence Program (GDIP), the FBI, and the State
Department—had to be shared with other standing committees, such as
the Armed Services Committee, the Judiciary Committee, and the
Foreign Relations Committee. In IRA, tactical intelligence was
specifically excluded from the SSCI's purview. However, the term
"tactical intelligence" was never coupled directly to "IRA." The first
years of the SSCI would see the rapid emergence of the question of
jurisdiction over programs in IRA that could be considered tactical
intelligence.

For the HPSCI—which had the advantage of a year to watch the
implementation of SRES 400—attempts were made to avoid potential
jurisdictional issues. In House Resolution 658, the committee was
given authority similar to that in the Senate over the DCI and the
NFIP. Other committees were likewise given authority to study and
review "any intelligence or intelligence-related activity affecting a
matter within their jurisdiction."[25] (This section of HRES 658 is, with
the exception of three words, a verbatim copy of the language in
SRES 400.) However, HRES 658 neither defined tactical intelligence
nor excluded it from the authority of the new committee (as did SRES
400), and the term "Intelligence Related Activities" was featured
prominently throughout the resolution. The HPSCI was given authority
not only over the IRA in the Defense Department, but over any
intelligence-related activities in the FBI and State Department as well.
IRA, therefore, was a potential tool for the HPSCI to use to identify
additional activities as subject to oversight.

In the first few years, jurisdiction became a significant issue in
the SSCI. In the SSCI's report for fiscal year 1979 (published in
September 1978), a special section on authority over the intelligence
budget consumed approximately one-third of the committee's
unclassified report. The report stated that "under Senate Resolution
400, the national foreign intelligence program is the sole jurisdiction of

the Select Committee on Intelligence." It also noted, however, that "the Senate Armed Services Committee and the Select Committee have been unable to resolve the issue of jurisdiction over intelligence related activities." The SSCI believed it had a role in a number of IRA programs with national-level importance, including systems that provided warning of attack by ICBMs, SSBNs, space weapons, and bombers.[26]

The Senate Armed Services Committee (SASC) asked for sequential referral of the SSCI's bill and issued its response several months later. The SASC's unclassified report devoted approximately one-half of its five pages to the subject of jurisdiction. It noted that SRES 400 excluded tactical intelligence from the SSCI's purview and stated that the Armed Services Committee had "exclusive jurisdiction" over the IRA. It also stated that the two committees "have concurrent authorizing jurisdiction over intelligence activities of the Department of Defense which serve national policy making functions." The latter statement was a clear signal that the SASC perceived the SSCI's sole authority in the NFIP as extending only to the DCI's staff and the CIA.[27]

The jurisdictional differences in the Senate were probably felt in the House of Representatives. In its first intelligence authorization bill (also published in September 1978) the HPSCI stated that its implementing resolution (HRES 658) gave it "authority to authorize annual appropriations for intelligence and intelligence related activities," probably as a pointed reminder to other committees of its power.[28] The House Armed Services Committee (HASC), however, published its report on the HPSCI bill a month later. The HASC noted that it "exercised its oversight jurisdiction, as shared with the Permanent Select Committee on Intelligence, with regard to . . . Intelligence Related Activities."[29] The area of disagreement may thus have been clearly marked for resolution, for a year later the HPSCI's annual report would state that it had "shared jurisdiction along with the Committee on Armed Services over the authorization of so-called Intelligence Related Activities." This report emphasized that "since Defense Department [IRA] programs also fall within the authorizing authority of the Committee on Armed Services, the amounts authorized [are] agreed to by both [committees]. It is important that the Select Committee on Intelligence be able to monitor both (NFIP and IRA) . . . because projects often are moved from one to the other."[30]

The House's move toward shared power probably came about in part because differences in jurisdiction over IRA spilled over from the Senate. The differences between the HPSCI and SSCI would also have created unusual organizational strain between the two houses in resolving differences in their authorization bills. In the Congress each House passes its own version of an authorization bill, and the responsible committees meet in conference to resolve differences and prepare a bill that both houses can pass. A conference on the FY 1979 authorization bill could have been delicate and confusing. The House Intelligence Committee would have had to negotiate with both the Senate Intelligence and Armed Services Committees. The Senate Intelligence Committee would have been reluctant to have Armed Services Committee involved in this very first year and therefore set a precedent for future years. The Senate Armed Services Committee would have preferred to deal with its House counterpart, maintaining traditional organizational arrangements. The House Armed Services Committee, on the other hand, would have been somewhat displeased that its Senate counterpart had more authority over IRA. In this situation the two armed services committees may have developed a coordinated approach to limiting the power of the two new committees.

Jurisdictional questions probably remained unresolved through the FY 1980 budget process. The HPSCI annual report in November 1980 indicates that it continued to struggle with the question of authority over IRA. Although the debate centered on IRA, questions as to the authority of the committees over the NFIP also began to appear. The House Intelligence Committee apparently preserved more authority over the NFIP, for no mention was made of Armed Service's interest in this area. In the Senate, however, Armed Services carefully pointed to the DoD component of the NFIP as an area in which it had a role.

Although these differences undoubtedly created strains in relationships (given that jurisdiction is an extremely sensitive, core issue among committees), it did not necessarily prevent cooperation among the committees. In the FY 1980 budget, for example, Senate Armed Services cut authorization for $150 million and five SURTASS ships based on the recommendation of the SSCI.[31] In the FY 1981 budget, Senate Armed Services added 300 manpower spaces to Army, Navy, and Air Force intelligence based on SSCI decisions.[32] Despite their differences, the two committees probably found it useful to tap each other's knowledge of defense programs.

THE PERFORMANCE OF THE COMMITTEES: 1976-1980

In contrast to the cursory review of intelligence budgets in the early 1970s, the two new intelligence committees took an aggressive stand in their first few years. The Senate Intelligence Committee held fifty hours of hearings for the FY 1978 budget, thirty hours for FY 1979, and twenty hours for FY 1980. The House Intelligence Committee held fifty-five hours and thirty-three hours for FY 1979 and FY 1980, respectively. Both built substantial records and files from the several thousand pages of material drawn from congressional justification books, written responses to questions, transcripts from hearings, and other collected reports and studies.

In FY 1978, the Senate Intelligence Committee produced an authorization bill for intelligence activities and a classified and unclassified report. The SSCI had not resolved whether to publicly disclose the intelligence budget, and consequently the bill itself contained amounts for only a few select activities (e.g., the DCI's Intelligence Community Staff). The specific funding levels for programs were provided in a classified report, and questions arose as to whether the executive branch would comply with budget limits not (technically) in the bill itself. The SSCI adopted the practice of identifying the classified report in the bill as the document that reflected the final actions of the Congress; in the public report, the committee noted that this "classified report will have the force of a Senate authorization bill." Both the SSCI and HPSCI would later determine not to publish the budget for intelligence, and a classified report became the standard practice in both houses.[33]

In its unclassified report, the Senate Committee concluded that the intelligence community was well managed, but that improvements were needed in automated data processing (ADP) and the quality of analysis. It also apparently decreased the budget over what the executive branch had requested, but even so, the committee's recommendations reversed the trend of allowing real funding for intelligence to decline by not requesting adequate increases to keep pace with inflation. Thus the Senate Committee provided for real growth and new initiatives that would appear in intelligence in the 1980s. The absence of a companion House committee resulted in no authorization bill being passed by Congress, and the first full exercise of budget oversight would occur in the following year.[34]

In FY 1979, according to the House Intelligence Committee, the executive branch substantially increased the budget for intelligence. This increase was centered in new equipment for combat units, upgrades of existing systems, and the starting of new systems. In this first year of the committee's existence, the HPSCI held 80 hours of hearings (25 hours of background, 55 hours on budgets) and posed more than 1,100 questions to the executive branch for written response. The House reduced the budget by deferring or decreasing the amounts for some projects while adding funds to others. However, the change may have been quite modest because the HPSCI stated its support for the level of effort proposed by the president. It also criticized some undefined management shortcomings.[35]

On the Senate side the SSCI concluded, as in FY 1978, that the agencies were in general well managed. Improvements were needed in the coordination of ADP resources and the analysis of projects as to their cost, benefits, and alternatives. Significantly, the SSCI appears to have taken an aggressive posture for expanding intelligence activities. It provided for a "number of major and highly significant new initiatives to meet the needs of national policymakers. These initiatives will have significant impact on the amount of resources devoted to intelligence over the next five years, but are considered . . . absolutely essential . . . to respond adequately to the needs of national policymakers in the 1980s."[36]

In FY 1980, according to the House Intelligence Committee, the executive branch again requested a substantial increase in the budget.[37] Both intelligence committees held a number of hearings, although the amount of time spent was less than that in FY 1979. Both also expressed concerns about management in the intelligence community. For example, in its annual report to the House, the HPSCI called attention to the lack of "coherent planning for new and improved collection and processing systems" and noted that "financial managers . . . are replacing both the policy maker and the professional intelligence program manager in deciding what kind and how much intelligence the U.S. Government requires."[38] The Senate stated its concerns that "in some key decisions [in allocating resources] a narrow rather than a broad view of intelligence needs has governed."[39]

The House decreased the budget from the president's requested levels although its annual report for the year states that several OMB cuts in the NFIP had to be overridden. Moreover, the House Committee reduced some programs and added funds to others (as in FY 1979). The Senate Committee's actions are unclear, although its review of the budget differed from the previous year in that more types of intelligence activities were analyzed. The Senate Committee continued to oversee ADP and to call attention to the need for planning and adequate justification of programs. It also examined airborne collection systems, analyst manpower, the tactical use of national systems, and U.S. capabilities to monitor SALT.

In FY 1981—the third year in which both committees prepared an authorization bill—the administration again "requested a substantial increase . . . over the amount Congress appropriated for" the previous year. The HPSCI held more than fifty hours of hearings and reduced the budget. It expressed concern over the management of intelligence and the "conduct of certain of the nation's intelligence activities." Improvements to these were discussed in the classified report.[40]

How the SSCI treated the president's request is unclear, but the committee's budget report suggests it was highly supportive of the requested increase. The report comments on the importance of both the Third World and the communist world to U.S. national security in the 1980s and the consequent need for "a robustness in collection and analytic capabilities." It describes the decade of the 1970s as having been characterized by a decline in dollars for intelligence and a "substantial retrenchment in manpower." The report states that "most of the major collection systems in being today are founded on late 1960s technology. . . . In large measure, the intelligence system has been sustaining itself from past capital investments. The Committee is recommending major investments over the next five years to ensure the availability of a new generation of systems." The report also noted that shortcomings continue to exist in the quality of analysis, management of ADP, and long-range planning.[41]

The authorization bills for FY 1981 also began including special provisions to benefit the intelligence agencies. Both committees, for example, authorized the Defense Intelligence Agency to award academic degrees through its Defense Intelligence School. CIA and NSA employees were given the same overseas privileges as State Department employees for housing benefits and dependent schools, and travel expenses. The General Services Administration (GSA) was authorized to post guards at non-GSA buildings. These actions mirrored the concerns of the Church and Pike committees some five years before the intelligence agencies were able to operate more efficiently with appropriate legislation. They also reflected the closer ties developing between the agencies and their principal sponsors in the Congress. After attempts to pass charters for the agencies had failed, the authorization bills became a vehicle to accomplish what charter legislation had not.

AN APPRAISAL

The period from 1970 to 1980 marked a major change in Congress's involvement in intelligence—particularly for its role in overseeing resource allocation. In the beginning of the decade, the analysis of budgets was cursory, fragmented, restricted, and seldom adversarial. The middle of the decade saw a traumatic investigative period, and the critical comments and recommendations of the investigative bodies hinted that the new oversight committees would be very attentive to the budget because of the power that comes from the control of moneys and because of the savings and efficiencies that could result. Two committees emerged that followed through on at least the first of these expectations. Despite jurisdictional issues, power did flow to the committees. However, regarding the second expectation, the HPSCI and SSCI appear to have been at least as aggressive as the executive branch in providing funds to intelligence. It is unclear from the public records as to whether savings or efficiencies resulted.

Growth in the Budget

The record of the investigations suggested that the first years of the House and Senate intelligence committees would be marked by reduced budgets and forced reallocation of resources. However, the public records of the HPSCI and SSCI indicate that they were highly supportive of a growth in intelligence programs that started in the Carter administration and reversed the trend of previous years. The HPSCI appears to have supported the overall growth, but it also cut the budget from the president's request in the three years from FY 1979 to FY 1981. The SSCI, too, appears to have supported the growth, and it may actually have added funds. The administration and the Congress seem to have shared common perspectives to the effect that the importance of intelligence to U.S. foreign policy in an uncertain world required that more funds be provided.

The committees also reallocated resources within intelligence. It is unclear as to which programs they shifted funds, but the committees expressed great interest in new systems, thus suggesting support for collection. They added manpower to the agencies and took initiatives to provide national intelligence to tactical commanders. They were also concerned about ADP and counterintelligence. Hence the spectrum of the committees' interests embraced most of the major activities of intelligence. Significantly, the committees do not appear to have altered the balance between investments in collection and those in analysis, although the investigating committees felt that collection had historically been overemphasized at the expense of analysis.

The records of the oversight committees in their first years seem to have been very conservative, supporting both the executive branch's requests and the historical allocation of resources among such intelligence activities as collection and analysis. Several factors may explain this. First, it is the nature of investigating committees to find faults, not strengths, and intelligence in the mid-1970s had many weaknesses that made good material for published reports. Moreover, the investigative committees were probably not adequately staffed to thoroughly analyze the multibillion-dollar complexity of projects and organizations that make up intelligence. Their reports, therefore, were oriented toward the critical and the general, and it should not be surprising that a more long-term, more broadly focused permanent committee could reach different conclusions.

Other factors that may explain the behavior of the new committees rest in the institutional milieu of the Congress. Congress entered into intelligence oversight with some degree of reluctance. Members on both sides questioned the ability of the legislative body to protect secrets, and, thus, to deal with a government activity so dependent on discretion. Some members also saw the new committees as a threat to their control and influence over the executive branch. In the first years of the committees, some conservatism in approach by their membership was probably necessary to placate these concerns. Dramatic changes in the allocation of intelligence resources could result in the formation of strong alliances among executive branch principals, the more powerful standing committees, and individual members of Congress.

A subtle partnership may have also emerged between the new committees sorting out their roles and new power centers in the executive branch establishing their positions. Concurrent with the committees' first years, the DCI was finally given major authority over the NFIP, and the DoD was consolidating its position over tactical intelligence. Close relationships with the intelligence committees constituted a means by which the DCI could demonstrate his newfound powers. For DoD, the preference for centralized management probably led to its uneasy cooperation with the new committees to help OSD-level managers oversee tactical intelligence. Neither of these informal partnerships—that is, between the executive and the DCI or the DoD—could have been adequately maintained if the committees had introduced dramatic changes into the budget.

A factor that may have weighed heavily on the behavior of the committees was the limited supply of outside information on intelligence. Congress relies heavily on constituencies, interest groups, and individuals for information. In contrast to other government activities (e.g., defense, social security), outside sources on intelligence are few, and they are usually centered on individuals (e.g., retired officials, ex-agency workers) rather than on groups. Moreover, the sources are even fewer on budget issues. Ex-officials can provide a broad perspective on the overall budget, but very few can speak with authority about specific funding levels, as they are unable to keep up to date after leaving the executive branch. Accordingly, the committees, in seeking information on the intelligence budgets in these first years, had to rely greatly upon the very agencies they were to oversee.

Finally, the growth in funding probably resulted from mutual concern in Congress and the executive branch over the real state of intelligence. Many members of Congress believed that the international posture of the United States was weak in one or more areas—military power, international trade, diplomatic relations, and so on. Adequate, and indeed strengthened, intelligence was an essential element to improving that situation, regardless of political preferences. The analyses published by the committees on such matters as U.S. capabilities to monitor SALT II did not conclude that intelligence should be less vigorous, build fewer systems, or hire fewer people. They called for more effort, not less.

Co-option of the Committees

Judging from the record, the executive branch seems to have adapted quickly to the presence of the new committees and may even have co-opted them to some extent. House and Senate changes and additions to the budget did not come out of nowhere, and considering the limited sources of information outside the agencies themselves, it would appear that the intelligence community learned quickly to bypass the executive branch to obtain funds for special projects.

Capture, of course, is not necessarily a bad thing. If the problems of intelligence were relatively clear, a commonality of goals between the agencies and the committees should not be surprising. Moreover, Congress may be more capable than the executive branch in dealing with deep-seated problems. For example, the FY 1981 Senate report noted a ten-year decline in manpower and an absence of major new systems initiatives since the late 1960s. Considering the increased criticality of intelligence in foreign affairs in the 1970s, the absence of significant action since the 1960s suggests rather profound impediments to constructive decisionmaking in the executive branch. Congress can be a very useful force for change under those circumstances.

Moreover, co-option does not mean that Congress submissively followed the instructions of the executive branch. The committees cut programs in their first four years and the agencies must have objected. Lengthy hearings and thousands of written questions probably strained relationships between the two branches, and repeated criticisms concerning ADP management, long-range planning, and the quality of analysis indicate that the committees maintained substantial independence. It would appear that, in essence, the issues at stake were what projects to fund and how fast to fund them, not whether to fund them.

The Administrative Burden

Deep congressional involvement in intelligence undoubtedly increased the work of the executive branch. But the exact nature of the impact is difficult to discern in the midst of the executive branch's own actions (e.g., centralizing the NFIP under the DCI and instituting ZBB). Yet the agencies of the community were suddenly thrust into producing thousands of pages of program descriptions and answers to questions, providing briefings to staffers and members of Congress, working with committees to protect secrets in congressional reports, and negotiating with and playing off committees for budget increases and decreases. Clearly, more work was created.

An issue for speculation concerns whether both the executive branch and the Congress created administrative mechanisms in these years that so burdened the development of a budget that the analysis of programs was weakened. Over a period of years, both committees criticized the absence of fundamental management steps such as long-range planning and systems analysis (e.g., in ADP). The Senate questioned the absence of a broad policy perspective, and the House criticized the dominance of the budget analyst in policy-level decisionmaking. Yet, neither the Congress nor the executive branch seems to have taken steps to streamline or change the complex administrative processes in which all participants had to play.

How to conduct such streamlining is a public-policy question that transcends the intelligence agencies and the committees. Changes in reports and systems do occur as a result of the recognition by administrations or senior officials that, say, a particular report or budget system has outlived its usefulness. But major changes in these systems are difficult to bring about because they affect the way in which the government shares power within its ranks. For example, modifications to the appropriations and authorization processes affected the balance of power among congressional committees, and the presence of the ZBB gave the DCI a lever to exert his new authority within the DoD. Hence those actions that might constitute good management are often crippled by the fact that government is not so much a form of management but an administration within a bureaucratic political framework.

NOTES

1. U.S., Congress, Congressional Research Service, To Create a Senate Select Committee on Intelligence: A Legislative History of Senate Resolution 400 (Washington, D.C.: Government Printing Office, August 1976), pp. 4-5 [hereafter referred to as History of SRES 400].

2. U.S., Senate, 94th Congress, Select Committee to Study Governmental Operations with Respect to Intelligence Activities, Foreign and Military Intelligence, Book I (Washington, D.C.: Government Printing Office, April 1976), p. 368 [hereafter referred to as Foreign and Military Intelligence].

3. Robin Berman Schwartzman, "Fiscal Oversight of the Central Intelligence Agency: Can Accountability and Confidentiality Coexist?" International Law and Politics 7, (1974): 493, 497-509 [hereafter referred to as International Law and Politics].

4. Foreign and Military Intelligence, p. 368.

5. Ibid., p. 3.

6. History of SRES 400, p. 6.

7. Foreign and Military Intelligence, p. 3.

8. Ibid., p. 2.

9. Ibid., pp. 4, 12.

10. Ibid., pp. 4, 425.

11. Aaron Latham, "The CIA Report the President Doesn't Want You to Read," Village Voice (February 16, 1976), pp. 70-92 [hereafter referred to as the CIA Report].

12. Foreign and Military Intelligence, p. 469.

13. Schwartzman, International Law and Politics, p. 500.

14. CIA Report, pp. 75-76.

15. Foreign and Military Intelligence, pp. 333-341, 465.

16. U.S., Congress, Senate, Senate Resolution 400 (May 1976), pp. 2-4 [hereafter referred to as SRES 400].

17. Ibid., pp. 5-6, 17, 18, 21.

18. U.S., Congress, Senate, Select Committee on Intelligence, Legislative Calendar (December 31, 1976), pp. 3, 9.

19. U.S., Congress, House of Representatives, HRES 658 (July 14, 1977), pp. 1, 3, 13, 14 [hereafter referred to as HRES 658].

20. Ibid., pp. 2, 12-13.

21. Foreign and Military Intelligence, p. 329.

22. U.S., Congress, Senate, Select Committee on Intelligence, Report to Accompany S2939, Report No. 95-744 (April 19, 1978), p. 8 [hereafter referred to as Report for S2939].

23. U.S., Congress, Senate, Report to Accompany S975, Report No. 96-71 (April 18, 1979), p. 3.

24. SRES 400, p. 7.

25. HRES 658, p. 5.

26. Report for S2939, pp. 6, 8.

27. U.S., Congress, Senate, Committee on Armed Services, Report to Accompany S2939, Report No. 95-1028 (July 20, 1978), p. 4.

28. U.S., Congress, House of Representatives, Permanent Select Committee on Intelligence, Report to Accompany H.R. 12240, Report No. 95-1075, part 1 (April 20, 1978), p. 3.

29. U.S., Congress, House of Representatives, Committee on Armed Services, Report to Accompany H.R. 12240, Report No. 95-1075, part 2 (May 9, 1978), p. 2.

30. U.S., Congress, House of Representatives, Permanent Select Committee on Intelligence, Annual Report, Report No. 96-1475, (November 21, 1980), pp. 2, 11.

31. U.S., Congress, Senate, Authorizing Appropriations for Fiscal Year 1980 for Military Procurement, Research and Development, Active Duty, Selected Reserve, and Civilian Personnel Strengths, Civil Defense, and for Other Purposes, Report No. 96-197 (May 31, 1979), p. 54.

32. U.S., Congress, Senate, Authorizing Appropriations for Fiscal Year 1981 for Military Procurement, Research and Development, Active Duty, Selected Reserve, and Civilian Personnel Strengths, Civil Defense, and for Other Purposes, Report No. 96-826 (June 20, 1980), pp. 9, 12.

33. U.S., Congress, Senate, Report to Accompany S1539, Report No. 95-214 (May 16, 1977), p. 2.

34. Ibid., p. 3.

35. U.S., Congress, House of Representatives, Report to Accompany H.R. 12240, Report No. 95-1075, part 1 (April 20, 1978), pp. 3-4.

36. U.S., Congress, Senate, Report to Accompany S2939, Report No. 95-744 (April 19, 1978), pp. 3-4.

37. U.S., Congress, House of Representatives, Report to Accompany H.R. 3821, Report No. 96-127, part 1 (May 8, 1979), p. 3.

38. U.S., Congress, House of Representatives, Report by the Permanent Select Committee on Intelligence, Report No. 96-1475 (November 21, 1980), p. 12.

39. U.S., Congress, Senate, Report to Accompany S975, Report No. 96-71 (April 18, 1979), p. 5.

40. U.S., Congress, House of Representatives, Report to Accompany H.R. 7152, Report No. 96-926, part 1 (May 7, 1980), pp. 3-4.

41. U.S., Congress, Senate, Report to Accompany S2597, Report No. 96-659 (April 23, 1980), pp. 3-4.

GROUP DYNAMICS, INDIVIDUALS, AND DECISIONMAKING

In this section, we look at the influence of small groups and individuals in the making and execution of national security decisions, and particularly at how those decisions are affected by intelligence. The focus of the section is an inward-looking one, directed to the world perspective of intelligence practitioners and decisionmakers and to their ability to influence events outside their circle of government. On the one side are the intelligence collectors and producers who form finished intelligence not only from the raw data available but also from the psychological filters in their minds through which the data must pass. On the other side of the intelligence product is the decisionmaker, whose frame of mind likewise conditions how he or she reacts to the intelligence presented. Graham Allison's Essence of Decision broke new theoretical ground in the area of decisionmaking by going inside the workings of government to create bureaucratic politics and organizational process models.[1] It was perhaps inevitable that this analysis be taken to its logical conclusion by delving even deeper into the motivations of small groups within the bureaucratic organization and, finally, to the individuals themselves.

The preceding section focused on the intelligence community as a subunit of the governmental structure, and necessarily on the members of that community individually as well as collectively. These bureaucracies were in the realm of Allison's organizational process model: the outputs of a given organization are seen at least partly as a function of both the structure of the organization and its standard operating procedures. From the point of view of Allison's bureaucratic politics model, what matters are the decisions that must be made by government leaders who represent different bureaucracies and are thereby constrained by their organizational roles. But these leaders are affected by other psychological influences as well. As members of decisionmaking groups—such as the National Security Council—they are particularly influenced by the psychology of small groups, including the impact of "groupthink."[2] At the same time, we should remember that small groups exist throughout large bureaucracies; indeed, large organizations are made up of small work groups, with which most people tend to identify as much or more than they do with the parent organization itself. Thus, given the pervasiveness of small groups, we can deal with their effects on decisionmaking in a general way.

Likewise, the specific leaders themselves can be treated either as individuals or as leadership types. This distinction has long been the forte of history. Much history, particularly that written in the middle ages and earlier, deals with historical events as if they were the doings of great leaders alone. Thus we speak of Caesar crossing the Rubicon or Hannibal crossing the Alps. Then, as we analyze these individuals and their influence upon history, we look for specific attributes that made them great, and so we arrive at leadership types. Less frequent, however, is the perception of leaders as human beings subject to the same psychological strengths and limitations as are all humans. In this light, their potential influence on events seems smaller.[3] In addition, the same psychological perspective can be used in general to analyze the possible actions of any and all persons involved in the production and use of intelligence.

When we speak in this section of the impact of personality, we mean only the general psychological tendencies; the study of individuals mentioned earlier is certainly a subject of intelligence in itself. The reader may note that we have also discussed the ethical implications for the individual of working in the intelligence profession in the section on intelligence in the open society.

Loch Johnson's chapter examines the intelligence production cycle from the theoretical perspective of decision costs, including the recognition that each decision made and each action taken is done at some cost, with a trade-off between competing solutions and answers. Thus the intelligence cycle, which at first glance appears to be a theoretically simple and smoothly flowing process, is in reality far more complicated; moreover, it produces pressures on individual producers and consumers alike that result in the loss and distortion of vital information. In order to understand this process, we will use the theories of organizational process, management, and administration--theories more often associated with the management and public policy disciplines than with intelligence, perhaps, but most useful in this context nevertheless.

Having looked at the problems endemic to decisionmaking, we then turn to the perceptual problems of the producers of intelligence. Here, and in the third chapter of this section, we will use theories of psychology in working toward an understanding of the sorts of problems that make the production and use of intelligence a far from simple task for the individual. In Jim Austin's paper, the psychological aspects of collection, analysis, counterintelligence, and covert action are described. Almost never do the facts speak for themselves in these areas; rarely does everyone agree even on what they might mean. How we interpret intelligence information is often largely a result of the mental lens we use in looking at the data.

The decisionmaker too—no less than the intelligence producer--has a set of perceptions that determines his or her view of the intelligence product and the importance to be assigned to it. William Dunn looks at the problems faced by the decisionmaker—some very much like those confronting the producer of intelligence and others conditioned by the fact that the decisionmaker must not only evaluate the intelligence product but frequently must also act on it. The relationship between collector and user is examined, as is the process of communication between the producer of intelligence and the decisionmaker.

NOTES

1. Graham T. Allison, <u>Essence of Decision</u> (Boston: Little, Brown, 1971).

2. For an exposition of groupthink, see Robert Jervis, <u>Groupthink: Psychological Studies of Policy Decisions and Fiascoes</u> (Boston: Houghton Mifflin, 1982).

3. For a discussion of Tolstoy's view of the influence of great leaders on history, see Isiah Berlin, <u>The Hedgehog and the Fox</u> (New York: Simon & Schuster, 1953).

Decision Costs in the Intelligence Cycle

INTRODUCTION

For over two decades, the U.S. intelligence agencies remained largely hidden in secrecy. In 1974-1975, however, investigative journalists and legislators lifted the lid and peered into the inner workings of these organizations, with the public taking a look, too, over their shoulders. One result was a bonanza of new information for scholars, leading to an outpouring of published studies on intelligence whose proportions, concluded Harry Howe Ransom, were "enormous and unprecedented." He found this fresh literature almost uniformly devoid of theoretical insight, though; and he lamented the "conceptual confusion." Ransom concluded his appraisal with the hope that "[p]erhaps the time is at hand for conceptual progress, inviting the first few steps down the long road to theories of intelligence."[1]

This chapter attempts a step in that direction. The objective is to examine the "intelligence cycle" from the theoretical perspective of "decision costs," as presented in a seminal work by Charles R. Adrian and Charles Press.[2] The authors identified eight costs involved in coalition formation, each of which seems to have explanatory usefulness for understanding the intelligence process: the costs of information, responsibility, intergames, division-of-payoffs, dissonance, inertia, time, and persuasion. Although Adrian and Press were interested in the dynamics of coalition building, their analytic framework lends itself well to the behavior of individuals in all institutions in which two or more people must make decisions.

Since individuals rarely agree perfectly, what they decide to do will be more in harmony with the views of some than with others. Whether a group is involved in voting on money for city sidewalks or deciding what intelligence (information) to provide national policymakers, decisions are made that will be more agreeable to some in the group than to others. One intelligence agency may defer to the judgment of another at an interagency meeting, perhaps because its chief is outranked in the bureaucratic hierarchy. Within an intelligence agency, a junior analyst--protective of a budding career--may suppress data that challenge a position taken by his or her superior. For a multitude of complex and elusive reasons, "coalitions" in support of (or opposed to) bits of intelligence will form or dissolve, in part according to the perception of economic and psychological costs for individual participants.

Theoretically, an algebraic summation of these costs could provide the observer with an estimate of the magnitude and direction of forces acting upon the intelligence as it makes its way from the field to the forums of policy decision. In practice, however, the efforts (costs) and motivations of participants are masked and difficult to discern; empirical data are lacking for the most part. The perspective of decision costs nevertheless highlights important aspects of the intelligence process often overlooked, and it therefore warrants consideration.

DECISION COSTS

At the front end of the intelligence cycle, intelligence officials face the chore of discovering what the policymakers need to know and, at the back end, the chore of persuading the policymakers to absorb and accept the fidelity of the estimates. In between lie several other challenges to intelligence officials, all of which entail costs.

Information Costs

If we adapt the Adrian-Press framework to fit the intelligence process, these costs may be divided into three categories: the costs of collecting information regarding the intelligence requirements of the policymaking consumers; the costs to intelligence officials of communicating their own sense of what data are relevant to the problems confronting the policymaker as well as the feasibility of gathering relevant data; and the more traditional question of costs involved in the actual physical gathering of the required data.

Collecting and digesting information is costly; communication, too, involves definite costs.[3] The benefits of being informed may be exceeded by the costs, or, as Adrian and Press have noted, it may be "uneconomic to be informed."[4] Yet without a flow of information back and forth between the producer and consumer of intelligence, neither is well served. As Sherman Kent once observed, without well-defined instructions from consumers, intelligence officials are "constantly in danger of collecting the wrong information."[5] Without adequate instructions from producers, policymakers sometimes have an unrealistic understanding of what information can be obtained and brought to bear on an issue in a timely manner. The question of morale enters the picture, as well. As organizational theorist Victor Thompson has emphasized: "When the subordinate is denied information, he is prevented from seeing the relationship between his immediate activities and the larger group of objectives, and therefore does not have the satisfaction of knowing he is part of a larger, important, co-operative effort."[6] In many situations, according to a CIA study, "intelligence analysts assert that they know more about our adversary's policy than they know about our own."[7]

The same CIA study stresses the importance of a producer/consumer exchange. "Within the intelligence working hierarchy," state the authors, "it must be understood that from top to bottom a certain amount of intelligence production time will be devoted to communication and dialogue."[8]   But are the costs too high to be worthwhile?

The literature on communications in large organizations reveals a variety of costs that may dissuade producers and consumers of information alike from engaging in an exchange.   As the CIA has recognized, the relationship between the two is "neither spontaneous nor self-perpetrating"[9]—the costs can be high.   The primary cost appears to be the investment of time on behalf of the producer in becoming better acquainted with the consumer.   "When a man wants to find out something, apparently, he turns first to a friend he knows and trusts . . . ," writes Herbert Kaufman, "or at least to someone who can be called by first name."   Once the channels are opened, Kaufman continues, "they tend to encourage additional use that deepens and widens them."[10]

This relationship between trust and communication has often been noted.   "The real organization of government at higher echelons is not what you find in textbooks or organization charts," former Secretary of State Dean Rusk once observed.   "It is how confidence flows down from the President."[11]   Administrative scientists Blau and Scott record the phenomenon of agents "reluctant to go to other agents with whom they were not particularly friendly."   When such "reciprocal-consultation channels" were present, however, they "reduced the effort and social cost required for obtaining advice."[12]   As Anthony Downs has phrased it: "In communications, unfamiliarity with one's communicants is a form of cost."[13]

Intelligence producers reportedly have been able to obtain only an "extremely limited" response from consumers with respect to finished intelligence estimates—except when the producers had established "routine and frequent contact with consumers."[14] Policymakers seems to be "more comfortable," suggests a CIA study, "when dealing with people with whom they work frequently and whom they trust."   So, the authors conclude, the producer "must be prepared personally to 'sell' and even hand-carry his product to the appropriate consumer."[15]

While an increase in rapport may decrease information costs, rapport building itself can be prohibitively expensive—especially with policymakers, who, as a group, exhibit high turnover.   At a mundane level, the matter of geographic space may be a cost consideration. "Typically geographic space is described in terms of distance between points within it," writes James D. Thompson, "but organizations usually measure this distance in terms of costs of transportation and of communication."[16]   The sheer inconvenience (cost) of establishing personal communications bonds in the widely dispersed structures of the national security apparatus in Washington works against such ties, with time lost in travel, parking problems (at downtown agencies), and the harassment of traffic congestion.

A more significant deterrent may be the boss's attitude.   "The superior has the right to monopolize communications," observes Victor Thompson; "the right to monopolize outgoing communications is often expressed by the insistence upon 'going through channels' and by bitter resistence to the use of specialist, nonhierarchical channels."[17] Preceding the Bay of Pigs disaster, the DCI and his deputy director for operations (DDO) effectively shut down the channels of communication between Agency Cuban specialists and policymakers in

the Kennedy administration, thereby barring estimates that called into
question the DDO's belief that Fidel Castro was vulnerable to a
spontaneous uprising against him by the people of Cuba.[18] Information
costs within the CIA between the Directorate for Operations and the
Directorate for Intelligence have always been high, in part because
they represent two separate cultures: the can-do, action-oriented,
clandestine operative and the Ph.D.-toting analyst—James Bond and the
ivory tower.

Status and ideological disparities between policymakers and
analysts can also be difficult to bridge. As Kaufman reminds us,
personal contacts (the informal communications network) are frequently
based on "shared experience and common strategic position," as well as
on a commonality of occupational specialities, ideological allies, similar
educational experiences, and ethnic identification.[19] "The
communication of information is complicated by the blurring effect
resulting from each individual's imperfect perception of reality," add
Adrian and Press, "and by the screening of all communications through
one's personal value system."[20] Sometimes producers and consumers
(including DCIs and presidents) will find they have similar value
systems and they will "hit it off"; but at other times they will not.

The most well-meaning attempts by producers to enhance a
dialogue with consumers is destined to fail, in the final analysis, if the
latter prove unwilling to appreciate the value of the intelligence
agencies. Policymakers often exhibit a tendency "to regard themselves
as their own best intelligence officers, especially on political issues,"
claims a CIA publication.[21] In calculating the costs of
communications between producer and consumer, one cannot take for
granted that policymakers want much in the way of messages from
analysts. And, indeed, some analysts would prefer to remain aloof
from the "contaminating" influence of policy and politics, with the
concomitant risks for undermining the analyst's claim to impartiality.

Compared to the subtle information costs in the web of
relationships between analyst and policymaker, the costs of actually
gathering targeted data have the advantage of at least being a more
familiar and tangible subject, although the precise amount of money
spent on intelligence-gathering remains classified[22]

Responsibility Costs

Responsibility costs, write Adrian and Press, stem "from having a
decision attributed in whole or in part to a given person."[23] When a
policy turns sour, its proponents may pay a high price—loss of prestige
at a minimum, perhaps even loss of a job. "Fear of losing face,"
suggest Blau and Scott, "is probably not much less inhibiting than fear
of losing one's place."[24] If the errant policy is based upon faulty
data—and this is often the case—the intelligence producer may face a
similar fate. Responsibility costs can be particularly high when borne
by a single individual or small group; they increase for the leader (or
chief analyst), too, as the decision approaches irrevocability. In
another intelligence cycle (for covert action), CIA Director
Allen Dulles and his DDO bore the responsibility for their faulty
forecasts regarding the Bay of Pigs invasion and were fired.
Intelligence analysts who have been wide of the mark on crucial

intelligence estimates have fared poorly as well.

To avoid the perils of this decision cost, organizations often attempt to spread responsibility as broadly as possibly; indeed, in unanimity lies the least cost to any individual. During the drafting of the most ambitious intelligence collection scheme to come from the White House—the notorious Huston Plan of 1970—agencies once reluctant to endorse sensitive collection operations of questionable legality were persuaded to agree to this top-secret blueprint, in part because other major agencies seemed prepared to go along.[25] Only at the last minute, when Director J. Edgar Hoover of the FBI balked, was the plan aborted. This episode also illustrates the "indispensable membership principle."[26] Without the presence of certain powerful members in a group, the aggregation fails in its objectives. Hoover's unwillingness to share the responsibility costs—even in a situation of unanimity—caused President Richard Nixon to rescind the Huston Plan; Hoover was too important a figure to ignore.[27]

Intelligence producers sometimes seek to reduce responsibility costs by hedging their bets—sprinkling their findings with mights, maybes, ifs, coulds, howevers, and other equivocators. This approach has occasionally led policymakers to "view the intelligence product as so cautious, so surrounded with caveats and qualifications, that it is virtually useless." Similarly, interagency intelligence may be "coordinated" (homogenized) to the point where the "process tends to mask alternative views or strong disagreements."[28]

Sometimes producers will hedge their bets in another way: by expanding the universe of possible calamities to include most everything. Dean Rusk remembers that when he was secretary of state, "the CIA predicted eight out of the last three crises!"[29] Steve Chan has stated the "significant costs" in this approach: "False alarms dull the audience's sense of vigilance, and reduce the credibility and reputation of the individual or organization initiating them."[30] Richard Betts refers to this as "alert fatigue."[31]

Conversely, Thomas L. Hughes, former director of Intelligence and Research (INR) in the Department of State, tells the story of the analyst in the British government who served from 1903 to 1950 and, in retirement, reputedly said: "Year after year worriers and fretters would come to me with awful predictions of the outbreak of war. I denied it each time. I was only wrong twice." With this methodology, Hughes observes, the estimator "can curl up in the luxury of a freebooting negativism. No reputation is staked, no career endangered."[32]

Responsibility costs may add to the information costs of the analyst. Traditionalists within the CIA remain wary of dissolving the distinction between producer and consumer. This wariness stems in part from a desire to avoid charges of bias or special pleading, but also (according to interviews with analysts) from the close affinity with policymakers, which might subject analysts "to pressures of policy and in some way put their jobs on the line."[33]

Intergame Costs

The theoretical idea here is a straightforward one: participation in one game incurs costs in another. Human activities and decisions are interrelated, connected one to another, with the costs of one game "discounted in relation to other games at different rates."[34]

We live out our lives with families, friends, bosses, allies, and opponents (who may become allies). How we deal with them at time t_a will influence how they deal with us at t_b, as every legislator who practices logrolling and compromise understands. These bargaining techniques are a part of all organizational life, not just legislatures. Successful bureaucrats, from beginning analysts to agency directors, understand the error of Cato's decision to destroy Carthage; instead, when possible, they normally try to mollify, soothe, and cajole competitors in the hope of protecting their current status and future bargaining opportunities.

In organizational settings, individuals are sensitive to questions of role and status; they hope to maintain cordial relations with powerful figures. "Nothing permeates the Cabinet Room more strongly than the smell of hierarchy," comments Wyden in his study of the Bay of Pigs decision.[35] In 1967, CIA Director Richard Helms endorsed an order-of-battle estimate on North Vietnamese and Viet Cong troops prepared by the Pentagon, even though his own agency's figures ran counter. The apparent reason was "he did not want a fight with the military, supported by [Walt] Rostow at the White House."[36] Three years later, Helms again went along with a Pentagon estimate on Soviet first-strike preparations, despite contrary CIA views, this time reportedly because "an assistant to [Secretary of Defense Melvin Laird] informed Helms that the [CIA] statement contradicted the public position of the [S]ecretary."[37] In the Huston Plan episode mentioned earlier, Nixon no doubt also perceived the intergame costs he would have incurred had he failed to retreat from Hoover's charge. As an aid to the FBI Director recalls: "Hoover had his files."[38]

Intergame costs can increase information costs for intelligence producers, for the simple reason that other games may strike policymakers as more important than their relations with intelligence officials. Kaufman reminds us that, among other games, the policymaker may prefer to concentrate on "[f]ormulating policy, introducing innovation, expanding jurisdiction, winning greater authority and appropriations, performing ritual and ceremonial functions, and representing the organization to higher headquarters and to Congress."[39]

The loftier the policymaker's perch in the hierarchy, the more games he or she is apt to engage in, with accompanying increases in information costs for those trying to serve that policymaker. Secretary of Defense Caspar Weinberger, for example, was reportedly "swamped," "overwhelmed," and "left with not enough time to think forward."[40] As James C. Thompson concludes in his study of U.S. policymakers during the Vietnam War, the end result for consumers of these spiraling intergame costs is often "executive fatigue," with the deadening effect this has on "freshness of thought, imagination, a sense of possibility and perspective. . . . The tired policymaker becomes a prisoner of his own narrowed view of the world and his own cliched rhetoric."[41]

The newest set of intelligence consumers, members of the congressional intelligence committees, acutely display the problems of information costs resulting from multiple games and systems overload. With all their various official duties and political obligations, representatives have limited time for intelligence reports and briefings.[42] Little wonder they were short on details regarding CIA covert action in Nicaragua and El Salvador in 1984; members probably took insufficient account of the (no doubt minimal) information provided by agency officials. Perhaps members learned a lesson over this flap. The CIA, too, may have learned a lesson: that intergame costs (earning the wrath of Senate Intelligence Committee Chairman Barry Goldwater, among others) can be higher than information costs (taking the time, and accepting the responsibility costs, to inform appropriate members, despite the difficulties of briefing fast-moving, often inattentive consumers). "[CIA Director William J.] Casey wouldn't tell you that your coat was on fire unless you asked him," complained House Intelligence Committee member Norman Y. Mineta.[43] In this era of New Oversight, with the two legislative intelligence committees engaged in authorization (funding) procedures, rational behavior for the intelligence community might well involve lowering intergame costs by increasing resources to enhance the flow of information to these committees.

Division-of-Payoffs Costs

Coalitions seek to win, with payoffs to be divided among the victorious members. The costs here are measured "by the loss of payoff to each member by the addition of members to the winning coalition."[44] For producers in the intelligence cycle, the payoff is credit (status, praise, promotion, salary increments, medals) for accurate, useful data and interpretation. Before the 1962 missile crisis, CIA analysts played down the likelihood of Soviet missile installations in Cuba; CIA Director John McCone, however, predicted their emplacement. He accrued negative costs (the profit of prestige); they accrued positive costs.

During the Bay of Pigs planning phase, the DDO evidently sought to keep matters largely to himself within the CIA. A recent study suggests that he took this course to maximize his credit for the successful mission—perhaps even to land the agency directorship as Dulles's successor.[45] Unfortunately for the DDO, his low payoff costs proved to be less significant for his career than his high responsibility costs.

As Adrian and Press have noted, individual payoffs can sometimes be increased by actually increasing the number of credit-takers (winners), contrary to Riker's size principle. This would be true, for instance, with interest groups, in which swelling membership roles can mean enhanced political clout.

In the Huston Plan episode, the intelligence community stood to gain greater resources by joining in a unanimous coalition of key agencies that, backed by President Nixon, could lay claim to the necessity for increased funding to meet White House intelligence requirements (specifically, on suspected Soviet ties to Vietnam War dissenters in the United States). One of two agencies trying to make this case alone would presumably have been less effective (especially in light of the questionable modus operandi envisaged); united, they may have strengthened the case. A high-ranking National Security Agency (NSA) official remembers the Huston Plan as "nothing less than a heaven-sent opportunity:" intelligence budgets were sagging in 1970 and the NSA saw the opportunity for expanded intelligence activities and increased funding.[46] Hoover, though, was less concerned (in 1970, at least) with payoffs than with responsibility costs. Already five years over the "mandatory" retirement age, Hoover served each year in a vulnerable position; his directorship was now reviewed for renewal on an annual basis. So, according to a senior FBI official, he became "very conscious of the fact that any incident that within his understanding might prove an embarrassment to the Bureau, could reflect questionably on his leadership of the Bureau."[47]

On other occasions, intelligence producers may prefer minimal coalitions. Within the CIA, long-time Counterintelligence Chief James Angleton seemed to be trying to maximize his payoffs in the organization by minimizing those with access to his counterintelligence (CI) data.[48] If information is power (or at least a vital currency) in the affairs of Washington, Angleton was clearly a powerful man, for he had a monopoly over specialized information in the intelligence community.[49] He kept his payoffs low and directly accrued most of the benefits that trading in this information could bring; his unique expertise, based upon a minimal coalition of only himself and a few close assistants controlling important CI files (as well as a few other specialized "accounts"), brought him status and high position in "the company."

During the Huston Plan proceedings, various agencies failed to realize that other agencies in the community were already (illegally) conducting some of the very intelligence collection operations that President Nixon now encouraged. The agencies apparently refused to trust one another to maintain the security of the operation.[50] High information costs (an unwillingness to communicate with candor) kept payoff costs low (no sharing of the take—and its benefits—was necessary). In this sense, generally speaking, the policy of limiting the distribution of information within the community (as well as within agencies) to small groups for security purposes—so-called compartmentation—creates a multitude of minimal coalitions controlling bits of valuable data. Compartmentation may decrease payoff costs, but it increases information (and responsibility) costs.

Dissonance Costs

Dissonance costs are costs of group dissent, stemming from the fact that internal discord grows with an increase in the size of a group or organizational membership. This proposition leads one to the literature on "groupthink," cognitive dissonance, and other psychological theories that help explain why mavericks and dissenters are usually discouraged from group membership—in short, beause their behavior is too costly to the long-term cohesion of the group. As Betts comments, "indulging dissent poses costs—first, for timeliness; second, for cogency."[51]

To ease the costs of conflict in the intelligence community, producers, hoping for consensus, often seek refuge in noncommittal, bland—and useless—language. The frequently extolled virtue of pluralism in the community, rather than providing diversity of opinion, may simply lead, in Wilensky's words, to "intramural negotiations" designed to blur policy discord.[52]   Hughes captured this classic statement from the Department of Defense, apparently offered to policymakers as they faced a crisis situation: "These basic characteristics of uncertainty will almost certainly continue to be operationally significant for the foreseeable future."[53]

Sometimes the unanimity principle will be evident: "the dynamics of intra-group interaction produces pressures for decision of the group to be formally unanimous," hypothesize Adrian and Press.[54]   And Hughes notes, "especially amid controversy, estimators will reach for extra ambiguities in the search for interagency unanimity."[55] Policymakers reportedly often dismiss this "consensus intelligence" without much regard.[56]

Unanimity proves harder to achieve, however, as the size of a group increases. Frequently, the easier course is simply to keep the decision group small, the dissenter out. In the Huston Plan case, payment of greater information costs to discover Hoover's views early on could have warned against attempts to include him in the spy-plan coalition, thereby reducing dissonance costs. In this instance, though, such an approach was infeasible: the FBI was an indispensable member (certain espionage capabilities required by the Huston Plan belonged to the FBI alone). According to the director of the Defense Intelligence Agency (DIA), the price paid by the White House and the other major intelligence agencies to DIA in order to quell its dissent to the Huston Plan was to allow language in the proposal that made it clear that the military intelligence agencies (Army, Navy, and Air Force, but not the NSA) would not engage in the illegal collection operations. The military agencies had just gone through a major legislative inquiry (led by Senator Sam J. Ervin, Jr.) into their domestic surveillance practices and had acquired a new shyness.[57]

One way to keep the group small is to forward estimates from a single agency, thus eliminating the costs of trying to coordinate the effort with others (with all the dissonance costs that may entail). During the important years of 1978-1979, estimates on Nicaragua forwarded to the National Security Council (NSC) were prepared almost exclusively by the CIA's Latin American Division.[58]   This form of intelligence, too, is viewed skeptically by many policymakers who "seek to obtain departmental intelligence from DIA or INR even though they are also receiving the 'national' [CIA] product"; rather than a narrow analysis, they prefer "inputs from all the experts."[59]

Dissonance costs, however, clearly work against this openness. In Modern Organization, Thompson addresses "the growing antipathy to idea men, to brilliance, that pervades our bureaucracies. The average person who will get along with others and go along with the system is preferred."[60]   Chan has observed this tendency within the intelligence bureaucracy:

> Like other bureaucrats, intelligence analysts have to conform to the regime's basic views about the nature and morality of international relations if they wish to be treated as "responsible" and "serious." Therefore, they refrain from asking the really "tough" but crucial questions such as [those concerning] the aggressiveness of the Soviet Union, the morality of the Vietnam War, and the validity of the "domino theory."[61]

Recruitment norms in the intelligence community reinforce the pressures that encourage conformity. In terms of class, education, ideology, and ethnicity, members of the community have been rather homogeneous with strong "waspish" leanings.[62]   A lack of opinion diversity has been shown to contribute to intelligence failures, as inaccurate Pollyannas force out accurate Cassandras.   In his analysis of India's failure to anticipate the 1962 Chinese invasion, for instance, Yaacov Vertzberger writes that the fact "Nehru was surrounded by a group whose members had a similar background and world view . . . made the presentation of dissonant information either impossible or not worthwhile."[63]

A common manifestation of this behavior is the driving out of qualified experts ("outsiders") who may raise dissonance costs.   This happened both during the Bay of Pigs planning phase, as both State Department and CIA intelligence analysts for Cuba were banished from decision councils ("This is being too tightly held," Secretary Rusk explained to an analyst at the time; indeed, the loss of such experts raised producer information costs beyond reach),[64] and with respect to the decisions regarding Vietnam during the Johnson and Nixon administrations and the Mayaquez decision in 1975, among others. Hence, as we have seen, such efforts to reduce dissonance costs through "concurrence-seeking" (Janis's phrase)[65] can lead to disastrous results as organizations drift away from reality.

Some argue that pluralism within an intelligence community nurtures a diversity of views.   While Chan demonstrates how this can be untrue,[66] organizational decentralization probably does encourage more diversity than would a single, monolithic intelligence entity (though the latter presumably would produce lower information and dissonance costs).   Concluding that decentralization remains "so essential to the national interest," Hughes reminds us that the "same subject matter may be analyzed differently under different auspices, and the differences may be highly relevant to policy in contrasting ways."[67]

Inertia Costs

Inertia costs stem from the proposition that coalitions, once formed, are difficult to alter; their dissolution can involve prohibitive costs.   Drift is fostered, as Betts notes, by the fact that "it is seductively easy for decision makers to wait for more [information]."[68]

Although Richard Helms had information from CIA analysts that President Nixon's invasion of Cambodia would fail to achieve its full objective, he suppressed the data apparently in part because the invasion plan seemed to have developed an inexorable momentum already.[69]   On the eve of World War I, last-minute efforts by policymakers to head off the conflict were submerged under the forces of inertia that made demobilization, once begun, impractical and improbable:

Agents at frontiers were reporting every cavalry patrol as a deployment to beat the mobilization gun. General staffs, goaded by their relentless timetables, were pounding the table for a signal to move lest their opponents gain an hour's head start.

Appalled upon the brink, the chiefs of state who would be ultimately responsible for their country's fate attempted to back away but the pull of military schedules dragged them forward.[70]

In his analysis of the Indian intelligence failure in 1962, Vertzberger attributes the outcome in part to inertia costs: "The need to prove methodically, all through the period in question, that the policy pursued had been the right one, and that the level of aspirations had been realized, made it necessary to ignore any information that contradicted this."[71]

Thompson's reflections on the Vietnam War emphasize "the central fact of human ego investment. Men who have participated in a decision develop a stake in that decision. As they participate in further, related decisions, their stake increases."[72] And as more and more American boys die in rice fields, what policymaker is willing to wonder aloud whether the deaths were the result of policy errors that ought to be fundamentally reexamined? The history of the Huston Plan demonstrates that even direct presidential orders against certain forms of collected intelligence can be ploughed under by the forces of inertia. The FBI and the CIA jointly continued their illegal mail-opening program (among others), despite President Nixon's withdrawal of his approval for this operation as part of the Huston Plan.[73]

The entire government of the United States displays high inertia costs; the accustomed way of doing things rarely changes, except when stimulated by crisis or scandal. Yet, as Hughes suggests, consistency is useful for the Supreme Court, not for the intelligence community.[74] Rather, intelligence producers must eschew the human inclination to move with the crowd; over consistency, they must value objectivity, skepticism, and reasoned nonconformity. In the summer of 1983, CIA analysts displayed these characteristics on at least two reported occasions. While the Reagan administration persisted with its public theme that the Soviet Union was arming Nicaragua with offensive weapons, the television newscasters at CBS stated that, according to a CIA estimate, 80 percent of all Soviet weapons bound for Nicaragua were defensive. The Reagan administration persisted with a second theme on Nicaragua, but the CIA again denied confirmation of this allegation.[75]

Pressure-of-Time Costs

"The worlds of intelligence and policy are always in motion," writes Hughes, "especially so in time of crisis."[76] Under pressure, time enacts a toll on all intelligence producers and consumers. Sometimes insufficient time exists to collect the required data; on other occasions, the data may be available—perhaps in superabundance—but the consumer has insufficient time to comprehend the information. "The quantity of current intelligence," confirms Hughes, "conspicuously exceeds the audience's capacity for absorption."[77]

Moreover, the fascination with current intelligence—as up-to-date timely—can drive out interest in the usually more thoughtful, long-range estimative intelligence. In place of the formal estimate, a document drafted over weeks of careful labor by area or functional experts, comes the raw report on whose side immediacy is to be found—possibly only a snippet of information from the field that tantalizes the eye of the policymaker.

Time costs increase, note Adrian and Press, as the decision process proceeds, for decisions become increasingly harder to change.[78] This is true during foreign policy and national security crises partly because decision responsibility is likely in such instances to rise through the organizational hierarchy. As this happens, cable-level experts are succeeded by harried senior policy chiefs, with all their multiple intergame commitments. The result: "frantic skimming of briefing papers in the back seats of limousines, . . . [which is] . . . no substitute for the presence of specialists."[79] Under time pressure, the forces of inertia accelerate, the full range of options narrows, fatigue increases, and imaginative thinking grows short of breath.

Beyond the banishment of analysts in times of crisis, pressures of time further dilute the quality of an estimate, given that the pulling together of the best judgments of the intelligence community entails time costs. The thoroughness of the search is diminished, or the results will be too late to be of any assistance. In at least one reported case, intelligence submissions to the NSC were so delayed that policy was formulated without this contribution.[80]

Downs posits that when "a bureau is operating under great time-pressure, it will tend to use subformal channels and messages extensively." Under time pressure, he continues, decisionmakers place a premium on communications from individuals "in whom they have great confidence."[81] If information costs between producers and consumers have been reduced through rapport building, the pressure of time costs will also be lower. Time costs are likely to increase information costs for yet another reason, as Downs notes: "The greater the time pressure upon decisionmaking within a bureau, the higher the total volume of messages per period."[82] By relying on trusted producers, consumers can gain valuable assistance in filtering through what might otherwise be an overwhelming—even numbing--increase in information flow.

Persuasion Costs

These are costs associated with "bringing a reluctant member of a group into a winning coalition."[83] The persuasion costs of bringing Hoover into the Huston Plan "coalition" proved to be too high, perhaps even priceless; he remained adamantly unwilling to accept the responsibility costs.

As Adrian and Press point out, persuasion costs can be related to ideological commitment. Richard Helms may have decided to give in to Melvin Laird on the Soviet military estimate mentioned earlier because he perceived the secretary of defense to be so closely identified ideologically with Henry Kissinger (who was Assistant for National Security Affairs at the time) and President Nixon, in public opposition to the CIA view that the persuasion costs had risen to a prohibitively high level. Policymakers generally may embrace only that intelligence conveniently corresponding to their Weltanschauung, while rejecting the rest. "Interested policymakers quickly learn," writes

Hughes, "that intelligence can be used the way a drunk uses a lamp post—for support rather than illumination."[84] This appears to be true especially with political intelligence. On technical matters (military weapons, for example) and with other "difficult" subjects (scientific or economic analysis), persuasion costs decline; the policymaker is reportedly more inclined to defer to the intelligence producer.[85] Hughes believes that "hardware estimates . . . have traditionally been first in acceptance and impact."[86]

CONCLUSION

The intelligence cycle appears to be a simple and smoothly flowing process, with essential and accurate data sweeping along from agents and machines to analysts and on to policymakers. This exploration of decision costs in the cycle, however, reveals a much more complicated reality. Throughout the cycle, information is lost and distorted.

This would happen to some degree regardless, as we understand from Gordon Tullock's model of hierarchical distortion.[87] Policymakers can take in only so much data from the organizational infrastructure--certainly not everything that is collected at the base of the hierarchy. In the winnowing process, as information travels upward it passes through various levels at which officials screen out "extraneous" data. This "condensation of information is an essential part of the bureau's communications process," states Downs. "Otherwise the top man would be buried under tons of facts and opinions."[88] Complicating this phenomenon, however, are the added omissions and distortions resulting from cost calculations of the kind discussed in this chapter.

Decision costs in the intelligence cycle are complex: They overlap and intertwine, and they are usually subtle and hard to calibrate. Scholars of intelligence policy have only just begun to think in more theoretical terms about the second oldest profession. As we learn more about the concealed portion of government, we will be in a better position to evaluate the various decision costs associated with the intelligence process.

The problem for researchers is compounded by the shroud of secrecy maintained over the intelligence community, keeping it hidden and inaccessible. This form of information costs isolates the intelligence producers and their findings from others who have data, brains, and experience to share. People outside the community (and often insiders, too, given compartmentation and bureaucratic politics) are shut off from information that could help them contribute to the national well-being.

In some cases, intelligence data may be too sensitive to share.[89] Great care must be taken, moreover, to protect fragile sources and methods of intelligence collection. But the evidence is persuasive: security costs have indeed been maintained at an artificially high level. Evidently only 10 percent of the intelligence product ever moves outside the walls of the intelligence establishment—not even to key executive-branch policy councils, let alone to the Congress, journalists, or academic specialists.[90] Studies repeatedly show that far more data are classified by the executive branch than is strictly necessary for security purposes.[91]

In the 1970s, the CIA experimented with lowering these information costs by publishing a few estimates (one on Soviet oil reserves received widespread attention) and by actually stirring something of a debate between analysts and outside consultants on the issue of Soviet strategic capabilities and objectives (the so-called A-Team, B-Team exercise). This debate, unfortunately, was limited in its usefulness because virtually all the outside consultants represented a single conservative view on the subject;[92] still, the basic idea was sound. On occasion, the CIA has used other recognized scholars and former government officials to review draft estimates.

A result of these experiments has been a rise in dissonance costs for the CIA, although both the policymakers themselves and the United States have been well served by the exchange of views. Underlying assumptions and methodologies can be examined in this way by a wider range of specialists; the cross-fertilization with outside opinion stimulates thought and offers new perspectives—all without jeopardizing security interests. Here are American democracy (which, after all, is a system designed to encourage debate about the future) and secret intelligence agencies working hand in hand, despite the contradictions and tensions each holds for the other. For the wise policymaker, here is the classic antidote for monopoly: competition. Openness without limits would naturally be too costly. But an inflation of information costs that serves only to quarantine the intelligence community from external influence may be, for the nation, the most expensive surcharge of all in the intelligence cycle.

NOTES

1. For these comments, see Harry Howe Ransom, "Being Intelligent About Secret Intelligence Agencies," American Political Science Review 74 (March 1980): 141, 147.

2. Charles R. Adrian and Charles Press, "Decision Costs in Coalition Formation," American Political Science Review 62 (June 1968): 556-563.

3. See Anthony Downs, Inside Bureaucracy (Boston: Little, Brown, 1967), p. 112; Herbert Kaufman (with Michael Couzens), Administrative Feedback: Monitoring Subordinates Behavior (Washington, D.C.: Brookings Institution, 1973), p. 53; Herbert A. Simon, Administrative Behavior, 3rd ed. (New York: Free Press, 1976), ch. 8; and Harold Guetzkow, "Communications in Organizations," in James G. March, ed., Handbook of Organizations (Chicago: Rand McNally, 1965), pp. 534-573.

4. Adrian and Press, "Decision Costs," p. 558.

5. Sherman Kent, Strategic Intelligence for American World Policy (Hamden, Conn.: Archon, 1965), p. 167.

6. Victor Thompson, Modern Organization (New York: Knopf, 1961), p. 95.

7. Arthur S. Hulnick and Deborah Brammer, "The Impact of Intelligence on the Policy Review and Decision Process—Part One: Findings," Intelligence Monograph TR 80-10002, Center for the Study of Intelligence, mimeo (Washington, D.C.: Central Intelligence Agency, January 1980), p. 15.

8. Arthur S. Hulnick and Deborah Brammer, "The Impact of Intelligence on the Policy Review and Decision Process—Part Two: A Framework for the Relationship Between Intelligence and Policy," Intelligence Monograph TR 80-10005, Center for the Study of Intelligence, mimeo (Washington, D.C.: Central Intelligence Agency, March 1980), p. 25.

9. Ibid., p. 17.

10. Kaufman, Administrative Feedback, p. 35.

11. Quoted in Life (January 17, 1969), p. 626; also cited by I. M. Destler, "National Security Management: What Presidents Have Wrought," Political Science Quarterly 95 (Winter 1981): 575.

12. Peter M. Blau and W. Richard Scott, Formal Organization (San Francisco: Chandler, 1962), pp. 133-136. See also Guetzkow, "Communications," pp. 555-556.

13. Downs, Inside Bureaucracy, p. 122.

14. Hulnick and Brammer, "Impact of Intelligence—Part One," p. 16.

15. Hulnick and Brammer, "Impact of Intelligence—Part Two," pp. 27-28.

16. James D. Thompson, Organizations in Action (New York: McGraw-Hill, 1967), p. 68 [original emphasis]. See also Guetzkow, "Communications," p. 536; and Simon, Administrative Behavior, p. 469.

17. V. Thompson, Modern Organization, p. 63.

18. See Peter Wyden, Bay of Pigs: The Untold Story (New York: Touchstone, 1979), p. 99.

19. Kaufman, Administrative Feedback, p. 35.

20. Adrian and Press, "Decision Costs," p. 557.

21. Hulnick and Brammer, "Impact of Intelligence—Part Two," p. 26.

22. See, for example, Harry F. Eustace, "Changing Intelligence Priorities," Electronic Warfare/Defense Electronics 28 (November 1978): 35.

23. Adrian and Press, "Decision Costs," p. 558.

24. Blau and Scott, Formal Organization, p. 133.

25. See Loch Johnson, "National Security, Civil Liberties, and the Collection of Intelligence: A Report on the Huston Plan," in Supplementary Detailed Staff Reports on Intelligence Activities and the Rights of Americans, Final Report of Select Committee to Study Governmental Operations with Respect to Intelligence Activities (Church Committee), U.S. Senate, Report No. 94-755 (April 23, 1976), pp. 921-986.

26. See Adrian and Press, "Decision Costs," p. 557.

27. On Nixon's reluctance to tangle with Hoover, see Johnson, "National Security," p. 960.

28. Hulnick and Brammer, "Impact of Intelligence—Part Two," pp. 11, 18.

29. Dean Rusk, interview with the author, Athens, Georgia (October 5, 1979).

30. Steve Chan, "The Intelligence of Stupidity: Understanding Failures in Strategic Warning," American Political Science Review 73 (March 1979): 172.

31. Richard K. Betts, "Surprise Despite Warning: Why Sudden Attacks Succeed," Political Science Quarterly 95 (Winter 1980-1981): 559.

32. Thomas L. Hughes, The Fate of Facts in a World of Men: Intelligence-Making (New York: Foreign Policy Association, Headline Series No. 233, 1976), p. 48.

33. Hulnick and Brammer, "Impact of Intelligence—Part Two," p. 21.

34. Adrian and Press, "Decision Costs," p. 559.

35. Wyden, Bay of Pigs, p. 315.

36. Thomas Powers, The Man Who Kept the Secrets: Richard Helms and the CIA (New York: Knopf, 1979), p. 240.

37. See the account in U.S., Senate, 94th Congress, Select Committee to Study Governmental Operations with Respect to Intelligence Activities, Foreign and Military Intelligence, Book 1 (Washington, D.C.: Government Printing Office, April 1976), p. 78.

38. Johnson, "National Security," p. 960.

39. Kaufman, Administrative Feedback, p. 66.

40. Theodore H. White, "Weinberger on the Ramparts," New York Times Magazine (February 6, 1983), p. 24.

41. James C. Thomson, Jr., "How Could Vietnam Happen?" Atlantic Monthly 221 (April 1968): 50.

42. On this point, see Loch Johnson, "The U.S. Congress and the CIA: Monitoring the Dark Side of Government," Legislative Studies Quarterly 5 (November 1980): 477-499.

43. New York Times (May 14, 1984), p. 10.

44. Adrian and Press, "Decision Costs," p. 560.

45. Wyden, Bay of Pigs, p. 96.

46. Johnson, "National Security," pp. 965, 973.

47. Ibid., pp. 931-932.

48. On counterintelligence as an art form, see Loch Johnson and John Elliff, "CIA Counterintelligence," Foreign and Military Intelligence, Book 1 (Washington, D.C.: Government Printing Office), pp. 163-178.

49. See the piece by the Angleton assistant Newton S. Miler, "Counter-intelligence," in Roy Godson, ed., Intelligence Requirements for the 1980s: Counterintelligence (Washington, D.C.: Consortium for the Study of Intelligence, 1980), pp. 47-60.

50. Johnson, "National Security," p. 964.

51. Richard K. Betts, "Intelligence for Policymaking," Washington Quarterly 3 (Summer 1980): 125.

52. Harold Wilensky, Organizational Intelligence: Knowledge and Policy in Government and Industry (New York: Basic Books, 1967), p. 54.

53. Hughes, Fate of Facts, p. 43.

54. Adrian and Press, "Decision Costs," p. 556.

55. Hughes, Fate of Facts, p. 43.

56. Hulnick and Brammer, "Impact of Intelligence—Part One," p. 22.

57. Former DIA Director Donald Bennett interview with the author, Hilton Head Island, South Carolina (June 5, 1975).

58. Hulnick and Brammer, "Impact of Intelligence—Part One," pp. 4, 11.

59. Ibid., p. 11.

60. V. Thompson, Modern Organization, p. 91.

61. Chan, "Intelligence of Stupidity," p. 178.

62. Benno Wasserman, "The Failure of Intelligence Prediction,"

Political Studies 8 (1960): 156-169.

63. Yaacov Vertzberger, "Bureaucratic-Organizational Politics and Information Processing in a Developing State," International Studies Quarterly 28 (March 1984): 86-87; see also Irving L. Janis, GroupThink: Psychological Studies of Policy Decisions and Fiascoes (Boston: Houghton Mifflin, 1982), p. 250.

64. Janis, Groupthink, p. 4.

65. Ibid., p. 243.

66. Chan, "Intelligence of Stupidity," p. 178.

67. Hughes, Fate of Facts, p. 50.

68. Betts, "Surprise Despite Warning," p. 561.

69. See Foreign and Military Intelligence, Book 1, p. 81.

70. Barbara Tuchman, The Guns of August (New York: Dell, 1962), pp. 91-92.

71. Vertzberger, "Bureaucratic-Organizational Politics," pp. 87-88.

72. J. C. Thomson, "How Could Vietnam Happen?" p. 52 [original emphasis].

73. Johnson, "National Security," p. 965.

74. Hughes, Fate of Facts, p. 49.

75. CBS television nightly news, July 29, 1983, and August 4, 1983.

76. Hughes, Fate of Facts, p. 46.

77. Ibid., p. 40.

78. Adrian and Press, "Decision Costs," p. 561.

79. J. C. Thomson, "How Could Vietnam Happen?" p. 49.

80. Hulnick and Brammer, "Impact of Intelligence—Part One," p. 20.

81. Downs, Inside Bureaucracy, p. 114.

82. Ibid., p. 129.

83. Adrian and Press, "Decision Costs," p. 561.

84. Hughes, Fate of Facts, p. 24

85. Hulnick and Brammer, "Impact of Intelligence—Part One," p. 21, and "Part Two," p. 18. Members of the new intelligence oversight committees on Capitol Hill are similarly inclined to accept (or ignore) technical aspects of intelligence, concentrating instead on the more comprehensible issues of foreign covert action and domestic civil liberties. See Johnson, "U.S. Congress and the CIA," p. 487.

86. Hughes, Fate of Facts, p. 45.

87. Gordon Tullock, The Politics of Bureaucracy (Washington, D.C.: Public Affairs Press, 1965), pp. 137-141; see also Downs, Inside Bureaucracy, pp. 116-118.

88. Downs, Inside Bureaucracy, p. 117.

89. Indeed, the data might "result in direct, immediate, and irreparable damage to our nation or its people," to use Justice Potter Steward's standard in the celebrated Pentagon Papers case. See the account in Sanford J. Ungar, The Papers and the Papers (New York: Dutton, 1972), p. 252.

90. Hulnick and Brammer, "Impact of Intelligence—Part One," p. 19.

91. See, for example, Morton H. Halperin and Daniel N. Hoffman, Top Secret: National Security and the Right to Know (Washington, D.C.: New Republic, 1977).

92. See the evaluation of this exercise by the Subcommittee on Collection, Production, and Quality, U.S. Senate, Select Committee on

198

Intelligence, <u>Report on the National Intelligence Estimates A-B Team Episode Concerning Soviet Capability and Objectives</u> (Washington, D.C.: Government Printing Office, 1978), pp. 2-6.

JAMES D. AUSTIN

The Psychological Dimension of Intelligence Activities

> Let us consider the nature of [intelligence], its want of trustworthiness, its changefulness, and we shall soon feel what a dangerous edifice War is, how easily it may fall to pieces and bury us in its ruins.
>
> —Karl von Clausewitz, 1832

Karl von Clausewitz warns us against placing too much faith in the calculability of war, because a "fog of uncertainty" obscures our ability to see what will happen.[1]   The history of warfare justifies his concern. Even a relatively easy matter such as detecting the presence and movements of an opponent's forces may be difficult. One's vision may be obscured by distance, rough terrain, and poor weather; moreover, one's opponents may use camouflage and deception to mask the movements and disposition of their forces.[2]

William Colby, at one time chief-of-station in Saigon and later director of Central Intelligence, testified in Congress in 1976 about the difficulty even of estimating the number of communist forces fighting in South Vietnam during the Vietnam War.

> Our experience in estimating enemy strength in South Vietnam is a classic example of many of the intangibles with which intelligence officers must wrestle in their day-to-day job. Working from incomplete and often conflicting data, the job of intelligence on this subject was . . . beset with . . . methodological and judgmental factors. These ranged from fundamental conceptual differences on the threat to be measured, to the choice of the proper methods for extrapolating uncertain and fragmentary data. Even if agreements could be reached on the groups to be included, there were problems in deciding on how to measure their strengths, their attrition, or their success in replacing manpower losses. Even if all of the definitional and quantitative factors could be resolved, there were any number of judgmental calls to be made on the qualitative aspects of these forces.
>
> In short, the problem of estimating the numerical strength of many disparate groups of organized manpower . . . was of necessity a highly imprecise art. Even to this day I doubt that there are experienced observers—in Washington or in Hanoi—who

would lay claim to having precise knowledge of the numerical strengths of most of the organized groups in South Vietnam on either side.[3]

Even when the movements of an opponent's forces are fairly visible, information on how and where the opponent intends to use them may not be. These are matters of doctrine and strategy. Because they are intangible elements of power, doctrine and strategy are hard to observe and estimate.[4] One can eliminate some uncertainty by piecing together facts about an opponent's weaponry and training, and about the past operations of the opponent's forces. Yet, in the end, one can only speculate about operational and strategic plans of an opponent's forces. That speculation can be wrong. In 1940, for instance, French commanders were well aware of the technical aspects of tanks but did not anticipate the use of mobile tank columns in the blitzkrieg campaign of the Germans.[5] In 1973, the Israelis were surprised by the novel use of SAMs by the Egyptians to neutralize Israeli air superiority over the battlefield.[6]

If war is uncertain, states of crisis and peace are even more so. At least in war, one does not have to worry so much about the ultimate intentions of the opponent. In peacetime, debates about an opponent's intentions often prove worrisome and time consuming. They lie at the heart of peacetime assessments because many subsidiary assessments are determined by one's view of an opponent's intentions. Yet plumbing the intentions of another nation's leaders remains one of the hardest tasks of all.[7]

A primal uncertainty, then, leads nations to create intelligence organizations. The intelligence organization in each country works to collect significant signals from events in the world, evaluate them properly, and fit them into a meaningful and correct picture of the situation faced, all the while preventing any foreign intelligence organization from penetrating or manipulating this ability. A fundamental problem, however, haunts this attempt to resolve uncertainty. The primal uncertainty that leads to the birth of intelligence organizations persists and bedevils any attempts by those organizations to create certain knowledge.[8]

The truth is that the world any nation faces is inherently uncertain. Most events that a nation might need to analyze happen in distance places. Distance limits the amount of information immediately available to analysts and policymakers. Some must travel to the area of interest and collect information. Yet which information should be collected? The events to be analyzed are often too extended in time and space for a quick, one-shot appraisal. Which information, out of all that is available, is relevant? One solution is to try to collect everything. But increases in collection activities can be costly, and the cost probably increases geometrically as one seeks additional facts. Moreover, "noise" surrounds the "signals" that one wants to collect.[9] If the collection of facts is increased, more noise will inevitably be picked up, resulting in more rather than less uncertainty.

Another problem compounds uncertainty. The world is a fluid, unpredictable, dynamic place. Technology advances. The mood of a country shifts. Opponents or allies change their minds. To the degree that an intelligence organization operates well, it will acquire new information that may seem to contradict what was previously known.

One must always ask, is there a true contradiction of facts, or has change simply occurred in the world? If change has occurred, how lasting is the change?

A third feature of the world further adds to uncertainty. Many variables are intangible. They are hard to see, difficult to count, and hard to weigh in terms of relative impact. One can look for and create indicators for these intangible elements, but the connection of the indicators to reality always remains conjectural. The difficulty involved in weighing intangibles means that one may have a rich store of information about an opponent's activities yet still fail to see them in their true light. Among the intangibles that are most important are the opponents' strategy and reasoning, their comprehension of their own strategy, their morale, the morale of their armed forces and their government, the morale of their allies, and the morale of their population.

Finally, uncertainty grows from the complex nature of events. For instance, in most cases, one's focus must go beyond events within one nation and take into account the interactions of several nations. Worse, each of these nations is itself a complex constellation of individuals, organizations, and groups interacting over time. Moreover, events that occur abroad present not one but several interwoven issues. Even when an analyst recognizes the complexity of an issue, he or she must still face questions not easily resolved. How tightly knit are the components of the event in question? Which features of an event are significant? How will changes in one feature ripple through the others? Which button should we push to get the changes that we want?

In sum, intangibility, distance, change, and complexity generate uncertainties that make intelligence an inherently psychological matter. At the primary level, one must fathom the psychology of foreign leaders. Beyond this, the mere collection of facts cannot provide answers to the most important questions. Only the piecing together of facts can do that. Such piecing together constitutes reasoning, and reasoning is psychology. Thus, intelligence is at its heart a psychological matter, and the study of psychology can help officials both understand the reasoning of their counterparts abroad and improve their own process of piecing facts together.

A PSYCHOLOGICAL PERSPECTIVE

Psychologists have not been able to provide a consensus on a single theory that explains human behavior. Over the years, many concepts and schools of thought have been created and explored. Personality theorists tend to believe that an individual's behavior is caused by internal dispositions that are fixed relatively early in life. Personality theories are probably most useful in political analysis when one is interested in the behavior of an extreme or deviant person or when one is interested almost entirely in the behavior of the top four or five leaders in a government. Unfortunately, personality concepts have not proven very reliable in predicting behavior.[10] Moreover, the usefulness of personality theories in understanding the behavior and reasoning of individuals in intelligence organizations is limited. Most personality theories focus on the behavior and internal dynamics of individuals. They are generally not flexible enough to be useful in studying the behavior of people working in organizations in which roles heavily shape reasoning behavior.

What one needs for the study of intelligence organizations are theories that take into account the effects of situational context on individual behavior. Indeed, theories of social psychology might be better suited than personality theories, as they focus on how factors external to the individual, such as groups and organizations, influence the judgment and behavior of individuals. Nonetheless, most theories of social psychology fall short of what is needed for the study of intelligence organizations. For one thing, many of these theories concentrate too heavily on the role of external factors and hence overlook internal factors such as an individual's beliefs and reasoning patterns. In short, they see an individual's judgment and behavior as determined by his or her role in the organization. Another problem with many theories in social psychology is that they tend to concentrate primarily on affective or emotional determinants of behavior rather than on processes of cognition and reasoning within the individual. In the study of governmental operations and especially in the study of intelligence activities, one needs psychological theories that take cognitive determinants of behavior into account as much as affective factors.

Cognitive theories seem to fit the bill for the study of intelligence activities. Cognitive theories emphasize the internal processes of perception and reasoning and presume that all individuals reason by means of systematic mental processes about which laws can be formulated. At the same time, most cognitive theories focus on the effects of situational context on individual reasoning.

For the most part, cognitive theories have adopted the view that human beings are problem solvers in their dealings with the world, and that people organize their perceptions, thoughts, and beliefs to arrive at interpretations of events and then use their interpretations to decide what to do. Thus, according to such theories, human behavior is determined neither by internal nor external factors alone. Rather, it is determined by the interaction between outside stimuli and the internal organization and interpretation of these stimuli. For this reason, one can say that an interactional paradigm underlies most cognitive theories.

The cognitive perspective holds that the meaning of events is not predetermined; it proceeds not simply from the possession of information but from our interpretation of the information. Even though our beliefs do not completely determine the world in which we live, they do shape what we see.

Most of us assume that the world is "obvious." We recognize that a number of things exist without our knowing about them; but we also believe that everybody else reasons as we do, that given the same information, everyone will reach similar conclusions. In short, we assume the world has an objective meaning independent of any one person's particular view.

Yet the world is not so unambiguous. Let us examine a fairly simple, straightforward event: holding a flame to one's foot. Is it foolish or wise? The answer seems fairly obvious: it is a foolish act to be terminated. But think for a moment. What if this event took place in a culture where enduring fire signaled adulthood? The change in cultural context changes the meaning of contact with fire from a foolish act to one that is brave or righteous. Thus, even in the case of an event that seems straightforward, one finds different interpretations—more than one meaning. Think how much more slippage exists when one tries to interpret social or political events of great scale and long duration.

If meaning is not obvious, where does it come from? Meaning grows out of the interaction between the stimulus information that is available and one's beliefs.

> Man looks at his world through transparent patterns or templates which he creates and then attempts to fit over the realities of which the world is composed. The fit is not always very good. Yet without such patterns the world appears to be such an undifferentiated homogeneity that man is unable to make any sense out of it. Even a poor fit is more helpful . . . than nothing at all.[11]

We make sense of situations by breaking them down and organizing them into meaningful patterns on the basis of our attitudes and beliefs. Thus an individual is "not simply a dutiful clerk who passively registers items of information" but an active interpreter who constructs meaning.[12] If two people possess different beliefs, they will see different realities.[13]

In coming to an understanding of the psychological factors in intelligence organizations, we are most concerned with the following issues: the scope and types of information collected, the ways in which information is coded, the beliefs through which information is processed, the structure of those beliefs, and, finally, the conditions that affect the quality and extent of reasoning. Let us now examine a few of these issues in each of the four major areas of intelligence activity: collection, analysis and estimates, counterintelligence, and covert action.

Psychological Factors in Collection

Intelligence officers and political leaders often proceed on the assumption that more collection will produce more information and more information will improve analysis. Or they keep collecting in an effort to find the one fact that will cause the jigsaw puzzle to fall into place.[14] The problem is that increased collection will not always produce better analysis.[15]

In fact, a dilemma of information may exist. To reduce the uncertainty of an intelligence report, one ideally seeks more information in order to fill in the gaps in the analysis. However, to the degree that one collects more information, one also picks up more of the uncertainty and confusion that naturally exists. Moreover, in collecting a larger stock of available information, we increase the cost and difficulty of analysis. Thus, as we collect more information, we may end up hindering analysis. Ultimately, we may actually end up increasing rather than decreasing uncertainty.[16] At the extreme, analysis degenerates into a series of current estimates, thereby creating a dilemma: If one cuts back on the amount of information collected, significant facts are more likely to be missed. On the other hand, an increase in the amount of information collected may bring about more "noise" in the form of trivial or irrelevant facts.

Illustrative of this dilemma of information is the case of the CIA's tap into underground cables in Berlin during Operation Gold. In 1954, the CIA tapped three cables used by Soviet military forces in Berlin. Each cable had 172 circuits and each circuit, a minimum of 18 channels. A total of 9,288 channels were monitored. The amount of information collected was enormous. Yet how could anyone sift through the miles of tape before the intelligence became outdated? The CIA had succeeded in a collection operation only to fall victim to its own success.[17]

A second problem can afflict collection. People perceive and interpret information in terms of what concerns them most immediately at the moment of perception. Whatever is at the front of their minds colors their perceptions and cognition. Psychologists call this phenomenon a "mental (or "evoked") set."[18]

Psychologists often depict the power of an evoked set by the use of an optical illusion—the drawing of a woman. Looked at in one way, the woman appears to be a young lady with a hat on, glancing over her shoulder. Looked at in a different way, however, the drawing appears to be that of an old lady looking down, with her chin buried in a shawl. If one expects to see an old lady, that is what the picture appears to be. Conversely, if one's mental set is altered by the expectation of seeing a young lady, the picture appears to change accordingly.[19]

Several factors can create or alter mental sets. The information last received can color the perception of new information. Immediate organizational concerns such as orders and directives can lead to the construction of a mental set. Finally, all jobs hold certain task incentives in the form of organizational doctrines and standard procedures. These, too, shape the mental sets that collectors and analysts have regarding the type of information to be collected, when to collect it, and how to evaluate it.[20]

Soviet collection activities prior to the German invasion of the Soviet Union in 1941 illustrate the impact of mental sets. Stalin feared that Britain and the United States were conspiring to provoke war between the USSR and Germany before the Soviets would be ready to fight a war. To gain the maximum amount of time for mobilization, Stalin wanted to avoid any provocative actions that might trigger a German attack. Thus, on several occasions when Soviet intelligence picked up information indicating that the Germans were already moving into position for an invasion of Russia, Stalin ordered that such provocative information should not be collected or circulated. For instance, nearly three weeks before the German assault, Stalin refused to send a directive to the army's political commissars warning of impending war. Indeed, he refused on the grounds that the directive was too provocative. Stalin's orders fairly quickly discouraged the reporting of field intelligence by the army and the Soviet secret police (NKVD), thus blocking the flow of vital intelligence about the deployments of German forces along the border.[21]

We see in this case two aspects of the mental set. First, because Stalin expected Britain and the United States to try to provoke a war between Germany and Russia, information about German force movements evoked a mental set in his mind of Anglo-American deception. His mental set to avoid becoming a victim of deception colored his interpretation of the information he received. Second, Stalin's orders to his collectors to cease reporting any provocative information operated not only as an order but also as a mental set for collectors.[22] Collectors in the field dismissed the reports of German defectors rather than reporting them. Operating under instructions to avoid provocation, the NKVD did not kidnap and interrogate German soldiers as they otherwise would have done. In short, the mental set for the Russians shut down collection activities that might have warned Stalin of impending disaster.

The Polish and Czech intelligence services offer an interesting contrast. Collectors and analysts in these services operated with a different mental set. Their hope for liberation from German occupation lay in a war between Germany and Russia. Accordingly, their mental set alerted them to any signs that war might occur. In contrast to the performance of the Soviet intelligence community, both the Polish and Czech services predicted fairly early on that Operation Barbarossa would take place.[23]

Mental sets can operate in another way. The doctrine and procedures peculiar to an organization (or the subunit of an organization) can predispose collectors in that organization to collect or trust only certain types of information. For instance, Jeffrey Race, who served as a military intelligence officer in Vietnam, writes that he had difficulty in reporting any information other than tactical order-of-battle data. Due to an emphasis on finding, fixing, and destroying enemy armed forces, the army, according to Race, felt that order-of-battle data were more important than information on political activities in villages.[24] To the degree this mental set existed and operated in the chain of command, it stopped the flow of a particular type of information.[25]

Another psychological problem can affect the collection of information. "Source-message interaction,"[26] or what psychologists call the "halo" or "forked-tail" effect,[27] occurs when a person's attitudes about the source of a message affect his or her attitudes about the content of a message. Attitudes about the source of information create an aura that colors the information. When this aura is positive, psychologists call the effect a "halo" effect; when it is negative, psychologists refer to it as a "forked-tail" effect.[28]

The forked-tail effect will be most pronounced when a message sharply contradicts a collector's view, when the source of the message has been wrong before, when the collector cannot cross-check the information, or when the source's beliefs sharply differ from those of the collector.[29] Conversely, we can probably expect that a pronounced halo effect will occur when a message confirms a collector's views, when the source of a message has been right before, or when the source holds values or beliefs very similar to those of the collector.

A good illustration of source-message interaction can be found in the earliest days of the Cuban Missile Crisis in 1962. Refugees from Cuba had been reporting the presence of missiles there for over a year and one-half prior to the crisis. When first checked out, however, these sightings by refugees turned out to be either groundless or sightings of surface-to-air missiles rather than medium-range ballistic missiles. Furthermore, intelligence officers recalled how, prior to the Bay of Pigs invasion in 1961, Cuban refugees had exaggerated anti-Castro sentiment in order to gain U.S. support for an invasion. These considerations about the refugees as a source of information colored the collectors' and analysts' judgments regarding the truth of information gained from the refugees.

This instance of source-message interaction became significant on September 9, 1962, when a Cuban refugee accurately reported the first sighting of a medium-range missile in the San Cristobal area. The sighting occurred a full thirty-three days before an American U-2 flight provided photographic evidence of the presence of Soviet ballistic missiles, yet the refugee's report was discounted. Even when another refugee matched the object he had seen with the correct photograph of an offensive missile, intelligence officers assumed he had simply made a mistake. Thus, a "history of mistaken observations by [other] refugees" led collectors and analysts to discount newer reports by refugees.[30] Clearly, the mental set that any refugee's report would probably be false had been established.

Source-message interaction can occur not only in assessing the truth of messages from agents but also in assessing information gained from liaison with foreign intelligence services. When an intelligence officer evaluates information from a close, friendly service, his or her positive attitude toward that service will probably augment the perception of the truth in the message, and a halo effect will occur. An additional factor may reinforce this tendency. In liaison with a friendly service, one's ability to cross-check information is likely to be limited, as will independent collection activities within that friendly country, in the interests of preserving the friendly liaison. To the degree that such limitations are incurred, one cannot easily check the information about a friendly nation provided by its intelligence service.

A halo effect might have played a role when U.S. officials underestimated the vulnerability of the shah of Iran. Savak, the shah's intelligence service, possessed a fairly good track record on internal dissent in Iran prior to the shah's overthrow, and Iran had maintained friendly liaison with U.S. intelligence. Moreover, the shah had limited independent activities by U.S. intelligence in Iran. The message coming from officials in the shah's government was one of optimism—namely, that the shah would weather the storm of protest. Perhaps intelligence officers and diplomats who maintained liaison with the shah's government allowed their positive views of the source of the message to color their views about the reliability of the message.

Source-message interaction can also operate in a negative direction in what psychologists call the forked-tail effect. When an intelligence service maintains limited liaison with a distant or hostile intelligence service, collectors and analysts will tend to degrade or discount the information collected when that information contradicts previously held beliefs. This happened in the case of Operation Barbarossa. Few military plans for a surprise attack have been so well reported to the intended victim as was the plan for Barbarossa. British, U.S., Czech, and Polish intelligence services specifically warned Stalin on numerous occasions. Yet Stalin refused to listen, refusing to trust nations that he considered to be imperialist. Their intent, he reasoned, was to deceive Soviet leaders and provoke a war between Germany and the USSR.[31]

The "consensus effect" can also affect the quality of intelligence. A study by Solomon Asch first established this concept. In Asch's study, subjects were seated one at a time in a room with a group of confederates. They were shown a card on which three lines varying in length had been drawn. They were asked to choose which line of the three best matched a fourth line drawn on another card. The correct answer was obvious and perceptible. The experimenter asked members of the group to state out loud which lines matched and instructed those who were actually confederates to answer first. The confederates had been secretly instructed prior to the experiment to answer incorrectly by matching two lines that were not the same size. Asch was interested in seeing whether the subjects would rely on their own judgment or conform to the group's judgment.

Asch discovered that most subjects will conform to the judgment of a group even when that judgment is perceptibly wrong. Drawing on Asch's interpretation, we can conclude that conformity occurs when people use group judgments in place of their own reasoning. Further experimentation by Asch and others has shown that conformity occurs for two reasons. First, people fear showing disagreements that will make them appear deviant or different. Second, people use group opinions as a source of information in forming their own judgments. When a group judgment differs markedly from an individual's judgment, the individual tends to assume that his or her judgment is somehow off the mark and thus accepts the group consensus. The consensus effect increases when group members are unanimous, when the size of the group is four or more, when others in the group are seen as experts, or when the group is highly cohesive.[32]

Collection activities can be hampered by the consensus effect. Once a consensus exists in regard to either the value of a source of information or the definition of a situation abroad, intelligence collectors may conform to the group consensus rather than disagree among themselves. In other words, they may not search as hard for facts that contradict the consensus and may not report those facts even when they find them. Furthermore, they may evaluate the credibility of facts in such a way that the group consensus is maintained rather than challenged.

The final issue in collection concerns the scope and depth of coverage of foreign events by collectors. Foreign policy problems, especially the important ones, usually have a number of dimensions—for instance, a military dimension, an administrative dimension, a dimension of leadership, a rural dimension, an international dimension, and so on. The key to understanding foreign policy problems lies in having adequate coverage in terms of collection from the critical dimensions. A continuous coverage of a variety of dimensions raises the probability that any narrow or partial preconception in the minds of analysts and policymakers will be challenged.

Psychological Factors in Analysis and Estimates

Analysis and estimates require analysts to sift through information that has been evaluated for credibility and to use the information to describe the world, report on current events, and project future trends. Three steps are involved in this process. First, analysts must decide how much to trust the various facts available to them and how significant each fact is to the overall picture. Second, they must integrate the assorted facts and dimensions of an event into an assessment or estimate. This is the step of production--an important step given that everyone can usually agree on facts, whereas the interpretation of facts tends to generate disagreement. Estimates provide the interpretive context for individual facts. The final step in analysis and estimates is the distribution of intelligence estimates to "consumers" within a government, the most important of these being the head of state. Distribution includes not only such procedural matters as formatting and classification of the report but also the use made of the report by consumers. It is in the understanding and acceptance of estimates by consumers that many, perhaps most, intelligence failures occur.[33]

Assessing the role of psychological factors in analysis and estimates can be difficult for two reasons. First, nations vary as to where they locate the analysis and estimates task. Some governments, such as that of the United States, hold a division of their intelligence organization specifically responsible for creating estimates. Other nations, such as the USSR, prefer to relegate intelligence organizations to collection and to assign analysis and estimates to top-level policymaking bodies. Even in such cases as the United States, where a specific directorate of the Central Intelligence Agency creates estimates, analysts in other governmental units—such as the military services, Defense Intelligence Agency, Department of State, and National Security Council staff—interpret facts available to them and write estimates. Thus it can be hard to decide where to draw the line in labeling someone an "analyst" or not. This difficulty is compounded when one realizes that it is hard to distinguish between the writing of an estimate and its appreciation by consumers. If an estimate fails to shake the preconceptions of a policymaker and a failure occurs, is this a failure of intelligence or policy? Drawing that line requires highly detailed evidence about the policy process that may not be available.

These two complications make for problems in the writing of illustrative case studies. Secondary sources that recount cases of analysis and estimates often do not provide enough detail to permit a researcher to draw conclusions about the role of psychological factors. Detailed case studies based on archival research offer the best route of remedy. But until these case studies are completed, one is left with the secondary sources that are available and the suggestion, not the proof, that psychological factors might have played a role in distorting the estimating process.

Psychological factors can operate in a number of ways in analysis and estimates. They affect the choice of questions that are asked, the thoroughness and seriousness with which questions are answered, the simplicity (or complexity) of analysis, and, finally, the amount of inertia and rigidity that beliefs might have in the face of contradictory evidence.

Mental sets can affect the type of questions that analysts ask. When an analyst turns his or her attention to an event happening abroad, that event can be assessed on any one of the three planes of analysis—the factual, the operational, or the strategic. The analysis created grows out of the analyst's mental set—a mental set derived from past training, experience, and job or task incentives. Task incentives originate from the organization in which the analyst works and from the directives handed down by superiors and policymakers.

One case that possibly illustrates the effect of mental sets on the questions asked was the problem of assessing the effectiveness of American bombing of the Ho Chi Minh trail. Communist forces were using the trails that ran down the western border of South Vietnam to supply their forces operating within South Vietnam. Bombing missions were flown by the United States to interdict the flow of supplies. The overarching question that needed to be answered was how well the bombing was working. But this question could be answered on a tactical plane ("Did we hit the specific targets?"), on an operational plane ("Has the coordinated effort reduced the flow of supplies during the last month or last year?"), or on a strategic plane ("Has the total effort weakened the will of the enemy to continue?"). In the DIA, analysts tended to approach their assessments from the tactical level up, counting the numbers of trucks destroyed, and so on, to arrive at an estimate of the extent to which operations were hurting the enemy. They were more optimistic about the bombing compared to the CIA, where the analysts tended to approach the issue from the strategic level down. In other words, the CIA analysts looked to see how the opponents had responded to the campaign and whether their will to continue had changed. They then worked downward toward pessimistic conclusions about the effectiveness of the bombing. Given the divergence in views, it seemed that one group of analysts had to be wrong. In fact, both groups were right. They were just operating on two different planes of analysis and answering two different sets of questions.

Mental sets can affect analysts and policymakers in another way. Events under an analyst's scrutiny occur in the context of other events, not in a vacuum. Hence the international context can operate as a mental set. An example of this can be found in the British experience prior to the Argentine invasion of the Falklands Islands. According to published reports, British analyses of Argentine intentions that reached the British Cabinet were far more reassuring than the raw information warranted. Analysts in the Current Intelligence Group of the Joint Intelligence Committee allegedly discounted the alarms in the raw reports because of the international context: relations between the Argentine government and Europe and the United States had been improving, and previous discussions with the Argentinians had been cordial. Because analysts assumed that Galtieri was preoccupied with the domestic problems of Argentina, they discounted Argentine statements that they would pursue "other means" of settling the sovereignty of the Falklands.[34]

One type of mental set deserves special mention because of its historic importance. This is the "dilemma of alerts," or what Betts calls the "growing used to the wolf at the door" fallacy and others call the "routinization of alarm."[35] Ideally, a nation wants to build an intelligence system that accurately alerts the country to a threat so that steps can be taken to deter the threat or limit the damage. If a nation does this and treats every warning seriously, it would seem that the nation's safety will be better assured. But the dilemma is this: to the degree that the individual takes alerts seriously, the sensitivity to alerts will be dulled and the individual will be led to take them less seriously. In the long run, one may actually become more rather than less vulnerable.

Another psychological phenomenon that may lead analysts and policymakers to give too little attention to an event or problem abroad occurs when officials underestimate or overestimate their leverage over events and so devote too little time to analyzing the information that is available. When officials feel that they cannot influence events, they psychologically withdraw from analyzing the issue. On the other hand, if they overestimate their influence, they tend to adopt the view that their current perspective is sufficient and no further analysis is needed.[36]

Analysis and estimates can be afflicted by another psychological factor as well—that of simplistic reasoning.[37] Reasoning that is cognitively simple does not really constitute a problem when the event being analyzed is simple. But if the events are complex, cognitively simple analyses increase the likelihood of surprise or failure.

Simplistic reasoning can come about in a number of ways. For example, analysts may leave out dimensions of events abroad that are critical to understanding what is happening, or focus on the personalities and statements of foreign leaders and ignore rural politics. Whenever significant dimensions are ignored, analysts become like the blind men and the elephant such that each analyst touches one or two parts of the problem but generates a mythical view of the whole by overgeneralizing from the parts.

Simplistic reasoning can also come about by projection, as when analysts overrationalize events and project a single personality, disposition, or plan to the actions of a foreign government.[38] Projection or overrationalization can occur in both a negative and a positive direction. When a positive projection is made, the analyst perceives a specific similarity between his or her perspective and that of the opponent and then projects a fundamental similarity in viewpoint.[39] Many observers feel that this occurred when analysts in the CIA in the late 1960s and early 1970s underestimated Soviet ICBM deployments by presuming a fundamental similarity in views of arms control and deterrence between the USSR and the United States.[40] When a negative projection is made, the reverse occurs. An analyst assumes that the disposition and plans of leaders in a country abroad have nothing at all in common with his or hers and, for that matter, are intentionally the very reverse. But projection in either direction is often simplistic both because it leaves out the situational causes of the other country's behavior and because it disregards the individual history of the country and its government.

Whatever the reason for its occurrence, cognitively simple reasoning creates problems, especially under conditions of extreme stress or at times when the political culture of a country or its government is highly ideological. It can also happen as the result of task incentives.

A final area of concern for analysis and estimates is the inertia or resistance of analysts' beliefs when analysts are faced with information that contradicts those beliefs. Cognitive inertia occurs when preconceptions of officials filter out or distort discrepant information, when the prior commitments of officials lead them to discount dissonant information, when discrepant information arrives gradually in bits and pieces that allow officials to preserve their beliefs by means of incremental adjustment, or when pressures on officials to conform to a consensus lead to a self-censorship and inhibition in examining alternative assessments.

Several conditions can increase the impact of cognitive inertia. For instance, highly centralized organizations make it more difficult for an analyst who adopts a dissenting point of view to argue against a prevailing consensus. Prior to 1973, Israeli military intelligence was set up in such a way that superiors could stop a dissenting point of view from circulating. A lieutenant, Benjamin Siman-Tov, had pieced together two correct assessments concerning Egyptian actions that constituted preparations for war concealed as exercises. His reports never made it up the chain of command, however, because they contradicted the dominant belief that Egypt would not go to war at that time. The centralized nature of Israeli military intelligence allowed the reigning preconception to rule unchallenged.[41]

An ideological political culture can also make cognitive inertia and rigidity more likely. Analysts working in a highly ideological setting are more likely to have strong preconceptions based on faith rather than evidence. Moreover, the fervor with which beliefs are held in an ideological culture increases the pressure on analysts to conform to the prevailing consensus.

Finally, the degree to which analysts must take responsibility for events and the severity of consequences should they be wrong can lead analysts, once they have committed themselves to a stand, to preserve their beliefs and discount any dissonant information. Even in the face of mounting evidence that their beliefs are wrong, analysts can believe all the more firmly in their initial beliefs, given that any reconsideration of their perspective would tend to overturn their growing commitment.

Psychological Factors in Counterintelligence

Counterintelligence activities center on the attempt to prevent foreign intelligence services from infiltrating or hindering one's government, especially one's intelligence service. Counterintelligence involves the identification, neutralization, and manipulation of foreign intelligence services. Counterintelligence activities can be divided into domestic and foreign counterintelligence. The domestic and foreign aspects may be combined in one organization, as with the KGB in the Soviet Union, or split between two organizations, as in the United States. Furthermore, many armies of the world possess counterintelligence units.

What sorts of psychological problems can beset counterintelligence? First, preconceptions or prior beliefs can lead to premature cognitive closure. This seems to have been a factor in the Philby case. Kim Philby was an intelligence officer in the British Secret Intelligence Service (SIS, also known as MI6). Philby came from the right class background and the right schools. Over time, he rose to prominence in British counterintelligence and was responsible for liaison with U.S. counterintelligence. Given Philby's class background, many thought it inconceivable that he would commit treason. Moreover, given his position in British counterintelligence, few, including even James Angleton of U.S. counterintelligence, ever considered the possibility that Philby might be a "mole" for the KGB when in fact he was.

We find a more serious problem in the mental set for counterintelligence. The ability to see and uncover deceit lies at the heart of the job of a specialist in counterintelligence. The nature of the job and the training for it establishes a mental set alert to the possibility of deception. The situation of the counterintelligence expert is not unlike that of the subjects in an experiment involving the training of radar operators. Subjects who played the role of operators were told to count the number of "enemy" and "friendly" blips on a radar screen. The number of enemy and friendly signals never changed across subjects, although one group of subjects was told to be sure not to let one enemy get through. A second group of subjects was told to make sure that no friendly blips were mistaken for enemy blips since accidental downings had to be avoided. The first group, the one with a mental set to catch all the enemies, counted more enemies than actually existed.[42]

Drawing on this research, we can posit that counterintelligence experts may begin to see more guile around them than actually exists. In a sense, to be good at the job one must develop a touch of paranoia. One must suspect conspiracy and trickery when all others least suspect it. But this is not irrational: conspiracy can exist. In fact, the risk always exists that the counterintelligence expert is right. Moreover, conspiracy can have psychological appeal as an explanation because it represents a single, all-encompassing explanation.

Unrestrained counterintelligence, then, can damage other intelligence capabilities. At the very least, it can create confusion and slow work throughout an intelligence service. The fear of penetration or manipulation by a foreign intelligence service can lead to a hesitancy in accepting facts or agents as genuine. As the standards of proof are increased before the existence of defectors or information is accepted as true, paralysis ensues. One finds a good illustration of this in the United States, where the head of U.S. counterintelligence, James Angleton, believed a high-level "mole" existed in the CIA. Angleton's nearly obsessive search for a possible "mole" crippled liaison with foreign services and reduced the number of clandestine operations that were undertaken. Which agents could be trusted? Which were genuine defectors? No one was certain. In fact, several years later, some observers have suggested that Angleton would have been the perfect mole given the debilitating effect of his search on CIA operations.[43]

Another problem with unrestrained counterintelligence lies in the state of continuous alarm. To the degree that the mental set involved in counterintelligence sets off too many alarms, the dilemma of alerts may occur. Too many alarms lead to their routinization. Intelligence offices classify a new alarm as simply another false alarm. They begin to lose their sensitivity to alarms and so may discount any that occur, thereby becoming vulnerable to foreign manipulation.

Finally, the fear of deception in counterintelligence can ultimately lead to what Angleton aptly called a "wilderness of mirrors,"[44] which occurs when an officer loses his or her bearings and sense of perspective. Kahneman and Tversky, two psychologists, offer a possible explanation based on their findings—namely, that the greater the availability or accessibility of events in memory, the greater the probability or frequency assigned to the event. Adapting this "availability heuristic" (as they call it) to the concerns here, one can posit that because counterintelligence experts are able to conceive of the possibility of some foreign intrigue, their conception changes their estimate of likelihood from a "possibility" to a "probability." Accordingly, counterintelligence experts may overdramatize the significance of foreign intrigue when they find it, seeing intrigue as the sole cause for events abroad. Worse, they may see intrigue where little or none exists.[45] In an extreme case, an intelligence officer might perceive every failure in intelligence and policy to be the result of foreign intrigue; so, too, every success, for he or she will believe success has been granted by the opponent as bait to set the stage for further deception. At this point, facts will begin to lose their weight and misconceptions will reign. Angleton's view that the Sino-Soviet dispute was a charade designed to lull the West into complacency seems to offer a good example of this problem.[46]

Psychological Factors in Covert Action

The area of covert action, unlike the other three areas, is used as a tool to accomplish the goals of a nation's foreign policy. In this area, intelligence organizations influence people and events in foreign countries by means of activities in which their hand is deliberately concealed. By acting through indigenous elements in a society, covert operators establish plausible deniability; that is, they limit the traceability of events back to their organizations.

Psychological factors can operate with especially strong force in this area. First, covert action brings an operating responsibility into play, such that cognitive dissonance and ego enhancement can be especially powerful. Second, the decentralized nature of covert activity and the greater compartmentation of the people carrying it out give freer reign to psychological factors. Small groups of people operate more independently in the absence of close day-to-day scrutiny.

Several of the psychological factors discussed earlier, such as premature cognitive closure, appear in this area of activity. Other phenomena are distinctive to the area of covert action. One such distinctive feature is "tactical fixation," which grows out of the mental set associated with operators. For operators, the implementation of a plan and the achievement of tactical goals must be paramount. Task incentives and the information of greatest concern frequently narrow an operator's cognitive focus to a short-term concern with getting the job done. Tactical fixation can occur both in the planning of operations and in the evaluation of the success of the operation after it is carried out.

Tactical fixation can create several problems. First, operators may not work long enough to build the local assets that are necessary for the covert action project. There is a tendency to want to use whatever assets are available and to try to get the job done as quickly as possible. Moreover, operators may fail to consider the effects of a "blown" covert action project on the collection and counterintelligence assets within a country.[47] The short-term covert action project, once it is publicly known, can damage or totally eliminate other intelligence capabilities that are long term in nature. Finally, operators working with a tactical fixation may lose sight of the fact that one can "win the battle but lose the war."[48] Operators may achieve the short-term goal of influencing or changing another government's policy or its leadership but fail to consider the long-term effects of covert action. Will covert action solve or worsen the country's problems? Will influence be greater or less in the future as a result of covert action? Operators often fail to ask these questions.

An incremental adjustment to new information can also hinder effective covert action. Operators in the field are more likely to receive information bit by bit rather than in one large batch. When this occurs, operators tend to adjust their views incrementally without reevaluating their basic premises.[49] They are also apt to dismiss as unimportant any dissonance they perceive between the information they receive and their prior beliefs and commitments. Thus information contradicting their views and even information indicating imminent failure may go unnoticed by operators.[50] Several retired operators have indicated that operations can continue, in some cases for several years, without any overall evaluation. To the degree that an intelligence organization adopts a graduated approval process for covert action, the probability of incremental adjustment increases.

In explaining the failure of the Bay of Pigs operation, many of those involved indicated that incremental adjustment played a role. Several of the planners have indicated that the project was based upon a key premise—the existence of an anti-Castro resistance network in Cuba. Although in this instance any invasion force of exiles would have been small, the plan was that it should serve only as a signal for a large-scale indigenous insurrection. Initially this plan seemed effective enough, but over time information came in that indicated the network of anti-Castro resistance did not exist. Rather than reexamining their basic premises, however, the operators simply altered their tactical plans to accommodate reality. No one put all the pieces together to see that the operational plan was unrealistic. Operators ended up trying to conduct a conventional military invasion with exile forces too small ever to succeed.[51]

A third psychological problem, known as operators' bias, can plague covert action.[52] Operators in the field have several advantages. They are closer to events and so have better information about them, and they usually have more experience in interpreting the information. Nonetheless, operators can be biased. First, their ego and the prestige of their organization are on the line. If they encounter information discrepant from their beliefs, they are more likely to reject the facts and preserve their beliefs. Second, operators best know their own plans and activities; that is, they have more information about their own activities than they do about their opponent's activities. Accordingly, they will more likely overestimate their degree of control (or leverage) over events.

This operators' bias produces what we might call a "paradox of operators." In strategic planning, when they survey the overall world scene, operators will tend to be overly pessimistic. Their task incentives (or mental set) and their uncertainty often introduce a worst-case logic into their thinking. Operators will overemphasize the degree of threat in the world and the need to utilize covert action capabilities to balance this threat. A worst-case logic can lead in the extreme to unnecessary escalation in covert action.

Paradoxically, operators often engage in a best-case logic in evaluating specific plans and operations; in particular, they tend to be overly optimistic in forecasting the likelihood of success and in evaluating their past records. This optimism proceeds in part from the ego-enhancing bias mentioned earlier. In other words, operators will tend to attribute any success to their skills and ability while attributing any failures to external factors such as chance, the failure of indigenous agents, or a lack of support by the leaders of a government. The more important the task and the greater the personal commitment of operators, the more likely this tendency is to destroy judgment.[53]

Best-case logic operates for a second reason as well. Operators generally overestimate their leverage or control over events.[54] Since they know their own plans best of all, and since they possess a faith in their ability to control events, operators tend to ignore or downplay factors not under their control. In many cases, operators simply fail to pay enough attention to the problem to solve it.[55] "Don't worry," they say; "we'll solve that part later." When this occurs, the results are overly optimistic reports of progress on current projects and unduly gilded evaluations of past projects.

Operators' bias occurs in many parts of a nation's government and armed forces, but it is in the area of covert action, given its organizational structure, that this bias has the freest reign. Because covert action projects are highly compartmented, activities are often insulated from outside advice and criticism. Operators may be the planners, implementors, and evaluators of their own projects with little other than a cursory review from their superiors.

Insulation of this magnitude suggests a final psychological problem: that of "groupthink."[56] According to Irving Janis, groupthink occurs when the members of a highly cohesive group allow their feelings toward the group to distort their individual capacity to reason. In other words, group processes interfere with individual reasoning. What happens, according to Janis, is that a consensus on the issue of discussion emerges within a group. This consensus is then protected from critical appraisal by collective rationalizations, self-censorship, a group pressure on deviants to conform, and the emergence of "mindguards" who protect the group consensus by attacking adverse information. When groupthink occurs, it produces assessments based on stereotyped views of opponents as weak, evil, or stupid. It also leads to an unexamined faith in the group's inherent ability and morality and to a shared illusion of invulnerability. As a result, members of the group approach problems simplistically and fail to look critically at their deliberations and beliefs.[57]

A major problem with the concept of groupthink is that it has been applied indiscriminately in research. It has been mistaken on occasion for bureaucratic consensus or national mood; and when (incorrectly) applied to organizations or nations, it stretches the concept to the point where its meaning in lost. Properly speaking, groupthink pertains only to deliberations within a small, informal group--not to large collectivities, such as nations, that never meet as a group. People in formal organizations or large collectivities may agree on a common set of beliefs that they fail to reexamine, but uncritical agreement is not sufficient for applying the concept of groupthink. In these cases, one can talk about individual compliance and obedience or about conformity and consensus, but not about groupthink. Hence the usefulness of the concept of groupthink in political analysis is somewhat limited.

Covert action task forces may be one of the few instances in government that does lend itself to discussion of groupthink.[58] Several authors, including Janis, have suggested that groupthink occurs in covert-action projects. In fact, one of Janis's case studies concerns the Bay of Pigs operation run.

Covert action task forces do have several of the traits that Janis believes cause groupthink. For instance, group members are similar in background and values. Task forces are usually small and highly cohesive. More important, due to compartmentation, these task forces are far more insulated from outsiders than are most groups in government.

To the degree that groupthink does occur in covert action, task forces will fail to survey adequately the alternatives, to plan realistically for possible obstacles and mistakes, and to reevaluate their plans when disconfirming evidence of failure emerges.

CONCLUSION

In the preceding sections of this chapter, I have described several of the concepts in psychology that are most useful in analyzing the management of intelligence activities and illustrated their operation in historical cases. Due to limits of space, however, I have not been able to provide either definitive case studies or an exhaustive survey of psychological concepts. Nonetheless, this chapter does demonstrate that a cognitive perspective is useful in understanding intelligence activities; ideally, it will inspire other researchers to develop further the scholarship in this area.

A psychological perspective might even highlight the reforms that are potentially available to us—including, for instance, competitive analysis, which can reduce the power of preconceptions. Yet there are limits to the reforms that can be made. Many of the reforms that might conceivably control psychological factors would be too costly in time or resources. Moreover, one cannot entirely eliminate psychological factors from intelligence organizations, because, in the end, intelligence activities are carried out by people who must reason, think, and act as best they can in a world that is inherently uncertain.

Even so, the psychological perspective can make an important contribution. Analysis of the psychological dimension of intelligence activities will sensitize practitioners to the operation of psychological factors, and their growing awareness of the "symptomatology" for congitive maladies will improve their reasoning—thereby rendering their management of intelligence more deft in the long run.

NOTES

1. Karl von Clausewitz, On War, edited by Anatol Rapoport (New York: Penguin Books, 1968), pp. 116-117, 140.
2. An increasing number of books and articles have analyzed

deception. See, for example, Donald Daniel and Katherine Herbig, Strategic Military Deception (New York: Pergamon Press, 1982).

3. U.S., Congress, House Select Committee on Intelligence, U.S. Intelligence Agencies and Activities: Risks and Control of Foreign Intelligence, Hearings before the Select Committee on Intelligence, 94th Congress, 1st Session (1975), p. 1689.

4. Another intangible element of power that can be difficult to estimate is morale. Morale is important on four levels: the morale of an opponent's forces, the morale of the government, the morale of an opponent's allies, and the morale of the population.

5. Richard K. Betts, Strategic Surprise (Washington, D.C.: Brookings Institution, 1983), p. 115.

6. Major Gen. Chaim Herzog, The War of Atonement: October 1973 (Boston: Little, Brown, 1975), pp. 9, 194; Ail Shlaim, Failures in National Intelligence Estimates, "The Case of the Yom Kippur War," World Politics XXVIII (April 1976): 178; Betts, Strategic Surprise, pp. 114-115. Betts describes the Egyptian use of SAMs as a substitute for offensive air superiority.

7. U.S., Senate, Select Committee to Study Governmental Operations with Respect to Intelligence Activities, Foreign and Military Intelligence, Book I (Washington, D.C.: Government Printing Office, 1976), p. 267.

8. See a discussion of the same point in Richard K. Betts, "Analysis, War and Decision: Why Intelligence Failures Are Inevitable," in Klaus Knorr, ed., Power, Strategy, and Security (Princeton, N.J.: Princeton University Press, 1983), p. 219.

9. See Roberta Wohlstetter, Pearl Harbor: Warning and Decision (Stanford: Stanford University Press, 1962); see also Barton Whaley, Codeword Barbarossa (Cambridge, Mass.: MIT Press, 1973).

10. For instance, see Walter Mischel, Personality and Assessment (New York: Wiley & Sons, 1968); and, by the same author, "Toward a Cognitive Social Learning Reconceptualization of Personality," Psychological Review 80 (1973): 252-283.

11. George A. Kelly, A Theory of Personality (New York: Norton, 1965), p. 26.

12. Fritz Heider, The Psychology of Interpersonal Relations (New York: John Wiley & Sons, 1958).

13. One can also say that beliefs serve as lenses or filters through which an individual sees the world.

14. U.S. Senate, Foreign and Military Intelligence, pp. 274-275. See also pp. 272-273 for a description of how pressure from top-level leaders in the U.S. government leads to a "current events syndrome" in the Directorate of Intelligence of the CIA.

15. Ibid., pp. 268-269.

16. Betts, "Analysis, War and Decision," pp. 219-220.

17. David C. Martin, Wilderness of Mirrors (New York: Random House, 1980), pp. 76-90.

18. Robert Jervis, Perception and Misperception in International Politics (Princeton, N.J.: Princeton University Press, 1976), pp. 203-218.

19. A sample of the drawing and a discussion of mental sets can be found in Albert H. Hastorf, David J. Schneider, and Judith Polefka, Personal Perception (Reading, Mass.: Addison-Wesley, 1970), pp. 4-5.

20. For a general discussion of the impact of mental sets within

organizations, see Daniel Katz and Robert L. Kahn, The Social Psychology of Organizations (New York: John Wiley & Sons, 1978), pp. 487-488, 494, 502-503.

21. Whaley, Codeword Barbarossa, pp. 45, 86, 118, 127, 202-203.

22. Collectors is a term used broadly to include personnel in the NKVD, the GRU (Soviet intelligence directorate), Foreign Ministry, and the Soviet armed forces.

23. Whaley, Codeword Barbarossa, pp. 47, 54.

24. Jeffrey Race, War Comes to Long An: Revolutionary Conflict in a Vietnamese Province (Berkeley: University of California Press, 1972.)

25. I am not so much addressing the appropriateness of standard operating procedure as simply making the point that directives and doctrines do establish mental sets that then affect the type of information collected.

26. Jervis, Perception and Misperception, pp. 122-128.

27. Jonathan L. Freedman, David O. Sears, and J. M. Carlsmith, Social Psychology (Englewood Cliffs, N.J.: Prentice-Hall, 1981), pp. 168-169, 189.

28. Presumably the references are to the aura of angels and the shadow of devils.

29. These conditions are adapted from Jervis's summary of psychological evidence, in Perception and Misperception, p. 122.

30. Roberta Wohlstetter, "Cuba and Pearl Harbor: Hindsight and Foresight," Foreign Affairs (July 1965), p. 699.

31. Whaley, Codeword Barbarossa, pp. 45, 63, 65, 68, 178, and passim.

32. See Freedman et al., Social Psychology, pp. 310-333. For a more elaborate concept of the consensus effect, see also Irving L. Janis, Groupthink: Psychological Studies of Policy Decisions and Fiascoes (Boston: Houghton Mifflin, 1982).

33. See Betts, "Analysis, War and Decision," p. 211, 218, 220; see also Chester Cooper's review of the appreciation of CIA estimates on Vietnam by top officials in "The CIA and Decision Making," Foreign Affairs 50 (1972): 223-236.

34. For instance, see the report in the Economist (June 19, 1982), p. 88.

35. For a description, see Betts, Strategic Surprise, p. 95.

36. See Jervis, Perception and Misperception, p. 344.

37. See a brief discussion of the problem of simplistic reasoning in organizations in Katz and Kahn, Social Psychology of Organizations, pp. 507-508.

38. For a fuller treatment, see Jervis, Perception and Misperception, pp. 319-328.

39. Richard Neustadt indicates that this can be a problem for policymakers as well. See his Alliance Politics (New York: Columbia University Press, 1970).

40. U.S. Senate, Foreign and Military Intelligence, pp. 76-78.

41. Shlaim, "Failures in National Intelligence Estimates," p. 184.

42. See D. Kahneman and A. Tversky, Psychological Review 80 (1973): 237-251; and Freedman et al., Social Psychology, pp. 122-123.

43. Martin, Wilderness of Mirrors, p. 206-212.

44. Martin, Wilderness of Mirrors, p. 205. (Martin uses the phrase as the title of his book.)

45. Ibid., pp. 209-210.

46. Ibid., pp. 149-150, 200-203.

47. See, for instance, Martin, Wilderness of Mirrors, p. 121.

48. This point was made by Richard Bissell in a personal conversation with the author, August 1981.

49. See Jervis, Perception and Misperception, pp. 308-310, for a discussion of the psychological evidence.

50. Ibid., pp. 382-399.

51. These points were made in conversations with the author by retired officers, including Richard Bissell.

52. See Betts's discussion of a similar point in "Analysis, War and Decision," pp. 214-215, 217.

53. See Freedman et al., Social Psychology, pp. 67-68.

54. For instance, see the summary in Freedman et al., Social Psychology, pp. 161-162.

55. See Jervis, Perception and Misperception, p. 234, for a general discussion of this concept.

56. For a full elaboration of this concept, see Janis, Groupthink.

57. Ibid., pp. 174-177, 242-259.

58. The other cases would seem to be (1) meetings of the top political leadership, such as those of the National Security Council and those of the top White House staffers in the United States or those of the Politburo in the Soviet Union and (2) meetings of interagency groups.

Intelligence and Decisionmaking

INTRODUCTION

This chapter[1] seeks to apply the findings of studies of misperception in international politics to the intelligence community. These studies of misperception have made extensive use of the findings of cognitive psychology. In particular, I will investigate the vulnerabilities of decisionmakers and analysts to misperception, the activities of community management and the collection and reporting of intelligence, the two principal modes of decisionmaking—the analytic and the cybernetic—and the implications of those misperceptions that seem most threatening to the principal activities in the intelligence community.

MODES OF DECISIONMAKING

The opportunities that intelligence and its nemesis, misperception, have to influence decisionmaking depend strongly on how those decisions are made. The analytic mode is the style considered the most familiar and the one most often presumed when the role of intelligence is being examined. The cybernetic mode, while less well known, is more commonly used by decisionmakers, especially for routine or well understood decision problems.

The Analytic Mode of Decisionmaking

This mode of decisionmaking is so well known that, rather than discuss it extensively, I will take the more interesting approach of describing how it is influenced by intelligence. The contribution of intelligence directly to the decision and to its context will both be discussed.

Intelligence is not essential to decisionmaking; knowledgeable decisionmakers can often make decisions without any additional information. Hence the contribution of intelligence is in improving the decisionmakers' ability to choose. Intelligence adds to the decisionmakers' understanding of their decisions by refining either their understanding of the choices that can be made or their understanding of the context of the problem. Refinement of understanding of the choice is accomplished by confirming or changing the number of alternatives, the consequences of the alternatives, the timing of the consequences, or the confidence that the number of alternatives and their consequences and timing is correctly understood.

The number of alternatives can be increased by intelligence that reveals a new possibility or decreased by intelligence that reveals that one of the alternatives under consideration is either infeasible or obviously unattractive. The estimated consequences of the alternatives can be revised on the basis of intelligence. Indeed, this is the classic view of the role of intelligence, although that view focuses too often on the narrowest view of consequences. The consequences of choosing an alternative include the expected outcome (as well as any other possibilities), the likelihood of each of the possible outcomes, their nature, and their timing. Timing is identified separately because of its importance in intelligence support to decisionmaking.

The timing of the consequences of an alternative often determines how quickly the decision must be made. If an attractive alternative must be selected quickly in order for its consequences to be realized, then both the intelligence support and the decisionmaking must be done quickly. Implicit in a quickly-made decision is the implication that the potential contribution of any additional information that would be gained by waiting is not sufficient to justify delay.

This leads to pressure on the intelligence community for prompt support. The need for timely support is often also inherent in the nature of the decision cycle itself. The planning of sorties by aircraft, for example, is done on a daily basis. To influence the current sortie planning cycle, intelligence must arrive early enough in that cycle to be of use in the decisions to be made that day—that is, hours in advance of the commencement of the mission. Thus intelligence in support of that mission is on a 24-hour cycle as well.

Another timing consideration that affects intelligence is perishability. Some information diminishes in value rapidly and must therefore be used quickly. Most transient events such as military exercises, weapon tests, or transport of material or equipment would fall into this category. Although the information to be gained from examining in retrospect the implications of the event can be gained long after the event, any value that such information might have in permitting some action to be taken during or prior to the event can be obtained only if the intelligence is promptly provided and acted on.

Finally, by refining the decisionmakers' understanding of the problem, intelligence can affect their confidence level. This can also be caused by information sources other than intelligence. However, if the intelligence is accurate, then diminishing the confidence of decisionmakers about any aspect of the decision they are confronting is as valuable as increasing their confidence about that same aspect. This is not the decisionmakers' view! Since they did not know they were overconfident until the intelligence arrived, the reduction in confidence is understandably seen as a loss, but they are genuinely better off correctly understanding the degree of uncertainty they face. The distinction to bear in mind is that the purpose of intelligence is to improve decisionmaking, not to make decisionmaking easier.

Three categories of uncertainty exist:

- Categorical uncertainty is actually more appropriately called certainty given the assumption that relations are deterministic (i.e., that an action will always lead to the same result). This is the view of uncertainty that the mind prefers.
- Known probabilities constitute the second category, which is also the favorite of game theorists.
- The third category of uncertainty concerns estimating the probability of an event occurring. Unfortunately for the mind's preferences, this is the category that is characteristic of most reality.

Intelligence also improves decisionmaking by providing a context for the decision. Refinement of the decisionmaker's understanding of the context of the problem is accomplished by confirming or changing the nature of the problem, the formulation of the decision, or the confidence that the nature and formulation are correctly understood.

An improved context makes the decisionmakers better able to judge that the problem is correctly formulated. The first step in making this judgment is to determine that the chain of events and contributing circumstances do in fact substantiate the importance of the problem and lead one to believe that the problem being addressed is the right one. It is in this step that confidence in understanding the nature of the problem is most important.

The next step is to examine the formulation of the decision to determine that the necessary actions will result from the alternatives that are presented. Confidence that the decision is correctly formulated is largely derived from understanding the nature of the problem and from analyzing the decision alternatives.

Intelligence can either contribute to or undermine the decisionmakers' confidence that the nature of the problem is correctly understood and the formulation of the decision is correct. Either case provides equal value to the decisionmakers, although the process of undermining may not be viewed as such. Any intelligence that changes the nature of the decision or the formulation of the problem will also affect the confidence levels associated with those matters; however, it is possible for intelligence to change the confidence levels without affecting the nature or formulation. Most commonly, this latter situation occurs when an important inconsistency is discovered that raises doubts without resolving them. There seems to be an asymmetry here; the discovery of reassuring consistencies is never as persuasive as the discovery of vexing inconsistencies is troubling.

The analytic mode requires value integration on the part of decisionmakers. It is complex and time-consuming to perform and requires intellectual acuity. The devoted users of analysis lack continuity in their decisionmaking if the problems that are being addressed are fluid, ambiguous, or incompletely known.

Even though the analytic mode is far more effective than the cybernetic mode for problems that are both complex and ambiguous, the interaction of complexity and ambiguity greatly increases the cumbersomeness of the analytic mode. Decisionmakers need to simplify. Analysis can provide this simplicity only if it is given ample time and resources. Eventually, analysis will often enable decisionmakers to focus on the few most salient variables and can characterize the extent to which the relationship among those variables is straightforward and stable. Finally, the analytic mode can identify which of the remaining multitude of uncertainties really make a difference to the decision, how they could affect the decision, and the likelihood that the decision will actually be affected.

The extravagance of resources required to apply the analytic mode well limits the number of problems that will be decided in this way. Other, more frugal, approaches are needed as well.

Cybernetic Mode of Decisionmaking

The cybernetic process of decisionmaking bases decisions on a few key variables for which there is information feedback.[2] An elementary example of the cybernetic mode is a thermostat that turns a heater on full blast if the room temperature falls below a predetermined level and keeps the heat on until the room temperature climbs to a predetermined higher level.

This mode is powerful, effective, and widely used. Much of the policymaking process can be viewed as a search for a few simple rules (standard operating procedures) that respond sufficiently well to the environment (information feedback on a few key variables) that the decisionmaking can be left to subordinates. More broadly, the cybernetic mode provides a means of removing or avoiding uncertainty to reduce the burdens of processing information and of dividing problems into segments to avoid organizational conflict. As a consequence, values are disaggregated by segmenting the problem, and thereby avoiding trade-offs among values. Information is used selectively—a great advantage where it is incomplete, ambiguous, or erratic in its availability or where continuity is more highly valued than other considerations. Outcome calculations are not made—a tremendous simplification, but one that can lead decisionmakers astray given that the cybernetic mode ignores what can be the most critical input to their decisions.[3]

Cybernetic Learning. In the cybernetic mode, learning is instrumental. Successful programs are retained and unsuccessful ones are dropped. Cybernetic learning is induced by changes in behavior rather than by the changes in the outcome calculation upon which the analytic mode lies. This learning is only initiated when the currently programmed sequence of actions is insufficient to maintain the critical variables within tolerances. The program is then modified (or a different one is borrowed from another, possibly dissimilar, process) and tried out. This modification continues until all of the critical variables are within tolerance.[4]

Intelligence Support to Cybernetic Decisionmaking. To support decisionmaking in the cybernetic mode, intelligence must recognize and either accommodate or challenge the narrowness of the cybernetic approach to a decision problem. In accommodating cybernetic decisionmaking, intelligence must restrict its support either to providing feedback on the critical variables that have already been accepted or to discovering the means to provide feedback on variables that would be acceptable if the information about them were available.

If the current program has failed to keep the critical variables within tolerance, then intelligence can be of assistance by shortening or otherwise improving the cybernetic learning process. Assisting in the development of a new program or identifying a workable variable to use in lieu of an unmanageable one are ways in which the learning process could be shortened. Demonstrating that the tolerances are inappropriately tight and that the current program is adequate would be another way of assisting.

It is necessary to challenge the appropriateness of the decision process in order to direct attention to intelligence that cannot be provided using aproaches that work within the cybernetic process. To challenge such a process as inadequate, intelligence must directly demonstrate either that the approach is inadequate or that it needs to be modified. Either of these approaches will require substantial evidence presented in terms that are understandable to a cybernetic decisionmaker, especially if the process has no critical variables out of tolerance.

TYPES OF MISPERCEPTIONS

Perception is automatic and not under conscious control.[5] The concern of this chapter is not with motivated distortions of reality (i.e., defense mechanisms), but with misperception caused by the nature of the cognitive factors that are intrinsic to perception. The danger of misperception is not just that it misdirects individual decisions. Misperception also leads to constrained learning. New information and new decision problems are forced to fit into already established conceptual structures without causing any general adjustment of the structure. The formation of new ideas, new inferences, and new perceptions occurs at a lower level of generality, resulting in a more stable but also a less complete understanding than would occur without misperception. Stability and consistency are preserved at the expense of learning.[6]

Cognitive Theory

The main pattern of operation of the mind in cognitive theory is to struggle constantly to impose clear, coherent meaning on events. As a part of this struggle, the mind tends to simplify by using categorical rather than probabilistic judgments. Accordingly, it attempts to identify a single outcome as certain to occur rather than to assign probabilities to a range of outcomes. This tendency is stronger under complex circumstances.

The following discussion focuses on those misperceptions most likely to threaten the effective operation of the intelligence community. Wishful thinking is not included, even though it is commonly presumed to be a problem, because research in cognitive psychology has not found it to be a significant source of misperception. Expectations are the most powerful force in forming misperceptions; when they are not consistent with wishes, it is expectations that dominate.[7]

Excessive Consistency

There is a strong tendency for people to see what they expect to see and to assimilate incoming information in a way that makes the new information consistent with pre-existing images. Rational ways of interpreting evidence (equivalent to the scientific method) are only a loose constraint on ambiguous situations, or data, that do not lead to a unique conclusion. Other methods of achieving consistency are often irrational (in the sense of violating the scientific method) and would be rejected by decisionmakers if they were aware of employing them.[8]

An extreme degree of excessive consistency occurs when a person adopts a number of beliefs, each of which would be sufficient by itself to justify his or her preference. The belief that the choice of constructs rests on many logically independent reasons is irrational when the multitude of reasons is not needed to justify the choice. When the goal is agreed upon, all that is logically needed to affirm a strategy is the belief that it is most likely to work at lowest cost.[9] Dean Acheson's description of Senator Vandenburg is an excellent example of this degree of excessive consistency: "He declared the end unattainable, the means harebrained, and the cost staggering."[10]

Cognitive Dissonance

Unlike the extreme degree of excessive consistency discussed earlier, such that the efforts to add justification seem unnecessary, cognitive dissonance springs from a genuine need to minimize conflict between the individual's own values. The resulting effect on behavior is similar, however, because cognitive dissonance leads to inertia; moreover, after a decision is made, the individual revises his or her value structure to make the relative weights of the values more consistent with the choice that was selected. As a consequence of this revision, the decisionmaker feels more confident that the choice made was the right one; hence the decision is difficult to reverse. The fewer the alternative justifications to force the decisionmaker to decide on a particular alternative, the greater the need to revise the value structure will be. This is because the compulsion to make the decision reduces the dissonance caused by the value conflict. Thus the absence of compulsion or other strong motivation preserves dissonance and leads to a more strongly entrenched attitude subsequent to the decision. This effect appears to be most powerful within the decisionmaker's personal staff.[11]

Differences in Evoked Set

What is on one's mind influences perception.[12] If circumstances or prior experience have stimulated different information and concerns (evoked sets) in the minds of two people, they will have difficulty communicating because their interpretations of ambiguous information or communications will be different.

When General Short, the U.S. Army commander in Hawaii in 1941, was warned of "hostile action," he thought the warning referred to sabotage because that had been the subject of earlier communiques.

Those writing the warning in Washington, D.C., were referring to attack from without and had on their minds the ongoing negotiations with the Japanese as well as the intercepted diplomatic communications of the Japanese that formed the basis for the warning.[13] Given that differences in classified access can also lead to differences in evoked sets, this misperception is more likely to be a problem for the intelligence community than for most other organizations.

In short, decisionmakers overestimate the extent to which each understands what the other is trying to say. They rarely take into account the degree to which the other may be concerned with different tasks and problems.[14]

Prematurely Formed Views

Prematurely formed views spring from a desire for simplicity and stability. When facing a new problem, people often find an idea that seems to put them on the right track. Subsequently, they organize their approach around modifying and testing that hypothesis. The new effect may be to lead them to adopt a view that is difficult to change. If this occurs, even a hint about how to solve a problem will have little impact, because most people will merely assimilate the new information into the approach they have already adopted.[15]

Presumption that Support for One Hypothesis Disconfirms Others

Evidence that is consistent with one's pre-existing beliefs is likely to be taken as disconfirming other views[16]—both a subtle and a common error, but one that is easily overcome. Discussion of a view in isolation from competitive views fosters such a misperception, but when the alternative hypotheses are explicitly included in the discussion, this misperception is readily evident.

Inappropriate Analogies

People often perceive certain past events as analogies because of characteristics of those events that are, from a rational standpoint, irrelevant. For example, they, or their nation, may have participated in these events; the events may have occurred at a time when the people were first forming their political ideas; or the event had important consequences. However, analogies chosen on the basis of irrelevant criteria are more likely to be inappropriate than useful.[17]

Superficial Lessons from History

Too often for decisionmakers, the search for causes is quick and oversimplified. The most salient features of the pre-existing situation and the actor's strategies are seen as causing the most obvious characteristics of the short-run outcome, and no careful examination is made of the links that he or she supposes are present. Few attempts are made to make the comparisons that are necessary to render a judgment on the causal efficacy of the variables. Although the quality of the analysis that precedes the decision can often be faulted, it is almost always much better than that involved in the attempts to understand the causes of past events. Neither immediately after an event nor later, when they use the event as an analogy, do decisionmakers engage in a thorough reconstruction and self-conscious effort to examine critically the proposed causes. When decisionmakers think they know the cause of a previous outcome, they rarely take the next step of looking for other cases in which this variable was present to determine its influence in other situations or of trying to locate additional instances of the same outcome to see whether other causes could produce the same result.[18]

People pay more attention to what happened than to why it occurred. They often mistake factors that are highly specific and situation-bound for more general characteristics. Since the immediate context is not stripped away in such situations, causality is not properly understood and the crucial characteristics of the situation (and the patterns that are likely to recur in the future) are not grasped. Accordingly, decisionmakers are led to apply an analogy from history to many disparate cases with dissimilar situations—the more general and abstract the previous learning, the more help and less barrier the learning is likely to be in future problems. Otherwise, rigidity results.[19] Nothing fails like success. A policy that has brought notable success is likely to be misapplied to a range of later situations.[20]

Presumption of Unitary Action by Organizations

Decisionmakers often see the behavior of others as more planned, centralized, and coordinated than it really is. This is the result of the mind's attempt to simplify and to seek causes, even when some of the perceived actions are accidental or unintentional.

Decisionmakers are also likely to fail to recognize that others will see them as more centralized, planned, and coordinated than they are. This misperception is a variation of the unitary actor misperception, but the variation in this case is the failure to recognize that others are also subject to misperception.

Decisionmakers are likely, as well, to overestimate their importance as a source of influence or as a target. The need to simplify again misleads. If every action is to be explained, an excessive number of the actions of others will be attributed to the decisionmakers, since many of the reasons for an action will not be evident to them, including accidents and actions taken without any thought at all of the decisionmakers. Those actions caused by accidents are very difficult to differentiate. It is easier to identify those intended to affect people other than the decisionmakers once that possibility has been recognized.

Conservatism in Probability Estimation

Given the general desire to avoid the risk associated with extremely confident predictions, a tendency exists to avoid estimating extremely high or extremely low probabilities. Events that are very likely to occur (for example, a probability above 95 percent) or very likely not to occur (a probability below 5 percent) are treated as less predictable than they actually are.[21]

Undersized Confidence Intervals in Subjective Probability Estimates

Tests have been conducted in which individuals are asked first to estimate a statistic they are very unlikely to know and then to bracket the estimate with a range outside of whose upper bound the true answer would be found only 20 percent of the time. When the ranges specified by a number of different respondents to a number of different questions were examined, the true answers were found to be outside the range significantly more than the 20 percent that the procedure should have produced if people were unbiased in their estimates. The implication is that the range is routinely undersized; in other words, people are overconfident about their subjective estimates.

RESISTANCE TO ATTITUDE CHANGE

The cognitive processes and misperceptions discussed earlier all contribute to attitude preservation. Nine distinct steps or gradations can be observed in an individual's attempts to protect against attitude change. These steps are likely to occur in association with any of the aforementioned misperceptions. These are listed below in the order in which they would be most likely to be taken:

1. Deny that the information is discrepant with the attitude.
2. Challenge the validity of the discrepant information.
3. Discredit the source of the discrepant information.
4. Admit that the discrepant information is valid, but do not incorporate its implications into the attitude; characterize the discrepancy as puzzling or as a mystery.
5. Develop new data and arguments to support the existing attitude. Referred to as bolstering, this step also includes rearrangement of attitudes to minimize the impact of the discrepant information.
6. Develop new data and arguments to attack the discrepant information. This is referred to as undermining. Attacking the source also contributes to undermining but occurs earlier in the sequence.
7. Split the attitude that is causing attitude conflict in a way that minimizes the amount of change. This is referred to as differentiation.
8. Combine rather than split up elements of the attitude being protected into larger units on a superordinate level. This is referred to as transcendence.
9. If the attitude must be changed, then change those elements that are least central to the attitude first. This is referred to as centralization.[22]

COMMUNICATING WITH DECISIONMAKERS

It is a truism to say that decisionmakers who use intelligence are busy and have little time to consider all of the ramifications of what they read, whether it is intelligence or other material. They still have a need for understanding many of the aspects and details of their area of responsibility. Only some of these aspects will be evident to intelligence analysts. As a result of decisionmakers' need for broad understanding and the little time that they have for reflection, they are particularly vulnerable to misperception. The analyst must assist the decisionmakers in avoiding misperception.

The problem of communicating to decisionmakers appears to have two aspects. First, the manner in which the intelligence is presented should not foster misperception. Misperception would be fostered if intelligence provided evidence that supported the decisionmakers' view, thus falsely giving the impression that others' views were disconfirmed. Second, the presentation of intelligence should anticipate existing misperceptions or decisionmaking modes by presenting the intelligence in a way that maximizes the likelihood the information will be used most effectively by the decisionmaker. For example, cybernetic decisionmakers will find it easiest to accept information that is cast in terms of the critical variables they are monitoring. If that is a feasible option, it should be elected.

To the extent that they affect the success of communicating intelligence, differences between middle- and upper-level decisionmakers should be noted. Middle-level users of intelligence require the detailed information and formal analysis that is characteristic of the bulk of the intelligence product. High-level decisionmakers may lack such expertise and have neither the time nor the inclination to develop it. The insights they require are varied. What they seek from intelligence is insight into the decision that they must make as well as information that is relevant to it but unavailable from other sources. Alternately, they seek support for a decision that has already been made. Because of their lack of background, they are more receptive than those of the middle level to new concepts and information. However, their need for brevity, pertinence, and timeliness is much greater. The result of these special needs is often a communication that is specifically directed to them.[23]

Excessive Consistency

Much additional information that decisionmakers need to know is likely to be incorporated into their understanding by presuming excessive consistency. If this tendency is recognized as the intelligence product is written, many potential errors of understanding can be anticipated and perhaps avoided.

Analytic decisionmakers are the more vulnerable to excessive consistency because they rely more on a greater variety of information and have a much more complex decisionmaking process. One aspect of excessive consistency is the way in which complex but strongly categorized information is recalled; another is the extension of the arguments in the report to other related matters.

Decisionmakers are likely to simplify systematically the

complexity by presuming consistency with categories and to remember with greater detail the relationships between the categories. A hypothetical example would be a report that discussed Soviet decisionmaking in great detail. Distinctions between the decisionmaking of the Soviet Army and the civilian leadership can be expected to be recalled more accurately and with a better understanding of fine distinctions than can distinctions within those categories.

The presumption of excessive consistency may underlie the original choice of the cybernetic approach over the analytic. If so, and if the decisionmakers consider all of the critical variables to be within tolerance, then it may become necessary to challenge the decision mode itself.

Cognitive Dissonance

Cognitive dissonance is one of the most dangerous misperceptions. An avoidance of it by decisionmakers requires knowledge of, or accurate surmise about, their value structures. Given the potentially serious consequences of cognitive dissonance, precautions should be taken whenever there is a reasonable likelihood that this misperception may be fostered by the intelligence product.

Difficult choices that require the resolution of conflict between important values are characteristic of analytic decisionmakers. In order for such decisionmakers to make a decision, the value conflict must be resolved. Once that occurs, the tendency will be very strong to revise the relative weight of the values to strengthen the decisionmakers' confidence that they did, indeed, make the right decision. Since the resolution of value conflict is the very essence of the decisionmakers' responsibility in this mode of decisionmaking, it cannot, and should not, be avoided.

The cybernetic mode attempts to avoid value trade-offs by decisionmakers. If such trade-offs cannot be avoided, the general reaction of the decisionmaker will be the same as that associated with the analytic mode.

Differences in Evoked Set

Pronounced differences exist between intelligence officers and the decisionmakers who rely on the intelligence provided by these officers in terms of their concerns and knowledge. The temperaments of analysts and decisionmakers often vary as well. These differences can become significant impediments to communication if the interpretations of meaning they provoke are not somehow anticipated during the writing of the intelligence product or remedied in subsequent personal interactions.

Prematurely Formed Views

This is another very dangerous misperception given that its result is the very antithesis of the purpose of intelligence. When decisionmakers are presented with an incompletely defined problem, there is always the danger they will adopt an approach or view that they will be reluctant to relinquish when additional evidence inconsistent with the preliminary view is made available. Although analytic decisionmakers are more likely to engage in activities that may lead to this misperception, they are also more likely to recognize the need to review additional evidence. Both types of decisionmakers are vulnerable, but the consequences are greater for the cybernetic decisionmakers. The precautions are different for the two modes as well.

Presumption that Support for One Hypothesis Disconfirms Others

Nothing about the decisionmaking procedures of either the analytic or cybernetic modes predisposes one more than the other to this misperception; however, analytic decisionmakers are more likely to be influenced in their decisionmaking. This presumption is primarily caused by the way information is presented. It is a fundamental responsibility of the intelligence community to avoid misleading consumers in this way.

Inappropriate Analogies

Both analytic and cybernetic decisionmakers are susceptible to the adoption of inappropriate analogies. It is very difficult to anticipate the experiences of individuals that might lead them to use inappropriate criteria for selecting an analogy, although it may be possible to discover after the fact that the criteria are inappropriate for the more senior decisionmakers. It is quite likely that other inappropriate analogies can be anticipated. Situations that have a superficial similarity to significant national experiences such as the landing of a man on the moon or the Cuban Missile Crisis are logical candidates.

Superficial Lessons from History

Both modes of decisionmaking are vulnerable to this misperception, but the consequences for each are very different. Analytic decisionmakers tend to be misled about individual decisions; however, if the cybernetic decisionmakers rely on a superficial interpretation of history in selecting the critical variables or in establishing their procedures, then the misperception may ultimately affect many of their decisions. In the case of this misperception, the precaution is similar for the two modes but the timing is different.

Presumption of Unitary Action by Organizations

This is an extremely common presumption. It is being used in this chapter, in fact, since it is more convenient to refer to decisionmakers as individuals than as groups, particularly when examining psychological conditions that can occur only on the level of the individual. For this reason, it is quite common to speak of individual action when the subject may be a group or even a collection of groups that are acting together. As a consequence of this practice, the presumption of unitary action is a common misperception affecting analytic and cybernetic decisionmakers alike.

The three common aspects of this presumption are the tendency to see the behavior of others as more planned, centralized, and coordinated than it is; the failure to recognize that others will see the decisionmakers as more centralized, planned, and coordinated than they are; and the overestimation of one's importance as an influence or target.

Conservatism in Probability Estimation

The tendency toward estimating probabilities in the region of 50 percent leads decisionmakers to be excessively uncertain. Analytic decisionmakers are most affected by this misperception, because their decisions are more precisely attuned to the information they are provided. Cybernetic decisionmakers are not likely to be affected by a modest reduction of a very high probability or the modest increase of a very low one.

Undersized Confidence Intervals in Subjective Probability Estimates

Analytic decisionmakers are more likely to be affected by excessive confidence about a subjective probability than are cybernetic decisionmakers. However, both can be misled, because the errors associated with this process can range much further. Where conservatism in probability estimation can be thought of as shading the probabilities toward 50 percent, the process of adding confidence intervals about the subjective estimate then becomes a matter of guessing about the accuracy of guessing and can occasionally result in large errors.

CONCLUSION

All of these misperceptions can lead to a resistance to attitude change that has great inertia. Analytic decisionmakers are most vulnerable to excessive consistency, cognitive dissonance, and the presumption that support for one hypothesis disconfirms others. All three misperceptions can significantly affect their ability to use intelligence to make effective decisions. Several precautions should be taken to minimize this effect. First, key inconsistencies should be emphasized to overcome the natural tendency to minimize them. Second, if additional information will soon be available, and if time permits, the decisionmakers should be encouraged to postpone their decisions until all the facts are before them. In this way, all of the information will be weighed by the same means, thus avoiding the effects of cognitive dissonance. Third, all contending hypotheses should be addressed in any analysis presented to the decisionmakers so as   to counter the tendency to conclude that the unaddressed hypotheses have been disconfirmed.

Cybernetic decisionmakers are most vulnerable to being misled by superficial lessons from history and by prematurely formed views. These misperceptions are most likely to occur when a set of standard operating procedures is being established or modified because the procedures have not worked. Two precautions exist that should be taken by cybernetic decisionmakers. First, obvious historical parallels to the issue under discussion should be addressed in the course of analysis. Those that are illogical should be explicitly identified as such, especially those superficial comparisons already known to be in use. Second, when the understanding of the problem under consideration is very incomplete, that incompleteness and the inadequacy of the available information should be acknowledged as such so that premature adoption of views can be avoided. If formed, these premature views may also influence the design of standard operating procedures.

Perhaps more than in most activities in which a large number of people need to communicate in order to get the job done, the intelligence field has a great deal of room for misperception and miscommunication. This chapter has pointed to some of the psychological causes of misperception and misapplication of intelligence by decisionmakers in the hopes of fostering such an awareness of these problems that they may actually become part of the solution.

NOTES

1. This paper is an abstract of a larger paper entitled Intelligence and Decisionmaking: Precautions Against Misperception, published by the Department of State's Executive Seminar in National and International Affairs. A copy of the larger paper can be obtained by writing to the author at the Intelligence Community Staff, Washington, D.C. 20505.

2. John D. Steinbruner, The Cybernetic Theory of Decision: New Dimensions of Political Analysis (Princeton, N.J.: Princeton University Press, 1974), p. 86.

3. Ibid., p. 78.

4. Ibid.

5. Robert Jervis, Perception and Misperception in International Politics (Princeton, N.J.: Princeton University Press, 1976), p. 10.

6. Ibid., pp. 137-138.

7. Jervis, Perception and Misperception, p. 361.

8. Ibid., p. 119

9. Ibid., pp. 130-131.

10. Ibid., p. 128.

11. Ibid., pp. 387-403.

12. Ibid., pp. 206-211.

13. Ibid., p. 209.

14. Ibid., p. 218.

15. Ibid., p. 190.

16. Ibid., p. 423.

17. Ibid.

18. Ibid., p. 229.

19. Ibid., p. 228.
20. Ibid., p. 278.
21. Ibid., p. 378.
22. Ibid., pp. 291-300.
23. The preceding points about high-level decisionmaking were made by David L. Aaron, former deputy assistant to the president for National Security Affairs, on May 18, 1984, to the Executive Seminar in National and International Affairs at the State Department's Foreign Service Institute. They are quoted with the permission of Mr. Aaron.

PART 2

Recurring Issues in Intelligence

STRATEGIC SURPRISE

Among the recurring issues of intelligence, the strategic information requirements of the United States deserve special attention. Specifically, the problems associated with efforts to minimize surprise and hence–reduce the effects of an adversary's deception endeavors are of paramount importance.

Michael Handel's study of strategic surprise begins with an historical evaluation of surprise as a force multiplier. He proceeds to identify and discuss methodological dilemmas—signals versus noise, uncertainty and the time factor, intentions and capabilities, estimating risks, self-defeating mobilizations—and ways to overcome perception problems—that is, detailed indications and warnings lists and worst-case analysis.

Handel also investigates the nature of the relationship between the intelligence community and civilian authority, arguing that maintaining the delicate balance between the former's independence and the latter's authority requires constant vigilance. Finally, Handel explores organizational and bureaucratic explanations of the issues of strategic surprise.

Katherine Herbig and Donald Daniel focus specifically on deception—its definition, its process, its likelihood and difficulties, the advantages accruing to the deceiver and the offensive—as well as on counterdeception and the ways to detect, deter, and foil deception efforts.

Handel, Daniel, and Herbig reach, at least in part, remarkably similar conclusions. Despite scholarly efforts to measure deception with precision, far-reaching technological advances in the means of intelligence information gathering, and greater political awareness of the perceptual mechanisms and efforts of the deceiver to undermine the intelligence process, deception remains a powerful tool—particularly in the hands of the astute practitioner—and little progress is apparent in our ability to anticipate strategic surprise.

How to cope with the reality of strategic surprise is the question that remains. Handel argues for a significant increase in our peacetime military capabilities in order to cope with surprise after it has occurred. This debate is an ongoing one, and it demands a knowledgeable electorate capable of making informed choices.

15

MICHAEL I. HANDEL

Strategic Surprise: The Politics of Intelligence and the Management of Uncertainty

INTRODUCTION

The study of strategic surprise can be rather disappointing for those who have always assumed that a better <u>theoretical</u> understanding of the subject at hand would logically lead to the discovery of more effective <u>practical</u> means to anticipate strategic surprise and alleviate its impact. Thus far in its application to the real world, improved insight into the causes and patterns of strategic surprise has made only a negligible contribution to the search for ways to warn of a sudden attack in an accurate and timely fashion. If anything, the increased scrutiny of this phenomenon in recent years has chiefly served to explain why surprise is almost always unavoidable—and will continue to be so in the foreseeable future—despite all efforts to the contrary.

Strategic Surprise as a Force Multiplier

From a military point of view, the advantages derived from achieving strategic surprise are invaluable. A successful unanticipated attack will facilitate the destruction of a sizable portion of the enemy's forces at a lower cost to the attacker by throwing the inherently stronger defense psychologically off balance and thus temporarily reducing the enemy's resistance. Stated in more general terms, the numerically inferior side is able to take the initiative by concentrating superior forces at the time and place of its choosing, thereby vastly improving the likelihood of achieving decisive victory. Thus, strategic surprise is a force multiplier. Clearly, then, the incentive to resort to strategic surprise (as well as to deception) is particularly strong for countries that are only too cognizant of their relative vulnerability. Stronger armies, however, lack the "natural incentive" to employ such methods, and must therefore make a conscious effort to exploit the full potential of strategic surprise if they are to maintain a superior position and achieve more decisive results at a minimal cost.[1]

Although strategic surprise in modern military history has seldom failed in terms of its initial impact, surprising the enemy per se does not necessarily mean that the attacker has reaped the fullest possible benefits or will be assured ultimate victory. There is, in fact, no positive correlation between the initial success of a strategic surprise and the outcome of a war. One reason for this is that the attackers are often so amazed by the effectiveness of their own attack that they are caught unprepared to exploit fully the opportunities it presents. For example, the Japanese did not follow up their success at Pearl Harbor with repeated attacks on U.S. oil depots and other naval and air installations in Hawaii, nor did the Allies take advantage of the opportunities created by their surprise landings in Salerno and Normandy. The same holds true for the Egyptian and Syrian armies in their 1973 attack on Israel: Rigidly adhering to their original plan of attack, they prematurely halted their advance following the first phase of the attack, when they could have continued to make considerable progress at little cost to themselves.

Benefits accruing from a strategic surprise will be maximized to the degree that plans for the attack become flexible and more initiative is delegated to field commanders, who are also encouraged to improvise and accept risks. For example, the Germans very successfully exploited the surprise gained in the opening of their attack on Norway and the West in 1940, and in the earlier stages of their attack on the Soviet Union in 1941, although they failed in this respect during the Ardennes offensive in 1944. In another instance, the Israelis came close to fully exhausting the potential of their unanticipated attack on Egypt in the opening phase of the 1967 war.

Thus accomplishment of the surprise itself is only the first phase of planning; the second phase must consist of detailed preparations for the best possible exploitation of the projected surprise attack. Frequently, this latter objective can be reached through a maxi-max (high-risk/high-gain) strategy as practiced by the Germans in Norway, the Japanese in Singapore, MacArthur in Inchon, and the Israelis in 1967. Yet the whole raison d'être of launching a strategic surprise will collapse if the first stage cannot be followed up by the second.

Surprise in Historical Perspective

Although surprise has always been possible on the tactical level, its feasibility on the strategic level is a relatively new, twentieth-century phenomenon. Before the technological-industrial revolution, rapid movement of large troop formations over long distances in a short period of time was virtually impossible. The slow pace of mobilization, not to mention that of troop concentration and movement, provided ample clues as to an adversary's offensive intent. Furthermore, such evidence could be gathered in time to countermobilize and make preparations to intercept the expected attack. Karl von Clausewitz recognized this, in the belief that strategic surprise was of greater theoretical interest than practical value.

Basically, surprise is a tactical device, simply because in tactics, time and space are limited in scale. Therefore, in strategy, surprise becomes more feasible the closer it occurs to the tactical realm, and more difficult, the more it approaches the higher levels of policy. . . . While the wish to achieve surprise is common and, indeed, indispensable, and while it is true that it will never be completely ineffective, it is equally true that by its very nature surprise can rarely be outstandingly successful. It would be a mistake, therefore, to regard surprise as a key element of success in war. The principle is highly attractive in theory, but in practice it is often held up by the friction of the whole machine. . . . Preparations for war usually take months. Concentrating troops at their main assembly points generally requires the installation of supply dumps and depots, as well as considerable troop movements, whose purpose can be assessed soon enough. It is very rare, therefore, that one state surprises another, either by an attack or by preparations for war [emphasis added].[2]

Indeed, Clausewitz was convinced that, in his time, strategic surprise was not powerful enough to overcome the inherent advantages of the defense.

The immediate object of an attack is victory. Only by means of his superior strength can the attacker make up for all the advantages that accrue to the defender by virtue of his position, and possibly by the modest advantage that his army derives from the knowledge that it is on the attacking, the advancing side. Usually this latter is much overrated: it is short-lived and will not stand the test of serious trouble. Naturally we assume that the defender will act as sensibly and correctly as the attacker. We say this in order to exclude certain vague notions about sudden assaults and surprise attacks, which are commonly thought of as bountiful sources of victory. They will only be that under exceptional circumstances.[3]

In the past, surprise was thus confined to the tactical and grand tactical levels. With the advent of modern technology came the ability to achieve strategic surprise, as well as a change in the modes and aims of surprise, which, in its strategic form, is a much more complex phenomenon. Surprise can now be achieved simultaneously on several different levels: in timing, place of attack, rapidity of movement, use of new delivery and weapons systems, frequent appearance of new doctrines and innovative tactics to match new technologies, as well as in the choice of political-military goals for war itself.[4]

As technological developments have made unprecedented contributions to the feasibility of strategic surprise, warning time has decreased dramatically. During the opening phases of war at the very least, technology significantly enhanced the power of the offense over the defense.

In this manner, then, advanced military technology opened up a highly destabilizing pandora's box. The fact that any country could clandestinely mobilize its armed forces and/or gain a tremendous advantage simply by starting to mobilize its forces first, created a situation in which the reciprocal fear of surprise attack[5] could, under crisis conditions, trigger automatic mobilization responses, loss of control, and preemptive attacks (i.e., become a self-fulfilling prophecy). Having produced optimal conditions for strategic surprise, technology emerged as one of the principal destabilizing factors in the international system of the twentieth century.

242

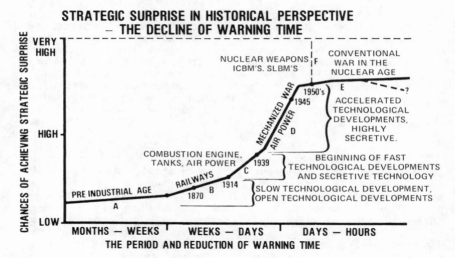

Figure 15.1

(Fig. 15.1 continues on next page)

Figure 15.1 (Part 2)

A. PREINDUSTRIAL AGE. SLOW MOBILITY, LIMITED FIRE POWER. CHANCES OF
A SUCCESSFUL STRATEGIC SURPRISE VERY LOW. (1870)

B. RAILWAY AGE. INCREASED MOBILITY, MOBILIZATION. SLOW INCREASES IN
FIRE POWER. CHANCES OF A SUCCESSFUL STRATEGIC SURPRISE LOW BUT
POSSIBLE. (1870 - 1916)

C. COMBUSTION ENGINES, TRACKED VEHICLES AND TANKS, RISE OF AIR POWER
AND FIRE POWER. MECHANIZED WARFARE BLITZKRIEG. CHANCES OF
STRATEGIC SURPRISE HIGH. (1916 - 1938)

D. FURTHER IMPROVEMENT IN MOBILITY AND FIRE POWER. CHANCES OF
STRATEGIC SURPRISE HIGH — BUT ALSO IMPROVEMENTS TO INTELLIGENCE.
(1939 TO PRESENT)

E. DEVELOPMENT OF NUCLEAR WEAPONS AND LATER ICBMs AND SLBMs
PAR EXCELLENCE THE WEAPONS OF STRATEGIC SURPRISE. WAR CAN BE
DECIDED—THEORETICALLY AND PRACTICALLY IN MINUTES. (1945 TO
PRESENT)

F. IMPROVEMENTS IN CONVENTIONAL MOBILITY AND FIRE POWER. INCREASED
IMPORTANCE OF AIR POWER. HIGH CHANCES OF SUCCESS FOR STRATEGIC
SURPRISE—BUT SLOWED INCREASE GIVEN THE TECHNICAL DEVELOPMENTS
OF RECONNAISSANCE (AIR PHOTOGRAPHY, SATELLITES, ELECTRONIC
INTELLIGENCE). POTENTIAL FOR SURPRISE IS SOMEWHAT LEVELED OFF BY
RECONNAISSANCE AND FAMILIARITY WITH TACTICS OF BLITZKRIEG. YET,
DESPITE ALL THE TECHNOLOGICAL IMPROVEMENTS THAT MAY HELP THE
DEFENSE, THE BASIC PROBLEMS OF ANTICIPATING AN ATTACK ARE
PERCEPTUAL AND PSYCHOLOGICAL AND REMAIN WITHOUT A SATISFACTORY
SOLUTION.

This trend reached its acme with modern nuclear weapons and ICBMs, whose staggering concentrated firepower, capable of being activated in minutes, meant that a strategic surprise could be both the beginning and the end of a war. That which Clausewitz considered to be a strictly theoretical possibility—the idea that a war might be decided by "a single short blow"[6]—has become reality. Technological progress in the last hundred years has reduced the time required for concentrating troops or launching weapons for a strategic surprise from months to weeks and days, and ultimately to hours or even minutes. (See Figure 15.1)

A significant by-product of the military-technological revolution was the tremendous increase in the importance and number of functions assigned to military intelligence. The connection between the rise of technology and that of military intelligence is a subject that has received very little attention from military historians.

In times of little technological progress or change, intelligence and up-to-date information were not of paramount importance because the behavior and strength of one's adversary did not change very frequently. The shape of each war differed only marginally from that of earlier wars. But this is not the case in a world of rapid technological change, where each new weapon and continually changing rates of military industrial production may give the innovator a critical unilateral advantage almost overnight.

Although military technology has revolutionized almost every conceivable aspect of military performance, the one area in which it has made little progress, ironically enough, is that of anticipating surprise attack. The warning gap between the attacker and defender has remained as wide as in the past and still favors the offense over the defense. This will continue to be so, mainly because intelligence work, despite access to electronic monitoring equipment, high-powered computers, and satellites, to name a few advances, is still based on the human factor. As it is labor intensive, intelligence work must reflect human nature, not technological excellence. Intelligence and strategic warning depend upon finding solutions to human problems that sometimes defy technological (or for that matter, any other) solutions. Among these are problems of human psychology and politics, wishful thinking, ethnocentric biases, perception and misperception of reality, conflicting interests, political competition over scarce resources, and organizational biases. As long as people interact with machines in the decisionmaking process, the quality of decisions will be most heavily influenced by the human factor, the complexities of which can be explained but not eliminated.

In the past, it has often explicitly or implicitly been assumed that intelligence work can be pursued by professional, detached experts working within an objective environment and that they will be able to present the truth, as best they can determine it, to policymakers. Policymakers in this scenario will recognize the quality and relevance of the data provided them, and will use this information in the best interests of their country. The "purely rational decisionmaking model" and the belief in the viability of a "strictly professional intelligence process" are but idealized normative fictions. Yet many scholars and even some experienced intelligence experts continue to believe in the possibility of creating—through the "right" reform—the perfect intelligence community. As with Clausewitz's war in practice, the realworld of intelligence is rife with political friction and contradictions, an environment in which uncertainty is the only certain thing.

Past failures in avoiding surprise cannot be blamed on a dearth of information and warning signals. Accordingly, we must look to the levels of analysis and acceptance for the cause of failure.

The major problems stemming from these two levels can be discussed under four principal categories, two of which are primarily related to the analytical process. These are the methodological dilemmas inherent in intelligence work, problems of perception, the level of acceptance of intelligence by leaders, and organizational and bureaucratic problems.

METHODOLOGICAL DILEMMAS

Signals and Noise

Basically, intelligence information can be divided into two types: correct or incorrect, or, as these forms are called in intelligence jargon, signals and noise.[7] Although this dichotomous method of classification is of great theoretical value, in reality it is often impossible to distinguish between signals and noise. To determine the reliability of any single piece of information, analysts need to corroborate it with many other bits of data. Analysis and evaluation is further hampered by the often contradictory nature of the information, which defies a quantitative analysis. Much important data does not lend itself to quantitative presentation because the criteria used to determine its selection, categorization, and corroboration are ultimately determined by human beings, who cannot detach themselves from their ethnocentric biases, preconceived ideas and concepts, and wishful thinking. As a result, in many facets of intelligence work, often no substitute exists for the experience and intuition of the expert. Intelligence must generally be described as an art despite the many scientific disciplines that make critical contributions to its success.

It has been observed that "if surprise is the most important 'key to victory,' then strategem is the key to surprise." The ever-present possibility of deception (defined as the deliberate and subtle dissemination of misleading information to an intelligence service by its adversaries) further complicates the already difficult task of the intelligence analyst.[8]

Since the deceiver intends to present noise as highly trustworthy information, most successful uses of strategem are based on the supply of largely accurate and verifiable data to the adversary. Having worked hard to obtain this information, the adversary is psychologically predisposed to believe it. Thus the intelligence analyst regards most information as suspicious until proven otherwise. This is especially true (1) when the intended deception victims frequently make use of it themselves, as they will be more sensitive to its possible use by adversaries, and (2) when an intelligence organization has been duped, as it thereafter tends to become overcautious. The latter situation can be summarized by this paradox: <u>The more alert one is to deception, the more likely he or she is to become its victim</u>.[9]

Additionally, the better information appears to be—the more readily it fits a neat pattern—the greater must be the analyst's caution. For example, Belgian intelligence obtained German plans for the invasion of the West when a German aircraft carrying two staff officers made a forced landing in Belgium on January 10, 1940. Upon receiving the information, the British and French excluded the possibility that it had been planted for their benefit.[10] The danger here is that the better the information, particularly when based on one source, the less credible it seems to be.

Deception, and uncertainty in general, creates an environment in which almost all information, at least in the short run, is accompanied by a question mark. This gives rise to yet another paradox: "As a result of the great difficulties involved in differentiating between 'signals' and noise in strategic warning, both valid and invalid information must be treated on a similar basis. In effect, all that exists is noise, not signals."[11] Attempts to separate the noise from the signals are aggravated by the fact that collection of additional information also contributes more noise to the system, and the higher the amount of data collected, the more difficult it becomes to filter, organize, and process it in time to be of use.[12]

To be successful, an intelligence organization must strike a balance between the collection and the analysis. If an intelligence organization operates an excellent acquisition and collection mechanism but lacks enough highly qualified experts to process the information in time, excellence in collection may come to naught so far as warning of a strategic surprise attack is concerned. Emphasis on acquisition in the United States and the USSR has resulted in American overreliance on technological intelligence and, in the case of both countries, has led to the collection of so much data that analytical capacities have no doubt been seriously taxed.

Uncertainty and the Time Factor

It is clear that the analytical process of distinguishing between signals and noises requires time. (See Figure 15.2.) Normally, a certain amount of time elapses before the intelligence organization of the "victims" gains some inkling of the attackers' plans. The lead time of the would-be attackers shrinks in direct proportion to the degree of excellence of the prospective victims' intelligence service. By the time the defenders seriously consider the possibility of an attack, the attackers are well ahead of them in their preparations for war. Even then, the defenders-to-be are not yet convinced that they will be attacked; therefore, despite the initial warning, they do not fully mobilize. While the attackers continue preparations, which become increasingly difficult to conceal from the defenders' intelligence, the "victims" may gradually become persuaded of the gravity of the threat and begin to mobilize their own forces. Meanwhile, the attackers have completed preparations and launch their attack. The time lag between the preparations of the two adversaries depends upon the warning received by the defenders and their speed of mobilization. The defenders' actual warning time probably will not coincide with the time required to complete their mobilization. This sequence is typical of strategic surprise that is not "out of the blue" and partly explains

Figure 15.2

THE NORMAL WARNING AND PREPARATION GAP BETWEEN THE ATTACKER AND DEFENDER.
(THIS CHART EMPIRICALLY REFLECTS MOST CASES OF STRATEGIC SURPRISE ATTACKS)

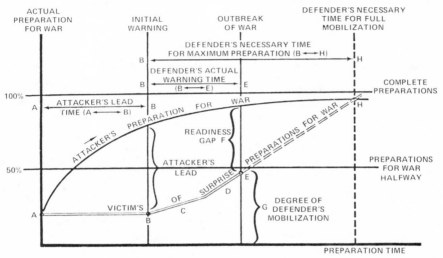

A. ATTACKER STARTS PREPARATIONS FOR WAR.

B. DEFENDER ISSUES INITIAL WARNING, BUT IS
   UNCERTAIN OF THE REAL PROBABILITY OF WAR.

C. DUE TO UNCERTAINTY THE INITIAL PHASE OF
   PREPARATION PROCEEDS RELATIVELY SLOWLY.

D. AS THE PROBABILITY OF WAR INCREASES AND
   BECOMES MORE CERTAIN THE DEFENDER
   ACCELERATES PREPARATIONS.

E. WAR BREAKS OUT, (E.G., SURPRISE ATTACK);
   DEFENDER'S PREPARATIONS INCOMPLETE AND LAG
   BEHIND THE ATTACKER.

F. THE READINESS GAP FAVORING THE ATTACKER.

G. THE DEGREE OF MOBILIZATION COMPLETED BY
   THE DEFENDER AT THE TIME OF ATTACK (E).

H. AT THIS POINT THE DEFENDER MAY HAVE
   REACHED HIS HIGHEST LEVEL OF PREPARATIONS.
   LINE A↔B REPRESENTS THE ATTACKER'S LEAD
   TIME; LINE B↔E REPRESENTS THE DEFENDER'S
   ACTUAL WARNING TIME; LINE B↔H REPRESENTS
   THE TIME THE DEFENDER NEEDS TO COMPLETE
   HIS PREPARATIONS. THE GREATER IS B↔H
   MINUS B↔E THE MORE INTENSE IS THE IMPACT
   OF THE SURPRISE ATTACK.

why surprise is not absolute, given that the defenders normally manage to mobilize at least some forces. In many instances, the defenders' preparations have been under way for a matter of hours, whereas the time required for full mobilization can be measured in days or even weeks. The ratio of the defenders' actual mobilization to the readiness gap (or the attackers' degree of preparation for war) is a good conceptual indicator of the intensity and effectiveness of the ensuing surprise attack.

Two possible exceptions exist to this otherwise typical sequence of events. In the first situation, the defenders, having acquired definitive, fully credible information concerning an imminent attack, may launch a preemptive attack even before their own forces have been fully mobilized. They thus seize the opportunity to begin the war on their terms by immediately using their most flexible and available forces (normally, their air force) to attack, even when their own actual preparations are less than 50 percent completed. This, for example, would have been the case in the 1973 Yom Kippur War, when the Israelis acquired incontrovertible information of an impending Egyptian-Syrian attack. Immediately placed on alert, the Israeli Air Force was instructed to make preparations for a preemptive strike on Arab troop concentrations. The attack was cancelled at the last moment, however, for political reasons.

The second exception occurs in prolonged crises when one side is the first to mobilize fully but then delays its attack. The opponents may then catch up and perhaps reach the point where they can attack first. This type of scenario occurred before the outbreak of World War I, and again when Egypt mobilized first in May 1967 but allowed the Israelis to eventually exceed Egypt's own preparations and even launch a preemptive surprise attack.[13] (See Figure 15.3)

Intentions and Capabilities

All intelligence information concerns either the intentions or the capabilities of the adversary. Although this sounds simple enough, actual sorting, evaluation, and corroboration of information is an extremely intricate and time-consuming process. An error of judgment in one phase may set off a chain reaction of errors causing potentially serious analytical distortions.

Perhaps the most fundamental problem concerns the difference in the collection and analysis of both types of information. It is far simpler to obtain information about capabilities than about intentions. Capabilities can be material or nonmaterial. Material capabilities (i.e., weapons), performance characteristics, and quantities are not easy to conceal. Nonmaterial capabilities, such as organization, morale, and military doctrine, are more difficult to evaluate precisely, although considerable knowledge about them can be obtained. A pitfall to be avoided at all costs is concentration on the measurable and quantifiable while neglecting the less precise characteristics.

Political and military intentions, on the other hand, are much easier to conceal; only a handful of leaders, and at times a single leader (e.g., Hitler, Stalin, Sadat), will shape the strategy of a state. Intentions, which can be changed at the last minute, defy evaluation in the absence of direct access to the adversary's political-military elite.

Figure 15.3

THE RELATIVITY OF SURPRISE

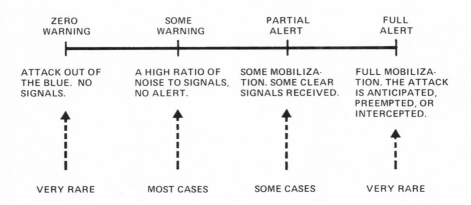

ZERO WARNING	SOME WARNING	PARTIAL ALERT	FULL ALERT
ATTACK OUT OF THE BLUE. NO SIGNALS.	A HIGH RATIO OF NOISE TO SIGNALS, NO ALERT.	SOME MOBILIZA- TION. SOME CLEAR SIGNALS RECEIVED.	FULL MOBILIZA- TION. THE ATTACK IS ANTICIPATED, PREEMPTED, OR INTERCEPTED.
VERY RARE	MOST CASES	SOME CASES	VERY RARE

Yet even the most secretive leaders can provide intelligence analysts with clues to their intentions in memoirs, speeches, briefings in closed or open circles, and the like. In addition, the adversary's intentions can be better understood through careful corroboration of all evidence pertaining to capabilities. (See Figure 15.4) In the long run, a leader harboring offensive intentions will have to invest in and expand his or her nation's capabilities, including heavy investments in military hardware and long-range offensive weapons. Limited capabilities may, however, force leaders to choose a defensive strategy in the short run. For example, Hitler needed to build up Germany's military strength before breaking away from the Versailles Treaty, reoccupying the Rhineland, or annexing Austria and the Sudetenland. In the absence of such strength, Hitler concealed his intentions behind the rhetoric of his peace offensives.

The process is further complicated when the adversaries state a need for capabilities comparable to one's own. For instance, Hitler demanded equality with, or disarmament for, everyone else, even as he was announcing German plans for conscription and rearmament. At other times, the adversaries may augment their capabilities in response to their perception of the hostile intentions of other nations. Such actions and reactions are intrinsic to every arms race. Furthermore, adversaries may assert that they are gearing their intentions to one's own, and actual or perceived changes in one's own capabilities as evaluated by the adversaries may trigger a change in their intentions out of fear and suspicion. These situations can heighten antagonism and, in extreme cases, may ignite a preemptive war. To complicate matters further, no direct correlation exists between capabilities and intentions; that is, a country with weaker capabilities may nevertheless

Figure 15.4

THE COMPLEXITY OF THE ESTIMATIVE PROCESS

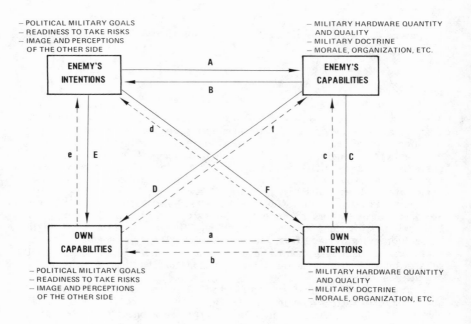

— POLITICAL MILITARY GOALS
— READINESS TO TAKE RISKS
— IMAGE AND PERCEPTIONS
   OF THE OTHER SIDE

— MILITARY HARDWARE QUANTITY
   AND QUALITY
— MILITARY DOCTRINE
— MORALE, ORGANIZATION, ETC.

ENEMY'S
INTENTIONS

ENEMY'S
CAPABILITIES

A

B

d

f

e   E

c   C

D

F

OWN
CAPABILITIES

OWN
INTENTIONS

a

b

— POLITICAL MILITARY GOALS
— READINESS TO TAKE RISKS
— IMAGE AND PERCEPTIONS
   OF THE OTHER SIDE

— MILITARY HARDWARE QUANTITY
   AND QUALITY
— MILITARY DOCTRINE
— MORALE, ORGANIZATION, ETC.

decide to go to war. Finally, the process just outlined requires exacting coordination and considerable time for analysis.

Although capabilities and intentions should undoubtedly be subject to equally careful collection and analytical efforts, it seems more prudent to emphasize the study of intentions for the following reasons: (1) Adversaries can still decide to attack even when their capabilities are relatively weak if they miscalculate the strength of the intended victim (as the Germans did in their attack of the Soviet Union in 1941, or the Arabs in their underestimation of Israeli capabilities in 1967). (2) The attackers may be more interested in applying political pressure or making political gains even at the cost of a military defeat. (3) The attackers might be gambling that their surprise attack will have a force-multiplier effect sufficient to compensate for their inferior capabilities. (4) War and surprise attack are determined not by the existence of capabilities per se, but by the political intention to use them. Mere possession of superior, equal, or inferior strength is therefore less important. A corollary of this observation is that while the adversaries' intentions can be influenced at any point (e.g., they can be deterred), it is impossible to have a comparable impact on capabilities immediately before the outbreak of war.[14] As it is much easier, of course, to determine capabilities than intentions, the temptation to concentrate on that which is simpler to identify or measure must be consciously resisted.

The Tricky Business of Estimating Risks

As Clausewitz has duly noted, "Boldness in war . . . has its own prerogatives. . . . Wherever it is superior, it will take advantage of its opponent's weakness. In other words, it is a genuinely creative force."[15]

Procedural, analytical, and methodological difficulties constitute only a small fraction of the problems involved in the intelligence-estimation process. Other, no less complex problems must also be discussed briefly. The first of these concerns the element of risk assessment in the planning of military operations.[16] The contradictory nature of risks in military operations adds another dimension of uncertainty to all intelligence estimates. Assuming rational behavior on the opponent's part, intelligence analysts may predict that a very risky operation, entailing very high costs and uncertain benefits, will not be implemented. Conversely, they might assume that an operation involving low risks and high benefits will be selected.

Although valid in theory, this premise is unreliable in practice. In the first place, a high risk in one culture may be acceptable in another. Thus there is the danger that an analyst's cultural values may be projected upon the adversary. In the summer of 1962, after U.S. intelligence received numerous reports that the Soviet Union was installing offensive missiles in Cuba, the National Security Council requested a National Intelligence Estimate (NIE) on the subject. "In early fall 1962, the NIE was completed. The estimate stated that it was highly unlikely that the Soviet Union would pursue a policy of such high risk as the placement of offensive missiles in Cuba. The estimate was made on the assumption that such a course of action would be irrational (at least from the American intelligence community's frame of reference)."[17]

Second, what sometimes appears to be great risk for an adversary may actually be less hazardous as a result of developments unknown to the intelligence analyst.[18] Before the Yom Kippur War, Israeli intelligence overestimated the risks the Egyptians would face from the superior Israeli Air Force, as did the Egyptian planners. Anticipating some 10,000 casualties in the initial crossing of the Suez Canal, they actually suffered about 200. Overestimating the risks caused them to adopt, perhaps wisely, a very cautious strategic plan. No rational Israeli planner would have gone to war against an enemy who maintained control of the skies. The Israelis were unaware, however, that the Egyptians had reduced the air threat by building an extremely powerful anti-aircraft defense system consisting of anti-aircraft guns and surface-to-air missiles.[19]

Intelligence analysts may also underrate the readiness of the enemy to take risks by assuming that their adversaries know as much as they do about their own strength. In 1941, the Russians may have felt confident that the Germans would not attack because of the extent of Russian strength. But they did not know that, in light of the Red Army's performance in Finland, German intelligence had grossly underestimated Russian strength by as much as 100 divisions.[20] On such occasions, the attackers-to-be underestimate their victims' strength, while the victims, sure of their own position, are more likely to be taken by surprise.

Assessment of a specific risk is further complicated by the estimated impact of strategic surprise itself. Although the Germans and Japanese in 1941, and the Israelis in 1967, knew that their respective adversaries possessed greater capabilities, they calculated that successful strategic surprise—as a force multiplier—would redress this imbalance. This expectation lowered the anticipated risks for the attackers. In contrast, defenders frequently underestimate the impact a surprise attack could have, and, instead, are confident that their retaliatory strength and capability to respond would not be diminished by such an occurrence (e.g., the USSR in 1941 and Israel in 1973).

In many instances, the stronger defender, interested in perpetuating a favorable status quo, does not fully comprehend the potential attacker's desperate frame of mind. On the eve of Pearl Harbor, the United States was unaware of the degree to which Japanese military and political leaders felt cornered. These leaders were cognizant of the United States' superior war potential and knew that unless the United States was ready to accept Japanese terms after the initial campaign, Japan could not win in the long run. Nevertheless, the Japanese felt they had no choice but to attack. For similar reasons, Egypt's President Nasser, in 1967, did not realize how desperate the Israelis felt; in 1973, the Israelis failed to understand how a lack of progress on the diplomatic front since 1967 caused mounting frustration in the Arab world, culminating in a decision to resort to war regardless of military consequences.

Estimating risks requires an intimate grasp of the culture, capabilities, and political and psychological frame of mind of one's adversaries—and above all, what they know and feel about the defender. But such detailed knowledge of one's opponents is rarely available and, even if obtained, is easily distorted by perceptual biases.

Finally, the paradoxical nature of risk should be considered. Superficially, it is rational to assume that very high-risk strategies, with low apparent chances of success, are normally unacceptable, whereas lower risks would be readily taken. In reality, such assumptions may be less than rational: Attackers may calculate that because attacking at a certain place or time would involve high costs, their adversaries would rationally conclude that the probability of this choice of strategy is extremely low. Paradoxically, then, opting for a high-risk strategy might be less foolhardy than is first assumed.

Many of the great captains of war have intuitively understood this principle, and it is associated with some of the most decisive strategic and tactical victories in history. The Allies' choice of Normandy as their landing beach despite its lack of harbors and its greater distance from their starting point than other possible landing sites, MacArthur's gamble at Inchon, Israel's attack on Egypt in 1967 and its rescue operation in Entebbe in 1976—these are but a few examples of the maxi-max strategies that actually reduced the risks involved.

No rational connection exists between the degree of risk on one hand and the choice of strategy on the other. The temptation to choose a high-risk/high-gain strategy is always present. Perhaps the only logical observation that can be made regarding this strategy is that although it can prevail in the short run, it is bound to fail in the long run. Napoleon and Hitler are the best known practitioners of this approach.

In war "the idea that something 'cannot be done' is one of the main aids to surprise. . . . Experts tend to forget that most military problems are soluble provided one is willing to pay the price."[21] Once someone is prepared to pay a high price, it may be added, that price is actually reduced. This leads to the following paradox: "The greater the risk, the less likely it seems to be, and the less risky it actually becomes. Thus, the greater the risk, the smaller it becomes."[22]

Why Mobilizations Can be Self-Defeating

The uncertain, politically sensitive nature of intelligence work is accentuated by deliberations concerning whether or not to declare an alert or a mobilization. Either would be the most critical policy recommendation an intelligence organization will ever have to make. If correct and timely, it may save many lives and significantly increase the chances of a vulnerable state's survival; if ill-timed, it can set off an uncontrollable chain of events and possibly lead to war through miscalculation. In the long run, such a grave mistake can also have harmful repercussions on the ability to make correct decisions in the future.

Every mobilization involves heavy political, material, and psychological costs in addition to greatly increasing the danger of war. A status-quo-oriented country not intending to go to war on its own initiative will, therefore, try to avoid mobilizing except in the most extreme circumstances. A single alert, let alone a series of alerts or a prolonged period of high alert not followed by war, will have a decisively negative impact on future decisions. A series of false alarms will undermine the credibility of the intelligence organization (the so-called cry-wolf syndrome), and when subsequent decisions on similar matters have to be made, prolonged periods of mobilization and the routinization of alerts will have brought about "alert fatigue."[23] A continuous or "permanent" state of alert can therefore be self-defeating.

The predicament of intelligence organizations is that many alarms deemed false in retrospect may actually have been justified. Although the cause for alarm is usually known, the defenders' intelligence may find it much more difficult to produce a timely explanation (before the next crisis occurs) as to why the predicted attack failed to materialize. The three basic explanations for this difficulty are as follows:

1. The enemy did not plan to attack in the first place. This is the outcome of an intelligence failure stemming from faulty information, incorrect analysis, and/or a low threshold for mobilization. In view of the normal reluctance to declare alerts or to mobilize, this type of faulty estimate is actually not too common. Of much greater interest and complexity are the remaining two explanations.

2. The enemy had decided to attack but at the last minute canceled or delayed because of bad weather, unsuitable political conditions, dissatisfaction with the plan, or a high level of alert on the defenders' side. The best known example of this sequence, consisting of a planned attack followed by a countermobilization and then the deferring of the attack, is Hitler's series of decisions to launch an offensive in the West: Attacks were planned and then canceled in November 1939 and January 1940, with the attack finally carried out in May 1940. Before each of the planned offensives, a number of timely—and in retrospect, reliable—warnings were received by British and French intelligence. Yet the Allies lost confidence in some reliable sources of information because the predicted attacks did not take place. By May 10, the day the Germans at last launched their offensive in the West, the Allies were completely surprised despite the multitude of warnings they had received but brushed aside.[24]

Failure in prediction does not necessarily mean something is amiss with an intelligence service or the information it has gathered. On the contrary, a correct prediction can be based on faulty information or a flawed analysis. For example, on September 25, 1962, the U.S. intelligence community agreed "on balance" that the Soviet Union would not install missiles in Cuba that were capable of reaching the United States. "The reason the intelligence community gave for its 'on balance' conclusion that the Soviets would not place 'offensive' missiles in Cuba was that according to its analytical framework, the Soviets were not prepared for this kind of confrontation. . . . In that event the Soviets got their confrontation and found a way to withdraw the missiles. . . . The intelligence community was wrong but for the right reasons: Khrushchev had miscalculated." Referring to this, a former senior U.S. intelligence officer said, "While it is most blessed to be right, it is more blessed in our business to be wrong for the right reasons than it is to be right for the wrong reasons."[25] In other words, a very small number of even significant intelligence failures may not constitute proof that something is intrinsically wrong with an intelligence organization; only a higher incidence of repeated failures indicates that reform or reorganization might be required.

3. Even more difficult to cope with is a situation in which the enemy prepares for an attack and the defenders react by mobilizing upon receiving a timely warning. The would-be attackers may then be deterred upon realizing that they can no longer reap the benefits of surprise. The prospective attackers might also fear that their secrets have been betrayed, thereby giving their adversaries precise knowledge of their plans. But even after such events have occurred, the defenders' intelligence can be hard pressed to determine whether the predicted attack was deterred by their countermobilization (which would justify similar measures in the future), or whether there was no attack planned in the first place. This was the dilemma faced by Israeli intelligence in the wake of a mobilization in May 1973 that was not followed by an attack, as summarized by the paradox of the self-negating prophecy: Information on a forthcoming enemy attack triggers a countermobilization, which, in turn, prompts the enemy to delay or cancel its plans. It is therefore extremely difficult—even in retrospect—to know whether or not the countermobilization was warranted.[26]

PROBLEMS OF PERCEPTION

The methodological problems discussed thus far have no perfect solutions. Intelligence experts are constantly searching for better ways to overcome the difficulties they face. Other than acquiring more and better information in real time, this search involves three basic strategies: The first is to "purge" the intelligence process (as much as possible) of human biases and perceptions. The second is a more costly approach in which the analysts take all threats seriously and implement the necessary precautionary measures. Finally, the last strategy calls for certain organizational reforms designed to improve the objectivity of the intelligence decisionmaking process by either reducing negative political influences or increasing the variety of participants and inputs involved in the process.

Indicators and Warnings

The most familiar methodological device capable of neutralizing the effects of the human element in the analytical intelligence process has been the development of a detailed list of Indications and Warnings (I & W). In theory, this device represents a simple and elegant solution:

> Essentially, the purpose of the method [is] to help the warning analyst pick and choose the significant from the massive amounts of ambiguous and possibly conflicting data that would be abundantly available in crisis situations. To do this, the analyst need only ask three simple questions: is it necessary (i.e., mandatory rather than optional to prepare for an attack); is it unambiguous (i.e., a move one takes only to prepare for war rather than for other purposes as well); and can we monitor it (i.e., can we observe the indicator we seek) [emphasis added].[27]

Warning indicators might include cancellation of all leaves, large-scale simultaneous maneuvers by several bordering countries, unusual levels of wireless communication, departure of foreign military advisers, distribution of live ammunition among units, mobilization of reserves, opening of civilian and other shelters, clearing of minefields and certain roads, and the emptying of large refineries of highly flammable materials.

Naturally, even a detailed set of warning indicators does not always speak for itself. If the changes occur slowly over a long period of time (i.e., through acclimatization),[28] they may be overlooked. Experience has shown that political leaders and analysts, if their concepts exclude the possibility of an imminent war, will go out of their way to dismiss as harmless all the warning signals they receive. "Even the best I&W scheme can only tell you whether and to what extent a government is prepared or preparing to act. It cannot tell you why or what its intentions are."[29] Moreover, an adversary who knows which indicators will be considered warning signals can deliberately manipulate such indicators to deceive the observer.[30] Of all the methodological devices intended to aid in the avoidance of strategic surprise, paying close attention to indicators and warnings appears to be the most promising.

In addition to simpler types of warning indicators, a number of other developments merit close observation. These include situations in which the adversaries or observers are frozen in a hopeless and unacceptable political deadlock that may encourage resort to war (Japanese in 1941; Arabs in 1973; Argentines over the Falkland Islands in 1982). Conclusion of a military treaty between former enemies (e.g., the Ribbentrop-Molotov agreement in 1939; Egypt and Jordan in May 1967), as well as the appearance of new leaders, unusual domestic pressures, and unexplicable anomalies in an adversary's pattern of behavior are also developments that should not escape scrutiny.

Worst-Case Analysis

A less elegant and more costly strategy involves lowering the threshold for taking precautionary measures in response to emerging threats. As a result of continual monitoring of actual and potential threats and because of professional socialization, intelligence analysts are a cautious lot. The resulting degree of pessimism and extreme caution will tend to be exacerbated by a major intelligence failure such as the inability to anticipate a strategic surprise, and is likely to lead to the adoption of a "worst-case" approach. This approach can be described as the belief that it is most prudent to base assumptions and analysis on the worst that the other nation could do; to assume, when presented with ambiguous evidence, that a threat will be carried out, even if the weight of indicators to the contrary appears to be greater.[31] According to Ken Booth,

> the worst case is more easily definable than the probable case, and so provides a firmer basis for a policy prescription. Worst case forecasting also frees individual analysts from blame if things go wrong. . . . To underplay what turns out to be a real threat may bring defeat: but to overestimate, and perhaps

provoke, a potential threat into an actual one, might only increase tension. In the past, when war was a less serious business, it nearly always made sense to defer to the alarmist. In the context of a nuclear confrontation, the balance of the argument should logically change. Risks should be taken for peace rather than war.[32]

The psychology behind the worst-case analysis is obvious, but the worst-case approach in its crude form may exact a heavy price:

1. It can be extremely expensive in terms of frequent mobilization and higher military expenditures.

2. It may bring antagonistic feelings to the boiling point and prove a major destabilizing factor when both opponents adopt a worst-case approach. Under such conditions, one party might mobilize prematurely, which could prompt an identical move by the other and then result in preemption as well as a war that no one wanted. Reciprocal fear of surprise attack played an important role in the loss of control over mobilization and countermobilization before World War I; the almost simultaneous German and British invasions of Norway; and the 1967 Six Day War.[33]

3. In the event this approach does not contribute to the loss of control or escalation, it may touch off many mobilizations and alerts that do not culminate in conflict, thus encouraging susceptibility to the "cry-wolf" syndrome and ultimately defeating its own purpose.

4. Frequent and facile resort to worst-case analysis can become an easy escape from analytical responsibility and reduce the quality of threat analysis.

Yet in spite of the social, material, and political costs of mobilization, it is advisable for more vulnerable states—those that are considerably weaker than their adversaries, lack strategic depth, or maintain only small armies—to lower somewhat their threshold for mobilization. The introduction of a flexible, modular, multistage alert and mobilization system would minimize the danger and costs entailed. If alerts and mobilizations occur repeatedly, care must be taken not to relax one's vigil. When survival is at stake, fewer risks should be taken. The high cost of false alarms is still lower than that of being caught unprepared.

Preconceptions, Ethnocentrism, and Misperception

Given the urgent nature of much intelligence work and the general process by which human learning takes place, all analysis must inevitably be based on preexisting concepts concerning, for example, the intentions of one's adversaries or their capabilities and military doctrines. Concepts, belief systems, theories, and images constituting the framework for assimilation of new information can be old or new, detailed or sketchy, rigid or flexible, static or dynamic.[34]

Generally speaking, perceptual errors are the result either of projections of one's own culture, ideological beliefs, military doctrine, and expectations onto the adversary (i.e., mirror imaging) or of wishful thinking—that is, molding facts to conform to one's hopes.[35]

Oversimplifications of reality can lead to underestimation of the adversary's will to resist, which in turn is responsible either for a hasty decision to become involved in a war or for a war that could be avoided if the costs and consequences are realistically calculated.

Correction of ethnocentric biases is the obvious answer to this problem, but the various measures toward this end are complex and should not be regarded as pat solutions. The most general suggestion is to "know thine enemy"—to intensify one's knowledge of the adversary's language, culture, political culture, ideology, and so on. This is always easier said than done, since even in the largest, most ethnically diverse societies there are few who are intimately familiar (in the Weberian sense of "Verstehen") with other cultures; moreover, such experts are not necessarily available for intelligence work.

More original is the suggestion calling for intelligence organizations to spend more time studying their own cultures and societies in depth to better comprehend (1) how the adversary reacts to or perceives the observer; and (2) how one's own environment can bias perception of another society. The need to know "thyself," according to this approach, is as essential as knowing the enemy.[36] After the Yom Kippur surprise attack in 1973, many Israeli intelligence analysts concluded that a principal cause of their misperception was the unconscious projection of Israeli society and its contentment with the status quo onto their Arab neighbors.[37]

However original and interesting, this proposal is highly impractical. Intelligence organizations often lack the resources necessary to properly analyze the adversary's intentions and capabilities, let alone to study their own society. In addition, whether intentional or not, an examination of one's own society and its politics will inevitably involve subjective political views and values, thus contributing to politicization of the intelligence community. Such studies are likely to alienate leaders (unless the observations are very flattering) and therefore become politically unacceptable. It cannot be assumed that the perceptual distortions leading to misperception of other societies will suddenly disappear during the examination of one's own society.

Perceptual analytical distortions can be formed either by individuals or by organizations. An individual's perceptual errors can at times be critical, but the mistake of a low-ranking individual is more likely to be counterbalanced and corrected by others working on the same problem. On the other hand, an individual at the top of the political or military hierarchy is not subject to such corrective procedures, which means that his or her errors are much less likely to be rectified. Thus, lower-echelon decisions can be examined most profitably in a bureaucratic, organizational context, whereas top-echelon decisions can be understood best in a psychological/political setting.

INTELLIGENCE/LEADERSHIP RELATIONS

The relationship between the military and civilian government is described by Huntington's model of "subjective control," which involves maximization of civilian power in relation to the military, reduces the professional autonomy of the military, leads to civilian interference in professional military affairs, and politicizes the armed forces by employing the military for narrow partisan interests.[38] Eventually, a pattern of subjective control may reduce the likelihood of having the best possible national security.

The relationship between the intelligence community and civilian authority requires a continuous search for careful balance between the professional independence of the former and the authority of the latter. For civilians in authority, the temptation to exploit the intelligence community's control over information for furtherance of political interests may be even greater than any desire to control the military.

Violation of the intelligence community's professional autonomy occurs not only for the sake of gaining access to critical information, but also because it is an important stepping-stone in facilitating subjective control of the military in general. Furthermore, the intelligence community's position is rendered even more sensitive to outside interference by the desire of <u>military</u> professionals to influence and control it to promote their special interests vis-à-vis those of the civilian authorities.[39] The intelligence community's professional autonomy may thus be compromised, and is constantly challenged, from two directions.

Correct and timely analysis of intelligence information is a necessary, but not sufficient, condition to guarantee intelligence community success. One of the most critical phases in the intelligence cycle lies in convincing the military and political leadership to make the best use of the information and analysis supplied to them.

Much depends on whether leaders are open-minded, encourage criticism, and want accurate, though possibly unpleasant, information. Leaders in a democratic system are generally more inclined to consider a wider variety of opinions than those in authoritarian or totalitarian political systems. In authoritarian countries, where the climb to the top is an unrelenting struggle for power, habits of cooperation and openness are usually less developed. The prevalence of ideology naturally restricts openness to variety, criticism, and consideration of contradictory ideas. Leaders in totalitarian countries ordinarily have little tolerance for ideas that deviate from the "party line," since such ideas are seen as personal criticism—as a dangerous element undermining the existing ideology. Among other reasons, this explains why the intelligence systems of the democracies, on the whole, performed better than those of the totalitarian nations during World War II.[40]

Of course, both kinds of leaders can be found in any type of state. Ultimately, each leader's idiosyncracies and personality play the definitive role. From the vantage point of intelligence organizations and their capacity to cooperate with a leader, two ideal types of leaders can be considered.

On the one hand, leaders such as Hitler or Stalin could not tolerate information that contradicted their own beliefs or policies. When such strictures are imposed, strategic intelligence is of very limited use. Hitler once told Ribbentrop that "when he had to make great decisions, he considered himself the instrument of the providence which the Almighty had determined. He . . . [added] that before big decisions, he always had a feeling of absolute certainty."[41] Having no habits of cooperation or orderly staff work, Hitler imposed his ideas on others. Early success in the face of senior military and foreign policy opposition had convinced him that his intuition was infallible. A look at the leaders and military assistants closest to Hitler—men such as Jodl and Keitel in the OKW, and Robbentrop, Goring, and Goebbels--reveals that almost all of them were sycophants. Ribbentrop and Goring (as well as others in Hitler's coterie) carefully ensured that he received only reports confirming his beliefs and images. At no point, even after the most serious defeats, did Hitler encourage another type of reporting. Good intelligence existed, but it was circumspectly filtered. "In light of Hitler's preconceptions and distorted images, one must question the usefulness of foreign reporting even if it had been one hundred percent correct."[42] Although Hitler is an extreme example, the danger involved in distorting information to suit a leader's policies exists in every type of government and between all leaders and their lieutenants.

Hitler made most of his important decisions without consulting anyone. Members of his entourage were often as surprised as were the victims of his moves, particularly during the period of diplomatic surprises in the 1930s, which, unlike his subsequent military surprises, required no material preparations. Such decisions, generally made on the spur of the moment, are very difficult to anticipate. Intelligence agencies are generally called upon to issue warnings before the adversary's leader has made up his own mind. The psychoanalytical study of leaders is beset by uncertainty and speculation: It can be difficult to make day-to-day predictions of an irrational leader's behavior, but in time a general pattern of behavior will emerge, thereby helping the observer gauge some of the leader's reactions and readiness to take risks, if not to make more precise forecasts.[43]

An "atomistic" style of leadership reaches more severe proportions when accompanied by dogmatic adherence to an ideology (especially if the ideology is irrational). Hitler dismissed intelligence reports on U.S. or Soviet behavior as an overestimation of Jewish, Bolshevik-Slav, or plutocratic groups that were racially or politically inferior and therefore could not be as motivated or efficient as German Aryans.[44] Similarly, Stalin's adherence to communist ideology, which viewed the world in zero-sum-game terms, led him to believe that any British or Western intelligence supplied to him (such as reports concerning, say, a German plan to attack in 1941) could not be genuine; indeed, Stalin refused to believe that delays in opening the second front in Europe stemmed from real difficulties and not from anti-Soviet sentiments.[45]

Although a modicum of interorganizational competition might actually be beneficial, Hitler's proclivity for pursuing a divide-and-rule policy was counterproductive in its politicization of German intelligence. An intelligence organization desiring recognition from the führer had to furnish him with the information that he wanted to hear. The dynamics of this competition encouraged a rapid deterioration in the quality of German intelligence and fostered mistrust between the various agencies.

In contrast, the relative openness of Roosevelt, Churchill, or Truman to intelligence reports seems to have yielded better results. From his early days at the Admiralty in World War I to his daily use of Enigma intercepts during World War II, Churchill certainly paid careful attention to intelligence reports.[46] His work habits have been described in this somewhat idealized way:

We see Churchill following up daily on the performance of

his subordinates. We see him emphasizing the importance of science and technology in the development of new weapons. We note his skill in using information acquired through the interception and decoding of German communications, and his success in keeping the knowledge of that decoding a secret. We note how effective was Churchill's insistence on transmitting instructions in writing, on keeping orderly track of every decision and on tracing the progress of decision to action. Such habits make for efficient administration.[47]

In reality, Churchill's handling of intelligence was far more complicated than is commonly realized. At times, he exaggerated in his insistence on personally reviewing "raw intelligence material" and on being his "own intelligence analyst" on subjects about which he had little expertise. In addition, once he rose to power, he did his best to closely control the use of intelligence information to advance his own political interests.[48] His own extensive use of classified information leaked to him while he was in the opposition during the 1930s certainly made him aware (more than any other political leader) of the danger of allowing his political adversaries to do likewise.

Beyond the problem of the psychological profile of leaders, more general political behavioral patterns can influence their attitude toward intelligence. For example, once leaders have invested substantial energy in promoting a particular policy direction—especially when their prestige is on the line or they have acted against the advice of their aides—they will be that much more reluctant to admit defeat even when presented with contradictory evidence. Under such circumstances, the most attractive course of action may be to ignore contradictory data and insist that subordinates supply them with the "right" information.[49] The greatest danger is when the leader supplants serious deliberation with wishful thinking. Chamberlain and appeasement advocates long resisted overwhelming evidence that their policies actually encouraged Hitler's aggressiveness and appetite. Leaders in democratic systems are particularly vulnerable to such wishful thinking before elections.

No perfect remedy exists for the problems discussed in this section of the chapter. However, two suggestions can be made in this context: first, that more time be devoted to the "education" of leaders on this subject before they rise to power (obviously not an easy matter, as it is often too much to expect to change the working habits of leaders), and, second, that the intelligence community be made more effective by gearing its presentation to the specific character of the leader.[50]

ORGANIZATIONAL AND BUREAUCRATIC EXPLANATIONS

As Charles Perrow has noted, "Complex systems are simply not responsive to warnings of unimaginable or highly unlikely accidents. Because they are complex, organizational routines must be carefully followed and off-standard events reinterpreted in routine frameworks."[51]

Much of an intelligence organization's professional integrity depends upon the degree to which (1) freedom of expression and criticism are encouraged; (2) the system of military and civil administration is based on merit; (3) corruption and favoritism are common, the educational system is a quality one, and the military has been involved in political matters. Of course, control of information and the possibility of manipulating it to promote the intelligence community's political influence or beliefs is an ever-present danger that gives rise to some serious ethical questions.

Despite powerful temptations, intelligence analysts ought to resist direct involvement in policymaking when, for example, after a briefing they are asked by senior politicians, " 'OK, that's your analysis; what would you do about it?' The temptation can be overpowering for the intelligence officer, but his reply should be 'Sorry, sir, that's your business,' even though he might have a pretty clear idea of what to do."[52] This is the point at which many good intelligence officers have committed themselves actively to one policy or another, with the result that their objectivity and judgment were severely impaired.

The purely "rational" or "professional" behavior of any organization is modified by parochial views, organizational interests and survival, the need for cohesion, and esprit de corps.[53] The neutral intelligence process, unencumbered by such complications, is a theoretical ideal that cannot be found in practice.

Military Patterns of Thought and Intelligence Analysis

Most intelligence organizations are either part of a larger military organization or include many members with military backgrounds. As a consequence, intelligence organizations are unavoidably imbued with a perspective that emphasizes such elements as military motives, capabilities, hierarchy, discipline, and worst-case analyses. These traits are not always the most suitable for intelligence work, which deals as much with political affairs as with military ones, and in which freedom of research and expression may be more important than rank and position.

The primacy of politics in strategic affairs can be ignored in subtle ways. Clausewitz's dictum that war must serve a political purpose is by now a cliché. Yet this logic merits further thought. Rational Western political and military leaders naturally assumed that war could be a political instrument only if, as Clausewitz said, we can compel our adversaries to do our will—that is, defeat them on the battlefield. In the Western tradition, it is usually and often correctly assumed that if it were impossible to win a war, starting one would be counterproductive and irrational. The Chinese, the Vietnamese, and the Arabs, for example, have taken the Clausewitzian primacy of politics one step further; for them, it makes sense to resort to war even if military victory is impossible, as long as they can win politically. This crucial point was repeatedly missed by Western analysts and policymakers regarding Indochina, Algeria, and the Middle East. In 1973, Israeli intelligence, believing from its own experience that a military defeat was also, by definition, a political defeat and a direct threat to survival, failed to recognize that Egypt and Syria would even contemplate initiating a war with the full knowledge that they could not win militarily, although they could triumph politically.

It is therefore crucial to devote more attention to the

corroboration and integration of military and political intelligence, especially at the highest levels of analysis. Focusing primarily on one area or the other may give rise to serious analytical distortions, as evaluation of military situations cannot be made in a political vacuum, and vice versa. It is not desirable for a preponderance of intelligence activity to be controlled by the military, as was the case in Israel before 1973. But this conclusion, though seemingly straightforward, has not been borne in mind by those who stand to profit most from it. The majority of cases of strategic surprise evince a prior lack of coordination between political-diplomatic and military activities on the part of the victim, and grave errors in judgment have resulted. Observed military warning signals are dismissed or underestimated as a result of the absence of corresponding political-diplomatic activity. The attacker takes care to maintain a facade of routine diplomacy, lulling the intended victim into suppressing military warning signals through optimistic political interpretations. States planning an attack no longer present their victims with ultimatums or declarations of war, nor do they initiate hostile diplomatic campaigns. Contemporary conflicts are often begun against a quiet diplomatic-political backdrop. This leads to the paradox of the sounds of silence. That is, a quiescent international environment can act as background noise that, by conditioning observers to a peaceful routine, actually covers preparations for war.[54] All meaningful changes in military warning signals should trigger an intensified probe into an apparently calm diplomatic-political environment. The obverse situation can be equally volatile, as when intensive diplomatic dialogue is deadlocked or abruptly terminated, yet is not accompanied by observation of unusual military activity (e.g., the United States before Pearl Harbor, or Egypt prior to the Suez and Sinai campaigns).

Organizational Parochialism, Compartmentation, and Excessive Secrecy

The analytical quality and objectivity of intelligence is also distorted by parochial views rising from an organization's specialized functions. Of course, a naval or air force intelligence agency will have a narrower focus than one that covers a broader area, such as the CIA; but even less specialized intelligence agencies often find it necessary to order priorities. Specialization can produce a better analysis of specific problems, but it may also hamper formulation of a more general outlook and increase the difficulty of coordination within and between intelligence organizations. Such trade-offs are, however, inevitable.

Before World War II, British naval intelligence focused on assessing German naval preparations for war. Far weaker than that of the British, the German Navy was unprepared for war in 1939. From the vantage point of British Naval Intelligence, therefore, Germany was unlikely to initiate war because of the high risk involved. Given Hitler's political intentions and the fact that Germany was a primarily continental power, Nazi intentions to go to war should not have been gauged by a naval estimate. "The Admiralty remained untroubled by German activity in every other sphere—foreign policy, internal policy, the economy, the air force, and the army. Naval intelligence drew from too narrow a field of information conclusions which were too broad, if eminently rational."[55]

Better coordination might correct somewhat the parochial biases of different intelligence organizations, but there is no perfect solution to the problem. Complicated and time-consuming, the coordination process itself can spur competition for influence and the search for acceptable compromise.[56]

Although each organization aspires to monopolistic control over its area of responsibility, some interorganizational competition can be constructive. The need for diversity in intelligence estimates to provide leaders with a wider choice of interpretations is obvious, but there is a price for competition. More organizations demand more resources: they duplicate efforts and require coordination. As in all other types of organizations, those in intelligence fight for greater influence and larger budgets. The drawback to such competition is that it can encourage politicization of the working process if protection and expansion of parochial interests is enhanced by supplying the executive with the "right" intelligence. These distortions are accentuated if the executive or military leadership practices a policy of divide and rule. The degree of objectivity achieved therefore depends largely on the character of the leaders in the political, executive, and military arenas, as well as on the integrity of those responsible for the intelligence community. It is the political culture in the wider sense (e.g., freedom of expression, tolerance of different opinions, respect for professional skills, respect for the law) that makes the difference.

Finally, the need for coordination and development of a political modus operandi between organizations also exists within each of them. It has been observed that individuals within groups feel compelled to develop a consensus, the maintenance of which may become a goal in its own right and can fulfill positive functions. Individuals working together often share similar educational and career backgrounds and common interests that need to be defended vis-à-vis other organizations. Moreover, any group that must achieve a common goal and implement a policy must also be able to arrive at an operational consensus that permits its members to work on a routine basis. No group can ever hope to implement the ideas of each of its members at the same time. Any collective action hence necessitates a political-social search for consensus.

The key question is this, however: How was the group consensus reached? Was it reached through open discussion of opposing opinions? Was it enforced by a single person who discouraged debate? Or was it brought about by submission to group pressure to conform? Agreement for its own sake prematurely stifles the expression of diverse, potentially valuable opinions. Of course, the pitfalls of groupthink exist in the intelligence evaluation process, particularly under crisis conditions. Groupthink may have been one reason for which U.S. intelligence adopted unrealistic images and concepts before Pearl Harbor and the Bay of Pigs, and during the Vietnam War.[57]

Excessive secrecy in handling information poses a related problem. Perhaps the most obvious symptom of this problem is the compartmentation within and among intelligence organizations, as well as between the intelligence community and other military and civilian agencies. Consequently, one organization often is not privy to the information held by another, an arrangement that may bring about failures to act, duplication of effort, or the inadvertent interference of one agency in the operations of another. Recent examples of such costly miscalculations are the Bay of Pigs operation and the ill-fated attempt to rescue American hostages in Iran.

The overall vice of excessive secrecy may leave actors unaware of the pressing need to coordinate actions, or even of which new issues require coordination. Furthermore, valuable information may not be used to the fullest possible extent. Particularly in times of crisis, information should be passed more readily to lower and parallel echelons, for in all failures to anticipate sudden attacks, much data is misinterpreted or improperly corroborated. In addition, information and exchange of opinions should flow both upward and downward in the intelligence hierarchy and with its political counterpart, and better coordination between tactical intelligence and its headquarters must be ensured.[58]

Tension will always exist between the desire to protect intelligence sources and the need to make the best and most profitable use of information. There is no formula to calculate potential costs and benefits or missed opportunities in such circumstances. Almost miraculously, the Allies managed to protect the secret of "Ultra" from the Germans, and in fact from the world, until the 1970s. Yet the decision to attribute Ultra information to spies or special operations in many cases descredited the information in the eyes of some senior field commanders, not informed of the actual source. A wider distribution of Ultra may have improved battlefield performance, thereby reducing the number of opportunities missed. Nevertheless, Ultra or the double-cross system are unique events in the history of intelligence and may confuse the issues involved. It seems that, in general, intelligence organizations tend to err in the direction of excessive caution and underutilization of information. This may be an innate professional bias—yet unused information is ineffective and has repercussions beyond the mere wasting of the collection effort.[59]

CONCLUSION

Far-reaching advances in the technical means of gathering intelligence information, and the greater awareness of political and perceptual mechanisms undermining the intelligence process, have not yielded corresponding progress in the ability to anticipate strategic surprise. Accordingly, understanding but not being able to avoid this phenomenon has led to a certain sense of futility. As Napoleon said, "Uncertainty is the essence of war, surprise its rule." If anything, history consoles us with the observation that there is no direct correlation between achieving the highest degree of surprise at the outbreak of a war and ultimately emerging victorious. The next best thing to avoiding surprise, therefore, is coping with it once it has occurred, thus requiring the judicious buildup of military strength in peacetime.

NOTES

1. See Michael I. Handel, "Intelligence and Deception," Journal of

Strategic Studies 5 (March 1982): 122-154, 145.
2. See the quotations by Karl von Clausewitz in Michael Howard and Peter Paret, eds., On War (Princeton, N.J.: Princeton University Press, 1976), pp. 198-199.
3. Ibid., p. 545.
4. For the impact of modern technology on warfare, see Michael Howard, War in European History (New York: Oxford University Press, 1979), in particular chs. 5-7; J.F.C. Fuller, Armaments and History (New York: Charles Scribner's Sons, 1945); J.F.C. Fuller, The Conduct of War 1789-1961: A Study of the Impact of the French, Industrial and Russian Revolutions on War and Its Conduct (London: Methuen, 1972); Tom Wintringham, Weapons and Tactics (New York: Penguin Books, 1973); Brian Ranft, ed., Technological Change and British Naval Policy 1860-1839 (New York: Holmes & Meier, 1977).
5. This apt phrase was suggested by Thomas C. Schelling in The Strategy of Conflict (Cambridge, Mass.: Harvard University Press, 1960), pp. 207-230, and in Schelling, Arms and Influence (New Haven, Conn.: Yale University Press, 1966), p. 221.
6. Clausewitz, On War, p. 79.
7. These terms were first applied to the study of strategic surprise and intelligence analysis by Roberta Wohlstetter in Pearl Harbor: Warning and Decision (Stanford, Calif.: Stanford University Press, 1962), pp. 336-338.
8. On deception see, for example, Barton Whaley, Codeword Barbarossa (Cambridge, Mass.: MIT Press, 1973); Whaley, Stratagem, Deception and Surprise, Journal of Strategic Studies 5 (March 1982) [special issue on intelligence and deception]; Donald Daniel and Katherine Herbig, eds., Strategic Military Deception (New York: Pergamon, 1982).
9. See Handel, "Intelligence and Deception," pp. 122-154.
10. For background on the numerous alerts preceding the German attack in the west in May 1940, see Telford Taylor, The March of Conquest (New York: Simon & Schuster, 1958); Erich von Manstein, Lost Victories (London: Methuen, 1958); Basil Collier, Hidden Weapons: Allied Secret or Undercover Services in World War II (London: Hamish Hamilton, 1982), pp. 78-96; Betts, Surprise Attack: Lessons for Defense Planning (Washington, D.C.: The Brookings Institution, 1982), pp. 28-34; Andre Beaufre, 1940: The Fall of France (London: Cassell, 1965); William L. Shirer, The Collapse of the Third Republic (New York: Simon & Schuster, 1969).
11. Michael I. Handel, Perception, Deception and Surprise: The Case of the Yom Kippur War (Jerusalem, Israel: The Leonard Davis Institute, 1976), p. 15.
12. Handel, "Intelligence and Deception," p. 154 (note 1.).
13. See Michael I. Handel, "Crisis and Surprise in Three Arab-Israeli Wars," in Klaus Knorr and Patrick Morgan, eds., Strategic Military Surprise (New Brunswick, N.J.: Transaction Books, 1982).
14. Handel, Perception, Deception and Surprise, p. 62.
15. Clausewitz, On War, p. 190.
16. Handel, Perception, Deception and Surprise, pp. 15-16.
17. W.D. Howells, "Intelligence in Crises," in Gregory R. Copley, ed., Defense 83 (Washington, D.C.: D and F Conferences, Inc., 1983) pp. 349-350.
18. See Ephraim Kam, "Failure to Anticipate War: The Why of

Surprise Attack," (Ph.D. dissertation, Harvard University, 1983), p. 182. For a discussion of the assessment of risks primarily on the tactical level, see Elias Carter Townsend, Risks: The Key to Combat Intelligence (Harrisburg, Pa.: Military Service Publishing Co., 1955).

19. Handel, Perception, Deception and Surprise, p. 46ff.

20. Barry Leach, German Strategy Against Russia 1939-1941 (Oxford, England: Oxford University Press, 1973), pp. 91-94 and Appendix 4, p. 270; Albert Seaton, The Russo-German War 1941-1945 (London: Praeger Publishers, 1971).

21. Waldemar Erfurth, Surprise (Harrisburg, Pa.: Military Service Publishing Co., 1943), pp. 6-7.

22. Handel, Perception, Deception and Surprise, p. 16.

23. The term is Schelling's. See Schelling, Strategy of Conflict, pp. 244-245.

24. For literature on this case, see Note 10 in this chapter.

25. Both quotations are from W.D. Howells, "Intelligence in Crises," pp. 351, 350.

26. Ibid., p. 54.

27. Howells, "Intelligence in Crises," pp. 359-361; Betts, Surprise Attack, pp. 190-192; Kam, Failure to Anticipate War, pp. 127-139.

28. For an interesting case, see R.V. Jones, Most Secret War: British Scientifics, Intelligence in World War II 1939-1945 (London, England: Hamish Hamilton, 1978), pp. 233-235.

29. Howells, "Intelligence in Crises," p. 361.

30. Robert Jervis, The Logic of Images in International Relations (Princeton, N.J.: Princeton University Press, 1970).

31. Betts, "Analysis, War, and Decision," World Politics 31 (October 1978): 73-75; Kam, Failure to Anticipate War, pp. 461-462.

32. Ken Booth, Strategy and Ethnocentrism (New York: Holmes & Meier, 1979), pp. 123-124.

33. See, for example, Luigi Albertini, The Origins of the War of 1914, vols. 2 and 3 (Oxford, England: Oxford University Press, 1952).

34. See, for example, Jervis, "Hypothesis on Misperception," World Politics 20 (April, 1968) and Robert Jervis, Perception and Misperception in International Politics (Princeton, N.J.: Princeton University Press, 1976).

35. See Chapters 12-14 of this volume for a detailed discussion of perceptual errors.

36. Zvi Lanir, Fundamental Surprise: The National Intelligence Crisis (Tel Aviv: HaKibbutz HaMeuchad, 1983) [in Hebrew].

37. Handel, Perception, Deception and Surprise, pp. 40-42.

38. Samuel P. Huntington, The Soldier and the State (New York: Vintage Books, 1964).

39. For an excellent discussion of this point, see Richard K. Betts, Soldiers, Statesmen, and Cold War Crisis (Cambridge: Harvard University Press, 1977), ch. 10, pp. 183-209.

40. See Michael I. Handel, The Diplomacy of Surprise (Cambridge, Mass.: Harvard University Press, 1981), pp. 1-31, 241-253; and Michael I. Handel, "Surprise and Change in International Politics," International Security 4 (Spring 1980): 57-85. On the failure of Japanese intelligence, see Harold L. Ashman, "Intelligence and Foreign Policy: A Functional Analysis" (Ph.D. dissertation, University of Utah, 1973), pp. 99-119.

41. Ashman, "Intelligence and Foreign Policy," p. 53.

42. Ibid., p. 61. On Hitler as a decisionmaker, see Walter Warlimont, Inside Hitler's Headquarters (London: Widenfeld and Nicolson, 1964); Percy Ernst Schramm, Hitler: The Man and the Military Leader (Chicago: Quadrangle Books, 1971); Franz Halder, Hitler as a Warlord (London: Putnam, 1950); Andreas Hillgreber, Hitler's Strategie: Politik und Kriegsfubrung 1940-1941 (Munich: Bernard Greife, 1982).

43. A well-known example is Walter Langer's psychoanalytical study of Hitler for the OSS during World War II. See Walter Langer, The Mind of Adolf Hitler (New York: Basic Books, 1972).

44. Gerhard L. Weinberg, "Hitler's Image of the United States," American Historical Review 69 (July 1964): 1004-1021.

45. See John Erikson, The Road to Stalingrad: Stalin's War with Germany, vol. 1 (New York: Harper & Row, 1975); John Erikson, The Soviet High Command (London: Macmillan, 1962). See also Seweryn Bialer, ed., Stalin and His Generals (New York: Pegasus, 1969).

46. Ronald Lewin, Churchill as a Warlord (New York: Stein and Day, 1982). For a different viewpoint, see A.J.P. Taylor et al., Churchill Revisited: A Critical Assessment (New York: Dial Press, 1969). More sympathetic is Martin Gilbert's Winston S. Churchill: The Prophet of Truth, vol. 5 (Boston: Houghton Mifflin, 1977) and Finest Hour 1939-1941, vol. 6 (Boston: Houghton Mifflin, 1983).

47. See Gaddis Smith, "How the British Held the Fort," New York Times Book Review (December 25, 1983), pp. 1-2, in which Martin Gilbert's Winston S. Churchill: Finest Hour is reviewed.

48. See Donald McLachlan, Room 39: A Study in Naval Intelligence (New York: Atheneum, 1968), ch. 6, pp. 124-143, and ch. 15, pp. 338-367.

49. Howells, "Intelligence in Crises," p. 364.

50. McLachlan, Room 39, p. 366.

51. Charles Perrow, "Normal Accident at Three Mile Island," Transaction (Social Sciences and Modern Society) 18 (July/August 1981), p. 21.

52. Howells, "Intelligence in Crises," p. 362.

53. A recently published article by a former senior Israeli intelligence officer tries to demonstrate that the "purely rational" decisionmaking process in intelligence analysis as well as in intelligence relations with policymakers can exist. See Brigadier General (Ret.) Yoel Ben-Porat, "The Role of the Political Level in Estimates," Haaretz (March 20, 1984), p. 3 [in Hebrew].

54. Handel, Perception, Deception and Surprise, p. 17.

55. Wesley K. Wark, "Baltic Submarine Bogeys: British Naval Intelligence and Nazi Germany 1933-1939," Journal of Strategic Studies 6 (March 1983): 60-81, 78.

56. Graham T. Allison, Essence of Decision (Boston: Little, Brown, 1971); Morton Halperin, Bureaucratic Politics and Foreign Policy (Washington, D.C.: Brookings Institution, 1974); and Patrick McGarvey, "DIA: Intelligence to Please," in Morton Halperin and Arnold Kanter, eds., Readings in American Foreign Policy: A Bureaucratic Perspective (Boston: Little, Brown, 1973), pp. 318-328.

57. Irving Janis, Victims of Groupthink (Boston: Houghton Mifflin, 1972).

58. Michael I. Handel, "Avoiding Political and Technological Surprise in the 1980s," in Roy Godson, ed., Intelligence Requirements for the 1980s: Analysis and Estimates (New Brunswick, N.J.:

Transaction Books, 1980), pp. 85–112, especially p. 105.
     59. McLachlan, <u>Room 39</u>, p. 366.

16

KATHERINE L. HERBIG
DONALD C. DANIEL

Strategic Military Deception

DEFINING DECEPTION

Deception is a broad concept that encompasses and goes beyond the ideas of cover, lying, and artifice. As in any research area, that of deception requires bounding the concept and analytically distinguishing it from related terms. Deception constitutes the deliberate misrepresentation of reality to gain a competitive advantage. (See Figure 16.1)

At deception's center is cover, the military term for secretkeeping and camouflage. It embodies deception's negative side because it entails the negation of knowledge of the truth. Cover is at the heart of deception because, no matter what their other goals, deceivers wish to protect a secret, be it information about an already existing reality (e.g., the capabilities of one's military systems) or an intended reality (such as the scenarios for their use).

The concept of "lying" encompasses that of "cover." Liars not only hold back the truth; they also act to deflect their victims away from it, thus highlighting deception's positive side. Liars create and perpetuate falsities and seek to draw their victims' attention to them. In a narrow sense, a lie involves making a statement that is untrue, but in a broader sense it can also involve manipulating the context surrounding the statement in order to enhance its veracity. This latter case is what is meant by artifice, an important element of nearly all strategic deceptions.

Just as lying subsumes cover, so does deception subsume lying in both of its textual and contextual senses. The terms are often used interchangeably, but deception and lying are not exact synonyms. Lying looks primarily to one side of the interaction between liars and their audience. It stresses the actions of the tellers of falsehoods. Deception is a term of wider scope because it also stresses the reactions of the receivers of falsehoods. Those whose false tales are not believed are still liars, but they have not deceived. One does not fail at lying because the audience is not convinced, but one does fail at deception if the audience does not believe the lie. Eventually almost all deceptions are exposed as events unfold; thus the trick for the deceivers is to ensure that their lies are accepted long enough to benefit them.

The question of benefits is important because they are a necess-

Figure 16.1

Deception's Subsidiary Concepts

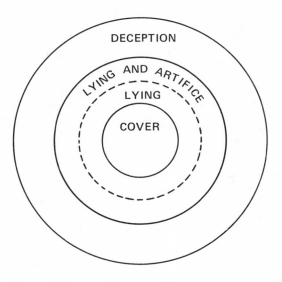

ary ingredient of deception. In our view, to be labeled deception an act must be committed to gain a competitive advantage. This means, in effect, that there are three goals in any deception. The immediate aim is to condition a target's beliefs; the intermediate aim is to influence his or her actions; and the ultimate aim is for the deceiver to benefit from the target's actions. Deceptions are often credited with success when only the first goal is achieved, but to evaluate the actual impact deception has on the course of events, its success should properly be measured against the third goal.

Variants

There are two variants of deception, and they may be viewed as end points on a continuum. The variants that deceivers intend may not match up with the actual outcomes. The less elegant variety is the "ambiguity producing" or A-type. Here deceivers act to confuse their targets by confronting them with at least two choices as to what the truth may be. One of these choices may be the truth itself, whose indicators the targets cannot completely hide. The greater the number of compelling alternatives, the smaller the possibility that the targets may by chance settle on the true one as the basis for their actions. If the deceivers' lies are to be compelling, it is necessary only that they be plausible enough and consequential enough to the targets' well-being that they cannot ignore them.

Deceivers can benefit from an A-type deception in two ways. Hoping to reduce ambiguity by awaiting additional information, the targets may delay decision, thereby surrendering the initiative to the deceivers and giving them wider latitude to marshal resources. If the deceivers can ensure that the situation remains confusing, then the targets may be forced to spread resources thinly to cover all important contingencies. They thereby reduce the resistance that deceivers can expect at any one point.

In contrast to those deceptions that increase ambiguity, there is a second, more complicated category, which we label "misleading" or M-type deceptions. These deceptions reduce ambiguity and fasten a victim's mind to one (false) version of the truth. Whereas in A-type deceptions the deceivers simply aim to have the targets not reject as untrue one or more alternatives to the truth, the aim in the M variant is to have the targets reject the truth itself and all alternatives to it except the one that suits the deceivers. Not only must the lie be plausible, it must also be so attractive, so convincing, that the victims are willing to concentrate the bulk of their operational resources on one contingency, thereby maximizing the deceivers' chances for prevailing on all others. This variant is particularly attractive in situations in which the deceivers believe that they can keep most indicators of the truth from even reaching the targets in the first place.

At least three types of misleading deceptions exist. The first, or M-1, variety seeks to have victims accept as true that which they are already inclined to believe. It is probably the easiest of the M deceptions to carry through to success. Conversely, the most difficult of the M deceptions is the M-2 variety. Here the deceivers swim against the tide of the victims' predispositions. They seek to have the victims believe that which the victims are inclined to doubt or to view as false. The M-3 version concerns those cases in which the victims' predispositions (prior to the commencement of the deception) are not directly relevant to or predictive of what the victims come to accept as true.

Although the two variants of deception, the M-type and the A-type, are conceptually distinct and can be initiated with different intentions in the deceiver's mind, in practice their effects often coexist or shade into one another as the deception evolves. In the latter case, the direction of change generally appears to be from M-type to A-type. Deceptions planned to mislead a target into choosing one possibility may degenerate and instead increase uncertainty if the target resists or postpones making the choice the deceiver intends.

Thus it is useful to consider the outcomes of the two variants as a continuum between convinced misdirection at the one pole and utter confusion, in which all looks equally likely, at the other. The Barbarossa deception (misleading Stalin about the German attack in June 1941) seems to be an unusually strong example of misdirection, whereas Fortitude South (the deception associated with the Normandy landing immediately before D-Day) would fall perhaps three-fourths of the way toward the misdirection pole. In the Barbarossa case, the Germans ultimately built on Stalin's expectation that the Third Reich would never attack the USSR without first issuing an ultimatum. This "ultimatum strategy," according to Whaley, "served to eliminate ambiguity, making Stalin quite certain, very decisive, and wrong."[1] In the Fortitude case, Hitler and many of his generals thought in late May and early June 1944 that the main Allied cross-channel invasion would come at Calais, but they continued to consider a range of invasion site possibilities along the English Channel coast, including Normandy.

In sum, the two deception variants differ in their intended effects. One seeks to increase a target's uncertainty and the other seeks to decrease it. It seems useful to view these variants as end points on a spectrum, with the outcome of actual deception usually falling between the two extremes.

THE DECEPTION PROCESS

For deception to occur, there must be deceivers, victims or targets, the communication channels linking them together, and signals transmitted within the channels. It also illustrates that each of these elements affects and is affected by environmental factors, some of which are deliberately manipulated by the targets as part of their deception. (See Figure 16.2)

On the deceivers' side are decisionmakers, planners, and implementers. Regardless of who had the inspiration, a deception does not begin until a decisionmaker agrees to it. (See Figure 16.3) The historical record reveals that wide-ranging strategic deceptions such as Fortitude or Barbarossa are cleared only by the highest authorities, but given their many responsibilities, these authorities were unable to devote much time to planning and implementation. During World War II such tasks were assigned to small cadres in intelligence-gathering and covert action organizations as well as to military staffs. These

Figure 16.2

Simplified View of the Deception Process

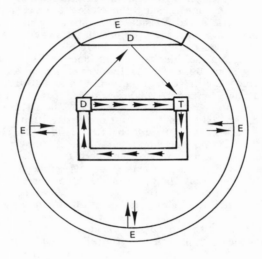

☐ = DECEIVER

☐ = TARGET

= = CHANNELS

⟹ = SIGNALS

➤ = FEEDBACK

E = ENVIRONMENT

E = PORTION OF ENVIRONMENT MANIPULATED BY DECEIVER
D

Figure 16.3
Deceiver and Target Elements in the Process of Deception

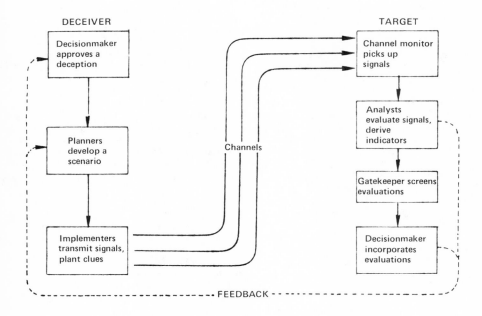

groups were often not a normal part of the civilian or military bureaucracy but rather, like the famous London Controlling Section, were specially formed during the war and disbanded or severely cut back at its conclusion. On an as-needed basis, implementers temporarily co-opted regular military personnel who generated false radio traffic, set up deceptive camouflage, and simulated large troop movements or encampments and the like. National political leaders, high-level diplomats, civil servants, businessmen, and news reporters also often played starring roles in strategic deceptions.

The initial target of a military deception is usually a state's intelligence organization. It consists of channel monitors who seek out and collect information and analysts who coordinate and evaluate it. Gatekeepers within the intelligence agencies and command staffs screen the information and analyses, and determine what is actually forwarded to civilian or military authorities—the ultimate deception targets. Presumably relying on information received, these leaders make the strategic or tactical decisions that the deceivers seek to influence.

The links, or "channels," between deceivers and targets make deception possible, and their variety is unlimited. A channel could be a newspaper monitored by the target, the target's reconnaissance satellites, electronic intercept systems, diplomats, or spies. Through these channels are transmitted signals—physical phenomena that can be observed or sensed by the target. A signal may be a news article on the activities of a general, a reduction in military radio traffic, or a staged unloading of ships. To a target preparing to repel an amphibious attack, these signals are (planted) clues of the attacker's interest. When put together they indicate that the attack will not soon occur because, say, the general expected to lead it is away on other business, radio traffic is too sparse to support an attack, and ships preparing to carry out an imminent landing usually on-load rather than off-load goods.

The flow of signals in a strategic deception is not only from deceivers to targets. Because these deceptions occur over weeks or months, the deceivers have time to monitor their targets' statements and actions in order to ascertain the effects of the deception while it is still ongoing. The statements and actions constitute return signals--"feedback"--that provide the deceivers with a basis for modulating their activities. In a successful deception, the targets are not aware that their actions and statements constitute this kind of feedback. Should the target realize it, the stage is set for a further permutation in the deception process, entrapment of the deceivers by their victim. By using the feedback channels to send deceptive signals to their enemies, the targets become the deceivers and the deception channels become feedback for this new layer of deception.

Implied in this discussion is a view of deception as a process of encoding, transferring, and decoding messages in which there are two categories of messages. The message feature is evident in the example used earlier. In it the target was concerned with repelling an expected amphibious attack, and the deceiver transmitted three signals to shape the target's estimate of the attack's timing: a news article on a general's activities, reduced radio traffic, and a staged unloading of ships. Each signal contained its own micromessage to the effect that "the general is away," "radio traffic is too sparse," and "ships are off-loading." The micromessages become important when the target properly interprets and conjoins them, for they convey the overarching macromessage—"an amphibious attack will not soon occur"—devised by the deceiver for the target's consumption. In a misleading deception, only one macromessage is intended. In the ambiguity-producing variant, a number of macromessages may be generated, each with its own micromessage subset.

LIKELIHOOD OF DECEPTION

Two groups of factors condition the likelihood of deception: aspects of the particular military situation and personal qualities. These factors may operate independently or in combination with one another. It is difficult to establish a priori which group is more important, although the second set probably has greater impact.

With respect to the first group, high-stakes situations can certainly influence willingness to deceive. When outcomes are critical, adversaries are encouraged to make use of every capability, every advantage, to ensure victory to stave off defeat.

Resort to deception can be particularly compelling if decisionmakers are not fully confident of a situation's outcome because of their own military weaknesses. Desiring to compensate for these deficiencies, they may seek through some ruse to induce their enemies to lower their guard, dilute their strength, or concentrate their forces on the wrong objective. For example, plans Bodyguard and Barclay for the invasions of Normandy and Sicily, respectively, both reflected the concern that until a beachhead was secured, amphibious landings would be highly vulnerable to being pushed back into the sea. From the attacker's perspective, it is thus imperative to ensure that the defender's response capability be as limited as possible. Weaker in mechanized forces, Hitler similarly wanted to limit Allied response to Case Yellow, the May 1940 push into France. He convinced the Allies that his main thrust would be through Holland and Belgium. While the British and French massed in that direction, the Wehrmacht's primary offensive was actually far to the south at Sedan. It then turned toward the channel encircling the very best of the Allied armies. The Dunkirk evacuation meant that the bulk of these would fight again, but for France the war was lost.

Even when optimistic of the outcome of a situation, an actor may be attracted to deception as one way to lower costs. The wish to avoid being viewed as an aggressor has inspired many a nation to fabricate evidence that its victim actually fired the first shot. The wish to avoid human or material losses has resulted in schemes such as the British plan in 1943 to protect their bombers attacking Peenemunde. Though confident that this German rocket facility could be destroyed, the British sought to minimize their own casualties. They succeeded in deflecting German fighters from their bomber streams by convincing the enemy's air defense that Berlin was the target instead.

Situations characterized by uncertainty can also induce deception. In those circumstances, actors often seek to mislead or confuse in order to keep their options open and to test the reaction to alternative policies. A state undecided as to whether to attack another, for instance, may still wish to be ready to do so. This was the case prior to the last-minute Soviet decision to invade Czechoslovakia. Having its troops "exercise" in border areas for the greater part of the summer allowed the USSR to proceed with preparations for an invasion while not openly committing itself to this step. It also allowed the Soviets to save face if they decided not to attack. After all, the Czechs might have backed down, making attack unnecessary, or they might have rallied the overwhelming support of the world community, making the invasion option even less attractive.

In any of these situations, not all states or individuals would resort to deception. Actors bring their own conditioned responses, their own predilections, to the problems they face. We see at least five factors possibly at play here.

First, there may be "deception styles," which vary from culture to culture, that would account for the differences in when and how nations use deception. The intriguing thought that some societies' values or expected modes of personal interaction condition individuals to understand and succeed at deception is to our knowledge largely unexplored.

It is conceivable that by studying cultural norms we may learn to predict how nations will employ deception in military contexts. One such analysis compares national patterns in the deceptive practices of the Soviets and the Chinese.[2] It describes the Soviets' use of the "false war scare" to overawe opponents, their penchant for "disinformation," and their efforts to induce overestimation of their military capabilities. This contrasts with the Chinese preference for the "deep lure," the multiple stratagem, and the anticipation of the enemy's intentions through acumen.[3] A study of this type suggests that by expanding systematic comparison of national deception styles, one can isolate patterns that could alert counterdeception analysts sooner to the deceptive ploys of a particular culture.

A second conditioning factor may be the nature of the political system in which an actor operates. Herbert Goldhamer, in developing this argument, contends that deception may be more common in states where political leaders take a strong, central role in military decisionmaking. He implies that politics either attracts individuals prone to deception or conditions individuals to practice it. As a corollary to his general argument, he adds that a tendency to deceive is particularly prevalent in dictatorships and authoritarian regimes. He reasons that the "secrecy and total control available [in these governments], and the reduced inhibitions that accompany such exercise of power, facilitate and provide incentives for the exercise of craft, cunning, and deception."[4]

Paralleling Goldhamer's perspective are two closely related factors. One is the bureaucratic imperative that organizations trained for particular tasks will seek to perform them. The other is the psychological trait that leads people to think in terms of what is available or familiar to them. These phenomena suggest that military deception is likely to occur if a nation maintains an apparatus to plan and organize deception, or if its military preserves, passes on, or at least debates a doctrine for deception. Conversely, nations having no such apparatus or doctrine, or those that allow them to atrophy, must overcome the inertia involved in creating or revivifying them—a situation characteristic of the United States' early strategic deception efforts in World War II.

Finally, there is the issue of a person's own predilection to deception. Clearly, even within the same cultural or organizational setting, individuals differ in this regard. Some leaders relish deception; others put up with it; still others resist it. Why this is so remains largely unexplored. Barton Whaley searched his historical data for evidence of a "deceptive personality type"—that is, a group of attributes or experiences that would account for these differences—but could find none. At present we must be content to observe that personal reactions to deception are at least self-consistent. In other words, a commander who has appreciated and relied on deception in the past is likely to do so again. Winston Churchill was an early proponent of deception in World War I and encouraged its elaboration again twenty years later; Douglas MacArthur used serial deceptions in his campaign across the Pacific, and succeeded with deception again at Inchon in Korea. In following the good advice to "know thine enemy," a nation might be well served to evaluate its opponent's experience with deception.

DIFFICULTIES OF DECEPTION

In theory, deception can fail. It is a fragile and risky enterprise. Succeeding at deception seems unlikely when we consider the many difficulties that plague deceivers. New problems attend each of the three stages of a deception, thereby causing a target (1) to receive signals, (2) to interpret them as intended, and (3) to act on them in a way that benefits the deceiver. These problems generate considerable uncertainty, which seems intrinsic to deception.

An amateurish formulation and transmission of clues is unlikely to fool an alert adversary. Even when signals are flawlessly crafted and implemented, however, deceivers may be undone by accidents in transmission that they could not have predicted or prevented.

The accidents that interrupt and corrupt a signal before it reaches its destination often resemble what communications theorists define as "noise." As William Reese points out, strict adherence to the definition of noise in communications theory would restrict our labeling as noise only the random accidents between transmission and reception of the signal. Accidents in interpretation, or those that result from deliberate, competing signals, do not meet physicists' standards of randomness, even though they might be equally devastating to the deceiver's plans.[5]

Accidents in interpretation sometimes cannot be avoided. Given that, by definition, deceivers wish to remain undetected, they must operate indirectly, at a discreet remove from their victims; they cannot risk overplaying their hands in order to guide their targets' analysis. The targets must inadvertently meet the deceivers halfway by figuring out for themselves what the evidence means. In effect, the deceivers must have the connivance of the target to succeed at deception. Thus, all deception includes an element of self-deception through the targets' active participation. (See Figure 16.4)

Two factors are especially pertinent to difficulties in predicting how an opponent will interpret a given clue: psychological perception and organizational processes. Richards J. Heuer points out that perception is more than a passive response to stimuli. It is an active

280

Figure 16.4
Possible Results of Transmitting a Deceptive Signal

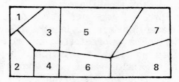

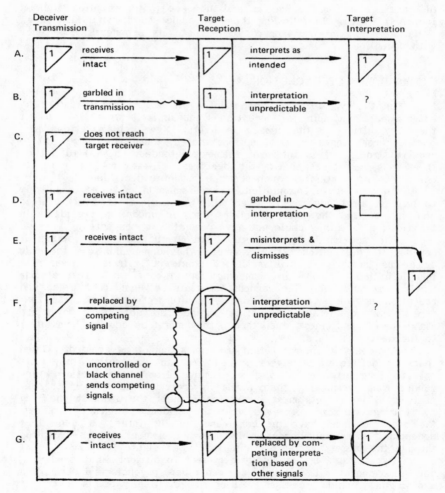

constructing of reality wherein one selects, arranges, and attaches meanings to certain stimuli from the great mass available. Individuals do this on the basis of rules and conventions learned over time. One's past experiences and training inevitably create a "mind-set," which, in Heuer's words, is "akin to a screen or lens through which we perceive the world."[6] A signal picked up intact by the target's sensors may be misperceived as it passes through the mind-set of the individual or group assigned to figure out what it means. What seems to the deceiver a clear and logical inference that anyone would draw from a clue may be filtered out or twisted by the target.

A second source of misinterpretations is the effect that organizations may have on the interpretation of data. Ronald G. Sherwin reminds us that intelligence organizations are the initial targets of deception. Ultimately, decisionmakers must be led into acting against their best interests for the deception to succeed, but this first involves fooling the organization that receives and interprets the signals going into an intelligence evaluation. In addition to the perceptual filters that individuals bring to their tasks, the organization is likely to have norms and assumptions about what certain things mean or portend. In effect, the organization often socializes its members into a group viewpoint, which, if known, can be played on by a deceiver.[7]

Should analysts resist the prevailing views of the group and raise a new possibility, another aspect of organizational life may prevent their dissent from succeeding. Despite a commitment to objectivity, most hierarchical organizations cannot escape seeing the importance of an interpretation as a function of the status of the person espousing it. Dissent from the top commands more attention than dissent from low-level analysts, no matter how well-founded their suspicions. The pressures toward group consensus in any organization tend to eliminate eccentricity, including an occasional offbeat but correct view.

These group processes can slant, block, or filter the meanings assigned by a group to a series of clues. If the signals sent by deceivers run aground on some bureaucratic sensitivity, or on the mind-set of the organization, they will fail to shape their targets' beliefs.

Further difficulties arise from the fact that even when decisionmakers are fooled by a deception, they may not always act on their false beliefs. Contingencies can intervene that prevent the targets from taking the action the deceivers are trying to elicit. On the one hand, new information or pressures may impinge on the decisionmakers, causing them to act in unexpected ways not consistent with their deception-induced beliefs. Bureaucratic competition for scarce resources, for example, sometimes prevents carrying out activities that in all other respects seem inevitable.

On the other hand, in the mere passage of time from the point at which the deceivers planned and executed their series of signals until the targets must take action, the situation may have changed and become something quite different. The original clues, once convincing and incorporated into the targets' interpretation, may not elicit the expected action if events overtake them in the meantime. Then again, chance in its many forms (e.g., bad weather or misplaced orders) can intervene to prevent action otherwise intended.

ADVANTAGES OF THE DECEIVER

The preceding list of difficulties suggests that deceptions should seldom work, and yet the evidence available to us has shown that they usually do. An analysis of 93 cases of strategic deception between 1914 and 1973 found the likelihood of achieving surprise by using two deceptive ruses was very high—.88, and with three ruses the probability rose to 1.00.[8] They aid the deceiver's cause even if they do not go strictly according to plan. In part, this paradoxical outcome may be an artifact of the familiar bias toward only documenting success. Bungled deceptions rarely appear in a deceiver's historical record, and they can seldom be proven after the fact by the target. The records suggest additional factors that help explain why deceptions succeed despite the difficulties we have identified. Some powerful elements in the relationship between adversaries, in human perception, and in the environment play into the deceiver's hands.

One source of this advantage is embedded in the basic goals of hostile competition. Each adversary eagerly seeks out information about the other while trying to deny access to information about itself. By opening up channels to the outside, and particularly to their opponents when possible, adversaries also open themselves up to being deceived via those channels. Although raw data about the enemy and the situation may flow into intelligence centers in enormous volume, highly reliable information is often scarce. A competitor is not able to dismiss information that may be true and, at the same time, portends serious consequences. As a result, the benefit of the doubt about the validity of such information is placed on the side of the deceivers, for it ensures that their deceptive clues will get a hearing by their targets.

On balance, the processes of human perception and cognition provide a second source of advantage for the deceivers. Although a few patterns in human thought favor the targets, particularly in cases where the deceivers must change the minds of their targets, most of these patterns appear to conspire against the targets, who are more often betrayed than served by their own processes of thought.

Psychologists characterize perception and cognition as organizing activities. Making what seems chaotic into a coherent, orderly, and at least partially predictable pattern is basic to human thought. The quantities of stimuli and types of information around us would overwhelm the senses were they not selectively ordered by perceptual processing. The stimuli which do pass through the filters of our senses are recognized and categorized using concepts evolved from past experience. The meaning assigned to any other stimulus depends in part on the meanings of the other events, objects, or ideas that exist with it and form its context. In Theodore R. Sarbin's view the best analogy for understanding human thought processes is the creation of a narrative which ties together the disparate elements into a plot.[9] By plotting a story which explains events chronologically, individuals keep the sense that they know with some confidence "what comes next" and can on this basis plan for the future. The drive for coherence is not a perfect process, however. Inevitably, simplifications result in the loss of some information. Often these biases favor the deceiver.

Initial impressions are extremely important in that they shape all subsequent understandings of an event. Apparently the mind works by taking incremental steps: what we first learn about a topic becomes the touchstone against which each new datum is compared. While some change in the overall concept does result from these later inputs, it is the persistence of the initial formulation and the resistance to changing it which are the striking features of the perceptual process. Thus targets of a deception can be at the mercy of their initial impressions if they are reinforced by a deceiver. This convergence on the psychological importance of first exposure and the presumptions brought to data suggests why studies consistently find that M-1 deception, wherein deceivers reinforce their target's existing views, are the most commonly tried, the most powerful, and the most likely to succeed of the deception variants. Barton Whaley's findings (1969) provide telling support for this: of 68 cases of strategic interaction he studied, he found that 79 percent of them succeeded by reinforcing what the target expected.

Deceivers can benefit from a third factor, the effects of inherent uncertainties. Especially in competitions where virtually all data are ambiguous and to some degree suspect, so often the case in war, the situation forgives most of the mistakes deceivers make. For example, security leaks, a major kind of mistake, seldom destroy a perception. If deceivers' true plans, or the fact that deception is afoot, reach a target, evidence suggests this is often not fatal to the deceivers' hopes. To explain this counterintuitive finding we must adopt the targets' perspective: faced with an array of evidence which can rarely be documented as completely reliable, they must use more-or-less ambiguous data. Leaks to them must seem just another species of potentially true or potentially false signals. Even leaks which come from well-placed sources or over channels which are usually reliable must still jostle and compete against the range of alternatives the targets' evidence supports. What seems to deceivers a glaringly bright give-away often seems to targets either too good to be true or only one more among their many monochrome clues.

A final advantage the deceiver holds is that although deception almost always inflicts costs on the targets, attempting it entails few penalties for the deceivers even if it does not transpire as planned. If the targets are deceived, they will probably act in a manner detrimental to their own interests; if they resist being taken in by the deception, they must still devote time and resources to evaluating the evidence and establishing probabilities for the future from the mass of clues. Efforts at deception, on the other hand, are often inexpensive because most illusions consume few available resources. Failure, even being caught red-handed, does not prevent future successes at deception against the same targets. The price of failure does entail the destruction of some "assets" for deception, such as double agents or covert channels that are "blown," but these are less net losses than the foregoing of future benefits. The deceivers are always cushioned by the elemental fact that they know the truth of their own intentions and, hence, can distinguish what is true from what is deceptive. The target does not and cannot know this with certainty, and the investment necessary to sort through yet another level of complexity introduced by deception falls with unequal force on the side of the targets.

ADVANTAGE OF THE OFFENSIVE

Being on the offensive provides a better position for succeeding at deception than being on the defensive. This is particularly true in the early stages of an attack. Defensive deception, however, can be effective under the right circumstances. The basis for this view is that the initiators of military action are defining the nature and timing of the encounter and thereby have a greater degree of control over it at the outset. Because they know what the truth will be—that is, the location, timing, and manner of the planned attack—they can better orchestrate the dissemination of untruth than the defenders, who, in a sense, have no similar "truth" of their own providing a baseline for devising untruths. The defenders obviously know what they want to defend, but they remain more or less uncertain as to specifically when and where an attacker will challenge them. They are also probably uncertain as to the magnitude and kind of attack they will face.

The attackers' deception advantage is usually greatest in the early stages of their offensive campaign. Once the campaign is well on its way, the situation often does not remain stable long enough for the attacker to devise and implement deception. A classic illustration is the relative nonuse of strategic deception by the Allies after the Normandy breakout. The rapidly changing strategic situation between September 1944 and May 1945 was not conducive to deception.

Although being on the defensive may not be conducive to engaging in deception, it would be wrong to say that defensive deceptions cannot occur. They can be very effective under the right circumstances, especially given adequate time and resources. The defending party may, for example, attempt to lay inviting axes of advance for enemy ground forces while remaining ready to ambush them should they take the bait. If the defenders fear enemy bomber or missile strikes, they can also engage in extensive camouflage and decoy aimed at drawing enemy weapons away from high-value targets to dummy sites instead. The British did this in 1940-1941, with limited results since they did not act to protect their assets until after war had begun. Their experience illustrates that defensive deceptions—at least those of that type--have the highest chance for success if they are undertaken before the need for them is obvious, because by then the time and resources needed to implement them may not be sufficient.

ASTUTENESS

Cleverness on the deceivers' part can reinforce their chances of successfully deceiving their adversaries. Certain behaviors distinguish expert deceivers from their mediocre counterparts. Experts seem to share a turn of mind useful for predicting the reactions of others, and they understand the demands that deception imposes on them.

The most successful deceivers rely on some individuals who have acumen, an ability to "de-center" or step outside one's own viewpoint into the mind-set of an opponent. People with a keen sense of acumen can empathize closely enough with their targets to predict with considerable confidence how they will see and respond to a given situation. British deception experts in World War II stressed the importance of individuals who could "get inside" the German mind and construct in their imagination how German analysts would piece together and interpret evidence.

Acumen seems to depend not only on logical ability; emotional and imaginative qualities also play important parts. Thus, in the British case during World War II, many of their most successful deception staffers brought their "flair" with them from diverse, nonmilitary backgrounds in literary, theatrical, and business fields. Sarbin suggests that although it may be difficult, one could conceivably develop the means to identify persons gifted with acumen, on the theory that this trait would be as valuable for counterdeception as it has proven to be for deceivers in the past.[10]

Assuming that potential deceivers can bring to bear keen insights into the perceptions of their victims, how should they proceed in order to maximize their chances of success? Deciding what the targets' basic goals are would seem to be the natural starting point. Knowledge of their goals should facilitate prediction of the options to which they will best respond. The deceivers should send clues that give impressions consistent with the targets' goals, for these, as noted earlier, will be most readily recognized and believed. If, as Paul H. Moose suggests, one side's goals are directed toward preserving the status quo, the other side can predict that they will be especially sensitive to signs that the current situation is stable.[11] Clever deceivers should then provide those signs while preparing to disrupt that stability. At the level of generality of change versus status quo, it appears that either an ambiguity-increasing or a misleading deception would accomplish the deceivers' object: If the targets are confused, they are likely to seize excuses to delay decision and action until they receive clarification; if they are misled by appearances that the deceivers have acquiesced to the status quo, they will likewise do nothing. As elaborated by Reese in his application of game theory to deception, doing nothing until the situation clears is often a fatally attractive option that leads to one's being surprised.[12]

Beyond concerning themselves with the goals of their targets, astute deceivers should try to determine their targets' beliefs and expectations vis-à-vis the impending encounter. As emphasized earlier, deceivers have a marked advantage if they spin a tale that their targets are already predisposed to believe. Experts at deception strike a balance between keeping their deception subtle enough so as not to arouse their targets' suspicions and intervening vigorously enough to have the desired reinforcing effect.

The greatest demands on the astuteness of deceivers are made when they must change their targets' beliefs. Deceivers should sequence their clues in ways that aim to shake the targets' initial ideas severely enough that the targets "reopen the case" in their minds. By overcoming the tendency to assimilate new evidence to existing views with an initial large, compelling piece of evidence, the deceivers may force the targets to reorient their views. Additional corroborating clues will then help to build up a plausible scenario of the deceivers' choice. The British <u>Mincemeat</u> ruse during World War II is an example of this sequencing to change the target's mind: Confronted by a drowned courier with plans suggesting invasion sites on Sardinia, Hitler and his generals deployed forces away from Sicily, the real site, even though they had initially guessed correctly where the invasion would come.

It is paradoxical but true that deceivers seeking to change the views of their targets should also aim to make them vigilant, even though that very vigilance may be instrumental in the rejection by those targets of the deceivers' false tales.

Why this is so requires distinguishing three emotional states associated with making important decisions. The first of these is relaxation: individuals feel no tension because no such decision is required of them. The second is that of moderate tension, or vigilance: some tension arises from the need for a decision, but it remains moderate as long as the individuals believe they have adequate time to evaluate alternatives before deciding on one. The third state is high tension, or rigidity. Here individuals feel great stress because time seems inadequate to evaluate properly alternatives.

Psychologists argue that individuals are most apt to follow their predispositions in either the first or the third emotional states: when they are relaxed, or when they are very tense. In the first case, facing no important decision, individuals see no disadvantage in giving head to their predispositions. Pressed for important decisions in a hurry, on the other hand, individuals fall prey to what they consciously or subconsciously choose to see. It is the second state of moderate tension, or vigilance, that elicits responses most likely to overcome predispositions. Individuals are then evidently most open-minded as they seek out information to make a rational decision. In short, deceivers should confront a target with the need to make an important decision but should avoid placing the target in a crisis situation if the aim is to change the target's beliefs.

In Operation Mincemeat the British organized their clues to suggest that Sardinia would be invaded in the coming months, but not immediately. Hitler and his intelligence staffs were given reason to doubt their expectations about Sicily. They had time to reassess the situation and put together an alternative scenario incorporating Sardinia. Had the British rushed them into crisis decisionmaking, they would probably not have shifted their forces so cooperatively.

In other circumstances astute deceivers will decide that they gain most by generating just such a crisis in decisionmaking for the target. Looking at how organizations function, Sherwin notes that increasing stress improves an organization's ability to process information only to a certain point. Thereafter, the internal system collapses and the organization cannot systematically process data. This "fibrillation" could be very useful to deceivers who need to paralyze the target's intelligence and command structures and subsequently move quickly against them.

However, the cost deceivers pay for deliberately provoking the false perception of crisis by their opponents is some inability to predict their responses accurately. What deceivers know about a target's normal behavior during steady state periods is undercut when the target moves into crisis and shifts to extraordinary coping behavior. It may be advantageous to deceivers to risk this unpredictability in order to reduce the target organization's efficiency. Many of the distracting deceptions connected with the Normandy landings, for example, such as dummy paratroops and multiple fake landing sites, served to stretch and overload the ability of German intelligence to sort out and respond to threat. There is some danger, though, that by generating crisis deceivers will find themselves facing some unexpected response which was saved just for such exigencies. Perhaps the key to assessing this risk is the quality of the deceivers' channels of information to the target, in particular the feedback channels we will discuss below.

In addition to seeing things through the targets' eyes, assessing their goals, and determining how much time pressure a victim should face, astute deceivers recognize that they should follow certain rules to maximize their chances of succeeding.

Past deception experts have left primers that distill the lessons they learned from experience. If not applied too rigidly, these lessons continue to be useful. For example, a scenario for deception on a strategic scale, which by definition is complex and persists for at least several weeks, must remain plausible to the target for as long as it is running. One aspect of establishing plausibility is making sure the target obtains confirmation of the crucial deceptive elements from various and reliable sources. Another is to ensure that the scenario adapts to changing circumstances and evolves in a "real-life" way. The best deceivers are sensitive enough not to overplay their hands: They knit false clues into a web of many truths that can be independently verified and found to "ring true." The more data points are determined by the targets to be true, the more likely they are to twist or ignore the remaining discrepant ones to fit their hypotheses. In addition, clever deceivers try to sabotage as many sources of disconfirming evidence as possible; they also strive to lay before their targets proof that they have the capabilities to carry out the operations suggested by the deceptive scenario.

Such expert advice reflects an intuitive understanding of the several psychological biases that people bring to the analysis of evidence of psychological factors in deception. In particular, deception experts seek to play on individuals' oversensitivity to consistency. Since people will tend to believe a small sample of consistent data more readily than a larger, more statistically reliable sample that is inconsistent, deceivers aim for a variety of clues that all reinforce and support one scenario. But there is yet another side to the need for consistency. People also tend to underestimate the importance of missing data in an array of evidence. What is there blinds them to the significance of what is not. Clever deceivers will realize that they need not, and probably should not, try to tie up every loose end and hypothetical possibility in their scenarios. The targets will work with the evidence they have and will tend to discount what is missing. An elaborate airtight case might excite suspicion if it looked "too good to be true" (i.e., was too consistent) and it may not allow sufficient flexibility to weave in chance events as they occur. Resisting the temptation to go too far in their desire to ensure that the targets make the right deductions is one of the hallmarks of astute deceivers.

FEEDBACK

If deceivers are to carry out an extended deception, they must adapt it to the changes inevitable in an evolving situation. Their most valuable asset for doing this is feedback. Feedback is accurate and timely information about an adversary's reactions. It can be direct or indirect; the former is more powerful, the latter more common.

Indirect feedback refers to observations about how the other side is responding to an action or event. It is available to anyone who systematically observes any sort of interaction, including deception. One acts and waits for visible signs of the opponent's reactions. If an action is specifically designed to test the reaction, indirect feedback is usually better focused and likely to be more useful in characterizing an opponent.

For strategic deception, however, a more precise form of feedback is usually desirable. Since military adversaries generally cover up their own reactions and simulate appearances to suit their needs, visible reactions can be unreliable. The side that achieves a reliable covert channel into its opponent's camp over which feedback can flow has, as spy novels often portray, a most precious advantage— namely, direct feedback consisting of systems such as Ultra in World War II or well-placed espionage agents. These systems pass information that, in effect, short-circuits the normal channels between sides. As a matter of course, adversaries eagerly seek such useful channels because the information obtained is usually more complete and unambiguous than indirect feedback would be. However, as demonstrated by the fates of most spies, direct channels are also inherently risky and usually temporary.

In addition to providing fuller, more reliable insight into the enemy's camp, direct feedback may allow deceivers to risk lying more frequently and to get away with it. Typically, deceivers must use many true signals in which a few lies are embedded in order to protect the impression of reliability of the channels held by their targets. If the targets find that the information from a channel is too often false (i.e., more often than the rate of error normal for such channels), they will stop relying on it. Direct feedback tells the deceivers quickly which of their lies the targets accept and which they question, what they find suspicious or inexplicable, and what they swallow without qualm. Thus the deceivers can at once back up the lies that are questioned, or soft-pedal them, so that numerous lies can be passed and protected without damaging the targets' perception of how reliable the channel is. The British use of their double-agent system in World War II is an extreme example of the rich possibilities for such a direct feedback system and its potential for passing lies. Many of the dangers from uncontrolled channels and from random accidents in deception scenarios can be eliminated by direct feedback, because these hitches can be detected and corrected quickly, before an alternative scenario has taken hold in the minds of the targets. Furthermore, direct feedback prevents targets from ambushing the deceivers, thereby removing the largest threat faced by the deceivers.

A third aspect of direct feedback's value for deception lies in its ability to overcome the unpredictability associated with crisis. Moose argues that indirect feedback may well suffice adversaries in situations where a competitive system persists over a fairly long period of time. When change is gradual and the parts of the system interact in stable ways, predictions of what the other side will do based on observations of past behavior can be quite accurate. Stability not only implies peaceful conditions; prolonged conflict between evenly matched adversaries could become similarly predictable.[13]

However, in times of transition or crisis, such as a surprise attack or warfare between opponents with rapidly shifting relative strengths, each side replaces its usual modes of operation with emergency routines. It no longer acts "normally." New pressures generate extraordinary exertions or desperate expedients, and the rapid changes each side undergoes prevent prediction based on observing the responses of the adversary. By the time one observes a response, the opponent may have changed in some crucial way and will not or cannot respond that way again in the future. Thus, in crises or transitions, when equilibrium and stability are lost, direct feedback with its shorter response time offers the only realistic means to predict the opponent's next likely move. By allowing deceivers to hold their fingers on the pulse of their targets even while the latter are changing rapidly, direct feedback permits the deceivers to keep up, providing new clues as needed to prolong and preserve the scenario's plausibility.

Deceivers themselves have viewed direct feedback as crucial for their success in elaborate, long-term deceptions. John Bevan, head of the British deception effort in London after 1942, credited their unusually intimate feedback through Ultra with supporting the complex, multilayered deceptions launched by the British against the Germans. Often by coordinating information from Ultra with their extensive network of turned German agents, British deceivers could incorporate the Germans' unexpected interpretations of their signals or sudden shifts in events into the deception scenario. This ability to touch on additional true reference points enhanced credibility considerably. The feedback also allowed the British to back off when a story wore thin, thereby preventing the enemy from concluding firmly that deception was at hand and allowed the deceivers to salvage their precious double agents and other resources for further deceptions.

COUNTERDECEPTION

The countering of deception is traditionally conceived of as a two-step process of first detecting and then foiling deception, but success need not always require the detection of deception.

Counterdeception is an extremely difficult task. Barton Whaley has analyzed 68 cases of attempted strategic military surprise occurring between 1914 and 1968. Fifty-seven of these instances involved resort to deception and, of this group, 50 (or 88 percent) resulted in some degree of surprise. It is necessary to emphasize that the cases Whaley studied were somewhat skewed in the direction of successful surprise; nevertheless, his data suggest that deception may be very difficult to foil, especially since the target in each case had the benefit of at least some warning.[14]

This conclusion is not surprising given that the deception variants that seem to occur most often—the M-1 and A types—are also those in which the targets are the most cooperative. The difficulty of countering M-1 deceptions is that the targets are inclined to accept the perpetrated lies before the deception starts; their perceptual and cognitive biases militate against their rejection of the lies. It is noteworthy that 79 percent of Whaley's cases involved exploiting a target's preconceptions.

In A-type deceptions, the deceivers need only send lies that are plausible and consequential to the targets' interests. If the lies go through to the targets, the latter's desire to make rational or good decisions helps to guarantee that they will not ignore the deceptive information. If they delay in making a final choice in order to await additional clarifying data, they surrender the initiative and leave themselves open to surprise. If they hedge by distributing resources to cover plausible contingencies, they face the prospect that their resources will be inadequate to deal with the contingency on which the deceivers will act.

Only in M-2 deceptions does an initial advantage lie with the targets. Their perceptual and cognitive biases incline them from the start to ignore deceptive messages and to doubt their veracity.

Detecting Deception

Sources such as Ultra or an agent in the enemy's headquarters are probably the best ways to establish whether that enemy is being deceitful. These sources, however, are generally unavailable and certainly not foolproof: Ultra, for instance, did not prevent the Allies from being surprised by Germany's Ardennes offensive during the winter of 1944.

Any state's attempt to harness more mundane intelligence assets to the counterdeception problem must be done delicately, for it is probable that attempts to sensitize intelligence analysts to the prospect of deception will incline them to find "deception" when it isn't there. Indeed, as Heuer suggests, intelligence analysts are generally predisposed to perceive deception without any encouragement to look for it. Heuer's conclusion parallels that of Sarbin who argues, in effect, that to encourage analysts to look for deception will probably lead them to subject intelligence data to particularly detailed or fine-grained scrutiny.[15]

In short, the sensitization of analysts to the possibility of deception can have pernicious effects, including a high false-alarm rate and a resulting "cry-wolf" syndrome, in which true deception is discounted. It can also lead to a situation in which analysts, no longer sure what they should accept as true, impose such rigid standards of proof that they suppress either the free play of intuition, which is so much a part of intelligence analysis, or the flow of intelligence from analysts to decisionmakers. Prior to the Cuban Missile Crisis, for example, CIA Director John McCone suspected that the USSR was emplacing missiles into Cuba and alerted President Kennedy several times. But the president grew impatient with McCone when the latter could produce no hard evidence. McCone reacted by drawing back; despite his suspicions he did not raise the issue again until the U-2 photos provided clear proof.

It is not enough for an intelligence organization to suspect strongly or detect traces of deception. A target must still separate the real from the lie. History is replete with cases in which the lie has been accepted as real and truth has been deemed to be deception. A classic example occurred prior to the Soviet summer offensive of June 22, 1944. Working to convince the Germans that the attack would be concentrated against Army Group North Ukraine, the Soviets actually prepared to strike Army Group Center instead. Between

May 30 and June 22, signs of a Soviet buildup off Army Group Center "multiplied rapidly as the deployment went into high gear, but they were not enough to divert the OKH's [i.e., the German Army High Command's] attention from Army Group North Ukraine. . . . The [Wehrmacht's] Eastern Intelligence Branch dismissed the activity opposite Army Group Center as an 'apparent deception.' "16

As a matter of course, intelligence agencies should seek to draw responses from a suspected deceiver that can help confirm or deny deceptive intent. For instance, by indicating rejection of a suspected lie, a target may trigger a measurable increase in deceiver activity aimed at reinforcing a lie. The increase should heighten suspicion that deception is afoot. Shortly after the Normandy landing, for example, the British learned that Hitler had ordered the transfer of troops from the Calais to the Normandy areas. The British feared that Hitler no longer viewed the Calais area as the ultimate main point of attack and Normandy as only a feint. Controlling all German spies in the U.K., they commanded one to send a special wireless message on June 9 to his German paymasters. The agent transmitted for two hours—a period of highly unusual length—as he argued that a large landing would soon occur at Calais. The message was instrumental in Hitler's cancellation of the troop transfer, but its special nature and length constituted a marked increase in the British deception effort, which could have aroused German suspicions.

Foiling or Deterring Deception

Targets may pursue two courses of action upon detecting deception. They can reveal their discoveries to the deceivers, thereby forcing them to abandon the deception and possibly also the military operation supported by it. But they can also try to keep the discovery a secret, stringing the deceivers along in the hopes of ambushing the latter's forces.

These actions are premised on the detection of deception first, but it is also theoretically possible to foil a potential deceiver without proof or even evidence of deception. The most realistic way a target can do this is to remain unpredictable, for uncertainty about whether a target is taking the bait, or how a target will deploy forces and react to an attack, can significantly increase a deceiver's fear of ambush. As suggested in Reese's application of game theory to deception, if rational deceivers rate the costs and prospects of ambush highly enough, they will probably be deterred from initiating or continuing deception.17 Ironically, (potential) targets could be well-served by engaging in their own deception in order to increase enemy uncertainties, thereby decreasing the enemy's probability of resorting to deception.

It is consistent with our earlier emphasis on unpredictability that deterring or foiling deception is often a by-product of maintaining the strategic military initiative. Although it would be folly to initiate an attack merely to avoid being deceived, the fact remains that strategic deceptions take weeks to implement and usually require that the victim be passive if not predictable during that time. The reason is that deceivers are usually thrown off balance, and their plans overtaken by events, if the victims engage in rapid large-scale or unpredictable changes of behavior. These are precisely the kinds of changes that occur when a state is pressing the strategic initiative.

In sum, counterdeception is extremely difficult to bring about. It is not enough merely to alert one's analysts to the possibility of deception, for such action may be dysfunctional. The institutional mechanisms (such as devil's advocates) so often suggested for avoiding strategic surprise are obviously and directly relevant for counterdeception. States fearful of being deception targets should look for opportunities to draw a response from a potential deceiver that helps confirm whether or not deception is afoot. Even when deception is not evidenced or ongoing, it may be possible to deter it by heightening a prospective deceiver's fears of ambush.

CONCLUSION

We now offer two final thoughts about the utility of deception. One is that deception's contribution to the outcome of any military campaign remains impossible to measure with scientific precision. Such precision would require verifiable answers to the following questions:

1. What did the targets believe before deception was attempted?
2. What did they come to believe because of the deception?
3. What did they decide to do as a result of their deception-induced beliefs?
4. What was the relative impact of those decisions and actions on the military outcome when compared to other factors such as generalship, quantity and quality of weapons, material resources, troop morale, and the like?

Each of these questions is progressively more difficult to answer. The second and third questions are especially problematic in cases in which only a fine line exists between perpetrated deception and target self-deception, or between perpetrated ambiguity and the ambiguity inherent in any wartime situation. The fourth question restates an analytical problem facing not only students of deception but also all strategic planners and military historians. Until one of them devises a model or formula for measuring accurately the impact of varying factors contributing to victory or defeat, and until adequate data become available so that such a model can be applied, it will remain impossible to estimate deception's relative impact with other than rough subjective precision.

With the preceding paragraph as a caveat, we believe that deception is a powerful tool, particularly in the hands of an astute practitioner. Barton Whaley's findings, while perhaps skewed toward cases of successful deception and surprise, support that conclusion.[18] The logic of the deception situation does so as well. The deceivers know the truth, after all, and they can assume that their adversaries will search for its indicators. As a result, the deceivers can expect their victims to pick up some of the signals intended to mislead or confuse. Should these signals be ignored, dismissed, or misinterpreted, the deceivers are probably not worse off. Should they be interpreted as intended, the deceivers stand to gain. The target must pay attention even to scenarios they suspect are untrue, if they are plausible and consequential to their interests. Although the targets may ultimately choose not to act on them, the additional time they spend evaluating deceptive scenarios or searching for further information should benefit their foes.

NOTES

1. Barton Whaley, Codeword Barbarossa (Cambridge, Mass.: MIT Press, 1973), p. 242.
2. Scott A. Boorman, "Deception in Chinese Strategy," in William W. Whitson, ed., The Military and Political Power in China in the 1970's (New York: Praeger Publishers, 1972), pp. 315-316.
3. William R. Harris, "On Countering Strategic Deception," draft R-1230-ARPA (Santa Monica, Calif.: Rand Corporation, 1973).
4. Herbert Goldhamer, "Reality and Belief in Military Affairs: A First Draft" (R-2448-NA, June 1977), edited by Joan Goldhamer (Santa Monica, Calif.: Rand Corporation, 1979), pp. 107-108.
5. William Reese, "Deception Within a Communications Theory Framework," in Donald C. Daniel and Katherine L. Herbig, eds., Strategic Military Deception (New York: Pergamon Press, 1982), p. 101.
6. Richards J. Heuer, "Cognitive Factors in Deception and Counterdeception," in D. C. Daniel and K. L. Herbig et al., eds., Multidisciplinary Perspectives on Military Deception, technical report 56-80-012 (Monterey, Calif.: Naval Postgraduate School, 1980), p. 52.
7. Ronald G. Sherwin, "The Organizational Approach to Strategic Deception: Implications for Theory and Policy," in Daniel and Herbig, Strategic Military Deception, pp. 73-77.
8. Ronald G. Sherwin and Barton Whaley, "Understanding Strategic Deception: An Analysis of 93 Cases," in Daniel and Herbig, Strategic Military Deception, p. 188.
9. Theodore R. Sarbin, "Prolegomenon to a Theory of Counterdeception," in Daniel and Herbig, Strategic Military Deception, pp. 167-170.
10. Ibid.
11. Paul H. Moose, "A Systems View of Deception," in Daniel and Herbig, Strategic Military Deception, p. 144.
12. William Reese, "Deception in a Game Theoretic Framework," in Daniel and Herbig, Strategic Military Deception, pp. 142-143.
13. Moose, "A Systems View," pp. 142-143.
14. Barton Whaley, "Strategem: Deception and Surprise in War" (unpublished manuscript, MIT, 1969).
15. Heuer, "Cognitive Factors," p. 64; Sarbin, "A Prolegomenon," pp. 168-169.
16. Earl F. Ziemke, Stalingrad to Berlin: The German Defeat in the East (Washington, D.C.: U.S. Army, Office of the Chief of Military History, 1968), p. 315. Ziemke is quoting from a German intelligence report.
17. Reese, "Game Theoretic Framework," p. 128.
18. Whaley, "Stratagem," p. 166.

INTELLIGENCE AND ARMS CONTROL

The technical and political aspects of the arms control issue raise serious intelligence questions. Experts disagree about the adequacy of our intelligence capabilities as well as about how formal arms control agreements contribute to United States' national security.

R. Joseph DeSutter is most concerned with distinguishing between intelligence and verification, demonstrating how the two processes are clumsily or cleverly confused, and reviewing some of the political consequences brought about by such confusion.

A crucial distinction between intelligence and verification identified by DeSutter is that intelligence occurs largely in the realm of technical monitoring and data collection, whereas verification, involving relationships between technical evidence and treaty language, deals with legalistic variables. Moreover, verification or compliance enforcement demands political judgments about both the seriousness or strategic significance of violations and whether proving such violations would be in the national interest.

For Herbert Scoville, on the other hand, a valuable partnership exists between intelligence and arms control. Intelligence is necessary to verify compliance with treaty provisions and, as such, suggests the need for arms control program priorities. Alternatively, arms control agreements greatly simplify the task the intelligence community faces. That is, the community's efforts can be reduced to finding violations to specific treaty provisions. However, Scoville is concerned that such a happy state is not guaranteed for the future. Specifically, new types of systems—namely, the cruise missile with its conventional and nuclear capabilities, which are virtually indistinguishable by present verification means—will immeasurably increase the demands on the intelligence community.

John Prados offers a third view on the tangled webs of intelligence and policy. The creation of independent intelligence authorities that report objective intelligence has been an elusive goal. In addition, even the best intelligence estimates contain discomfiting uncertainties.

Doubts and uncertainties characteristic of the intelligence process will continue to interact with the political process as we wrestle with the issues of arms control and effective management of the U.S.-Soviet rivalry. The great hope is that we will find the appropriate answers. Otherwise, we may find ourselves victims of deception and strategic surprise that could lead to devastating policy consequences.

Intelligence Versus Verification:
Distinctions, Confusion, and Consequences

Other contributions to this text have dealt with the specifics of intelligence—what it is, how it is done, and who does it. This chapter discusses one thing that intelligence is not—it is not arms control verification. Because the verification process employs the same monitoring machinery that is used for traditional threat assessment, the confusion seems to persist that the two processes are either the same or very similar. They are not. Such confusion is not only semantically incorrect in itself, and therefore detrimental to analytical rigor, but also quite pernicious in its policy implications. I will first strive to clarify the distinction between intelligence and verification, then demonstrate how the two processes are clumsily or cleverly confused with each other, and finally review some of the political consequences brought about by that confusion.

DISTINCTIONS

Conventional wisdom has it that U.S. participation in arms control regimes was made possible by the maturation of technical monitoring skills—particularly space-based reconnaissance—beginning in the early 1960s.[1] According to this logic, the U.S. compliance-monitoring capability was inadequate to sustain agreements before the emergence of technical reconnaissance, because the Soviet Union had persistently refused to permit on-site inspection. But the emergence of "national technical means" (NTM), so goes the argument, enhanced monitoring skills sufficiently to "enable" previously impossible agreements with the closed Soviet political system.

This logic process posits a certain cause and effect relationship between high-confidence intelligence-monitoring capability and arms control agreements that might serve U.S. security interests. The principal problem with this model is that it implies not just "necessity" but also "sufficiency" with regard to monitoring capability and treaty enforcement power. In so doing, it equates observation and detection of noncompliance with indictment and conviction of the violator. In short, it is a form of reductionism that oversimplifies the complex process of verification and encourages unwarranted optimism in the capacity of arms control to serve traditional U.S. national security interests.

The seemingly widespread understanding of an identity between intelligence and verification appears intellectually seductive if one weighs the benefits of meaningful arms control against the inherent difficulty of negotiating with a secretive, frequently deceptive political adversary like the USSR. The asymmetry between Soviet and American access to information about one another's defense postures is profound. Furthermore, whereas the U.S. Constitution assigns inviolable legal status to a ratified treaty, the Soviet party/government structure is equipped to orchestrate a campaign of clandestine noncompliance with the most dignified obligations assumed in the name of the state. Thus, whether U.S. intelligence monitoring is used in support of compliance adjudication or traditional threat assessment, the United States is at an incalculable disadvantage by comparison with the Soviet Union. Anxiety that compliance might be purely unilateral is therefore a burden that is effectively borne unilaterally by the open democracies when their negotiating partner represents the Soviet political system.

Although it is inarguably true that reliable monitoring skills are essential if the United States is to bear the disproportionate security risks associated with compliance uncertainty, monitoring is only one part of the verification process. Correctly understood in an arms control setting, monitoring is an essentially technical undertaking. Verification, however, is a much broader category involving perceived relationships between technically garnered evidence and carefully crafted treaty language. This relationship takes verification decisions out of the purely technical realms of monitoring and data collection and adds legalistic variables to the equation; but the compliance analyst must ask a variety of additional questions that render the verification or compliance enforcement process far more political than either technical or legal in nature.

Verification, as opposed to monitoring in particular or intelligence threat assessment in general, is a decisionmaking process for making compliance related judgments. In theory, verification, by supporting arms control, is a servant of the same national security goals as those traditionally informed by intelligence collection. In practice, however, the powerful urge to sustain arms control's "momentum" generates process preservation interests for the verifier that are foreign to the threat assessor—goals that are part and parcel of arms control but are also potentially at variance with traditional national security concerns. Verification, then, is not the same as intelligence because arms control enforcement is not the same as traditional national security management. Intelligence specialists examine information collected from many sources and with many possible meanings, and they offer conclusions regarding potential threats to national security. Verification specialists examine similar information, compare its multiple meanings with their understanding of a treaty's language, and suggest tentative conclusions as to whether or not observed conditions represent compliance from an arms control standpoint.

If noncompliance is suspected, a series of painfully difficult questions must be answered. Does the infraction appear serious enough to be raised directly with the Soviets? Can the case be argued (or even raised) without compromising assets necessary for threat assessment? Is the activity in question "strategically significant" enough to risk such a compromise? If the Soviets do not agree with our conclusion, is U.S. abrogation of the agreement in the national interest? Under what conditions should the United States "go public" and risk charges of overreaction from the population at large, from political opponents, or from the media? These are not simply intelligence or threat-measurement questions; they are matters of fine judgment with potentially volatile political overtones. They are political questions because a variety of conflicting domestic and allied value orientations are staked to their answers, because Soviet ire is likely to be invoked if those answers are particularly assertive, because "proof" of one's case is often in the eye of the beholder, because commercial and ideological interests are at stake, and because bureaucratic momentum and professional careers will rise or fall on their resolution. In short, compliance questions are political questions because verification, unlike intelligence or intelligence monitoring, is a political decisionmaking process.

These distinctions should not be regarded as particularly controversial. It is fairly self-evident that intelligence analysts examine monitoring data and ask threat-assessment questions, and that verification analysts examine monitoring data and ask compliance questions. In a variety of official settings, the U.S. government has even directly acknowledged these distinctions. Regarding the differences between intelligence and verification, for example, the Arms Control and Disarmament Agency (ACDA) has explained:

> For the very reason that verification and intelligence are so intimately connected, it is important to emphasize the differences between them. What distinguishes verification from arms related intelligence most of all is its method of approach. While the chief mission of military intelligence is to determine the characteristics and activities of an opponent's weapons and forces, verification must assess whether those characteristics or activities exceed the limitations imposed by an agreement. Accordingly, the task of verification can be more demanding than that of traditional intelligence. . . . Hence, the evidence indicating that violations are occurring will have to be of a higher quality than the evidence needed to react to comparable actions by an adversary without an agreement [emphasis added].[2]

Reflecting on the broad range of issues on which such fine political judgment must be exercised with regard to compliance questions, R. W. Buchheim, a former U.S. commissioner to the SALT Standing Consultative Commission (SCC)—the official forum in which compliance issues are (or are not) raised with the Soviets—maintained:

> Problems of implementation can arise, among other ways, from tentative signs of possible noncompliance which could indicate that a party might be setting out upon a course not consistent with the provisions of an agreement as understood by either or both of the parties, or upon a course of action not fully contemplated in the explicit provisions of the agreement, or upon a course involving circumstances substantially different from any anticipated by the parties when the agreement was formulated [emphasis added].[3]

These acknowledgments of the intensely judgmental nature of

compliance adjudication are not parochially held perspectives. On the contrary, they are typical observations from officials who have been associated with the verification community. Confusion between intelligence and verification, however, can often be as convenient as it is intellectually dishonest for the following reasons:

- The technological processes by which monitoring is conducted are impressive from almost any perspective.
- Descriptions of these monitoring methods in the unclassified literature can give short shrift to technological limitations and encourage invalid political generalizations from nonpolitical data.
- Projection of the resultant favorable image of monitoring technology onto verification in general makes otherwise contentious arms control issues appear much simpler.
- Presentation of arms control as a plausible, low-risk alternative to an otherwise necessary military buildup is a politically marketable enterprise.
- Counterarguments that highlight nontechnical complications inherent in the verification process are not only unwelcome to the arms control advocate but often uninteresting to the lay electorate in general.

CONFUSION

Evidence of this semantical confusion exists in several studies seeking to document the capabilities of NTM in an unclassified format.[4]   Perhaps the first of the postwar scientists to relate monitoring with verification was J. Robert Oppenheimer, whose thoughts on the subject were important underpinnings for the 1946 Baruch Proposal.[5]   Another, from shortly before his appointment as chairman of President Kennedy's Scientific Advisory Committee until the present, is Jerome B. Wiesner, who has consistently argued that the technical efficacy of monitoring enables full confidence in the verification of various arms control proposals.[6]   As scientists who participated in the initial development of the United States' nuclear arsenal, Oppenheimer and Wiesner evidently expected to connect causes and effects so as to enable disarmament as well. Both of these scientists therefore advanced well-developed theories of verification from purely technological perspectives: good monitoring would enable good arms agreements.

Working from the same logical premises in the 1970s, several students of monitoring technology developed policy recommendations from their impressions of the optical perspicacity of reconnaissance satellites. Jeremy Stone, for example, after a brief discussion of then emergent technical espionage skills, boasted in 1971 that given the U.S. "unilateral arms inspection system . . . it is hard to imagine that Soviet leaders . . . would think they could get away with cheating—by building, for example, large numbers of missiles, submarines, or antimissile defenses. . . ."[7]   Stone had, in effect, equated good reconnaissance (the technical process) with the "detection" of "cheating" (the hardly self-evident political-assessment process). Similarly, Ted Greenwood, a widely cited unclassified chronicler of NTM, asserted in 1973 that the major conclusion that can be drawn from the analysis presented here is that the U.S. can, with its observation satellites and missile-test surveillance systems, verify Russian observance of the SALT I ABM Treaty and Interim Agreement with high confidence. . . . [Furthermore,] [t]he conclusion of verifiability is not dependent . . . on Russian cooperation in nonconcealment. . . .[8]

Not surprisingly, the Nixon administration's principal congressional witnesses would commonly utilize this technical-political leap in logic on behalf of SALT I. Thus, Secretary of Defense Melvin Laird advanced the argument during ratification hearings that "I am completely satisfied that our national technical means of verification are adequate to verify Soviet compliance with the provisions of the agreements."[9] Similarly, in response to widespread concern at the time that SALT I had merely "frozen" the Soviets to the unconfirmed force levels estimated by U.S. intelligence, Chief Negotiator Gerard Smith expressed his own "confidence in our national technical means of verification's capability to reveal the current number of Soviet ICBM's." Although SALT I had limited silos instead of ICBMs precisely because NTM could not count missiles or weapons with high confidence, Smith allowed: "We do not need Soviet confirmation of our intelligence. . . ."[10]

Carter administration officials would invoke the same logic in their efforts to sell SALT II. Speaking to a media association in April 1979, for example, Carter himself first inquired rhetorically: "How can we know whether the Soviets are living up to their obligations under this agreement?" He then answered with an assertive appeal to his listeners' impressions of NTM:

Our confidence in the verifiability of the agreement derives from the size and the nature of the activities we must monitor and the many effective and sophisticated intelligence collection systems which we in America possess . . . . The sensitive intelligence techniques obviously cannot be disclosed in public, but the bottom line is that if there is an effort to cheat on the SALT agreement . . . we will detect it, and we will do so in time fully to protect our security.[11]

What the president was telling the media representatives, of course, was that because we can monitor, we can verify; that because we can verify, we can "protect our security"; and that, in this light, SALT II should be ratified. Although the distinction between verification and intelligence may appear obvious, it is easily obscured in the heat of debate over the merits of a particular agreement.

Arguments emanating from the alleged technical efficacy of NTM have also been buttressed from the outset by legalistic claims dealing with the enforcing power of a treaty itself. As a result of these two traditions evolving side by side, a well-developed technical-legal logic system seems to have matured, replete with its own vocabulary, grammar, and policy premises. Some have argued that, aside from whatever detective or deterrent powers inhere to NTM with regard to Soviet cheating, international law, as manifested in a treaty, imposes constraints that law-abiding nations are wont to ignore regardless of the monitoring's thoroughness.[12] A more dominant and more recent theme has stressed the legal dignity purchased for NTM by specific provisions of an agreement. The thrust of this position is that, in conjunction with NTM's technological marvel, further status in a legal setting anchors the effectiveness of monitoring and gives verifiability still greater credibility. Thus, each of the SALT agreements has featured the following interestingly phrased terms: "For the purpose of providing assurance of compliance with the provisions of this Treaty [or Interim Agreement], each Party shall use National Technical Means of verification at its disposal in a manner consistent with generally recognized principles of international law."[13] Not only did this provision render NTM "legal" (so long as it was used "in a manner consistent with generally recognized principles of international law," which are vague by any standard), but the same articles also made bilateral "cooperation" a central requirement:

> Each party undertakes not to interfere with the national technical means of verification of the other Party operating in accordance with paragraph 1 of this Article.

> Each Party undertakes not to use deliberate concealment measures which impede verification by national technical means of compliance with the provisions of this Treaty [or Interim Agreement]. This obligation shall not require changes in current construction, assembly, conversion, or overhaul practices [emphasis added].[14]

This legal requirement for "cooperation," which Ted Greenwood and Gerard Smith had said was not even necessary, in conjunction with the quasi-legal status purchased for NTM by the agreements, elevated monitoring to new heights of efficacy in the minds of many. Because monitoring had long since come to be equated with verifying, and because verification was understood to have been the principal inhibitor of serious arms control, these provisions of SALT I and SALT II were presented as virtual breakthroughs in the long-sought effort to achieve security through diplomacy. Pushing this technical-legal logic to its extreme during ratification hearings for SALT II, Secretary of Defense Brown argued that "all of the [multiple] uncertainties we face in SALT II would be far worse without an agreement because Soviet concealment practices would then be unconstrained."[15] The statement revealed just how far down the technical-legal road the United States had traveled since the pre-NTM days when more stringent but allegedly non-negotiable provisions for verification had been demanded. Instead of an agreement's monitoring provisions being so thorough as to permit the negotiated relaxation of U.S. defenses, treaties could now be defended on the basis of how well they facilitated monitoring. The achievement of these "legal" constraints on Soviet interference with U.S. NTM had, in short, become an end in itself. The credibility of NTM had, according to Carter himself, enabled SALT II; but SALT II, according to Carter's secretary of defense, had enabled NTM's credibility. Logically, the two processes could "enable" one another into infinite regress, but behind this tautology lay an entire belief system—a technical-legal ethic that sustains itself to this day against all logical challenges, against all demands for actual enforcement provisions, and even against considerable empirical evidence of its shortsightedness. Thus, one frequently hears the argument that "while it isn't perfect, it's all we've got, and, more importantly, it is negotiable."

CONSEQUENCES

The distinction between verification and intelligence—one that would appear fairly straightforward on its own merits—turns out to be no simple matter. Nor is persistent confusion between the two concepts a matter of mere semantics. On the contrary, the conceptual ambiguity often carries over into <u>policy</u> ambiguity, with notable consequences for the national security process. Specifically, when intelligence or threat-assessment questions are treated as verification or compliance-adjudication questions, three major changes in the conflict-resolution process tend to follow. First, a new set of players becomes central to the management of crises, and an entirely different set of response options becomes likely. As a result of this "regime change," a whole new analytical framework is used to define, and hence to resolve, security dilemmas. Second, the verification framework imposes new and different requirements on intelligence-monitoring assets, actually increasing the risk of their compromise. More important, the newer regime diverts the attention of NTM <u>away from</u> activities that might otherwise be considered worthy of attention from a traditional security standpoint. Third, since the verification framework involves fairly rigid <u>legal</u> formalities, it demands standards of "proof" that are often beyond the scope of NTM. Whereas traditional threat assessment requires its own high standards of proof in support of any assertive action contemplated by government, <u>compliance</u> judgments involve the comparison of technically garnered evidence with carefully crafted words on paper—a difference not simply in degree but also in kind.

The net result of these three changes is that, if a favorable compliance judgment is reached, the same logic that first confused verification with intelligence often confuses "nonviolations," in treaty terms, with "security" in threat-assessment terms. Thus, the conceptual ambiguity comes full circle. So that we might understand this process more fully, the following discussion elaborates the impact of these three changes.

In January 1984, responding to a bipartisan demand by ninety-three senators, President Reagan forwarded a fifty-page report to Congress detailing "an expanding pattern of Soviet violations or possible violations of arms control agreements."[16] The president summarized the report with the following carefully structured assertion:

The United States Government has determined that the Soviet Union <u>is violating</u> the Geneva Protocol on Chemical Weapons, the Biological Weapons Convention, the Helsinki Final Act, and two provisions of SALT II: telemetry encryption and a rule concerning ICBM modernization. In addition, we have determined that the Soviet Union <u>has almost certainly violated</u> the ABM Treaty, <u>probably violated</u> the SALT II limit on new types, <u>probably violated</u> the SS-16 deployment prohibition of SALT II, and is likely to have violated the nuclear testing yield limit of the Threshold Test Ban Treaty [emphasis added].[17]

Reactions to these declarations were interesting. The statement had identified just four Soviet activities as definite "cheating" because the monitoring means (NTM) could not sufficiently "prove" any other suspected violations. A report by the president's General Advisory Committee on Arms Control and Disarmament would later document seventeen Soviet activities that it considered "material breaches."[18] Although the president would cautiously allude to only ten of these, Joseph Harsch was comfortable with the conclusion that "both sides have obviously padded their lists of complaints with everything they could think of to make it more impressive."[19] Newsweek magazine agreed with Harsch that "both sides had overstated the case," that the issue was merely "the latest skirmish in a propaganda war," and that, in any case, the accusations were "esoteric," "premature," and would not "significantly alter" the balance of power.[20]

News media responses of this genre thus gave equal billing to a hastily released Soviet list of U.S. "violations" widely believed to have been assembled for that purpose. The "debate" held media attention for a very brief period of time and focused almost entirely on the strictly legal merits of the matter rather than on any strategic implications that may have underlain them. Secretary of Defense Weinberger elaborated the greater concern that several of the violations "must have been planned by the Soviet authorities many years ago, in some cases at the very time the Soviet Union entered into the agreements"; moreover, Assistant Secretary Richard Perle pointed out that there were "serious potential security risks from Soviet arms control violations."[21] The issues had already lost any sting they may have had from a purely strategic standpoint, however, because they were addressed from the outset merely as verification and compliance controversies. SALT II negotiator Paul Warnke and SALT I negotiator Gerard Smith, who would refuse the administration's offer of classified briefings on the accusations, promptly criticized elevation of the dispute above established secret bilateral channels and argued that, in any case, none of the allegations qualified as technical "violations."[22]

The pattern was a fairly familiar one even though it was the first time in the history of postwar security negotiations that a U.S. president had formally accused the Soviets of outright violations. "The politics of this is tough," one SCC official explained to the New York Times; "arms control is popular and you have to have a tremendously good case of violation to present to domestic and world public opinion."[23] The "politics" is tough indeed; as the Times elaborated, "The technical complexity of the evidence and the fact that it is gathered by remote electronic sensors that people outside the Government must take on faith make the presentation of such a case difficult."[24]

Although such new developments in the Soviet threat are debated as "complex compliance issues," the United States nevertheless remains bound by the strict terms of an agreement's intent. If compliance-related Soviet activities do raise genuine security questions for the United States, assertive reactions are nevertheless all but impossible from a political standpoint until all remedies available within the provisions of a relevant treaty have been exhausted—and that may take years. Outright treaty abrogations are not absolutely impossible under verification regimes, but they are out of the question in constitutional democracies until there is a consensus that various counterarguments defending Soviet activities as compliance have been ruled out. In the meantime, the mere presence of an arms control agreement can change the character of what is acceptable from a political standpoint in response to Soviet behavior patterns that would probably have taken place with or without an agreement.

A useful comparative case is the 1962 Cuban Missile Crisis. In that instance, as with those to which Reagan referred, U.S. intelligence analysts using technical collection devices spotted a new development in the Soviet threat. The liquid fueled SS-4 "Sandal" IRBMs, deployed at fifteen sites throughout Cuba, were reported to be accurate to within a mile and a quarter; they held one-third of the United States within their 1,200-mile range, and they carried one-megaton warheads.[25] After examining this intelligence information and discussing its strategic implications with professional analysts, President Kennedy publicly identified the situation as a "crisis," called the Soviets "liars" for arguing that the missiles were purely defensive in nature, imposed a naval quarantine around the island, and demanded immediate removal of the missiles.[26]

Kennedy's actions, of course, had nothing whatsoever to do with any international agreement, but that is precisely the point: he justified his public assertiveness solely on the basis of evidence that U.S. security had become unacceptably jeopardized by the IRBMs. He appealed to no legal tradition, no contract that had to be abrogated, and no "process" of negotiations that had to be disrupted. He was acting simply "in defense of our own security and that of the Western Hemisphere, under the authority entrusted to [him] by the Constitution."[27] Today, however, when Soviet weapons deployments in Cuba are governed by the Kennedy-Khrushchev Agreement that culminated the 1962 crisis, the following Soviet activities are regarded as commonplace:[28]

1. Soviet offensive capabilities deployed to Cuba:
   (a) a combat brigade;
   (b) Golf and Echo Class nuclear-missile-equipped submarines;
   (c) the Cienfuegos strategic submarine base with a nuclear warhead storage facility;
   (d) nuclear delivery-capable aircraft: MIG 23/27 Floggers, Bear/TU-95 Ds and Fs; and
   (e) a regional military communications center.
2. Use of Cuba as a revolutionary base to export subversion and aggression, including:
   (a) the training of neighboring terrorist and revolutionary forces; and
   (b) equipment to supply these revolutionary forces.
3. A probable biological and chemical warfare facility.

Like the SS-4s in 1962, these activities have evidently been persuasively monitored by NTM. Unlike the SS-4s, they have also been evaluated as "compliance" rather than just "threat" questions, and found to be "not offensive," compatible with the relevant arms control agreement, and therefore no apparent cause for action. The presence of an agreement thus activates an entirely different framework for the analysis of threats to U.S. security. That framework activates legalistic and interpretive policy guidelines, making assertive (traditional) crisis-management solutions considerably more difficult to justify to an open democratic society than would have been the case without an agreement. The first of several pernicious consequences that arise when policymakers confuse threat assessment with verification is therefore clear: to do so converts normal intelligence questions into legalistic compliance questions and spawns the illusion that U.S. security concerns are served equally by either approach. In reality, however, the latter framework merely provides a different set of policy players with a politically more palatable set of responses to the same problems that would have to be faced with or without formal agreements in place.

The urgencies of verification do not simply alter the _framework_ in which threat questions are evaluated. They also impose higher demands on technical monitoring devices (NTM) and thereby place those assets at considerably greater risk of being compromised. Intelligence collection is difficult enough when the object of one's attention is as secretive and elusive as the USSR. Arms control actually complicates that problem still further by requiring the United States to specify how successful it has become in penetrating that societal closure and by demanding higher standards of evidence.

This occurs for a variety of reasons. In formal negotiation settings, U.S. negotiators cannot even _discuss_ limitations on Soviet weapons that are beyond the purview of U.S. intelligence—thus inviting Soviet "probing" at the negotiating table and necessitating certain disclosures about U.S. monitoring capabilities. Two additional complementary realities of modern bilateral negotiations, however, further complicate the situation. First, the Soviets categorically refuse to provide the needed "data" about their arsenal, from which logical negotiations might proceed. Second, U.S. negotiators have nevertheless been willing to conduct discussions on the basis of _their_ _own_ intelligence estimates on the Soviet arsenal. The Soviets, by refusing even to confirm the _validity_ of these U.S. estimates, thereby position themselves to refute any related argument referencing those numbers during the implementation phase of agreements. This is evidently what caused the "ambiguity" during the mid-1970s when Soviet SLBM deployments began to exceed the "ceilings" to which the two sides had "agreed" in SALT I.

Obviously, if it is Soviet ignorance about the specifics of U.S. collection skill that makes the monitoring assets reliable in the first place, this kind of magnanimity on the part of the United States degrades threat-assessment capability for the sake of "verifiable" arms control. But since a "verifiable" agreement must then be subject to regular monitoring, the Soviets to some extent actually participate in the U.S. intelligence community's allocation of its scarce monitoring assets.

In establishing such resource allocation priorities itself, the United States proceeds on the belief that those portions of the Soviet arsenal designated in an agreement are the same objects to which one must attend from an overall threat-assessment standpoint. To whatever extent this assumption is valid, Soviet "compliance" with treaties leads logically to a favorable evaluation of U.S. "national security." To the extent that it is not valid, however, monitoring assets have been diverted away from the principal purpose of their existence; accordingly, the Soviets have actually helped the U.S. intelligence community to focus on these less relevant targets. If the result of these monitoring activities leads to a judgment of Soviet compliance with a treaty, any resultant leaps in logic about overall U.S. security could clearly be quite dangerous—however subtly those assessments are officially digested.

The assumption that an agreement's subject matter is worthy of disproportionate attention from a traditional security standpoint is, of course, highly speculative. Because of the asymmetric position in which the U.S. finds itself regarding relative access to defense information, the substance of negotiations in bilateral arms control becomes not so much that which is threatening from a security standpoint as that which is observable, stationary, and measurable from a verification standpoint. In both SALT I and SALT II, for example, the United States agreed to define ICBMs as the equivalent of the "silos" with which most of them were necessarily associated at the time. Large silo-launchers were observable, stationary, and measurable, but they are not in themselves threatening. ICBMs, which do not require silos in order to be launched, were quite threatening but not necessarily observable. If the United States had felt at the time that it could have reliably counted and measured the missiles themselves, then negotiators of SALT I and SALT II would have been instructed to limit the weapon system itself rather than its silo. It is indeed fortunate when those components of the Soviet arsenal considered most threatening from a strategic standpoint are also easily observable from a monitoring standpoint. In the case of ICBMs, the United States sought to force a solution to that disparity—between what was threatening and what was observable—by placing limits on (observable) symbols of (threatening) Soviet weapons.

The unhappy consequences of that decision are well known. Today, all of the most frequently cited strategic balance computations in the unclassified literature (IISS, Air Force Magazine, Library of Congress, etc.) routinely report SALT's "data base" on silos as the precise measure of Soviet ICBM strength. But the confusion is hardly limited to unofficial literature. In his defense of SALT I before leaders of Congress, Henry Kissinger explained that agreed terms would prohibit the Soviets from "significantly increasing" their large SS-11 silos' size.[29] Two years later, a full-blown "compliance controversy" developed when the Soviets increased the size of the SS-11 silo by 52 percent and quadrupled the SS-11's throw-weight with the SS-19s that replaced them.[30] The debate became quite heated as to both the meaning of "significantly increased" and the legal admissibility of a U.S. Unilateral Statement that, according to Kissinger's 1972 remarks, had clarified the meaning of those words in the agreement. But while the official and unofficial debate focused on the subtleties of nuance associated with the "compliance controversy," the Soviets MIRVed the upper stage of the new missile and dramatically improved its guidance system.[31]

Although the latter improvements were far more threatening to the United States and its retaliatory deterrent than were any increases in the size of the silo, they were unrelated to the debate at hand and, for quite some time, were overlooked or understated throughout the U.S. threat-assessment community. Furthermore, the compliance argument itself had little to do with the quality of monitoring. Even if the United States had been permitted to conduct <u>physical inspections</u> of the enlarged silos, the verification process would have produced the same outcome because the size of the silos was never seriously disputed. The compliance debate was focused entirely on what the words of the treaty said, meant, and were intended to mean. Recalling this and other examples of diverted attention and restricted utilization of monitoring assets during the implementation of SALT I, the Senate Armed Services Committee recommended rejection of SALT II by a 10 to 0 vote. Unimpressed by familiar arguments from the Carter administration about U.S. ability to monitor the specific terms of the treaty, the committee cautioned:

> Ironically, the threat to the United States and its allies would be diminished if the Soviets were to go on building ICBMs. By doing so they would have to divert resources from other weapons programs in areas such as antisubmarine warfare, cruise missile defenses, medium range weapons and the like, where the balance of power is more responsive to additional investment.[32]

Besides risking the compromise of important national security assets and diverting attention from potentially threatening Soviet activities, the existing ground rules for compliance enforcement make verification much more difficult than is commonly understood. In fact, if a judgment is made that the Soviets are <u>not</u> in compliance with an agreement, then precious monitoring assets may be placed still further at risk. "Prosecution" is an elusive notion in international law, where the "courtrooms" are more often unofficial than formal, where "litigation" is frequently adjudicated by public opinion and negotiation, and where the burden of proof rests squarely with the accuser. To a certain extent, of course, proof is pursued in the day-to-day conduct of routine intelligence, but in verification regimes the presumption of innocence rests with the accused government and must be proved to the contrary by much more demanding forms of evidence.

Evidence of an adversary's noncompliance with a security treaty must be convincing not only to the president and his national security advisers but also to Congress, to the public, to the media, and very often to allied governments and the "world community" at large. This may well be the most fundamental distinction between intelligence and verification, and also the least commonly understood one. Proof is difficult enough within communities that share common languages and value systems, but it is made easier by conventions like process, juries, and "reasonable man" standards of evidence. Proof is nearly impossible in the adversarial cross-cultural setting of modern arms control where none of these conventions apply.

Therefore, before a decision is officially taken to designate a given activity as a "violation" instead of merely a "compliance question," a virtually self-evident case must be assembled and then presented to the public with utmost clarity. If the most persuasive available evidence emanates from secret collection assets, as was the case when the Soviets destroyed a civilian airliner in 1983, then the decision might be made simply to live with the "violation" by downgrading it to a "compliance question," to present a lesser case that does not compromise assets, or to ignore it altogether. Political expediency is likely to be as much a factor in this decision as the strategic implications of its ultimate resolution. A halfway case invites ridicule from arms control advocates; ignoring it altogether invites ridicule from arms control skeptics. No matter how convincing the case may be, the Soviets can be expected to "probe" U.S. collection skills still further by calling the "proof" inadequate or by arming administration critics with plausible counterexplanations. Neither a "jury" nor a "reasonable man" standard exists in these proceedings, and the SCC is a purely deliberative intergovernmental organization without powers of enforcement or even of official judgment. Even if the Soviets themselves feel the case for "violation" has been established, a "so what?" response can force the United States either to drop the case altogether or to take politically painful measures on the basis of "evidence" that is normally too technical and complex to generate anxieties among the democratic population that must coalesce behind assertive reactions.

Classic examples of this train of events can be found by reviewing the history of any of the violations cited by President Reagan in January 1984, but one will suffice as a case in point for this discussion. Reagan's observation that "the Soviet Union is violating the Geneva Protocol on Chemical Weapons [and] the Biological Weapons Convention" followed from a case the administration had been developing for several years. The State Department began publicizing its suspicions (and its evidence) with two reports to Congress made public in 1982.[33] The two reports assembled a fairly cautious argument citing[34]

- testimony of those who saw or experienced chemical weapons attacks;
- testimony of doctors, refugee workers, journalists, and others who had the opportunity to question witnesses or victims;
- testimony of those who had engaged in chemical warfare [Soviet Army defectors] or were in a position to observe those who did; scientific analysis of physical samples taken from sites where the attacks had been conducted;
- documentary evidence from open sources; and
- intelligence derived from National Technical Means.

On the basis of these sources, the State Department advanced the following somewhat historic observations:

> taken together this evidence has led the U.S. Government to conclude that Lao and Vietnamese forces, operating under Soviet supervision, have since 1975 employed lethal chemical and toxin weapons in Laos; that Vietnamese forces have, since 1978, used lethal chemical and toxin agents in Kampuchea; and that Soviet forces have used a variety of lethal chemical warfare agents, including nerve gases, in Afghanistan since the Soviet invasion of that country in 1979.[35]

Furthermore, since the two agreements said to have been violated were multilateral rather than bilateral in nature, complementary investigations by Canada, France, West Germany, Britain, Sweden, Denmark, Israel, South Africa, Australia, New Zealand, and China--some of the 111 signatories—all yielded the same findings.[36]

Given these many interlocking bits of evidence from so many different sources of intelligence and so many different national governments, why has it remained virtually impossible to achieve the kind of consensus needed in the U.S. political system for assertive reaction? This is an important and troublesome question, because technical-legal means of verification, according to their proponents, were supposed to be enough by themselves to deter or discover cheating—and with far less monitoring than has been used in this case. Furthermore, these agreements are unusually trenchant as to the activities they proscribe. The 1925 Geneva Protocol, to which both the United States and the USSR are signatory, is an outright prohibition on the use of any "asphyxiating, poisonous, or other gases, and of analogous liquids, materials, or devices." These substances, according to the agreement itself, are also "condemned by the general opinion of the civilized world."[37] Similarly, the 1972 Biological Weapons Convention, which was signed and ratified under UN auspices by 111 nations including the United States and the USSR, was described by President Nixon as "the first international agreement since World War II to provide for the actual elimination of an entire class of weapons."[38] Indeed, the agreement specifically prohibits "the development, production and stockpiling of chemical and bacteriological (biological) weapons. . . ."[39] The clarity and legal footing of the provisions, as well as the extensiveness of the monitoring, have therefore been as straightforward as one could reasonably expect— especially by comparison with either of the SALT agreements.

The Soviet response to these charges, however, has been both muted and evasive. At first, they argued that the toxins were produced naturally in Southeast Asia, then blown by prevailing winds onto various Soviet enemies in the region. Later they asserted that it was the CIA that was responsible for the spread of the poisons in Afghanistan.[40] Still later, when asked to respond to State Department allegations, the first deputy of the Soviet Mission to the United States simply dismissed all of the evidence as "hearsay." When asked by an American television reporter if he felt any obligation, beyond simply denying the charges, to prove that the allegations were false, the Soviet official's response was enlightening: "Well, I would say that sort of a habit in this country [i.e., the United States] is that anybody innocent of anything shouldn't have to <u>prove</u> anything. So the <u>burden of proof</u> is on the government of the U.S. [emphasis added]."[41] This argument defies the logic according to which verification is necessary in the first place. It suggests that a presumption of innocence should be exported intact to the bilateral political setting, even while other standards and conventions remain unique to domestic proceedings. Prosecution in this context would retain the burdens designed to protect the accused while enjoying none of the traditions— such as the "reasonable man" standard—by which proof of guilt is commonly accepted. In short, the injured government must present a case that, on its own merits, categorically rules out all evidence of innocence, and it must do so in a political setting where "justice" is in the eye of the beholder.

The Soviet official's logic has been precisely the standard that many arms control advocates and most media observers have applied to this allegation. Shortly after President Reagan's formal accusations regarding Soviet employment of chemical weapons in Indochina and Afghanistan, the New York Times began giving widespread coverage to a counterexplanation advanced by Mathew W. Meselson of Harvard and Thomas W. Seeley of Yale. According to this theory, the substance known as yellow rain is so similar in color and texture to excrement from bees that it may be the consequence of "massive defecation flights by wild honeybees." According to Meselson and Seeley, they were once personally bombarded with "bee feces that left yellowish splotches on them and their land rover." Unexplained in any of the Times' many reports on the subject, however, was why these scientists were spared all of the symptoms reported by the victims of attacks in the region. As the Wall Street Journal once described these reactions:

> the mycotoxin breaks down the immune response as white blood cells are no longer produced. The lungs go within 48 hours. Bone marrow ceases to replenish the blood with nutrients. The gastrointestinal system collapses. Doctors say the kidneys would go next, though so far none of the patients has lived to this stage.[42]

Any disparity between official reports of various populations' reactions to the attacks, on the one hand, and the Meselson–Seeley account on the other, was lost in the noise level of ensuing "debate." The fact that there was a counterexplanation had by itself become a highly relevant factor in the verification process. Virtually every official and unofficial treatment of the proclaimed violations that followed would have had to deal either directly or indirectly with "the counter argument"—regardless of how weighty or shallow the relative merits of the case may have been. One editorial written for the Washington Post, for example, condemned a subsequent administration proposal for a new treaty on chemical weapons for these reasons:

> By way of warming up the Russians, while not actually mentioning them by name, [Reagan] referred to what he regards as the fact that they used chemical weapons in Afghanistan and in Southeast Asia. The charges on Soviet use of "yellow rain" are in dispute. A foremost expert on chemical warfare, Dr. Mathew Meselson of Harvard, says that the fatalities came from nature—the excrement of honeybees—not from Soviet planes. But, as always, Reagan fears right wing suspicion.[43]

Clearly the irrefutable proof being demanded by opponents of the Reagan administration—proof that absolutely rules out all counterarguments—goes beyond the presumption of innocence demanded by the Soviets. More important, however, is the fact that such a degree of proof is completely beyond the monitoring capacity of NTM. Such proof is evidently unattainable even when the prohibitions are spelled out as clearly as they were in the 1925 and 1972 agreements in question and are all the more so with the highly complicated provisions found in the SALT agreements. What is particularly ironic about the abnormally stringent proof requirements is that such a tradition could derive from verification's scientific and legal heritage, because proof "qua proof" is known to be unachievable in both professions. Indeed, it is taken as common knowledge among most scientists that outright proof of any general principle is logically impossible. Traditional philosophies of science resolve this epistemological trap by demanding prompt rejection of accepted "laws" when disproof, which is possible, is encountered, and by holding established wisdoms as tentative in the meantime. The Western legal tradition faces up to the same logical dilemma by building a similar conservatism into its proceedings, by demanding similarly reproducible routes to conclusions, by submitting most criminal proof verdicts to the biases of a jury of human beings, and by reserving final decisions for an appeals process that reexamines the evidence and the procedures behind an indictment. Scientific and legal traditions impose these rigorously conservative standards on their practitioners because the consequences of error are so vital that error on the side of caution is specifically designed into both methodologies.

In spite of these built-in precautions, however, the discovery of truth is still possible in both science and law. Science sustains its tentative paradigms by periodic corroboration and reluctant toleration of unexplained anomalies. Domestic law faces up to the logical impossibility of proving "intent" by employing such cultural traditions as the "reasonable man" standard and leaving ultimate decisions to a jury; but neither "the standard" nor "the jury" is available to the verifier. The only tradition exported from domestic criminal law to international compliance adjudication is thus the presumption of innocence.

It would seem that if there is any way out of the proof trap in which the West finds itself in responding to known violations, it would arise when the UN is involved as a neutral arbitrator of compliance disagreements. If the 1983 Korean airline disaster is any indication, however, it would appear, once again, that political interests will normally rule out any objective evaluation of facts and events. Even though the United States and Japan compromised several previously secret intelligence-monitoring assets in order to establish their case--that a Soviet military pilot knowingly destroyed a civilian aircraft in flight—they could still muster only nine supporting votes from among the fifteen Security Council members, and these nine could agree only to condemn "the act," without naming "the actor." When asked later why his government could not formally object to such a presumably unconscionable act, one head of state explained:

> [T]he fact that it was taken to the United Nations and argued by the United States in the manner in which it has been argued tends to create the impression that it's now a matter of international politics. . . . The feeling of some is that it's no longer in the category of a mere act of inhumanity; it's now raised to the sphere of . . . rivalry between the two superpowers, [and] that perhaps there was some degree of using this as an instrument now for being critical of the Soviet Union and of intensifying the usual posture of opposition to the Soviet Union.[44]

This explanation would rule out any assertive reaction by the United States against the USSR, even in the UN, because these are always "matters of international politics."

By this logic, even when the United States does have a provable case to present, the mere fact that the violator is a political adversary rules out objective prosecution. If cases like the Korean airliner and the chemical-biological warfare issue—two inherently repugnant activities regardless of one's politics—cannot be neutrally judged by the UN, it is hard to imagine how bilateral or multilateral entities could deal with truly complicated violations involving ABM radars or ICBM throw-weights, no matter how effectively the activities are monitored, no matter how thoroughly compromised the collection asset that witnessed them, and no matter how transparent the sophistries employed by the violators or their apologists.

CONCLUSION

The problems with modern arms control are many and varied, and verification remains one of its more poignant ones. Arms control is not a problem, however, merely because it places constraints on U.S. weapons programs; likewise, verification is not a problem merely because the closed Soviet society is so hard to monitor. Weapons programs need some constraints, and modern technology permits the United States to monitor many parts of the USSR. The real problem is that our verification ethic conditions our minds far more than arms control constrains the arms race. Some would argue that verification is still quite reliable so long as the violation in question is "strategically significant," but this serves only to cloud the issue still further. For Jimmy Carter, just one Poseidon submarine was "overwhelming" in its strategic significance;[45] for Henry Kissinger, the SS-19 deployments were "permissible," regardless of strategic significance, because they were not precisely prohibited by arms control.

To be called "verifiable," a treaty's terms need not be foolproof. Such absolutism was discarded a generation ago along with all serious talk about thorough on-site-inspection provisions. Logic alone, let alone intrusiveness and negotiability, rules out any coherent demands along these lines today. Hence widely understood euphemisms for "enough" call for something between "adequate" and "effective" monitoring provisions. What started out as an asymmetry in openness between the negotiating partners thus becomes an asymmetry in compliance uncertainty during the treaty implementation phase. These compromises are openly acknowledged and, to varying degrees, accepted for purposes of negotiability. Significantly, however, this logic also preordains that uncertainty will reign over compliance judgments that are linked to the monitoring data.

Beyond monitoring, verification can be termed "adequate" only if a treaty's provisions are continually enforced—enforced, that is, with the uncertainties that necessarily emanate from a negotiated monitoring regime. If an airtight case comes to be required for the verification of noncompliance, then better means of monitoring and much broader provisions for cooperation will be required for future arms control treaties. If negotiability is a necessary precondition of all monitoring proposals surfaced at the bargaining table, then less than perfect evidence of noncompliance must be regarded as "adequate" during the

implementation phase of an agreement as well. None of this is meant
to propose compliance policies that react reflexively to each suspected
infraction. The intent is merely to contend that the notion of
"compliance" has so many meanings that it has lost meaning, but that
in any case it has little to do with threat assessment. One hopes the
business of intelligence is conducted in a separate corridor.

NOTES

1. Indeed, it is true that the Limited Test Ban Treaty of
1963--the first serious attempt of the postwar era to impose genuine
mutual restraints on U.S. and Soviet weapons developments—followed
closely on the heels of the first successes in space-based
reconnaissance technology.
2. Verification: The Critical Element of Arms Control
(Washington, D.C.: Arms Control and Disarmament Agency Publication
No. 85, March 1976), pp. 4-5.
3. R. W. Buchheim, "The U.S.-USSR Standing Consultative
Commission and Its Work," address presented by Ambassador Buchheim
(Washington, D.C.: Arms Control and Disarmament Agency, April 22,
1981), p. 9.
4. See, for example, any of the following: E. Asa Bates, "National
Technical Means of Verification," RUSI Journal (May 1978); Bruce G.
Blair and Gary D. Brewer, "Verifying SALT Agreements," in William C.
Potter, ed., Verification and SALT (Boulder, Colo.: Westview Press,
1980); J. S. Butz, Jr., "Under the Spaceborne Eyes," Air Force and
Space Digest (May 1967); Hubert Feigl, "Satellitenaufklarung als Mittel
der Rustungskontrolle," Europa Archiv 34 (September 25, 1979); Ted
Greenwood, "Reconnaissance and Arms Control," Scientific American
228 (February 1973); Ted Greenwood, Reconnaissance, Surveillance, and
Arms Control, Adelphi paper #8 (London: International Institute for
Strategic Studies, June 1972); Philip J. Klass, Secret Sentries in Space
(New York: Random House, 1971); "Spies in Space," U.S. News and
World Report (September 9, 1968); Russell Spurr, "Enter the Super
Spooks," Far Eastern Economic Review 95 (February 25, 1977); Jeremy
Stone, "Can the Communists Deceive Us?" in Abram Chayes and
Jerome B. Wiesner, eds., ABM (New York: Harper & Row, 1971); and
Peter T. White, "The Camera Keeps Watch on the World," New York
Times Magazine (April 3, 1966).
5. Oppenheimer's Baruch era thoughts on verification are spelled
out in J. Robert Oppenheimer, "International Control of Atomic
Energy," in Morton Godzins and Eugene Rabinowitch, eds., The Atomic
Age (New York: Basic Books, 1963). Modifications of his early
thinking, after the Soviets had rejected his preferred methods of
verification, can be found in J. Robert Oppenheimer, "Atomic Weapons
and American Policy" (July 1953), in Godzins and Rabinowitch, eds.,
Atomic Age.
6. Wiesner's thinking on the verifiability of security agreements
evolves step by step, from very demanding measures of monitoring to
more permissive provisions as the technology of intelligence monitoring
devices matures. For examples, see Jerome B. Wiesner, "Inspection for
Disarmament," Arms Control Issues for the Public (Englewood Cliffs,
N.J: Prentice-Hall, 1961); and Jerome B. Wiesner, "Comprehensive Arms

Limitation Systems," in Donald G. Brennan, ed., Arms Control, Disarmament, and National Security (New York: George Braziller, 1961). The latter article appears in Daedalus 89, no. 4 (1960) as well as in Jerome B. Wiesner, Where Science and Politics Meet (New York: McGraw-Hill, 1961). It actually predates "Inspection for Disarmament," but was less specific about methods of verification. See also Jerome B. Wiesner, "Russian and American Capabilities," Atlantic Monthly, (July 1982).

7. Stone, "Can the Communists Deceive Us?" p. 197.

8. Greenwood, "Reconnaissance and Arms Control," p. 24.

9. U.S., Congress, Senate, Committee on Armed Services, Military Implications of the Treaty on the Limitations of Anti-Ballistic Missile Systems and the Interim Agreement on Limitation of Strategic Offensive Arms [hereafter referred to as Military Implications], testimony by Melvin R. Laird, "National Security Assurances in a Strategic Arms Limitation Environment" (June 20, 1972), p. 153.

10. Military Implications, statement by Ambassador Gerard C. Smith (June 28, 1972), pp. 287-288.

11. Remarks of President Jimmy Carter before the Annual Convention of American Newspaper Publishers Association, New York (April 25, 1979); Weekly Compilation of Presidential Documents (April 30, 1979), p. 696.

12. For early examples of legal arguments on how monitoring enables verification, see Richard J. Barnet, "Inspection: Shadow and Substance," and Richard A. Falk, "Inspection, Trust, and Security," both of which appear in Barnet and Falk, eds., Security in Disarmament (Princeton, N.J.: Princeton University Press, 1965).

13. These provisions appear as Article XII of the 26 May 1979 ABM Treaty, Article V of the 26 May 1972 Interim Agreement on the Limitation of Offensive Arms, and Article XV of the unratified 18 June 1979 Treaty on the Limitation of Strategic Offensive Arms (SALT II).

14. Ibid.

15. The quote, which comes from Brown's SALT II testimony, is also cited in "U.S. Drops Turkish U-2 Plan," Baltimore Sun (September 13, 1979), p. 1.

16. Wall Street Journal (January 25, 1984), p. 6.

17. U.S., Congress, Senate, Subcommittee on Defense Appropriations Committee, transcript of testimony of the Honorable Richard Perle, Assistant Secretary of Defense for International Security Policy (March 28, 1984).

18. "A Quarter-Century of Soviet Compliance Practices under Arms Control Commitments, 1958-1983" (Washington, D.C.: General Advisory Committee on Arms Control and Disarmament, October 1984).

19. Joseph C. Harsch, Christian Science Monitor (February 2, 1984), p. 16.

20. Marc Frons and John J. Lindsay, "Charges of Cheating Over Nuclear Weapons," Newsweek (February 13, 1984), p. 38. It is probably worth pointing out that this response to the president's charges did not occur in an editorial format. The Newsweek rejection of these charges is reported as "news" under the heading of "Arms Control."

21. U.S., Congress, Senate, Subcommittee on Defense Appropriations, testimony of Assistant Secretary of Defense Perle.

22. Ibid. Perle makes reference in this testimony to remarks by Smith and Warnke.

23. New York Times (October 5, 1983), p. 8.

24. Ibid.

25. John M. Collins, The U.S.-Soviet Military Balance, Concepts and Capabilities 1960-1980 (Washington, D.C.: McGraw-Hill, 1980), pp. 438-451.

26. John F. Kennedy, "Soviet Missiles in Cuba," Annals of America, vol. 18 (Chicago: Encyclopaedia Britannica, 1968), p. 140.

27. Ibid.

28. See Congressional Record, Proceedings and Debates of the 98th Congress, Second Session, vol. 130, no. 8 (February 1, 1984), p. 1. See also "Cuba's New Missiles," Richmond Times-Dispatch (July 5, 1982), p. 26, which cites empirical and circumstantial evidence accumulated by Christopher Whalen of the Heritage Foundation; Ralph Bennet and Jay Mallin, "The Increasing Threat of a Sovietized Cuba," Washington Times (July 26, 1982), p. 8; "Cuba: Yesterday and Today," Grand Strategy 2 (January 1982), pp. 2-6.

29. See Congressional Briefing by Dr. Henry J. Kissinger, Assistant to the President for National Security Affairs, The State Dining Room, Office of the White House Press Secretary (June 15, 1972), reprinted in Military Implications, p. 121.

30. John M. Collins, The U.S.-Soviet Military Balance, Concepts and Capabilities 1960-1980 (Washington, D.C.: McGraw-Hill, 1980), pp. 438-451.

31. Ibid.

32. U.S., Congress, Senate, Committee of Armed Services, Military Implications of the Proposed SALT II Treaty (Washington, D.C.: Government Printing Office, December 20, 1979), from the introduction to that report; reprinted by the Coalition for Peace Through Strength, p. 10.

33. Chemical Warfare in Southeast Asia and Afghanistan, report to the Congress from the Secretary of State, Special Report No. 98 (Washington, D.C.: Bureau of Public Affairs, U.S. Department of State, March 22, 1982); and Chemical Warfare in Southeast Asia and Afghanistan: An Update, report to the Congress from the Secretary of State, Special Report No. 104 (Washington, D.C.: Bureau of Public Affairs, U.S. Department of State, November 1982).

34. As summarized in Security and Arms Control: The Search for a More Stable Peace (Washington, D.C.: Bureau of Public Affairs, U.S. Department of State, June 1983).

35. Ibid.

36. As noted by Sterling Seagrave, "Yellow Rain's Year: 'Like Laughing at Guernica,' " Wall Street Journal (September 16, 1982), p. 30.

37. "Protocol for the Prohibition in War of Asphyxiating, Poisonous or Other Gases, and of Bacteriological Methods of Warfare (1925)," Arms Control and Disarmament Agreements: Texts and Histories of Agreements (Washington, D.C.: U.S. Arms Control and Disarmament Agency, 1982), p. 14.

38. "1972 Biological Weapons Convention," Arms Control and Disarmament Agreements, p. 122.

39. "Convention on the Prohibition of the Development, Production and Stockpiling of Bacteriological (Biological) and Toxin Weapons and Their Destruction," Arms Control and Disarmament Agreements, p. 124.

40. See "Evidence from the Battlefield," St. Louis Post Dispatch,

(December 3, 1982), p. 18. The Soviets have argued that fungus-producing toxins colonized spontaneously in Vietnam because competitor fungi were capriciously destroyed by American napalm during the Vietnam war. A different U.S. plot, according to this argument, spread the poisons in Afghanistan. As spelled out in the Literatunaya Gazeta of February 2, 1982, the Pakistan Malaria Research Center is a CIA-financed effort to breed mosquitoes that "infect their victims with deadly viruses as part of U.S. plans to introduce biological warfare in Afghanistan." For a related discussion, see Department of State Bulletin (October 1982), p. 44.

41. "Soviet Use of Chemical Weapons," transcript from the Today Show, NBC Network (August 5, 1983). The exchange cited is between Beverly Beyer, NBC Radio News correspondent for the UN, and Richard Ovimnikov, first secretary of the Soviet Mission to the UN.

42. Repeated by William Rusher, "Liberals Try 'Bee Dropping' Excuse," Gazette Telegraph [Colorado Springs] (April 10, 1984), p. 11.

43. Mary McGrory, "Peace Through Poison Gas," Washington Post (April 8, 1984), p. C-1.

44. McNeil/Lehrer News Hour, interview with Robert Mugabe (September 14, 1983), Transcript #2078.

45. Jimmy Carter, State of the Union Address, transcript reprinted in the New York Times (January 24, 1979).

Intelligence and Arms Control—
A Valuable Partnership

Effective intelligence is an essential ingredient in the achievement of arms control. Without it, arms control cannot remain a viable element of U.S. national security policy for any protracted period. In the first place, reliable information is needed on existing and potential military capabilities in order to determine what weapons it would be in our national security interests to control. Intelligence suggests the priorities that should be given within any arms control program. Second, intelligence is vital for verifying that other parties to any agreement are complying with its provisions. We must have confidence that we could detect any violation that would have a significant effect on our security. In the nuclear age we cannot rely on trusting the Soviet Union or any nation when the fate of our country and of humankind is at stake.

What is not so often realized is that arms control can be an important aid to the intelligence process. In the absence of any agreement limiting the forces of the Soviet Union, we need extensive information on the nature of the Soviet threat and how it might develop in the future. This information must be much more detailed than that required to verify compliance with an arms control agreement. Without any limitations on the development and procurement of a specific weapons system, intelligence has the difficult task of gathering vast amounts of data on the specific characteristics of weapons deployed or under development. With an arms control agreement, intelligence has only to find evidence of single violations of specific treaty provisions. Intelligence requirements are greatly simplified and reduced. For example, if cruise missiles were totally banned, then only one cruise missile need be spotted. Without such a ban intelligence must procure a reasonably accurate count on the number of such missiles deployed and data on such characteristics of the weapons as accuracy, speed, range, flight profiles, and warhead yield.

Furthermore, arms control agreements can contribute to our ability to obtain otherwise unavailable information on secret Soviet weapons development. For example, one provision in the SALT II Treaty forbade the encryption of missile flight telemetry that would impede verification of compliance with the provisions of the treaty. Although this does not mean that all telemetry of missile tests could not be encrypted whether or not it was related to limitations in the treaty, it did reduce the scope of the task that intelligence would have were there no restrictions on missile test encryption. The broader the treaty, the easier would be the intelligence job. The SALT II Treaty also required advance notification of certain missile tests and the limitation of flights to specific test ranges, thus allowing the intelligence community to focus its resources to obtain the maximum data on the nature of any test. In the SALT II Treaty alone, more than a dozen provisions facilitated the task of obtaining intelligence on the Soviet threat. The failure to put the SALT II Treaty into effect has reduced our intelligence capabilities.

The value of intelligence in verifying arms control agreements is frequently underestimated—particularly by the public, who have no access to classified information and little knowledge of today's extraordinary capabilities; but this is true even of the people who have had access to classified information. A strong tendency exists to believe that the ability to send inspectors for on-site observation within the Soviet Union is critical to adequate verification. In actuality, on-site inspection can rarely add significantly to our intelligence capabilities. In 1955 President Eisenhower offered to the Soviet Union an "Open Skies" proposal, which would have permitted the overflight and photographic observation of potential military sites in that country. He felt that if only the Soviets would accept this proposal, all our problems for verifying arms control agreements would be solved. But the Soviets, not surprisingly, rejected the proposal without serious consideration.

Today, however, we have intelligence capabilities that far surpass those that would have been available through "Open Skies." Furthermore, the Soviet Union has formally agreed in international treaties that such "national technical means" (the polite diplomatic jargon for technical intelligence) are permitted and that it is a violation of the agreement to interfere with them. Camouflage of missile launchers, for example, is forbidden.

It is useful to highlight in some detail a few examples of how national intelligence can be used in conjunction with the arms control negotiating process to provide a satisfactory means of ensuring compliance. It may also be useful to demonstrate the relatively minor part that on-site inspections play in this process. Many have the naive belief that on-site inspections can prove to be a boon to our intelligence. The Soviet Union accuses us of seeking such inspections for their espionage value. But in the real world, it is almost certain that no inspection team would be given the opportunity to see installations or get information from individuals that is of any great security value. Similarly, no nation would allow an inspection team to obtain data that would prove a violation. Thus, the function of on-site inspection is primarily to provide reassurance that an ambiguous event is not a violation. In a few cases, perhaps, it could provide some deterrence against noncompliance if the potential violator felt that the onus of refusing or blocking a meaningful inspection overrode the gains from the violation.

An excellent example of how national intelligence can be employed to support the objective of an arms control agreement is the case of MIRVs (multiple warheads on a single missile, which can be directed at separate targets). In 1968 the United States started testing MIRVs and began deployment in 1970 when the SALT I negotiations were in a relatively early stage. Within the government, policymakers vigorously debated whether we should attempt to negotiate controls on MIRVs in the SALT I agreement. Many senators strongly supported such a move, and the administration felt a need to appear at least to be doing something in this area.

After much discussion, the United States put forward a proposal at SALT to ban the testing and deployment of MIRVs and to verify with on-site inspections whether the deployed missiles had more than a single warhead. The inspections were justified on the basis that there was no way in which satellite observation could determine how many warheads were carried in a missile deployed in a silo. However, it was almost equally obvious that no conceivably negotiable on-site inspection could determine how many warheads a given deployed missile contained. By the time an inspection team had arrived at the scene, a single warhead final stage could easily be substituted for the MIRVed one. The inspection would have required inspectors at every missile launcher with the ability to inspect the highly secret internal components of the missile warhead(s) on short notice. Such procedures would be clearly unacceptable in the Soviet Union as well as in this country. Accordingly, it was generally recognized that the United States was not serious in its attempt to limit MIRVs in SALT I. After the Soviets made an equally unacceptable offer to ban the production and deployment of MIRVs without on-site inspection and with no limitations on testing, no further discussions of the matter followed under SALT I. A MIRV race with resultant decreased stability in the strategic balance was the inevitable consequence.

The need to proceed with the problem of limiting MIRVs became much more acute as negotiations for SALT II commenced in 1973. The Soviets carried out their first MIRV test in the summer of that year and their first deployment in 1975. It was increasingly recognized that the widespread deployment of such weapons and the potential provided by improved accuracy obtainable in second generation systems could gravely enhance the incentives for a first strike and magnify the risk of the outbreak of a nuclear conflict. Those interested in obtaining verifiable MIRV controls proposed an ingenious solution involving national technical means, which, without on-site inspection, could provide confidence that significant clandestine MIRV programs would not escape detection.

Extensive testing of complete MIRVed missiles is essential if a nation is to have a reliable operational system that can be used to threaten the deterrent of the other side. Fortunately, MIRVed missile flight tests are easily detectable by our national intelligence. Observation of the missile launch—particularly the high-altitude post-boost phase, when the individual warheads are being dispersed—is observable from surface stations outside the Soviet Union. Telemetry required by the developers from such tests can also be picked up by our intelligence, and a determination can be made as to whether MIRVs are being dispensed. Even were our intelligence to fail at the launch stage or be negated, as some feared, by the loss of such listening stations as those in Iran, we could still determine that MIRVs were involved by observations from international waters during warhead reentry into the atmosphere. During this phase, one can literally count the number of reentry vehicles and also obtain a wealth of data on their characteristics. Thus it would be almost inconceivable that the Soviets could develop an operationally reliable MIRV system for a specific type of long-range missile without our intelligence being able to detect it.

The United States took advantage of this intelligence capability in detailing the specific limits on MIRVed missiles in SALT II. Any missile of a type that had ever been tested with MIRVs would be considered a MIRVed missile and subject to the limitations within the treaty regardless of whether it was actually deployed with single or multiple warheads. This simple procedure circumvented the difficulties in verifying whether a deployed missile contained one or more warheads. Furthermore, in order to put a cap on the number of warheads that any missile could carry, a ban was placed on the future testing of specific types of missiles with more reentry vehicles than had been tested at the time the treaty was negotiated. Hence the Soviet SS-18 was limited to ten warheads even though it had the payload capacity for delivering twenty or perhaps even thirty.

These provisions were particularly advantageous to the United States in that, at the time the treaty was signed, the United States had no missiles deployed, nor any plans to deploy any, that in some cases could have had a single warhead and in other cases, MIRVs. The Soviet Union, on the other hand, was deploying missiles with such a capability. Some SS-18s and SS-19s were operational as a single-warhead system, others as multiple-warhead systems. This provision forced them to count their single-warhead missiles under the ceiling of MIRVed missiles even though they were not so deployed. Thus we have an example whereby the verification provisions relying on national intelligence not only provided effective assurance of compliance but also were favorable to the United States. On-site inspections would never have provided adequate assurance, and, for that matter, could have caused serious security problems for this country as well as the Soviet Union.

A second area in which our national intelligence capabilities have been a tremendous boon to the achievement of ensuring treaty compliance has been the nuclear test ban. In the early 1960s, our national intelligence systems were capable of detecting all significant tests in the atmosphere, underwater, and in outer space. However, uncertainty remained over the ability to identify underground nuclear tests by their seismic signals, since for many relatively low-yield seismic events, explosions could not be differentiated from natural earthquakes. Because of this difficulty, it was proposed that on-site inspections be conducted at the locations of unidentified seismic events to determine whether such events were produced by clandestine nuclear explosions.

The United States offered to accept an underground test ban if it could have seven inspections per year within the Soviet Union; the Soviets agreed to accept only three. It would have seemed that this relatively small difference could have been negotiated to some median number and that a total ban on nuclear tests might have been achieved. However, even had this difference between three and seven inspections been resolved, it is unlikely that the negotiations would ever have been successful, given that the U.S. concept of an inspection involved widely different procedures than those the Soviets had ever indicated they might accept. We had in mind inspection teams of twenty or more people with drilling equipment and other instrumentation as well as the right to explore over a hundred square miles. Since an unidentifiable event, such as a natural earthquake, might occur in a secret sensitive area, this type of intrusion would probably have been unacceptable. In any case, no agreement was reached and the Limited Test Ban Treaty of 1963 did not halt underground tests.

During this same period, extensive research programs were conducted in an effort to improve our technical capabilities for discriminating between earthquakes and underground nuclear tests. The criteria for identification available in 1963 were crude, at best, because there had been so few underground explosions; indeed, those criteria were later shown to be unreliable. However, the research program proved to be extraordinarily successful. Through careful analysis of the records of large numbers of earthquakes and underground tests, it was possible to develop a means of identifying a seismic event as either a nuclear test or an earthquake. This, together with improvements in seismic instrumentation and the use of multiple arrays of seismometers, made discrimination between natural events and explosions of very low yields possible. Potential evasion tactics were studied and ways of disclosing such tactics developed. At one time it was feared that explosions in very dry, soft earth (alluvium) would reduce the intensity of the seismic signals to the point that discrimination might not be possible for tests as high as ten to twenty kilotons. However, it was found that such explosions—unless carried out at very great depths, usually below the depth at which such types of soil existed—would produce subsidence craters, which could easily be spotted by technical collection means.

As a result of these improvements, the requirement for on-site inspections has been minimized. Ambiguities in the seismic signals would rarely occur except in events at very low yield. However, since an occasional event might occur in which the data were ambiguous, the negotiators of a Comprehensive Test Ban agreed, that if after all avenues had been explored through consultation and exchange of data, an inspection team could be invited to the scene of the event to provide added confidence that a violation had not occurred. The Soviet Union has agreed in principle to this procedure as well as to the placement of unmanned seismic stations within the USSR to improve the quality of the data on low-yield events. Regrettably, negotiations on a Comprehensive Test Ban Treaty have now been broken off because the United States wished to continue testing. The groundwork, nevertheless, has been laid for the successful negotiation of such a treaty should the pursuit of a comprehensive test ban again become our national policy.

These are only two cases among many in which our national intelligence has provided the verification of compliance needed to ensure that our security would not be threatened by a Soviet violation. One factor that makes the verification problem manageable is that the United States and the Soviet Union have such large stockpiles of nuclear weapons and have conducted so many tests, not only of the explosive systems but of the delivery systems as well, that a small violation is of little security significance. Thus, the deployment of a single secret additional missile when the Soviet Union already has thousands is of little consequence.

If we were to agree with the Soviet Union to halt production of fissionable material for weapons, this eventuality would also be easy to verify within acceptable limits, given that it would take a very large secret production program to add significantly to the hundreds of thousands of kilograms already available. Our intelligence would certainly detect such a program. This, of course, is not the case if one is talking about a non-nuclear nation procuring a single weapon, perhaps using a peaceful nuclear power program to shield its intentions. In such circumstances, national intelligence cannot be thoroughly reliable, and more rigorous inspection procedures such as those now carried out by the International Atomic Energy Agency under the Non-Proliferation Treaty would be required.

In conclusion, it is clear that at the present time our national intelligence capabilities provide extraordinary tools for verifying arms control agreements. On-site inspections rarely add significantly to this capability, although they might in some cases increase confidence in compliance. Such a happy state cannot, however, be guaranteed for the future. The development of new types of systems, particularly those with dual capabilities (i.e., both nuclear and conventional) may make verification much more difficult. Cruise missiles are an excellent example because they are small, do not require much logistic support, and can have a nuclear payload virtually indistinguishable from that of a conventional one. Once cruise missiles are deployed extensively, verification will be much more intractable. Today verification is possible because the Soviets have no such missiles, and a total ban can thus be monitored. However, the freezing of such a program at some high level would tax our intelligence capabilities—and on-site inspection can probably do little to alleviate this problem. Thus we must give an added priority to reaching agreement on limitations on new weapons systems at an early date. In the absence of any such agreement, the Soviets will certainly proceed with cruise missile deployment as they did with MIRVs. Second and additional generation types will be developed with increased danger to our survival. It follows that the intelligence task of evaluating the Soviet threat will then have been made immeasurably more demanding.

Central Intelligence and the Arms Race

Whether arms control in any form can endure through superpower hostility is still an open question. Whether a policy of confrontation will lead to nuclear war is also unknown. The historical precedents are not encouraging. Whatever the chances for peace, it is clear that U.S. intelligence authorities will have a key role in predicting international behavior. The prospects for arms control will be critically affected by intelligence coverage of forces restrained by treaties. In turn, perceptions of negotiators are to a large extent conditioned by the accuracy and objectivity of intelligence information.

The odd tangle between national policy and intelligence is a subject that former intelligence officials are reluctant to discuss, partly because intelligence can get in the way of policy, as illustrated in the intelligence-informed tabling of SALT II ratification. The topic is also sensitive because former officials, in both intelligence and from the State and Defense Departments, as well as the White House, may be fearful of the charge of conducting "policy without intelligence," as Kissinger's endeavors were once described by Ray Cline, his own chief of Intelligence and Research.

Intelligence has often been excluded from policy discussions, and some members of the intelligence community are reluctant to influence policy. Vigorous advocates also have insisted upon presenting their views: In 1962 the voice of John McCone from CIA was among those recommending the use of force to remove Soviet missile bases from the Caribbean island. More recently, CIA's Admiral Stansfield Turner exercised a policy role at certain points in the negotiation of SALT II. Conclusions on the role of the intelligence community in postwar U.S. policy must remain tentative, for there is much that is unknown and much that will not be declassified for many years. Nevertheless, some attempt must be made to grapple with the issue of policy versus intelligence.

Ideally, intelligence informs policy. Through intelligence, decisions can be made on the basis of reasonably accurate and objective knowledge of existing conditions. Clearly good intelligence contributes to good policy. Unfortunately, intelligence not only informs policy but also restricts the range of policy choices as well. This may mean in practice that only uninteresting or counterproductive choices are available to the president when the decision has to be made. Because of the orderly progression of the bureaucracy from threat analysis to weapons development to engineering development and then deployment, mistaken intelligence may dictate requirements for worthless weapons or suggest impractical military strategies by seeming to make other weapons or other strategies irrelevant to the discussion. During the "missile gap" period, President Eisenhower was under intense pressure to approve major accelerations in the U.S. missile program as a result of false air force reports that the Russians already had numerous ICBMs. The options Eisenhower chose had the effect of delaying ICBM deployment until the appearance of the new generation of Minuteman ICBMs while approving a sizable missile program (1,100 ICBMs) that enabled Kennedy to go full speed on deployment, with the result that the real "missile gap" faced the Soviet Union and not the United States.

Intelligence information also conditions the public debate over national security policy. Most information, particularly if it is of an alarming nature, generally reaches the public in more or less watered-down fashion within six months to a year of its appearance at the intelligence-community level. Such information normally appears in a scattered and desultory way; moreover, because, by and large, the public is not really equipped to evaluate it, it usually helps to create or to further reinforce a hostile image of the adversary. The intelligence dispute over the Backfire bomber resulted in such a changed perception. As the general image became more hostile and the specific claims as to the Backfire's performance became progressively more extreme, a point was reached at which legislators, who are public representatives after all, were insisting that such a powerful weapon had to be included within the arms limitation treaty.

Throughout the seven presidential administrations since the formation of the CIA, no easy interaction between "policy and intelligence" has yet appeared. The best measure would seem to be the presentation of accurate and objective intelligence but, since 1947, this has proved to be an elusive objective. Especially in the area of intelligence on strategic nuclear forces, objectivity has proven a very difficult goal.

The United States has repeatedly tried to create independent intelligence authorities as part of the search for objective intelligence. The National Intelligence Estimates (NIEs) have been national precisely because they have transcended the parochial interests of the individual intelligence agencies. Since 1947, there have been many experiments in drafting estimates as well as two distinct organizations responsible for NIEs and three governing boards supervising the intelligence community as a whole. In the mid-1950s, the Intelligence Advisory Board lacked jurisdiction over the National Security Agency. Interestingly enough, however, the greatest expansion in NSA activities occurred only after the agency's inclusion in the United States Intelligence Board (USIB) in 1958. Significantly, this expansion proceeded concurrently with intense interest in Soviet missile and space activities—an interest generated by the "missile gap" perceptions of Soviet capability.

The USIB always retained the prerogative of rejecting NIEs brought before it. Nevertheless, for many years the task of actually drafting the national estimates was delegated to the Board of National Estimates and its subsidiary Office of National Estimates (ONE). The most important attribute of ONE was that it was an office—an institution, that is, albeit one within the CIA. This meant that an individual analyst drafting an estimate was at least insulated to some degree from partisan pressures applied by service interests and others within the Department of Defense. During his tenure in office, Henry Kissinger led a campaign to dismantle the Board of National Estimates (BNE) and was successful when, in 1973, the board was abolished and replaced by what is known as the National Intelligence Officer system. Unfortunately, the single NIO is inherently more susceptible to manipulation than the corporate BNE had been. The SALT "hold" items, the Backfire case, the B-Team episode, and the intelligence differences on Soviet directed-energy weapons development all involved certain manipulations of the NIO system and do not encourage confidence with respect to this new system.

To support his criticisms of national estimates by ONE, Kissinger charged that the papers were bland and like "talmudic documents." Unfortunately he was right. The price of "central" (i.e., generally approved) intelligence was that individual differences in opinion were often submerged in an NIE by agreeing upon sufficiently ambiguous language to incorporate all views. One result of such an estimate process was a paper with a large amount of general knowledge—almost nothing the Soviets could do would surprise <u>all</u> the intelligence agencies. On the other hand, such consensus NIEs were also likely to be of little value to the White House policymaker confronted with a specific question or option. Kissinger wanted intelligence to be more relevant. Under the NIO system, it has been. Under the law, intelligence is responsible specifically only to the president, and presidents have made frequent use of their powers to reorganize intelligence as they wish. It is therefore significant that despite the widespread intelligence organizational changes made by the Carter administration, nothing was done to move away from the mechanism of the NIO system begun under Nixon, or the National Foreign Intelligence Board, which replaced the USIB during the Ford administration. The need to choose between corporate integrity or policy relevancy in intelligence seems to leave responsible government on the horns of a dilemma.

As far as the actual collection of information is concerned, it is clear that a massive amount of data flows through the intelligence community. One might even suspect that intelligence is collected too well, that with all the data analysts are swamped in a veritable flood of ambiguous but suggestive indicators. Neither the original intelligence requirements systems nor their successors have proven to be very effective in day-to-day collection guidance. Many former analysts have been concerned that the process for generating intelligence requirements is overbureaucratized and insufficiently informed about the real gaps in information that confront intelligence analysts.

Even with all the information, a carefully coordinated mechanism for national estimates, and an efficient organization for intelligence analysis, there have been numerous disputes over the nature and strength of Soviet strategic forces. During the last decade, conservative critics have repeatedly charged that U.S. intelligence systematically "underestimates" Soviet strength. These arguments have contributed to political demands for "unleashing the CIA" in the expectation that unrestricted central intelligence can avoid the systematic errors attributed to the national estimates.

The story of the Soviet estimates clearly includes numerous cases of both "underestimates" and "overestimates." Intelligence underestimated the pace of the Russian ICBM buildup in the late 1960s and that of Soviet SLBM construction in the 1970s. Underestimates of Soviet achievements in missile accuracy also evidently occurred in the late 1970s and it has been admitted that there was a substantial underestimate of the size of the Soviet defense budget. On the other hand, there have been overestimates such as those pertaining to Soviet bomber forces and initial deployment of ICBMs in the 1950s. The 1960s' underestimates do not "dwarf" the "missile gap" in size or duration: The bomber gap dispute raged for three years, the "missile gap" overestimates for five. Intelligence underestimated the pace of Russian missile emplacement only between 1967 and 1972. During that same period there were other overestimates: of Soviet MIRV capability; of the appearance of a mobile ICBM; of the ballistic missile defense capacity of the Tallinn SAM; of the appearance of a new Soviet penetrating bomber; and of the quantity of defense goods purchased by the "defense ruble." Those who charge systematic underestimating draw their conclusions from only one category of intelligence and assemble their proof purely from quantitative analysis.

Representative Les Aspin (D-Wisconsin), chairman of the Oversight Subcommittee of the House Select Committee on Intelligence, has pointed out a number of factors responsible for mistaken intelligence.[1] Among these are preconceived notions, "mirror-imaging," misjudgment of Soviet strategic priorities, political and bureaucratic pressure, spurious learning, and a failure to use Soviet sources. Preconceived notions were clearly involved in the Cuban Missile Crisis and later in the assumption that because the Soviets emphasize defense they would immediately expand their ABMs to cover the entire Soviet Union. The effects of bureaucratic and political pressure are endemic and have often been observed at work in Aspin's study. With misjudgment of Soviet strategic priorities Aspin accounts for the 1960s' underestimates of Soviet ICBM numbers, pointing out that intelligence believed the Soviets would focus on quality over quantity, rapidly deploy MIRV, and emplace large defenses. As for spurious learning, the community overcompensates for its errors rather than correcting the methods that produced them such that the 1960s' underestimates could again be said to have occurred as a reaction to the exaggerations of the "missile gap."

It is important to note that intelligence disputes occurred because of the possession of suggestive information and not in a vacuum caused by a total lack of information. Intelligence information was concrete and useful enough in most cases for bureaucrats to fight over its dissemination or interpretation. A review of the major disputes shows that key pieces of information on Soviet weapon performance reached intelligence before the deployment of those weapons in almost all cases.

Why did the Soviets put missiles in Cuba after all? Why did they build precisely 1,513 ICBMs? Why do the Soviets so vigorously continue their civil defense, air defense, or strategic defense programs? Is their MIRVed missile force intended to pose a threat to our Minuteman land-based missiles? Do the Russians intend to deploy a generation of energy-based ABM weapons? These and a myriad of other questions require not only analysis of real capabilities, but postulation of adversary intentions as well. The question of capabilities versus intentions is the thorniest of conceptual problems because intentions are in the realm of the unknowable, even more so in a closed society like that of the Soviet Union. Russia has historically maintained large military forces. Large forces today do not necessarily indicate an intention to seek war with the United States, although they may. The evidence is ambiguous once again.

Intentions may themselves be inchoate in the minds of the opponents. They may be imperfectly thought out, irrational, or only partially formulated. Furthermore, observers' perceptions of them are conditioned by their own assumptions and preexisting beliefs as well as, in the military, a measure of service bureaucratic interests. Many years ago Secretary McNamara conceded that intelligence had to make projections even in advance of Soviet decisions on the programs in question.

Many would agree that drafting intelligence estimates is similar to assembling a jigsaw puzzle, as far as conceptual processes are concerned. Indeed, the puzzle analogy was used in the 1966 Cunningham Report, which warned that the necessity for sifting through all the information gathered could make it increasingly difficult to find the missing pieces. Even if information is found, its reliability must be established beyond the shadow of a doubt and, despite the "real" reliability of data, analysts from other organizations with specific and possibly conflicting interests must become convinced of that fact—a difficult task if colleagues are "victims of groupthink."[2] Moreover, the entire exercise must be accomplished under conditions in which intelligence is under considerable pressure to deliver daily "current" intelligence as opposed to long-range and carefully conceived estimates. Estimates themselves may be intended for any of several different purposes that entail different uses of information in the elaboration of conclusions.

Consideration of the problems of intelligence analysis leads to a healthy notion of the limitations on estimates, both conceptual and evidentiary. No matter how valid the information collected, however unambiguous it may be, however rigorous the estimating procedures may be, and regardless of whether an intelligence community can eliminate its biases and bureaucratic interests, a residual uncertainty remains in even the best intelligence estimates. This is discomfiting, to be sure.

Both the United States and the Soviet Union are at the brink of a new round of arms competition that promises to be very expensive and potentially very destructive. In the absence of formal arms control and with mutual hostility between the superpowers, the military competition will intensify and may explode into military conflagration, with incalculable consequences for all of humankind. The United States is currently deploying a new submarine-launched ballistic missile, the C4, in the Trident submarine as well as in older Poseidon boats. The new missile has equivalent accuracy and greater range (or greater accuracy at equivalent range) than the Poseidon. Land-based Minuteman III missiles with improved warheads and a "real-time" retargeting capability have counterforce capability against Soviet land-based missiles, which represent 75 percent of the throw-weight in the Russian nuclear arsenal. Under development is a new land-based missile, the MX, with more warheads and even greater accuracy. Moreover, a nuclear-tipped cruise missile now under development will be mounted aboard bombers in large numbers, further increasing the arsenal. At the same time, the advent of "terminal guidance," in which satellites will aid delivery vehicles in course corrections during the last moments of flight, promises pinpoint accuracies from half a world away in addition to eliminating the accuracy differences between land-based and sea-based missiles (land-based missiles have traditionally been preferred because of their greater accuracy). Work is also proceeding rapidly on the development of a laser directed-energy weapon for ballistic-missile defense and other applications.

The Soviet Union is evidently also pursuing a directed-energy beam weapon. A new generation of ballistic missiles, presumably with pinpoint accuracies as well, is under development, but whether the present SS-18 family of Soviet missiles can improve its accuracy to this extent is still unknown. The Soviets have continued to spend substantial amounts annually on air defense, missile defense, and civil defense. Currently, they have also deployed their first MIRVed SLBM missile, the SS-N-18, as well as a satellite inspector/destructor system with some degree of capability against low-orbit objects in space, such as reconnaissance and navigation satellites.

With land-based missile forces on both sides vulnerable to a first strike plus a plethora of highly capable weapons on both sides, the incentive for either in a nuclear confrontation to preempt (i.e., to launch land-based missiles before they can be destroyed in their silos or shelters) grows. The command and control requirements for a force posture capable of executing a preemptive response are such that both superpowers would have to assume hair-trigger stances. This is particularly true if a policy of "launch on warning" is adopted, as some have advocated. The risk of an accidental nuclear war then rises precipitously. Alarming failures have occurred in the networks that warn of a nuclear attack, such as SAC's mistaken alerts in December 1979 and June 1980, the latter of which was reputedly caused by one 46-cent microchip circuit that failed. These examples should serve as salutary reminders of what can go wrong with hair-trigger postures.

A complementary weakness of the present strategic balance is that it is becoming increasingly unstable. Nuclear strategies have traditionally been predicated upon the absence of any effective ways to defend against atomic attack. Beam energy weapons in combination with a new generation of very high-speed computers may change the terms of the offense-defense equation. The advent of ultrahigh-precision warheads and new sensors may enable a superpower to target sea-based as well as land-based forces, thereby becoming capable of wholly disarming the opponent rather than merely being restricted to disarming land-based missiles and nonalert bombers. Alternatively, a combination of civil defense capability, missile defense, and hard-target forces may lead the adversary to the (delusionary) notion that nuclear war could be fought in the face of an acceptable toll in human destruction.

The strategic balance of the 1980s could be extremely volatile. A revolutionary weapons breakthrough by either side could convince the opponent that the innovator was on the verge of achieving real strategic superiority. The opponent might then be tempted to avert inferiority by launching an immediate war. Hair-trigger force postures under these circumstances could serve to encourage a decision for war by helping to give statesmen the confidence that they will actually be able to plan and execute a thermonuclear strike. Even if pressures for war were averted in the case of a technological breakthrough, at the very least a "Sputnik" effect might occur in which the opposing superpower would redouble its efforts at a military buildup in order to close whatever "gap" had developed.

It is intelligence that must bring in the first notice of a Soviet technological breakthrough. In this connection, it is comforting to remember that the main outlines of Soviet technical development have been known long in advance, even if analysts disagree on precise details or future trends. On the other hand it is disturbing to recall that what knowledge there is remains continually subject to the doubt embodied in residual uncertainty. Ultimately, the beginning of wisdom lies in the realization that one must go beyond intelligence to cope with the problems of the arms race.

NOTES

1. Les Aspin, "Debate over U.S. Strategic Forecasts: A Mixed Record," Strategic Review 8, no. 3 (Summer 1980), pp. 29-43.

2. See Irving Janis who, in Victims of Groupthink (Boston: Houghton Mifflin, 1972), describes how officials as members of the team become infected with common biases and are subject to peer-group pressures to conform.

COVERT ACTION

Covert action is perhaps the most controversial activity that has been carried out by the U.S. intelligence community. In the introduction to this book, we stated that covert action is not a proper intelligence function. This assertion must be further qualified, but, to do so, we must first define exactly what covert action is. In a general sense, Roy Godson has defined covert action to be "the attempt by a government to influence events in another state or territory without revealing its involvement."[1] Some of the types of involvement uncovered by the Church and Pike Committees ranged from influencing newspapers in Chile to raising a full-fledged secret army in Laos to plotting the assassinations of heads of state. These types of activities can be divided into political and propaganda actions on the one hand, and paramilitary operations on the other.

Such "fifth-column" activities are probably as old as statecraft, and few would argue that the state needs to perform these activites on some occasions when it feels that its national interests are threatened. However, the consensus ends there. What began under the OSS during World War II continued under the CIA during the 1950s and 1960s until the Church Committee branded the intelligence community a "rogue elephant" out of control—a characterization that was largely the result of covert activities. Since that time, many have felt that the United States should not engage in covert activities of any kind. In making that decision, however, we should recognize that the Soviet Union places a premium on influencing other countries' beliefs about both itself and the United States, and that the Soviets make little distinction between overt and covert means.[2] In the final analysis, then, it seems that the United States, no less than any other country in the modern world, should not foreclose the option to use covert action when necessary.[3]

That said, the question remains as to how covert action, if used, should be conducted. Recent events show that both the Congress and the executive branch will play a role in the authorization and conduct of covert operations. Furthermore, certain types of covert action, such as assassination, are far less acceptable than others, such as supplying arms to insurgent groups. If the United States engages in covert action, who should control it? That is another way of asking whether covert action is an intelligence function. Those who say covert action properly falls within the intelligence sphere argue that the clandestine nature of intelligence, as well as special placement and contacts, makes the intelligence community a logical choice.[4]   On the other hand, opponents argue that the high-risk nature of covert operations threatens more traditional intelligence collection and tends, in the end, to overshadow it.

A solution, we feel, may lie somewhere in the middle ground. Certainly the intelligence community is well equipped to deal with the political and propaganda aspects of covert action.   It is less clear, however, as to whether they are equally well suited to deal with the paramilitary aspects.   It is this issue of paramilitary operations that David Charters examines in the chapter following. Without making any moral judgment on the use of covert operations, Charters recognizes that Western democracies have used covert means in the past and will probably do so again in the future.   That being the case, is there an alternative to handling paramilitary operations as the United States has done?   Charters thinks there is, and he cites the British experience since World War II to show that the paramilitary aspect of covert operations, at least, is best separated from the intelligence community and given over to military formations.

It is true that we have not addressed the parallel issue of political and propaganda operations beyond this introduction. It is our feeling that most of the writing in this area is rather polemical and that the balanced viewpoint that Charters brings to paramilitary operations is difficult to find, most writers being either former practitioners or sharp critics. We hope that his example may inspire others to take a fresh look at the whole question of the propriety and use of covert actions.

NOTES

1. Roy Godson, ed., Intelligence Requirements for the 1980's: Covert Action (Washington, D.C.: National Strategy Information Center, 1981), p. 1.

2. Ibid., p. 2.

3. See, for example, the discussion by Angelo Codevilla, "Covert Action and Foreign Policy," in Godson, Intelligence Requirements, pp. 81-86.

4. See, for instance, Godson, Intelligence Requirements, p. 3.

The Role of Intelligence Services in the Direction of Covert Paramilitary Operations

INTRODUCTION

The dispute between the Reagan administration and Congress over American support for the Nicaraguan Contra rebels reopened the debate on the ethics and efficacy of "covert action." Much of the public debate is focused on the thorny but central ethical issue: whether covert action is an appropriate tool of U.S. foreign policy.[1] The moral-based argument against it, which can be very persuasive, states simply that the United States should get out of the covert-action business altogether, because such activity is not congruent with constitutional government, American democratic ideals, or the letter and spirit of the United Nations Charter. The equally persuasive utilitarian view suggests that the United States cannot afford to leave the back alleyways to its opponents. The mere fact of being a member of the international community often presents the United States with a choice between several unsatisfactory alternatives. Sometimes doing nothing may be the worst option of all, whereas a covert initiative may offer the least unsatisfactory course. Therefore, the argument goes, to foreclose the covert option in advance, in perpetuity, may be as unwise as it is impractical.

These are clearly the most important and the most difficult considerations, but they are not the only ones. This chapter will address the closely related efficacy issue—whether the direction of covert paramilitary operations constitutes an appropriate field of activity for the Central Intelligence Agency. This is not, of course, the first time the ground has been covered, but in view of the current controversy the present moment seems an opportune one to reengage the intellectual debate.

After attempting a clarification of terminology, the chapter will examine two issues. The first concerns the extent to which covert action might conflict with the CIA's principal mission—"to collect, produce and disseminate foreign intelligence and counter intelligence including information not otherwise obtainable"[2]—in particular, clandestine human source intelligence collection. In this connection, the chapter will explore both the requirement for such sources in the current strategic environment in light of U.S. national security objectives and the operational conditions that facilitate it. These conditions will then be compared with those of covert paramilitary operations in order to determine whether there might be a conflict of operational priorities, styles, and methods that could jeopardize the clandestine collection mission. This leads to the second matter under examination: If there is a potential conflict of operational conditions, what alternatives are available, and what is the appropriate role for the CIA? The British experience of covert action since 1939 will be explored with a view to identifying potentially applicable "lessons." These, in turn, will be considered within the context of existing U.S. constitutional and bureaucratic arrangements in order to determine what options are available to the U.S. government. From this it should be possible to draw some conclusions about the place of the CIA in covert paramilitary operations.

As a cautionary note, however, it should be stated initially that there may be no neat and tidy answers, no resolution of the problem that is wholly satisfactory to all concerned. This dark underside of international affairs is inherently untidy and unpleasant. It leaves little room for comfortable moral, political, or operational positions. That said, to the extent this chapter can clarify the role of the CIA in covert paramilitary operations, it may be able to make a positive contribution to the larger debate over the place of covert action in U.S. diplomacy.

This should not be taken to imply that the chapter starts from the a priori assumption that covert action does have a place in the repertoire of American extradiplomatic tools. Rather, it starts with an "if": If covert action were seen to be necessary, then what should be the role of the CIA?

DEFINING THE PROBLEM

It may be useful to start by attempting to clarify the central concept: covert paramilitary operations. The commonly used term covert action, which is widely used to describe activities such as the Contra campaign in Nicaragua, is insufficiently specific. Traditionally, and in official parlance, it has been something of a catch-all phrase, including within its scope a wide spectrum of activities. These range from the relatively benign political influence operation—channeling funds to an opposition newspaper, for example—to the singularly violent—such as assassination of foreign leaders or the overthrow of a government.[3] The term covert, while literally synonymous with clandestine or secret, actually refers to the concept of "plausible deniability." This means that the action itself may be visible and verifiable, but that the links between the real initiator and the events themselves are concealed to the extent that the initiator can plausibly deny involvement.[4] The adjective paramilitary has been inserted here to indicate that subsequent discussion will be confined to that category of covert activity which involves the active direction, deployment, or support of regular or irregular armed bodies of men employing unconventional military means to achieve their (or their sponsor's) political objectives.

The reference to unconventional means leads the semantic quest into the military dimension of what is called "Special Operations," which in fact might prove to be a more appropriate label than covert action. In its military or paramilitary context, the concept of Special

Operations embraces a variety of activities, which could include the following:

1. Raising, training, financing, and arming an indigenous insurgent movement;
2. Foreign Internal Defense (i.e., military training and technical assistance to a foreign government for the purpose of countering internal unrest or insurgency);
3. Counterterrorist "direct action" missions;
4. Assistance to a foreign army plotting to overthrow its government by means of a coup d'état;
5. "Executive-action"-type assassination missions against a hostile foreign leader or other foreign persons;
6. Military assistance to a "third-party" actor engaged in any of the above against a mutually agreed target;
7. Paramilitary direct-action missions in support of conventional war operations, including sabotage and assassination; and
8. Combat Rescue/Services Protected Evacuation operations.[5]

The CIA has been involved for several decades in many of these categories of operations.[6] Recently, the counterterrorist role has also been suggested for the agency in conjunction with other U.S. security forces.[7]

CLANDESTINE COLLECTION AND COVERT ACTION IN THE CONTEMPORARY STRATEGIC ENVIRONMENT

In the latter part of the 1970s, it became fashionable to argue that the clandestine human source was of declining importance and that most, if not all, of what American analysts needed to know about their opponents could be collected by National Technical Means.[8] Without denigrating the importance of such means, particularly in the strategic forces dimension of intelligence analysis, it is possible to make a case for continued, even increased, reliance on human sources. The reason for this is quite clear and simple. The national security strategy of the Reagan administration commits the United States (1) to protecting U.S. interests and citizens abroad; (2) to preventing coercion of the United States, its allies and friends; (3) to maintaining access to critical resources; (4) to opposing Soviet expansion; and (5) to encouraging long-term political and military changes in the Soviet "empire."[9] Ranged against these strategic objectives is a vast array of "threats," the least likely of which is probably a direct military conflict between the United States and the Soviet Union in Central Europe. The threats to U.S. objectives in the 1980s seem most likely to arise in the low-intensity spectrum: local and regional conflicts of a guerrilla, limited conventional, or revolutionary nature and internal instability of U.S. allies or clients.[10] The current conflicts in Lebanon, the Persian Gulf area, and Central America are cases in point. Terrorism is another problem with which U.S. foreign policy has to cope. American citizens and installations have been the principal targets since the 1970s. Recent trends suggest that state-sponsored terrorism, such as that ascribed to Libya and Iran, rather than terrorism by substate groups, may prove to be the predominant terrorist problem of the 1980s.[11]

Regardless of location and specific political circumstances, these situations share at least two common features. First, and above all, they are political conflicts; military means are employed to achieve a political objective. That is as true for a coup d'état as it is for political terrorism or revolutionary war. The second common feature is that the political and military aspects of these conflicts are planned, organized, and conducted by clandestine means. Those who plan coups plot in secrecy; political terrorist organizations operate in small, self-contained cells; and revolutionary groups are often organized in multiple layers of overt and covert levels of leadership and membership. These two factors combined point to a major intelligence requirement, even if the object is merely to be well informed about developments. If the United States is to engage these forces in a political/military struggle, then the task is more difficult still. For, as Frank Kitson has observed about low-intensity conflict, "the problem of defeating the enemy consists very largely of finding him."[12]

This, in turn, points the intelligence task in the direction of clandestine collection, for obvious reasons: the target is essentially political, not military/technical, and it is largely human and clandestine. National Technical Means, at which the United States excels, has limited application in low-intensity conflict. Aircraft can photograph some arms shipments or training camps, and electronic listening posts may be capable of listening in on phone calls or radio transmissions. Yet it is in the nature of revolutionaries, guerrillas, or terrorists not to be dependent on such means for operations and communication. Couriers, cut-outs, and letter drops are more secure. In other words, not just buildings, but the minds of men must be penetrated. The arena is one of clandestine intelligence, and whether the task involves planting a bug, photographing a document, meeting a deep-penetration agent, or cultivating a defector, the human element is predominant. But such intelligence sources take time, patience, effort, and resources to develop. It may be that the United States depends upon clandestine sources for no more than 5 percent of all of its intelligence input.[13] Yet, in a given situation, the successful prosecution of policy may depend more upon that slender thread of intelligence than upon all the weaponry deployed on the battlefield. It is not just a question of being able to anticipate the next guerrilla ambush or to identify the planners of a coup. It is a matter of being able to make reliable assessments about the politics and direction of the conflict as a whole. In a polarized and militarized situation, clandestine means may be indispensable.

The question thus arises: Does the renewed emphasis on covert paramilitary action, characterized by the Contra operation in Nicaragua, place clandestine collection efforts at some risk? Obviously, secrecy is the first operational consideration with respect to human source collection on hostile territory. Not only must the sources of information be protected from exposure and "neutralization" by more or less violent means, but the means and methods by which each source is acquired, developed, contacted, and exploited must also be kept secure.[14] The operational style of clandestine collection is clearly and completely at odds with that of covert paramilitary operations. Whereas the former amounts, in the strictest sense, to observation of a target, in which success may be predicated on watching or listening while remaining undetected, the latter are inherently activist. By definition they involve active, often violent manipulation of the politics of a foreign country or region. Yet, although such actions are supposed to be "covert," their very nature carries the risks of exposure and, hence, failure. There are at least two reasons for this. First, paramilitary operations exhibit a high "noise" factor, either immediately or afterward.[15] This is due largely to the scale of many such operations (often hundreds or thousands of people are involved); to the requirement for a logistic infrastructure, which can be complex and costly; and to the multitudinous opportunities for human error and carelessness that can breach operational security. Furthermore, the use of violence, in whatever form, is simply bound to attract attention. Second, covert paramilitary operations are frequently undertaken as the weapon of last resort, when all other means have been exhausted and/or are not available to assist the operation. Consequently, they have a very uncertain likelihood of success, an assertion that seems amply supported by the historical record.[16] In every sense of the term, then, they are "high-risk" operations.

The two operational styles and requirements could not be more dissimilar. Yet within the CIA the two tasks—clandestine collection and covert operations—are grouped together under the same directorate (that of Operations), and overseas they are frequently run out of the same CIA station, if not by the same people.[17] Indeed, the advocates of CIA involvement in covert action argue that this is an operational advantage; that by virtue of its intelligence work the agency has usually built up the contacts, networks, and infrastructure (safe houses, front organizations, couriers) that make effective covert action possible. Furthermore, the agency station personnel account for a great deal of accumulated in-country experience and language skills.[18] This may be perfectly true, but it seems to raise a number of important questions. First, given that the CIA's clandestine service is not large to start with, and that the bulk of recent expansion nas been assigned to covert action,[19] it seems only fair to ask whether any of the delicate skeins of clandestine intelligence networks, built up painstakingly over long periods of time, have been jeopardized by exploitation for covert paramilitary operations? If so, what were the consequences for the agents or informers thus exposed and compromised; for the agency, in relation to its ability to recruit other local sources, when the risks of exposure seemed so great; and for the United States, in terms of acquiring vital information? Could any of the so-called intelligence failures[20] of recent years be attributed to a conflict of priorities between paramilitary operations and clandestine collection?

Those questions cannot be answered here; indeed, it is not clear whether the subject could be properly researched without access to documents that are normally too sensitive for declassification. Even so, consideration of alternative arrangements for covert paramilitary operations is not precluded. In the search for answers there may be something to be learned from the British experience.

COVERT PARAMILITARY OPERATIONS: THE BRITISH EXPERIENCE

With their long imperial history, the British also have a long history of political warfare and covert paramilitary action, to preserve the empire, to oppose foreign enemies, and to futher foreign policy objectives by unconventional means, and not without some considerable success. The Arab uprising against the Ottoman empire in 1916-1918 is a case in point: in return for a relatively modest investment of money, weapons, and personnel—in particular, the enigmatic but effective Colonel T. E. Lawrence—the British government effectively liberated the Arabian peninsula from Turkish rule, thereby allowing Britain to divide up the region and install client regimes.[21] In the postimperial era, Britain has continued to rely on clandestine means to maintain its residual interests, in addition to maintaining, according to Anthony Verrier, the illusion of power where the substance is lacking.[22] Indeed, it may be fair to suggest that as its real economic, political, and military power has receded, Britain has been forced to rely increasingly on bluff, deception, and unconventional means to achieve its objectives.

The significant aspect of the British experience is the extent to which Britain has relied on organizations outside its intelligence service to undertake covert paramilitary missions. MI6, the Secret Intelligence Service, was not excluded altogether; in fact, it initiated both the abortive rebellion against the Albanian communist regime and the coup against Mossadegh in Iran—in both cases, some time before the Americans became involved.[23] In the 1970s, however, under the stewardship of Sir Maurice Oldfield, MI6 discarded the paramilitary mission. Oldfield, who as the senior British intelligence officer in Washington from 1960 to 1964, had numerous opportunities to observe the CIA's paramilitary efforts, did not approve of such activity. As director-general of MI6, he insisted that if an intelligence service was to be respected, it should never confuse the collection of information with sabotage and assassination.[24] By and large, then, the British approach since 1939 has been to create separate specialized organizations for such tasks.

During World War II, the largest of these was the Special Operations Executive (SOE), a secret service created in 1940 "to coordinate all action, by way of subversion and sabotage, against the enemy overseas."[25] The SOE effectively hived off MI6's covert action branch for the duration of the war.[26] The British Army established the Special Air Service (SAS) Regiment, which operated behind enemy lines independently or in cooperation with local resistance forces.[27] These constitute but a small sample of the numerous clandestine special organizations established by the British during the war. Virtually all, the SAS and SOE among them, were disbanded at the end of the conflict.

The capabilities were not allowed to lapse for long, as the Albanian operation indicates. The early postwar efforts, however, tended to be ad hoc, with all the problems and risks that entailed. The "Farran case" in Palestine (then a British mandate territory) in 1947 illustrates this point. Confronted by the ruthless and effective terrorism of the Irgun Zvai Leumi and the "Stern Gang," two Jewish underground movements, the British government authorized the Palestine police to create "countergangs" of specially recruited ex-SOE, ex-SAS men who would hunt down and eliminate the terrorists by covert means. Owing to the lack of clear guidelines and accurate intelligence, the operation apparently got out of control and exceeded its mandate. Roy Farran, leader of one of the teams, was accused of murder and, after a series of escapes, was brought to trial, but was later acquitted. The counterterrorist teams were disbanded and the investigation of Captain Farran was played out in the media of the day, adding sensationalist embarrassment to Britain's already difficult political and military task in Palestine.[28] Surprisingly, however, the countergang technique was not completely discredited from an operational point of view. It was used by the British Army (on a small scale) with considerable effect in Kenya against the Mau-Mau and with more limited effect in Aden in 1966-1967.[29]

Herein lies the crucial difference between the British and American approaches to the problem: the British have tended to rely on the armed forces, not the intelligence community, to provide the necessary paramilitary skills. Those skills have been concentrated increasingly in the SAS. Recreated as a regular regiment of the British Army in the 1950s to provide specialized counterinsurgency techniques for the Malayan Emergency, the SAS has since become the overt/covert special-operations arm of the Foreign Office.[30] In this capacity it has carried out counterterrorist and hostage-rescue operations and has provided training teams to foreign governments.[31] In war and situations short of war, it fills the gap left by SOE. A highly secretive force, it relies on superior training, intelligence, professionalism, and stealth to get the job done. The SAS was instrumental in one of Britain's least publicized victories of the postwar period: the defeat of the Dhofar rebellion in Oman in the 1970s.

Time and space do not permit me to describe the campaign in detail; it started in the mid-1960s as a largely indigenous rebellion against the reactionary rule of Sultan Said bin Taimur and became a classic revolutionary struggle, supported from South Yemen by the USSR and China. The British, with a long-standing defense commitment to Oman, intervened to protect the flow of oil through the Straits of Hormuz, by ensuring that a friendly government remained in power in Oman.[32] This involved the British in some rather unorthodox covert actions. The first of these was the removal of Sultan Taimur in a virtually bloodless and highly popular coup that placed his progressive, Western-educated son on the throne.[33] Other elements of the British campaign included the following: first, operating under the thin official cover of British Army Training Teams, elements of several SAS squadrons were instrumental in raising, training, and leading the Firquats, Dhofari irregular forces composed of loyal tribesmen and surrendered guerrillas who had been turned to fight for the new sultan. By the end of the campaign they numbered some 3,000, of whom about one-third were surrendered guerrillas. The Firquats provided the counterrevolutionary infrastructure that bought time for the regular forces to defeat the insurgents.[34] Second, British Army Information Teams both played a significant role in military psychological warfare and deception operations and also contributed to the larger political warfare and information program (to which the BBC lent unofficial assistance).[35] Third, the sultan's armed forces were strengthened considerably by the secondment and contracting of British officers to key training and leadership positions. Airwork Services Limited, a commercial firm with close links to the Ministry of Defense, served as the contracting agency for those military personnel not lent under normal secondment arrangements, over and above its primary task of providing training and technical support to the Omani air force.[36] Finally, British officers (apparently including some ex-MI6 personnel) staffed and ran the Omani intelligence and security services, with considerable success.[37]

British involvement in the Dhofar campaign, while significant in political and military terms, was—for public consumption in Britain--distinctly low profile. News media coverage was not prevented, but neither was it encouraged. Two examples should suffice to illustrate this point. First, in July 1970 the British-officered security forces deliberately suppressed news of Qaboos' coup d'état, largely for internal security reasons. It was first reported in British newspapers on July 27th, four days after it occurred. The already substantial British military presence in Oman was acknowledged, but Whitehall "expressed amazement" at suggestions in the <u>Manchester Guardian</u> that the British forces there might have had anything to do with the coup.[38] There were no questions asked in Parliament or directed to the prime minister in the week following the coup, and as late as December 1970 the British government was steadfastly maintaining the fiction that the SAS was in Dhofar for training purposes only.[39] The second example is perhaps more telling. On July 19, 1972, at Mirbat, an eight-man SAS "training team," along with the local <u>Firqa</u>, Dhofar Gendarmerie, and Askari irregulars, fought a four-hour pitched battle against a rebel force 250 strong before being relieved by helicopter-borne SAS reinforcements. The Mirbat SAS team suffered two killed and two seriously wounded.[40] Mirbat is now regarded as a milestone in the Dhofar war, but by the end of July 1972 the battle had still gone unreported in the major British papers.[41]

The silence about Mirbat may have been facilitated by the fact that most British media attention was focused on the then escalating conflict in Northern Ireland. Yet it is clear that the British government was able to uphold the covert approach to the Dhofar war generally by taking advantage of both the SAS regiment's tradition as a "silent service" and the British parliamentary tradition that discourages public discussion of the activities of the secret services.[42] The all-party parliamentary committee on foreign affairs, moreover, lacks the influence and investigative power normally attributed to its U.S. congressional counterparts (of which more will be said later). Furthermore, the use of the Airwork company as a civil/military contractor cum participant helped effectively to blur "the distinction between commercial activity and government-inspired foreign policy initiatives."[43]

Consequently, although the British government took some political heat for its involvement in the war, mainly in the form of Soviet propaganda and British-based prorebel agitprop,[44] it was able to ride out the storm. Criticism did not focus on MI6 and thus did not put at risk any intelligence efforts in the region. The covert paramilitary operations themselves were effectively kept under wraps and were not compromised.

If there is a single lesson to be drawn from the British experience, it is that covert paramilitary operations need not be run by intelligence services. Indeed, the British example suggests that such operations ought to be conducted by the organization best trained, equipped, and qualified to do so—the armed forces. Granted that the experience of one country cannot be applied easily to another, but to what extent might this lesson be applied to the United States?

COVERT PARAMILITARY OPERATIONS: U.S. OPTIONS AND OBSTACLES

On the face of it, the lesson should be easily applied. In a 1975 article, Harry Rositzke asserted that "all that is needed to make [the Department of] Defense effective in covert operations is to convert a small section of its command structure into a special operating unit which can be given congressional authority to move funds, personnel and equipment outside the bureaucratic system."[45] This, he said, would also bring future paramilitary operations under established congressional oversight and review. To a limited extent this has been done. The U.S. Army's Special Forces and Rangers have been brought together under a single unified command.[46] Moreover, many of the missions currently assigned to the Special Forces—unconventional warfare (guerrilla warfare, subversion, and sabotage), psychological operations, and foreign internal defense[47]—go to the heart of covert paramilitary operations as they are presently practiced by the CIA. Furthermore, the Joint Chiefs of Staff have established a triservice "Special Operations Agency" to carry out counterterrorist operations in a covert manner.[48] The relevant military resources, expertise, and organizational structures are thus already in place.

In theory, at least, the same could be said for the policy formulation, decisionmaking, and oversight dimensions. Covert paramilitary action is manifestly a foreign policy activity, and the president has stated that he regards the secretary of state as his principal foreign policy adviser, responsible for the formulation and execution of that policy.[49] Given, therefore, that covert action is legitimately part of the secretary's "turf," it would appear only logical to assign to the State Department, under the secretary's direction, the authority to act as the "lead agency" for covert paramilitary action. By this I do not mean conversion of the State Department and its diplomats into specialists in the "Black Arts"; rather, I refer to placement of the Defense Department's Special Forces resources at the State Department's disposal and under its direction and responsibility when some form of covert action is deemed necessary and advisable. The State Department, working closely with the National Security Council, would have to play the major role in deciding when those conditions exist in relation to broader foreign policy objectives. Planning would have to be the responsibility of an interdepartmental committee or task force (chaired by the State Department) on which each of the contributing agencies or departments—as well as the executive branch—would be represented. Operational control would then be exercised by a Pentagon staff with advisers from State and the other relevant organizations. Regarding oversight, the charters of both the Senate and House Foreign Affairs committees give them the congressional review and oversight role with respect to foreign affairs.[50]   It would be only logical, therefore, to transfer the oversight of covert paramilitary activities to these committees from the intelligence committees where it currently resides.   In view of the intention to use the armed forces in this role, moreover, the House Armed Services Committee would probably have to be consulted as well.

Giving the State Department and the Department of Defense joint responsibility for covert paramilitary operations might produce several practical advantages.   First, it would free the CIA to concentrate solely on its primary mission—intelligence collection and production. When called upon to support paramilitary operations the agency would be acting properly in an _advisory_ capacity, rather than its current policymaking _and_ policy-enacting role.   Thus, in an operation such as that in Nicaragua, the CIA would concentrate on clandestine intelligence-collection tasks, including "[d]eveloping sources in Managua (such as dissidents and cooperative foreign diplomats or military attachés) to clarify the Nicaraguan regime's ability to deal with the rebels; [and] nailing down the precise nature and quality of arms arriving in the area from the Soviet Union and Cuba."[51]   This sort of largely human source intelligence would be essential to a successful paramilitary operation, and the CIA is the only agency that has the capability to provide it.   Far better, then, that it should be able to conduct its clandestine collection efforts discreetly without simultaneous responsibility for running the operation it is trying to advise.

Second, the U.S. Armed Forces personnel engaged in directing or supporting a paramilitary operation would be subject (as CIA personnel are not) to military law and discipline.   While hardly foolproof, these safeguards should go some way toward discouraging the kind of "cowboy" or freelance initiatives that have characterized some past CIA operations.

Finally, making the State Department the "lead agency" for policymaking and planning with respect to covert paramilitary operations would probably introduce an element of caution and selectivity into their use.   Moreover, it would facilitate the integration of covert operations with both the outlook and the other components of foreign policy.

However sensible or practical this might appear, it seems unlikely to occur in the foreseeable future.   To exchange existing arrangements for anything like the system suggested earlier would, in fact, require a major reorganization of the foreign policymaking structure.   More important, it would require a radical change in bureaucratic thinking. However, the obstacles to such fundamental organizational, bureaucratic, and conceptual reform are simply too formidable.   The first of these is the predominant role of the president and his immediate advisers, especially the National Security Council (NSC), in the making of foreign policy.   As Robert Hunter has noted:

> [T]he success or failure of U.S. foreign policy is the responsibility of the President . . . to the degree that the United States itself can be instrumental in determining its own fate.   The President must set the central vision of U.S. foreign policy, . . . work with it, set priorities based upon it, relate it to domestic affairs, put it into political terms, and communicate it most effectively to the

Congress, the American people, and nations abroad.[52]

Furthermore, it is the NSC, and not the State Department, that in recent administrations has become the principal forum for the development and conduct of foreign policy. The president's public assertions notwithstanding, only under Henry Kissinger as secretary of state did the State Department and its secretary carry genuine authority in the foreign policy field, and then only because of the force of Kissinger's personality. Under the Carter administration, power passed back to the NSC. The State Department was criticized for being oversensitive to the reactions of other nations, whereas the White House was concerned with "getting things done." The State versus NSC/White House struggle continues under the Reagan administration, having not as yet been wholly resolved.[53] The main point here is that neither the State Department nor its head carries sufficient political clout to wrest from the president and the NSC the right and the power to direct such a sensitive area of foreign policy as covert paramilitary operations.

Nor is the president likely to delegate that authority to the State Department so long as he has access to and authority to direct an "action-capable" agency such as the CIA. The CIA is regarded as "the president's" intelligence agency.[54] It comes directly under the NSC, and the director of Central Intelligence is the president's principal adviser on matters pertaining to foreign intelligence. Assuming that the president supports it, this position gives the CIA considerable leverage to resist modification of its charter or restrictions on the scope of its activities. The CIA could be expected to resist strongly, and probably successfully, any attempt to take paramilitary operations out of its hands.

Moreover, the president is likely to reject any reform that would strengthen the relatively weak hand of Congress in the foreign policy process. Constitutional theory, the power of the purse and of declaring war notwithstanding, Congress has little genuine authority in the foreign policy field. In addition, under existing arrangements there are simply too many loopholes through which the president can exercise his prerogative—the recent "fudging" of the briefing of Congress on the mining of Nicaraguan ports being a case in point.[55] Transferring the paramilitary role to the armed forces and the oversight task to the Senate Foreign Relations Committee, however, might restrict the president's freedom of action and significantly enhance Congress's foreign policy role. By means of negative votes, procedural delays, committee hearings, and appropriation amendments, an assertive Congress, as in the mid-1970s, can set limits on presidential action.[56] This largely negative, restrictive, intrusive, and embarrassing role has resulted in a tug-of-war between the executive and legislative branches over foreign-policymaking through several recent administrations. If it chose to be obstructive, Congress could insist on applying the War Powers Act, in the full, to each and every occasion on which the president deployed the armed forces overseas on a covert paramilitary mission. This could have two limiting effects on such operations.[57] First, the requirement to notify Congress within 48 hours of the start of a mission could potentially violate operational security, place the lives of the soldiers at risk, and possibly contribute to the failure of the operation. Second, the War Powers Act provides for a 60-day limit to commitment of U.S. forces, beyond which the president must receive from Congress either an extension or a declaration of war. Yet it is in the nature of low-intensity conflict that some paramilitary operations might not achieve visible and satisfactory results within 60 days; although a declaration of war might be wholly inappropriate in some circumstances, Congress might not have either the stomach or the patience for a mere extension of the operation. As few conflicts are fought to rigid timetables, premature application of the War Powers limit could, under certain conditions, prove prejudicial, if not disastrous, to U.S. foreign policy interests.

This should not be construed as an argument for unlimited presidential power in foreign policy or covert operations. Rather, it should be viewed as an attempt to see the problems of reforming the system as the executive branch would be likely to see them. In this way, the reasons for presidential resistance to change can better be understood.

Of course, where one sees problems another may see opportunities. It could be argued that the pursuit of a bipartisan consensus on foreign policy—and, by inference, on covert paramilitary operations--might be better served (as suggested earlier) by assigning the oversight role to the prestigious and supposedly influential Senate Foreign Relations Committee. Yet the committee in its present incarnation might not be the best forum for such a difficult policy issue. Critics say that the administration's failure to consult Congress and the committee's poor relations with the executive branch have eroded the committee's authority. The liberal-conservative split in committee membership has made it difficult to achieve bipartisan consensus; issues and personalities have become politicized, and opposition to the president continues to make the news, whereas support for his policies does not and might even be regarded as a liability. Furthermore, the committee has had poor relations with the State Department; each regards the other as camping on its turf and views its own expertise as superior.[58] Clearly this sort of situation would not be regarded by the current (and possibly subsequent) administrations as satisfactory for the purpose of conducting oversights of sensitive and politically controversial operations.

Finally, it must be acknowledged that there are doubts about the ability of U.S. military forces to handle these missions with the subtlety and sophistication they demand. To their credit, the Special Forces have apparently performed well as instructors overseas, and at first glance the Rangers appear to have passed the test of combat in their parachute assault on Grenada.[59] Moreover, bringing all of the army's unconventional warfare units together under one command was probably a wise decision, as it should reduce to a minimum duplication of effort and clashes over roles and missions. Still, the doubts linger--and not without reason.

Ideally, every Green Beret or Ranger is an airborne-qualified volunteer, cross-trained in the necessary skills and able to speak a foreign language. In reality, operational effectiveness and readiness is adversely affected, first of all, by the absence of a clear doctrine of employment, constantly shifting operational and training priorities, and (until the formation of the Special Operations Command in 1982) a lack of guidance from higher commands to relate training to potential missions. Second, reduced training standards throughout the rest of the army have pushed all skill levels below requirement. A lack of career incentive for officers has caused a leadership shortage. Manpower shortages generally are particularly noticeable in communications and medical slots. Some first-term men are filling NCO positions, and many positions are filled one or two grades below authorization. Finally, the reserve groups, which constitute nearly half of the army's Special Forces, are poorly trained and equipped and are not ready for deployment.[60]

With the exception of the doctrine and training aspects, these problems tend to afflict the Special Forces rather than the Rangers. They are, nonetheless, no less serious for either element. The weaknesses identified earlier provide a recipe for failure, if not for disaster. They make the reasons for the collapse of the Iran rescue mission easier to understand, and they provide little incentive for a president to employ these forces instead of the CIA on highly sensitive, high-risk covert missions.

CONCLUSIONS

The foregoing suggests that for the foreseeable future there will be no viable administrative alternative to current arrangements whereby the CIA functions as the lead agency for the direction of covert paramilitary operations. The imperatives of U.S. politics rule out, for the time being at least, the kind of wholesale institutional reform in both the executive branch and the Congress that would make possible the transfer of the covert paramilitary role from the CIA to the armed forces. What this means for the U.S. government is that the CIA will continue to be the focus of controversy and exposé, with the corollary that its covert operations may be rendered ineffective and its clandestine collection efforts compromised. It raises the question as to whether the concept of "covert" operations can have any meaning in today's politicized, information-consuming climate, for to deny involvement when the evidence is there for all to see is foolish and counterproductive. Moreover, although the official term Special Activities appears to be a more neutral concept, the accompanying definition explicitly implies a deliberate effort to conceal certain activities[61] that cannot or need not always be concealed.

If in the field of paramilitary special operations the U.S. government is thus condemned to "muddling through" the existing arrangements, all the while gritting its collective teeth in the face of criticism, then perhaps it should think carefully about how such operations should be conducted in future. Indeed, I might usefully close this chapter by suggesting some guidelines for future paramilitary special operations that could enhance, rather than detract from, the conduct of foreign policy by unconventional means.[62] First, to the extent that a country can choose the conflicts in which it becomes involved, special operations planners should pick their opponents, battles, and means with care. This calls for considerable strategic and political sensitivity, subtlety, and sophistication, and it leads, in turn, to the second point: special operations are tools of diplomacy, not substitutes for it; integration of these methods with other foreign policy instruments is essential, thus suggesting a need for effective coordination, high-quality intelligence, and sound political/diplomatic advice. Third, and directly related to the foregoing, it is a mistake to stake too much prestige on a single operation. Covert operations can be kept in perspective by being realistic about goals, requirements, and limitations. Furthermore, if an operation is unlikely to remain covert, then the government should be prepared to live with overt status from the outset while making every effort to keep it low profile. Politically, it should be possible to be candid about strategic intentions while preserving operational security at the tactical level—rendering "secure" only that which is vital to the mission's success. Finally, although this cannot be a hard and fast rule, it may be fair to suggest (counterterrorist and hostage rescue missions notwithstanding) that special operations should rarely be considered a last resort. Chances are that if all other means have failed, the odds are stacked against a special operation success as well.

The purpose of this chapter was to contribute to the debate on the appropriate role for the CIA in covert paramilitary operations. The evidence suggests that the CIA might benefit from withdrawal from the paramilitary role, which could be handled instead by the armed forces. However, domestic U.S. political considerations—especially the bureaucratic politics of the executive branch—make such a change unlikely. Continued use of the CIA in this role, then, is testimony to the fact that democratic societies invariably have to make choices and compromises in the conduct of domestic and foreign affairs that inevitably fall short of perfection.

NOTES

1. See, for example, "Is Covert Action Necessary?" Newsweek (November 8, 1982); "Arguing About Means and Ends," Time (April 18, 1983); "Another Public Covert Action," Chicago Tribune (April 12, 1984); "The Trouble with Covert Operations," Washington Post (April 24, 1984).

2. U.S. Executive Order 12333, "United States Intelligence Activities," Part I.8(a) (Washington, D.C.: Government Printing Office, 1981).

3. Memorandum from Special Counsel to the Director of Central Intelligence, in House Select Committee on Intelligence, Hearings (December 9, 1975), quoted in Tyrus G. Fain et al., eds., The Intelligence Community: History, Organization, Issues (New York: Bowker, Public Documents Series, 1977), p. 4.

4. Hugh Tovar, "Covert Action," in Roy Godson, ed., Intelligence Requirements for the 1980s: Elements of Intelligence (Washington, D.C.: National Strategy Information Center, 1979), p. 69.

5. Extracted largely from David Charters and Maurice Tugwell, "Special Operations and the Threats to United States Interests in the 1980s," in Patrick J. Garrity, ed., Special Operations in United States Strategy in the 1980s (Washington, D.C.: National Defense University Press, 1984); see also M.R.D. Foot, "Special Operations, I," in Michael Elliott-Bateman, ed., The Fourth Dimension of Warfare, Volume One: Intelligence, Subversion Resistance (Manchester, England: Manchester University Press, 1970), p. 19; Bernard Gwertzman, "Covert Action: Debating Wisdom and Morality," New York Times (April 8, 1983).

6. In "Black Ops 1963-1983," Harpers (April 1984), pp. 17, 20,

forty-five major and minor operations, successful or otherwise, are
listed for that twenty-year period in which CIA involvement has been
either proven or alleged. The majority of these operations were in the
paramilitary category. A comprehensive list covering the period 1950-
1974 is contained in "Reported Foreign and Domestic Covert Activities
of the U.S. Central Intelligence Agency: 1950-1974," in Fain et al.,
The Intelligence Community, pp. 695-706.

7. National Security Decision Directive (NSDD) 138, promulgated
April 3, 1984. According to "Preemptive Anti-Terrorist Raids Allowed,"
Washington Post (April 16, 1984), NSDD 138 would permit use of force
by FBI, CIA, and military counterterrorist teams. This was later
denied by senior U.S. government officials (see Washington Times [April
17, 1984]).

8. The problem of the relative importance and priority of National
Technical Means versus clandestine human sources is discussed by
Richard K. Betts, "American Strategic Intelligence: Politics, Priorities
and Direction," in Robert Pfaltzgraff, Jr., Uri Ra'anan, and
Warren Milburg, eds., Intelligence Policy and National Security (London:
Macmillan, 1981), pp. 253-254.

9. As outlined in July 1981 by Secretary of Defense Caspar
Weinberger, "U.S. Military Strategy for the 1980s," in The 1980s:
Decade of Confrontation? 1981 Proceedings Eighth National Security
Affairs Conference (Washington, D.C.: National Defense University
Press, 1981), p. xi.

10. William J. Taylor, The Future of Conflict: U.S. Interests--The
Washington Papers No. 94 (Washington, D.C.: Center for Strategic and
International Studies, 1983), pp. 41-45; Michael Carver, War Since 1945
(London: Weidenfeld and Nicholson, 1980), p. 282; David Charters,
Dominick Graham, and Maurice Tugwell, Trends in Low-Intensity
Conflict: ORAE Extra-Mural Paper No. 16 (Ottawa: Department of
National Defense, 1981), pp. 11-12; Robert A. Scalapino, "The Political
Strategic Outlook for International Violence," in Tunde Adeniran and
Yonah Alexander, eds., International Violence (New York: Praeger
Publishers, 1983), pp. 166-167.

11. See Brian Michael Jenkins, New Modes of Conflict (Santa
Monica, Calif.: Rand Corporation, 1983), pp. 10-14; Frederick Kempe,
"Violent Tactics," Wall Street Journal (April 19, 1983);
Caroline Moorehead, "This Alien Scourge," The Times [London] (March
12, 1984).

12. Frank Kitson, Low Intensity Operations: Insurgency,
Subversion, Peacekeeping (London: Faber, 1971), p. 95.

13. Estimate from William Barnds, "Intelligence and Policymaking in
an Institutional Context," in Fain et al., The Intelligence Community,
p. 80.

14. The assassination of CIA Station Chief Richard Welch stands
as ample testimony to the risks facing the exposed, unprotected agent.

15. Harry Rositzke, The CIA's Secret Operations: Espionage,
Counterespionage and Covert Action (New York: Reader's Digest
Press, 1977), p. 166.

16. The ill-fated rescue attempt in Iran in 1980 might have been
atypical, but it stands out as a rather desperate effort, dependent on
slender, high-risk, and, in some aspects, unproven resources, undertaken
under political duress. See U.S., Joint Chiefs of Staff, Special
Operations Review Group, Report on Aborted U.S. Rescue Mission to

348

Iran (Washington, D.C.: Department of Defense, 1980). For an insider's view, see Colonel Charlie A. Beckwith, Delta Force (New York: Harcourt Brace Jovanovich, 1983), which strengthens rather than diminishes this impression.

17. See Barnds, "The Policy Context," in Fain et al., The Intelligence Community, p. 71; and Mark M. Lowenthal, U.S. Intelligence: Evolution and Anatomy, The Washington Papers No. 105 (Washington, D.C.: Center for Strategic and International Studies, 1984), p. 91.

18. Roy Godson, "Covert Action: An Introduction," in Roy Godson, ed., Intelligence Requirements for the 1980s: Covert Action (Washington, D.C.: National Strategy Information Center, 1981), pp. 2-3.

19. Angelo Codevilla, "The Substance and the Rules," Washington Quarterly 5, no. 3 (Summer 1983): 36; see also "America's Secret Warriors," Newsweek (October 10, 1983), pp. 38-39.

20. The events that come to mind include the bomb attacks on the U.S. Embassy and Marine Compound in Beirut, the declaration of martial law in Poland, the Soviet invasion of Afghanistan, and the Iranian revolution and hostage crisis. The extent to which the United States' inability to predict with precision any of these incidents constitutes a genuine intelligence "failure" remains a matter of considerable debate.

21. Michael Elliott-Bateman, "The Age of the Guerrila," in Elliott-Bateman, John Ellis, Tom Bowden, eds., The Fourth Dimension of Warfare, Volume II: Revolt to Revolution (Manchester, England: Manchester University Press, 1974), p. 9.

22. Anthony Verrier, Through the Looking Glass: British Foreign Policy in the Age of Illusions (London: Jonathan Cape, 1983), pp. 1-6.

23. See ibid., pp. 51-77, 105-108; see also Kermit Roosevelt, Countercoup: The Struggle for the Control of Iran (New York: McGraw-Hill, 1979), pp. 3, 15.

24. David A. Charters, "Sir Maurice Oldfield and British Intelligence: Some Lessons for Canada," Conflict Quarterly 2, no. 3 (Winter 1982): 48.

25. M.R.D. Foot, SOE in France (London: Her Majesty's Stationery Office [HMSO], 1966), pp. 8-9. The quotation comes from a secret cabinet memorandum.

26. F. H. Hinsley et al., British Intelligence in the Second World War, Volume 1 (London: HMSO, 1979), and Resistance, Volume 2 (London: Granada, 1976), pp. 137-141.

27. Tony Geraghty, Who Dares Wins: The Story of the Special Air Service 1950-1980 (London: Arms and Armour Press, 1980), pp. 10-15.

28. David A. Charters, "Special Operations in Counter-Insurgency: The Farran Case, Palestine 1947," Royal United Services Institute Journal for Defense Studies 124, no. 2 (June 1979): 51-61.

29. On Kenya, see Frank Kitson, Bunch of Five (London: Faber, 1977), pp. 29-56; for a distillation of his earlier work, see Kitson, Gangs and Countergangs (London: Barrie and Rockliff, 1964); on Aden, see Geraghty, Who Dares Wins, pp. 79-82. No sources are given, however, for Geraghty's assertions.

30. Geraghty, Who Dares Wins, pp. 165-166; Eliot S. Cohen, Commandos and Politicians: Elite Military Units in Modern Democracies (Cambridge, Mass.: Harvard Center for International

Affairs, 1978), pp. 85-86, 98-99.

31. See Geraghty, Who Dares Wins, pp. 162-167, 169-173; see "Britain World Leader in Anti-Guerrilla Methods," Manchester Guardian Weekly (May 17, 1981).

32. There is a small but growing body of literature on the Dhofar campaign. The book by Tony Jeapes, SAS: Operation Oman (London: William Kimber, 1980), is the most complete account of operations at the field commander's level, with particular emphasis on the SAS work with the Firquats. John Akehurst, who commanded the multinational Dhofar Brigade, provides a senior commander's view of the campaign as a whole, in We Won a War: The Campaign in Oman, 1965-1975 (Salisbury, U.K.: Michael Russell, 1982). Articles by Penelope Tremayne, a freelance journalist for the RUSI Journal and Brassey's Annual in the mid-1970s, provide useful insights on the various stages of the campaign. See also D. L. Price, Conflict Studies No. 53 Oman: Insurgency and Development (London: Institute for the Study of Conflict, 1975); and Ranulph Fiennes, Where Soldiers Fear to Tread (London: Hodder and Stoughton, 1975).

33. Akehurst, in We Won a War, p. 15, is not very forthcoming about the details of the coup. Jonathan Block and Patrick Fitzgerald, British Intelligence and Covert Action (London: Junction Books, 1983), pp. 136-137, provide a more complete account but give no sources for any of their assertions.

34. Jeapes, SAS: Operation Oman, pp. 36-68 and passim.

35. Maurice Tugwell, "Revolutionary Propaganda and Possible Countermeasures" (Ph.D. dissertation, Department of War Studies, King's College, University of London, 1979), pp. 286-288; "Dhofar Campaign Briefing Notes" (Oman File, Centre for Conflict Studies Data Bank, University of New Brunswick, 1977). See also Jeapes, SAS: Operation Oman, pp. 34-37, 131, 138-139, 232.

36. Akehurst, We Won a War, pp. 31-36, 38-40, 42; Bloch and Fitzgerald, British Intelligence, pp. 50-51.

37. Akehurst, We Won a War, p. 44; Bloch and Fitzgerald, British Intelligence, pp. 137-138; Geraghty, Who Dares Wins, p. 122; Jeapes, SAS: Operation Oman, pp. 33-34.

38. Times (London) (July 27 and 31, 1970); Manchester Guardian (July 27 and 28, 1970).

39. Financial Times (London) (December 20, 1970), quoted in Geraghty, Who Dares Wins, pp. 122-123.

40. Jeapes, SAS: Operation Oman, pp. 143-157.

41. Ibid., p. 157; Geraghty, in Who Dares Wins, pp. 131-132, says no account ever appeared in the British press.

42. Christopher Andrew, "Whitehall, Washington and the Intelligence Services," International Affairs 53, no. 3 (1977): 390; see also M.R.D. Foot, "Britain—Intelligence Services," Economist (March 15, 1980).

43. Bloch and Fitzgerald, British Intelligence, p. 51.

44. Propaganda techniques and themes of the prorebel Gulf Committee and of Soviet broadcasts are discussed in Tugwell, Revoluntionary Propaganda, pp. 283-286.

45. Harry Rositzke, "America's Secret Operations: A Perspective," Foreign Affairs 53, no. 2 (January 1975): 344-345.

46. Richard Halloran, "Army Plans New Command to Curb Leftist Insurgencies," New York Times (September 17, 1982). The 1st Special

Operations Command (SOC) is a U.S. Army formation.

47. Mission statements extracted from official publications (training circulars and field manuals), quoted in David J. Barratto, "Special Forces in the 1980s: A Strategic Reorientation," Military Review 63, no. 3 (March 1983): 5-8.

48. The Joint Special Operations Agency (formerly Command) functions under the direct operational control of the Joint Chiefs of Staff. It is separate and distinct from the Army's 1st SOC, although both are based at Fort Bragg. See "Elite Secret U.S. Unit Trains to Foil Terror," Washington Post (February 7, 1982).

49. See "Statements on Issuance of a Presidential Directive, 12 January 1982," quoted in Captain James T. Strong, "Covert Activities and Intelligence Operations: Redefining Congressional and Executive Responsibilities," USAFA Conference Paper (June 1984).

50. U.S., Congress, Senate, Standing Rules, No. 25, 1(j) (April 2, 1983); House, Rules of the House of Representatives, No. 10, quoted in Strong, "Elite Secret U.S. Unit."

51. Harry Rositzke, "If a War Is Big Enough to Mine Ports, Let the Pentagon Run It, Not the CIA," Washington Post (April 15, 1984).

52. Robert E. Hunter, Presidential Control of Foreign Policy: Mismanagement or Mishap? The Washington Papers No. 91 (Washington, D.C.: Center for Strategic and International Studies, 1982), pp. 90-91.

53. Roy M. Melbourne, "Odyssey of the NSC," Strategic Review 2, no. 3 (Summer 1983): 59-60. According to the New York Times (June 11, 1984), the State Department has played a major role in conceiving and supporting the Central American operations, but interdepartmental consultation has been minimized and expert diplomatic and military advice excluded from the planning sessions, which are run by a subgroup of the NSC.

54. Lowenthal, U.S. Intelligence, p. 91.

55. Washington Post (April 27, 1984); "The CIA Sues for Peace," Newsweek (May 7, 1984).

56. Richard Cheney, "U.S. Foreign Policy: Who's in Charge?" SAIS Review (Winter/Spring 1984): 110-112; William Bader, "Congress and the Making of U.S. Security Policies," in America's Security in the 1980s, Part I, Adelphi Papers No. 173 (London: International Institute of Strategic Studies, 1982), pp. 14-16.

57. John G. Tower, "Congress Versus the President: The Formulation and Implementation of American Foreign Policy," Foreign Affairs no. 2 (Winter 1981-1982): 238. As Cheney notes, however, the requirements of the act are so restrictive that it has never been fully applied (p. 110).

58. This critical view of the committee can be found in Patricia Cohen, "A Blunt Instrument," Foreign Service Journal (April 1984): 26-33. The House Foreign Affairs Committee has suffered similar problems in recent years. See "Fascell Gives New Life to Foreign Affairs Panel," Congressional Quarterly (April 28, 1984): 967-970.

59. Drew Middleton, "The Grenada Conquest: How Forces Performed," New York Times (October 28, 1983); "D-Day in Grenada," Time (November 7, 1983); see also Charles Corddry, "Pleased by Grenada Operation, Army Plans More Elite Forces," Baltimore Sun (November 8, 1983); and Richard Halloran, "Army's Special Forces Try to Rebuild Image by Linking Brains with Brawn," New York Times

(August 21, 1982).

60. Barratto, "Special Forces in the 1980s," pp. 9–11; Lieutenant Colonel Tom Hamrick, "The Black Berets," Army 27, no. 5 (May 1977): 31; Richard A. Gabriel, "Can U.S. Unconventional Forces Meet the Future?" Conflict Quarterly 2, no. 2 (Fall 1981): 4–7; Howard Graves, "U.S. Capabilities for Military Intervention," in Sam C. Sarkesian and William L. Scully, eds., U.S. Policy and Low Intensity Conflict: Potentials for Military Struggles in the 1980s (New York: National Strategy Information Center, 1981), pp. 73–75; Robin Moore, "The Green Berets Are Back," Washington Post Parade Magazine (August 2, 1981); U.S., Joint Chiefs of Staff, United States Military Posture for FY 1983 (Washington, D.C.: Government Printing Office, 1982), p. 99; Richard Halloran, "Military is Quietly Rebuilding Its Special Operations Forces" and "Army's Special Forces," New York Times (July 17 and August 21, 1982).

61. U.S. Executive Order 12333, Part III.4(h).

62. Adapted with some modification from Arthur H. Bair et al., "Unconventional Warfare: A Legitimate Tool of Foreign Policy," Conflict: An International Journal 4, no. 1 (1983): 54.

CONCLUSION

Intelligence, as Richard Betts suggests, remains an important ingredient for U.S policymakers as they seek to "understand the nature of the challenges in the international arena and know the full implications of their own policy initiatives and reactions."[1] Despite such significance, consensus has not as yet emerged on the true nature of intelligence and its proper uses to enhance the quality of policymakers' actions in pursuit of the national interest.[2]

The purpose of this book has been to explore the issues of intelligence as a process of collecting, processing, analyzing, and evaluating information and to seek out the intelligence/policy relationships that do and should exist.[3]

No clear lines can easily be drawn between the type of intelligence that searches for policies to influence and the government officials who turn to intelligence as they decide policy intended for a complex world.[4] One way to frame the intelligence/policy relationships is with the systems model.[5] When this approach is utilized, the relationship between intelligence and policy in the decisionmaking process appears to be ongoing and in flux. As Betts argues:

> Simple logic suggests that intelligence should precede the decision process: estimators should turn out their products and only then should officials read and use them. In the real world of international politics, though, apart from long-range analyses of problems that have not yet become critical, the division of labor can rarely be so logically neat and discrete. In crises or on rapidly developing issues, the formal process of producing National Intelligence Estimates (NIEs) is too slow, and useful contributions from intelligence may have to come in the form of quick memos. Complicated and pressing issues are in flux, not frozen in time. The information available, its significance or meaning, the process of policy choice, change, implementation, and adaptation are all constantly changing—feeding into, and altering, each other. Estimates themselves can be self-fulfilling or self-negating prophesies, by prompting leaders to take actions that change the situation and change the facts behind the prediction. Intelligence pushes decision-makers' ideas in one direction, and their decisions affect the environment, thus changing the intelligence picture again. In short, there is a political Heisenberg effect: measuring

the phenomenon changes it. Intelligence assessment and the policy process become one big ball of wax.[6]

Like it or not, that is the reality. Intelligence and its relationship to policy is more—much more—than mere transmission of facts intended to inform decisionmakers as they determine the direction of policy. Equally important, domestic, personality, bureaucratic, and international environment variables influence the relationship--setting limits on appropriate means, defining the agenda, and so on. The interdependent relationship between producer and user—between analysis and decision—becomes further muddled. What is acceptable in pursuit of the national interest becomes further entangled in a complicated web from which direction to policy must emerge. For if it does not, intelligence collection and analysis will drift aimlessly[7] and only coincidentally will it support the national interest. Further, even with policy guidelines, differences will exist between the world that committee policymakers picture and the murkier perceptions of intelligence. As a consequence, major problems are created for good intelligence officers (who will persist in telling policymakers what they should know) and policymakers (who are often resistant to modification of their world views).[8]

The potential magnitude of this dilemma creates profound implications for this study. On the one hand, policymakers may choose to use intelligence for support rather than illumination. Alternatively, intelligence officers may hesitate to push forward displeasing analyses or information thought to be unpalatable to policymakers. Both sets of actors may choose to withhold information from each other, with potentially disastrous policy implications.[9] More subtle psychologies can also fuzz the lines between facts and judgment.

The multiplicity of actors involved in the intelligence process demands proper management. However, many of the issues raised in this book point not to the case of managing such a bureaucracy properly, but rather to the diversity of perspectives on the distribution of power and the most effective organizational structure. Moreover, such discussions quickly encompass debate about the demands for secrecy and the requirements for openness in a democratic society. Congress has a role to play as the people's representative. Yet, congressional oversight has led in the past to serious intelligence compromises, as have media investigations. No easy answers appear to us, although we recognize that both sets of demands are legitimate. Beyond such claims lies an even less examined dimension—the morality of those who act on our behalf. In this context, the questions revolve not around which particular institution or institutions should direct the intelligence functions but, rather, around the moral character of those who act on our behalf and the standards to which they should be held accountable.

As for the threat the United States faced in the international system, we see no major changes in the immediate future. Thus the United States will continue to be challenged by an adversary whose ideological and great power interests remain antithetical to ours. This competition will continue to take place in a world dominated by nation-state actors and in an environment similar to the anarchical society of Hedley Bull.[10]

We will continue to ask intelligence to do the impossible--to keep policymakers perfectly informed about threats to our national security in an environment flooded by the deceptions of our principal adversaries. We will also continue to require information about our foes' present and future developments and capabilities as we search for strategies and tactics that can lead to a world order supportive of our national interests. What specifics that will include, such as arms control, nuclear deterrence or defense capabilities, or disarmament, remains to be seen. However, we cannot afford to be surprised, for in the world of today and tomorrows, surprise might bring with it the destruction of the world.

In our endeavor, we have not sought to provide answers. Rather, we have raised questions—questions that must continue to be researched, explored, and examined as we wrestle with the difficulties now confronting us.

NOTES

1. Richard K. Betts, "Intelligence for Policy Making," Washington Quarterly 3, no. 3 (Summer, 1980): 118.
2. National interest itself remains an ill-defined and ambiguous concept. In addition, we recognize the possibility that not all government decisions may be consistent with the national interest.
3. The prominent work in this area remains Thomas L. Hughes, The Fate of Facts in a World of Men (New York: Foreign Policy Association, Headline Series No. 233, 1976). Many of the thoughts that follow have found their seeds in this stimulating work.
4. Hughes, The Fate of Facts, p. 6.
5. See the works of Etzioni and Easton, among others, for a more complete description of the analytic value of the systems approach.
6. Betts, "Intelligence for Policy Making," p. 119.
7. Steve Chan, "The Intelligence of Stupidity: Understanding Failures in Strategic Warning," American Political Science Review 73, no. 1 (March 1979): 178.
8. See Alexander George, Presidential Decision Making in Foreign Policy, for a treatment of the many psychological impediments to effective information processing.
9. Hughes, The Fate of Facts, pp. 23-30.
10. Hedley Bull, in The Anarchical Society (New York: Columbia University Press, 1977), describes a certain sense of order that exists despite the absence of world government. We share this view.

Appendix: Literature on Intelligence

INTRODUCTION

To be able to think realistically of intelligence as having a body of literature akin to other disciplines is a relatively new development, hardly over twenty years in the making. During the last decade or so, the number of published works on intelligence has increased substantially. One can only speculate as to the reasons why. Perhaps changes in societal values concerning secrecy have had some influence. There can be little doubt that freedom-of-information statutes, such as the Freedom of Information Act, have provided writers with mechanisms through which they may now obtain information previously denied to them. But whatever the reasons, today's student of intelligence can turn to numerous books devoted to intelligence and closely related matters.

Now that intelligence has a substantial body of literature, the study of intelligence has been greatly facilitated. It is no longer uncommon, for example, to see intelligence studies being offered at colleges and universities.

It is important to recognize that studies designed to increase one's understanding of intelligence, its policies, and its process require investigation of a wide variety of subjects and disciplines, agencies, and organizations. The need to recognize the expansiveness of intelligence can quickly be appreciated if one considers the rather self-evident interdisciplinary and interdepartmental nature of intelligence and whether intelligence is being thought of in terms of a subject for study or as a function to be performed. To fully study intelligence as a subject per se, one must recognize the necessity to study history, economics, and political science. To acquire a comprehensive understanding of the purposes for and roles played by intelligence communities related to matters of national interest in general, or national security specifically, one must investigate the means and ways of government, military capabilities, and technological advancements.

The expansiveness of and cross-dependencies within intelligence become obvious when one considers the subterranean makeup of the intelligence complex itself. Compartmentation notwithstanding, the distinct components of an intelligence complex, frequently existing as if they were independent of one another, should be viewed in relation to the whole; otherwise, one's perception and understanding of intelligence can only be incomplete. Scientific intelligence may encompass biological, chemical, and nuclear intelligence. Geographic intelligence may be subdivided to include hydrographic, topographic, and weather intelligence. Military intelligence has many components under its umbrella, not the least of which is the strategic/tactical dichotomy. Political intelligence is composed of comparisons and differences between domestic and foreign intelligence.

In the study of intelligence, as in the study of other subjects, it is useful to establish a working point of reference—that is, a definition of intelligence. Purists among intelligence analysts posit that intelligence is primarily, if not exclusively, the act of gathering, analyzing, and processing information in a way that ensures the information is reliable, timely, and useful. Keeping this in mind, we find that the most important result of intelligence is generally accepted to be information products that enable an organization, a group of people, or individuals to know the direction of the future political, economic, and military activities of others, especially adversaries. For our present purposes, intelligence will be considered kaleidoscopically, the idea being that because the act of intelligence is not intended to exist for its own sake, as if in a vacuum, intelligence might best be understood if studied in the context of multiple relations. Accordingly, this bibliographic essay provides a list of materials that investigate the whys, hows, and wherefores of intelligence, as well as the significance of its semantic definition.

Given the expansiveness of intelligence as a topic for study, we can clearly see why no single essay on the literature of intelligence could possibly be all-encompassing, up to date, or capable of doing justice to so vast a topic. The following list of materials represents an eclectic coverage of materials on intelligence, primarily directed to undergraduate readers. The intent of this list is to provide readings that will stimulate the interest of the reader while offering various viewpoints. If the reader derives a degree of pleasure, in addition to pedagogical benefits, from one, some, or all of the books listed, so much the better!

REFERENCE

The most helpful bibliography for the undergraduate is Constantinides's annotated Intelligence and Espionage: An Analytical Bibliography. This bibliography lists and reviews approximately 500 nonfiction books. Constantinides offers considerable evaluative information, the result of which is authoritative guidance. Coverage begins with the seventeenth century, with a primary focus on twentieth-century English-language sources. Constantinides draws upon more than twenty-five years of working experience in intelligence to direct attention to significant events and fallacies. Smith's The Secret Wars: A Guide to Sources in English details the noteworthy results of the author's prodigious research. His three-volume work represents the most comprehensive bibliography on intelligence to date. In it there are nearly 10,000 indexed citations to English-language nonfiction books, periodicals, government publications, and scholarly papers. Subjects covered include military special forces, psychological warfare, and transnational terrorism. Unfortunately, The Secret Wars is not annotated; it does, however, serve as an index for important and available sources relevant to the study of intelligence.

The student of intelligence would be hard pressed to find a truly comprehensive bibliography that would completely satisfy a demanding scholar. For want of such a work, one may be partially satisfied by the Scholar's Guide to Intelligence Literature: Bibliography of the Russell J. Bowen Collection. This collection is deposited at Georgetown University. Prepared under the auspices of the National Intelligence Study Center, the Scholar's Guide to Intelligence Literature identifies more than 5,000 titles, covering such subjects as military intelligence, state security, paramilitary operations, and secret weapons programs. Global in scope, its coverage begins with events before Christ and ends well into the 1980s. Harris's Intelligence and National Security: A Bibliography with Selected Annotations stands out for its candor and, evidently, for the author's sound opinions on deception. Another bibliography of substance is the Library of Congress's Soviet Intelligence and Security Services: A Selected Bibliography of Soviet Publications, with Some Additional Titles from Other Sources. This two-volume publication offers a conspectus of over 3,000 pieces dating from the mid-1960s to the early 1970s.

Blackstock and Schaf's annotated Intelligence, Espionage, Counterespionage and Covert Operations: A Guide to Information Sources is helpful. The reader will appreciate the interesting narrative. Two primer-like bibliographies also come to mind: Devore's Spies and All That: Intelligence Agencies and Operations—A Bibliography, and the Defense Intelligence College's Bibliography of Intelligence Literature: A Critical and Annotated Bibliography of Open Source Intelligence Literature. The former cites over 500 sources, including U.S. Senate and House reports; the latter cites half as many items, but it includes important intelligence works produced by congressional committees and foreign commissions.

There are many published bibliographies that offer information useful to the study of intelligence. Many of these bibliographies do not have obvious designations drawing attention to the subject of intelligence in their titles; yet they include between their covers considerable information that is germane to the study of intelligence. One example to illustrate this point is Sugnet's award-winning, comprehensive, and annotated Vietnam War Bibliography (VWB). This bibliographical register, with its companion index, is an invaluable source of information for anyone researching the role of U.S. intelligence—both political and military—during the thirty-year involvement of the United States in Southeast Asia (1945-1975). The 4,000 items listed in VWB have been selected from Cornell University's Echols Collection. VWB is fast gaining respect within the academic community for its thoroughness and reliability. It is interesting to note, for example, that the Murphy's Report (1967, Saigon?), described in the past as a report of a U.S. operations officer interviewing Vietnamese (in South Vietnam), is correctly identified by Sugnet as a report of interviews with Laotian refugees (in Laos) concerning Pathet Lao activity in Laos villages. Such accuracy is of obvious benefit to the student-scholar.

Two encyclopedias are worth noticing: Seth's Encyclopedia of Espionage, and the Buranellis' Spy/Counterspy: An Encyclopedia of

Espionage. Together they offer an array of biographical sketches, descriptions of intelligence organizations, explanations of historical events, clandestine techniques, and vocabulary defined. Both volumes are packed with fascinating tidbits. Spy/Counterspy is confined to modern history, beginning with Elizabethan England, with a concentration on the United States and Europe. It has 1,100 citations with publication dates ranging from 1732-1980. The Buranellis draw relationships between espionage, politics and wars, and successes and failures.

GENERAL AND HISTORICAL

The study of intelligence cannot properly be advanced without some familiarity with the basic publications in the general areas of intelligence. Basic readings lay the foundation for understanding specific policies and procedures. The list that follows has been assembled to suggest the contents of a basic collection of readings for the student interested in the history, nature, and development of U.S. intelligence.

Two excellent lead-ins to the study of modern U.S. intelligence are William V. Kennedy's Intelligence Warfare (IW), and Jack Haswell's Spies and Spymasters. Although Intelligence Warfare focuses on military intelligence, it has broader applications. IW offers a great deal of information that is applicable to an understanding of the workings of the intelligence machine in general, as well as of the more specific role it plays in protecting free societies. Topics covered in IW include the meaning of intelligence in relation to worldwide intelligence exchange, espionage, counterespionage, and war in space, in the air, on land, and at sea. Spies and Spymasters serves as a quick and general introduction to intelligence. Its literary instructional sketches make for delightful reading.

There are several studies that when taken together represent several authors' attempts to provide, through the eyes of history, comprehensive explanations of the ins and outs of intelligence. Because it has been said by scholars that all of history since the times of classical antiquity has been no more than a matter of historical footnotes, one might be well advised to begin a reading of intelligence history with Starr's Political Intelligence in Classical Greece, a work that describes intelligence-collection handling and its evaluation by politicians and military personnel in Ancient Greece. A companion piece of scholarship on the making of intelligence prior to the coming of the modern world is Thompson's Secret Diplomacy: Espionage and Cryptography, 1500-1815, which introduces the reader to undercover intelligence diplomacy and techniques of political manipulations associated with the Middle Ages and the means-justifying-the-ends concept developed during the European Renaissance.

Useful histories and analytical studies on intelligence during the transition from the Old to the New World include Ford's A Peculiar Service—an outstanding work, marked by solid research and good documentation, on the history of intelligence during the American Revolution. Among other references, A Peculiar Service contains excellent accounts of Benedict Arnold, Nathan Hale, and the Culper Ring. Complementing A Peculiar Service is the insightful The Armies of Ignorance, by William Corson, who explains the formation of U.S. intelligence, describes the competitiveness between various agencies, and reviews issues that have plagued intelligence communities from their earliest days. Attention is specifically given to the struggles and counterproductive relationships between the U.S. intelligence community, Congress, and the executive branch of government since World War II. Recommendations for the future are offered. With the advantage of hindsight, one can appreciate the author's sense of vision. For those people who wish to fill a reading gap between American Revolution intelligence history and its evolution into the world wars of the twentieth century, there is Stern's Secret Missions of the Civil War. The special value of this book lies in the comments on the documentation unearthed from the U.S. National Archives.

Those who wish to obtain a sense of what intelligence was like in the Western world between the sixteenth and twentieth centuries would do well to turn to the classic The Story of Secret Service, by Richard Rowan. This general study represents a single author's attempt at comprehensive explanations. For more specialized coverage of secret services, especially those in existence between the world wars, readers can refer to the following: Mashbir's I Was An American Spy, Poretsky's Our Own People, and The Rote Kapelle. I Was an American Spy offers a personal approach. The author reveals his personal views on the intelligence efforts of the United States as directed against post-World War I Japan. The author of Our Own People takes the biographical approach in describing Soviet intelligence during the 1920s and 1930s. The Rote Kapelle is the CIA's view. It is recognized as an authoritative explanation of the intricacies and practices of Soviet intelligence and espionage networks in Western Europe between 1936 and 1945. For a current study of Soviet intelligence in pre-World War II Japan, see Prange's Target Tokyo: The Story of the Sorge Spy Ring.

The events leading up to World War II have been the subject of many investigations. Perhaps no event has caused more embarrassment to the U.S. intelligence community than Japan's successful attack on Pearl Harbor. In the time since that attack, there have been numerous investigations underlying the attempt to understand the nature and cause of strategic surprise. One such investigation, certainly one of the most comprehensive, is Wohlstetter's Pearl Harbor: Warning and Decision. The attack on Pearl Harbor signaled the need for the U.S. intelligence community to increase its activities, not only in the Pacific but in Europe as well. With respect to the European theater, a superb description of the U.S. intelligence buildup is Persico's Piercing the Reich. This work also introduces the reader to the early roots of today's Central Intelligence Agency.

No study of World War II intelligence could really be adequate in the absence of an investigation into the roles played by the German intelligence services. Two of the best surveys and interpretative studies on German intelligence during the days of the Third Reich are Paine's German Military Intelligence in World War II: The Abwehr, and Lewin's Ultra Goes to War. The former describes in detail the Abwehr, in contrast to the SS, Gestapo, and the Secret Service (SD). Ultra Goes to War is an academic qualitative presentation on the successes of cryptographers, as well as an account of interceptive services generally.

Following World War II, the world witnessed its division into two super factions: pro-West and pro-East. Out of this political schism developed academic, analytical attention to "democracy," as opposed to "international communism." One of the best investigations into the role of intelligence in a democratic society was executed by the venerable academic warrior, Harry Howe Ransom. In The Intelligence Establishment, Ransom systematically describes and critically analyzes the U.S. intelligence community. Ransom's work can justifiably stand alone. However, the issues covered therein may be better considered if viewed in comparison with those analyzed in Meyer's Facing Reality. Meyer offers an explanation for the existence of intelligence in the face of the communist threat to the free West. Facing Reality received an award from the National Intelligence Study Center for its coverage of numerous significant events and activities, including events pertaining to the use of Radio Free Europe as an instrument of foreign policy.

U.S. involvement in Southeast Asia during the 1950s, 1960s, and 1970s culminated in great internal political unrest. Americans, more than ever, questioned the raison d'être of the country's political, military, and intelligence policies, all viewed as common threads dominating national diplomatic policy. The critical mood of the nation during those years is exemplified in Snepp's controversial Decent Interval: An Insider's Account of Saigon's Indecent End. In contrast to Snepp's negativism, De Silva in Sub Rosa chooses to defend the need for and the ways of the intelligence community, in spite of its apparent behavioral inconsistencies with cherished democratic values. Lyman Kirkpatrick offers another positive stand. In The U.S. Intelligence Community: Foreign Policy and Domestic Activities, Kirkpatrick attempts, with considerable success, to persuade his public of the necessity for intelligence.

Intelligence is never absent from the sensitive deliberations between warring countries. This fact is borne out conclusively in Walters's Silent Missions, which takes the reader into the world of diplomats and their secret negotiations. The role of intelligence in conducting the secret talks between the United States and North Vietnam is partially exposed for all to see. Finally, for those interested in considering the role of intelligence in and for the 1980s, the recommended readings include five sequential works of collected papers edited by Roy Godson: Elements of Intelligence, Analysis and Estimates, Counterintelligence, Covert Action, and Clandestine Collection. These works are the result of colloquia proceedings sponsored by the Consortium for the Study of Intelligence. Collectively, they reflect on crucial intelligence matters; given their purpose--to stimulate an interest in the study of intelligence—they should not be overlooked.

In view of the relationships between intelligence agencies, policies, and procedures, and internal or domestic political intelligence, the following titles offer insights on the elusive political intelligence problems that continue to exist in the United States. Cox's The Myths of National Security expounds on the notion that democracy and secrecy are incompatible. It is the author's contention that the government of the United States has unnecessarily operated in secrecy and that to the extent it does so, it breeds arrogance, self-righteousness, and corruption. The scope of The Myths of National

Security includes views on the growth of the U.S. secrecy system and on executive secrecy, secrecy and the media, and Congress. Another work that represents well the challenges to the notion of the necessity of domestic political secrecy is Wise's The American Police State. This particular book was one of countless reactions to Richard Nixon's resignation from the presidency as a result of accusations by the House Judiciary Committee of abusing the powers of his office. The American Police State looks at wiretapping, the clandestine machinery of the U.S. government, break-ins, FBI, CIA, and government action against individuals who dissent from established policy. One may wish to peruse Theoharis's Spying on Americans: Political Surveillance from Hoover to the Huston Plan. This examination focuses exclusively on U.S. internal security policy for the years after 1936. Included in what amounts to a wide-sweeping investigation of domestic surveillance are surveys of relevant intelligence activities of the FBI, CIA, NSA, IRS, and various military intelligence agencies.

For a candid study of surveillance by a civil liberties lawyer, the reader can refer to Donner's The Age of Surveillance. Donner expresses the belief that intelligence in the United States serves as an instrument for resolving a major contradiction in the U.S. political system: how to protect the status quo while maintaining the forms of liberal political democracy. Donner posits that the nature of the interest protected by intelligence, the very life of the United States as a nation, encourages and justifies repressive overkill. The Age of Surveillance analyzes political intelligence in the United States from its formative years to 1980.

AUTOBIOGRAPHIES AND BIOGRAPHIES

The history of intelligence is not just a chronicling of events; it is also one of personalities and individuals. Accordingly, both autobiographies and biographies are discussed in this section. As the emphasis is on the genres themselves, the order of books named is strictly random. The autobiography, as a genre, is well represented by Twenty-Five Years in the Secret Service: The Recollections of a Spy. Under the nom de plume of Le Caron, Thomas Beach tells the story of his life as an agent following the American Civil War. Beach worked undercover in Irish revolutionary organizations in the United States. Another recommended autobiography is Lotz's The Champagne Spy: Israel's Master Spy Tells His Story. An illegal in Egypt after World War II, Lotz passed himself off as a German as he spied for Israel. For insights into the life of a double agent in the 1960s, one might wish to read Double Eagle: The Autobiography of a Polish Spy Who Defected to the West. The author (Mr. X), a member of the Polish intelligence while working for the CIA, discusses the psyche of the defector. Trepper's The Great Game: Memoirs of the Spy Hitler Couldn't Silence is an autobiography written by the head of Russia's military intelligence in Western Europe during World War II. This work contains many facts about espionage. Finally, Philby's My Silent War should not be missed. Philby reveals many secrets associated with his work in British intelligence as a Soviet mole. His book is also a story of what Philby took with him back to Russia.

Biographies abound, but, unfortunately, only a few can be

considered here. Masson's Christine: A Search for Christine Granville is the story of a Polish spy who worked for Britain during World War II. With the British cover name of Christine Granville, this daughter of a Polish count carried out missions under the direction of the Special Operations Executive (SOE), including one that required Granville to parachute into France in 1942. Clark's The Man Who Broke Purple: The Life of the World's Greatest Cryptologist, Colonel William F. Freidman. Purple was the name of the principal Japanese code, considered by Tokyo to be unbreakable. Freidman broke it in 1940, enabling the United States to read Japanese messages throughout World War II. Colonel Freidman was the first cryptologist to be hired by the National Security Agency. The White Rabbit, by Bruce Marshall, chronicles the life of F.F.E. Yeo-Thomas, who was a British spy in France during World War II. Prior to working for SOE as its liaison person with the BCRA (Central Bureau of Intelligence and Operations, de Gaulle's intelligence department), Yeo-Thomas had served in the French Army and later with the Polish forces. Captured by the Russians, he subsequently escaped. Captured by the Gestapo, he again escaped. Yeo-Thomas lived to testify against the war criminals of Buchenwald.

William Sevenson's A Man Called Intrepid is the captivating biography of Sir William Stephenson, the Canadian coordinator of Anglo-American intelligence during World War II. Stephenson's life epitomizes adventure, patriotic fervor, and control of intelligence at the highest levels. Stephenson was a flying ace in the Royal Flying Corps. He was captured by the Germans during World War I, only to escape to safety. A Man Called Intrepid focuses on Stephenson's activities during World War II, including his workings with Churchill, Roosevelt, Hoover, and Donovan. Goulden's The Death Merchant is a biography of a different color. It represents an investigation into the life of the rogue agent Edwin P. Wilson. During the 1960s, Wilson built a reputation within the CIA as a master at creating and operating what is known in the intelligence world as a "proprietary company." Wilson was eventually dismissed from the CIA. Subsequently, he applied the skills he had learned in the CIA to become an international arms dealer supplying Libya's Qaddafi. Eventually, Wilson was sentenced to federal prison.

OPERATIONS

Intelligence per se is the collection, evaluation, and dissemination of information. But the process of collecting, evaluating, and disseminating information requires active doing. The doing is frequently the domain of intelligence operatives, working in concert with the "nonoperatives." The books listed and described in this section focus on operations, the Jekyll side of intelligence. Works are identified according to a specific focus or function of intelligence operations.

Philosophy

In Honorable Men, William Colby writes about his long career in the CIA, beginning with his years in the OSS. He also presents his personal philosophical rationalization for secret operations. Allen Dulles, a strong advocate of clandestine intelligence operations, offers in Craft of Intelligence a popularized philosophical treatise. His Craft of Intelligence also serves as a vocational text.

General Survey of Secret Operations

Rositzke, a twenty-five-year veteran of CIA, describes in The CIA's Secret Operations: Espionage, Counterespionage and Covert Action a number of secret operations, especially those directed against the Soviets.

Forming A New Intelligence and Underground Organization

The Pledge by Leonard Slater reveals the underground efforts that supported the formation of the new Jewish state in Palestine. Topics include arms smuggling and violation of embargo laws.

Technical Support

Perhaps one of the first books in modern times to concentrate on technical support of the operations side of intelligence, Lovell's Of Spies and Strategems serves as an excellent introduction to the subject.

Handbooks

For good and obvious reasons, the how-to handbooks and other kinds of materials useful to operatives are not normally listed, and are certainly not described, in bibliographies intended for public reading. An example of items that approximate classified professional handbooks and other forms of materials is Colonel Herbert's The Soldier's Handbook. It covers numerous operative techniques, aggressive as well as defensive. For academic purposes the student may wish to read Che Guevara's Guerrilla Warfare. According to I. F. Stone, this book is the revolutionary's bible; on the other hand, Stone opined that it serves as an antibible of the Green Berets. Lotz's A Handbook for Spies offers advice for those who are contemplating a career in espionage. Orlov's Handbook of Intelligence and Guerrilla Warfare, though somewhat dated, continues to be currently relevant; its value lies primarily in its coverage of operating methods of illegals.

Psychological Warfare

As an outline of Allied psychological warfare during World War II, Cruickshank's The Fourth Arm is authoritative and informative. Howe's The Black Game describes World War II British propaganda activities classified as "black." Activities covered include BBC broadcasts to enemy-occupied Europe and dropping of leaflets. There is a discussion, as well, of the shades of nigritudes—that is, comparisons between black and white special operations.

Censorship

Koop's Weapons of Silence describes U.S. censorship (during World War II) of mail and media, all in the interests of national security, intelligence, and other warfare efforts.

Black Radio

Macdonald's Undercover Girl and Delmer's Black Boomerang together describe what propaganda and black operations were like during World War II. One might also refer to Short's Film and Radio Propaganda in World War II, a 1983 account of the struggle for the control of minds.

Clandestine Entry

Willis's Surreptitious Entry is considered a timeless classic in the special operations field. The work is certainly of historical importance. Contents include discussions of experiences of wartime secret agents, entry teams, and training techniques.

Exploitative Use of Sex

Lewis's Sexpionage looks at the use of sex by the Soviet government to obtain secret political and military information from another government. This topic is too often sensationalized beyond credibility, but Sexpionage serves to raise one's consciousness.

Kidnapping

Harel's The House on Garibaldi Street: The First Full Account of the Capture of Adolf Eichmann Told by the Former Head of Israel's Secret Service serves as an instructive guide for anyone interested in interrogation and contains considerable information on military intelligence.

Retaliation

Tinnin's The Hit Team is a journalistic account of an eye-for-an-eye operation planned and sanctioned by the Israeli government and military. The decision to seek out the leaders of the Black September terrorist movement was a response to the massacre of Israeli atheletes at the 1972 Olympics in Munich. The Hit Team is a true story about the war of reprisal that the Mossad aggressively waged. For additional reading on this subject, see the current explication by Jonas, Vengeance: The True Story of an Israeli Counterterrorist Team.

Escape and Evasion

Hutton's Official Secret: The Remarkable Story of Escape Aids--Their Invention, Production and the Sequel may have been written primarily as a history of the production of escape aids. Nevertheless, Official Secret should be appreciated as a basic handbook on learning devices for practical application. This work offers several illustrations—for example, of button compasses, cigarette-holder telescopes, saws in led pencils, pocket-guns with darts, and so on. Anderson's Bat-21 documents the trials and tribulations of Lt. Col. Iceal E. Hambleton, USAF, from the time his plane was destroyed over Vietnam to his rescue twelve days later; it also describes a number of U.S. Air Force escape and evasion techniques. Escape From Laos is an incredible documentary of Navy pilot Dieter Dengler's capture by and escape from the Pathet Lao. Indeed, the book contains a bagful of escape and evasion (E&E) tricks.

Camouflage

An investigation into the art of concealment and deception might begin with the reading of Sun-Tzu's The Art of War (500 B.C.). Sun-Tzu stated centuries ago that "all warfare is based on deception." The fundamental principles of camouflage have not changed since. For a contemporary description of the use of camouflage, Hartcup offers Camouflage: A History of Concealment and Deception in War.

Deception

Military strategists have long believed that by holding out bait to entice the enemy, they could crush the opposition. The importance of deception as a tactic is clearly shown in Montagu's The Man Who Never Was, a true account of an operation carried out in 1942 and 1943 to deceive the Germans prior to the landing of the Allies in Sicily. Whaley's Codeword Barbarossa is regarded by many academics as perhaps the most significant analysis of deception on a grand scale. Whaley's work is still treated as a model for others to follow. Deception Maxims: Fact and Folklore, produced by the CIA and Mathtech, Inc., should not be overlooked. A number of historical cases are studied to illustrate the maxims. Not enough acclaim can be expressed for the comprehensiveness and authoritative analysis provided by Brown's Bodyguard of Lies, whose theme is that deception is the ultimate secret weapon. Bodyguard of Lies makes its point most emphatically.

Drugs

Marks's The Search For the "Manchurian Candidate": The CIA and Mind Control is an investigative study into the CIA's experimentation with hallucinogenic drugs, hypnosis, psychosurgery, and the like—all in the hope of controlling the minds of enemy agents.

Counterinsurgency

For a good introduction to this subject and for insights into the future, the reader is referred to Shackley's The Third Option: An American View of Counterinsurgency Operations. Shackley is one of many who envision wars of the future to be wars of low intensity, capitalizing on irregular warfare. There are many political scientists, in particular, who believe that the main defense for the United States in the future will necessitate unconventional warfare, covert action, and counterinsurgency.

Counterintelligence

This activity has been covered well in a number of the works cited herein. Special mention must be made of Masterman's classic, The Double-Cross System. This important historical document describes a number of episodes and cases of people ostensibly working for the Germans during World War II. Unknown to the Germans, the agents were working for the British.

Unconventional Warfare and Intelligence

Readers interested in the history of the uses of the U.S. military to pursue the policies of the U.S. government regarding clandestine intelligence objectives are referred to Lung's Intelligence and Paddock's U.S. Army Special Warfare—Its Origins: Psychological and Unconventional Warfare, 1941-1952. Lung has attempted to record all of the most significant facts concerning intelligence activities, its organizations and coordination procedures, and its successes and failures during the period from 1965 to 1975. Paddock's book covers the origin of the U.S. Army's special warfare capabilities related to intelligence service requirements.

CRYPTOLOGY

Cryptology is the "crème de la crème" of the intelligence process. As a science, it is concerned with the methods and equipment used in secret communications. Closely allied with cryptology are its sister sciences, signal security and signal intelligence. The former deals with protecting one's own signals; the latter deals with acquiring intelligence by intercepting and solving the cryptosignals of other countries, especially those of enemies. Cryptoanalysis involves inductive and deductive reasoning, and strong mathematical powers. Given the scientific and technical nature of cryptology, this section will not attempt to include works directed primarily to experts in the field.

The single most important historical and analytical review for the general reader is unquestionably David Kahn's The Codebreakers. This superb scholarly work is a comprehensive account of secret communications from ancient times well into the 1960s. A good supplement to The Codebreakers is the pictorial Way's Codes and Ciphers, published ten years after Kahn's pioneering study. By publishing The Ultra Secret, Winterbotham opened new doors for the public. For the first time the general public was informed about the Enigma Cypher and how German World War II codes were intercepted and used to the advantage of the Allies. Top Secret Ultra by Calvocoressi adds to the information first provided by Winterbotham. Both books on Ultra are essential readings for the student of cryptoanalysis intelligence. A classic in cryptology literature is Yardley's The American Black Chamber, an account of the establishment in 1919 of the U.S. cryptologic organization. Mention should also be made of Tuchman's The Zimmerman Telegram, a popular account of the cryptoanalytic achievement of the British that led the United States into World War I.

Two extraordinary books about ciphers and codes are Lorain's Clandestine Operations and Paul's The Navajo Code Talkers. The former offers descriptions of and comments on weapons used by clandestine services, the nuts and bolts equipment of agents. One value of Lorain's work lies in its provision of details about the cryptosystems used between the French Resistance networks and Great Britain's SOE. The Navajo Code Talkers refers in detail to the plan recommended to the U.S. Marines to prevent communications from being decoded by Japanese cryptographers and discusses the acceptance and implementation of a plan to employ a code based on the Navajo tongue.

INTELLIGENCE ORGANIZATIONS

Literature about the various intelligence agencies in the world is essential to an understanding not only of the workings of the individual agencies themselves but also of the myriad relationships between the temper of given times, or periods in history, and their influences on the various intelligence communities, international as well as domestic.

An appropriate lead into the literature on intelligence agencies is Dvornik's Origins of Intelligence Services. Dvornik points out that intelligence is not the modern invention that some may assume it to be. The early history of intelligence agencies began in the Ancient Near East. Dvornik's book traces the origin of intelligence services from their beginnings in Egypt and Babylonia up to their development as political instruments of the sixteenth-century Muscovites. For a concise analysis and description of and comparison among modern intelligence agencies, the popular The Espionage Establishment, by David Wise, serves the purpose. This well-written book includes comparisons among intelligence agencies in the United States, Soviet Union, Great Britain, and China.

The works listed in this section will be arranged according to national affiliation. The scope of the category itself necessitates the listing of only a limited number of descriptions.

United States: CIA, NSA, FBI, and IRS

For a brief overview of U.S. intelligence agencies in the face of controversy, readers can turn to The Lawless State, edited by Morton Halperin. This book, of some 300 pages, provides a sober presentation on the administration and coordination of the intelligence services of the CIA. The services of the Army, Navy, Air Force, and State Department can be found in the report prepared by the U.S. Commission on Organization of the Executive Branch of the Government (1953-1955) Intelligence activities. Although this report is nearly thirty years old, it continues to shed light on historical conclusions and recommendations concerning U.S. intelligence.

Concerning the CIA specifically, a survey of the literature can easily lead one to believe that there are more books about this agency than anyone would wish to read. The purpose of the listing that follows is to include a representative sample, but with some mercy on the reader! For an interesting and pleasant introduction to literature on the CIA, Marchetti and Marks's The CIA and the Cult of Intelligence is readily recommended. Advertised as the first book that the U.S. Government went to court to censor before publication, it attempts to answer the following questions: What is the CIA really up to? What does it do, and why? The main thesis of The CIA and the Cult of Intelligence is that the CIA is obsessed with clandestine missions and that this obsession has largely supplanted the agency's original and proper mission. Cline's Secrets, Spies, and Scholars: Blueprint of the Essential CIA, another authoritative account, provides many explanations of intelligence processing. Troy's Donovan and the CIA: A History of the Establishment of the Central Intelligence Agency is a thorough study and detailed history of landmark events in which the author covers virtually every issue of importance.

There are two monographs that serve as supplementary reading on the question as to what may be the proper role of the CIA. The first of these was produced by the Africa Research Group. Entitled The CIA's Global Strategy: Intelligence and Foreign Policy: The Complete Text of a Document Never Intended for Publication, this document claims to enumerate the mechanisms that allow the United States to interfere in the internal affairs of sovereign nations throughout the world. The second monograph, entitled Foreign Intelligence, Legal and Democratic Controls, is the edited transcript of an American Enterprise Institute forum consisting of a presentation of competing views on problems of national and international importance. This document reflects public opinion regarding the role of CIA in the aftermath of the Iranian crises of the late 1970s.

A fitting conclusion at this point is to recommend B. F. Smith's The Shadow Warriors, a recent historical survey of secret intelligence in the United States in which its role regarding the causes of the spread of sabotage is explained.

Soviet Union: KGB

The author of KGB: The Secret Work of Soviet Secret Agents, John Barron, prepared his study with the assumption that one cannot fully understand the Soviet Union without also understanding the KGB. Accordingly, this work represents an extensively documented investigation of the KGB and how it has continued since its inception to support the Soviet politico-economical system. Rositzke's The KGB: The Eyes of Russia portrays the KGB as being the best intelligence service in the world. Examples to support this contention include evidence of KGB agents in the British Parliament, NATO, Pentagon, U.S. Congress, and technical research facilities. Rositzke considers motives, the use of terror and violence, and grades of treason.

Great Britian: Special Operations Executive

Howarth's Undercover: The Men and Women of the Special Operations Executive is an excellent compendium of information previously made available in various publications. It serves well as a recommended introductory text. Undercover offers condensed historical data, but it has added information of its own to make this account of the SOE historically accurate and relatively up to date. Laska's Women in the Resistance and in the Holocaust is the full story of female SOE agents—a powerful account that should not go unread.

Israel: Mossad

Two books come to mind: Deacon's The Israeli Secret Service, and Steven's The Spymasters of Israel. Both are popular, journalistic-like accounts. Even so, they provide the reader with plausible descriptions and useful information. A more recent work, broad in its historical scope, is Blumberg's The Survival Factor. The focus of this work is survival in the face of a potential nuclear holocaust and the important role played by Israeli intelligence. Topics covered include the Zion Mule Corps, Lavon Affair, Irgun, Shin Bet, and Mossad.

Canada: RCMP Security Service

Judging by what is available in the published literature the Mounties have remained extremely close-mouthed. Sawatsky's Men In the Shadows, a history of RCMP—or the GRCs, as they are often called—is a rare find that sheds light on RCMP intelligence, its organization, and its practices.

France: Second Bureau

Readily available introductory reading in English on the "deuxieme bureau" is scant. To fill the gap there is Stead's Second Bureau, which is essentially an account of French counterintelligence during

World War II.

Cuba: General Directorate of Intelligence (DGI)

The best-known work in the eyes of the American public is Spy For Fidel, written by the DGI defector Orlando Castro Hidalgo. Spy For Fidel includes a brief history and comments about DGI's organization, policies, and practices.

Poland

Woytak's On The Border of War and Peace is a work that offers considerable information on the role played by Polish intelligence along with Poland's allies during the late 1930s. Topics covered include Enigma, Czech-Polish intelligence exchange, and diplomatic intelligence regarding Great Britain, France, Germany, and so on.

Japan

The history of Japanese intelligence is also a history of secret societies. Deacon's Kempei Tai is a historical description as well as an analysis of both. Beginning with the spy-master who unified a nation, Hideyoski, Kempei Tai marches through the 16th century all the way into 1980. Although this account is primarily a history of the Japanese secret service, much about the history of Chinese intelligence is also included. Robertson's The Japanese File is a description of the successes of Japanese intelligence in its covert-network development and its penetration in Southeast Asia, especially in Malaya before the outbreak of the war in 1941.

Switzerland

The Swiss Corridor serves as a history of espionage networks and an analysis of the problems of intelligence resistance and security. This book has excellent chapters on Allen Dulles and foreign intelligence services during World War II.

CASE STUDIES

Case studies of intelligence are important in that they are frequently prime examples of "pieces" of intelligence coming together or not coming together, as the case may be. Frequently, case studies are eye openers, second in this respect to no other type of literary examination.

Schemmer's The Raid describes the making of a successful mission against the Son Tay POW camp in North Vietnam, even though the raid was not successful. In The Raid the successes and failures of intelligence are examined, and the reader is introduced to the workings of the intelligence community as it relates to operations. For another account of the operations side of intelligence, one can turn to Operation Overflight. The U-2 pilot Frances Powers reveals his feelings about high-altitude intelligence surveillance over Russia, and what it was like to be shot down and interrogated by the Russians. If one wants to read about a prime example of intelligence SNAFU, there are several books on the Bay of Pigs. One example is Meyer's The Cuban Invasion: The Chronicle of a Disaster, which depicts the Bay of Pigs invasion of Cuba as one of the great fiascoes of intelligence gathering and military/CIA leadership. Howard Hunt, in Give Us This Day, offers a personalized analysis of how the Cuba Project was organized, and why it failed. Operation Zapata concludes that the impossibility of running the Bay of Pigs invasion as a covert operation under the CIA should have been recognized.

Other case studies that describe and analyze intelligence, running in tandem with operations, are Varner's A Matter of Risk, an account of the CIA's attempt to steal a sunken Soviet submarine; Barron's MIG Pilot: The Final Escape of Lieutenant Belenko, the story of Belenko's defection; Armbrister's A Matter of Accountability: The True Story of the Pueblo Affair; Ennes's Assault On the Liberty: The True Story of the Israeli Attack on an American Intelligence Ship; and Dabringhaus's Klaus Barbie, an exposé explaining why and how a Nazi war criminal was knowingly hired to work for the U.S. Army counterintelligence corps.

Leary's Perilous Missions: Civil Air Transport and CIA Covert Operations In Asia is, as the title suggests, an historical account of the growth of the CIA's "air force." The CIA, in its capacity of stewardship with respect to foreign intelligence and policy support, used Civil Air Transport (CAT) to carry out its intelligence/clandestine missions. It also used CAT to deliver weapons to anticommunist forces, to transport operatives, and to evacuate the wounded. One may say that Perilous Missions is a case study of airline pilots who were secret-intelligence special-operation soldiers. Another clandestine intelligence operation to consider is the one that was carried out, unsuccessfully, in the hopes of freeing the American hostages from Iran in April 1980. For a personal recollection of the intelligence work involved in the preparation and execution of the rescue attempt, the reader is referred to Beckwith's Delta Force, a welcomed analysis. Delta Force is also an account of the creation and building of the United States' primary military counterterrorist unit.

TECHNICAL BOOKS

More and more technical means are being used in the intelligence process. This section lists works that concern themselves with the use of the latest high technology to carry out scientific intelligence. Three excellent works, classics by now, are Prince's Instruments of Darkness, Klass's Secret Sentries in Space, and Jones's The Wizard War. Together they chronicle the developments and progress regarding electronic warfare, modern intelligence collection in its various forms, and reconnaissance satellites of the United States and the Soviet Union. Karas's The New High Ground: Systems and Weapons of Space Age War deals primarily with what the U.S. military is currently doing in space. To some extent, The New High Ground looks into the future. This work is an informative source on matters directly related to scientific intelligence, especially its chapter on spy satellites. On the same subject, Gunston's An Illustrated Guide to Spy Planes and Electronic Warfare Aircraft can be most useful. The narrative, complementing the illustrations, provides considerable information on intelligence capabilities. Finally, the reader is referred to Ra'anan's International Security Dimensions of Space. The importance of this work lies in its attention to topics concerning U.S. security in the near and distant future. More than a dozen contributors have come forward with papers that concur in their recognition of the need for a coherent national space policy, encompassing both military and civilian objectives, that ensures national security in the face of continuous threats, at home and from abroad. International Security Dimensions of Space should be required reading for anyone investigating the role of scientific intelligence in the making of a free and secure world.

SOURCES

The search for truth about intelligence is a dynamic process. The core questions about the process may be where to look and how to proceed. Information-searching techniques vary and, to a great extent, are determined by the purposes of the search, available resources, and the level of sophistication of the searcher.

Books are an obvious source of printed information on intelligence, its policies, and its process, especially for the kind of information that serves to form a knowledgeable base from which to proceed. The best bibliographic sources for current information on intelligence are domestic and foreign newspapers. Academic and professional journals, special-interest publications, and magazines from around the world also provide relevant information. Special collections of materials, housed in libraries, government agencies, research institutes, and public and private buildings, often yield fruitful finds. Special collections may include archival records, private papers, manuscripts, government publications, and primary as well as secondary sources.

A search for truth about intelligence may first begin in one, or more, of the standard encyclopedias. Encyclopedias are generally helpful, particularly to the novice, in that they can guide readers properly to the next level of inquiry or investigation—in part, by providing bibliographies and suggestions for further reading on specific subjects. Another way to initiate an inquiry or a search for information on intelligence is to work through library public inventory tools, such as card catalogs, and periodical and newspaper indexes. Similarly, computerized information-retrieval services can facilitate efficient and effective access to information. Their selective dissemination of information capabilities are continually increasing. As the search for truth continues, one can only conclude that the truth is where one finds it.

WORKS CITED

1. AFRICA RESEARCH GROUP. The CIA's Global Strategy: Intelligence and Foreign Policy: The Complete Text of a Document Never Intended for Publication. Cambridge, Mass.: 1972.
2. ANDERSON, William C. Bat 21, based on the true story of Lieutenant Colonel Iceal E. Hambleton, USAF. Englewood Cliffs, N.J.: Prentice-Hall, 1980.
3. ARMBRISTER, Trevor. A Matter of Accountability: The True Story of the Pueblo Affair. New York: Coward-McCann, 1970.
4. ASPIN, Les, et al. Foreign Intelligence, Legal and Democratic Controls, Paper presented at a conference held on December 11, 1979 and sponsored by the American Enterprise Institute for Public Policy Research. Washington, D.C.: AEI, 1980.
5. BARRON, John. KGB: The Secret Work of Soviet Secret Agents. Pleasantville, N.Y.: Reader's Digest Press, 1974.
6. BARRON, John. MIG Pilot: The Final Escape of Lt. Belenko. Pleasantville, N.Y.: Reader's Digest Press, 1980.
7. BECKWITH, Col. Charlie A. Delta Force. New York: Harcourt Brace Jovanovich, 1983.
8. BLACKSTOCK, Paul W., and Frank L. Schaf, Jr. Intelligence, Espionage, Counterespionage, and Covert Operations: A Guide to Information Sources. Detroit: Gale Research Co., 1978.
9. BLUMBERG, Stanley A., and Gwinn Owens. The Survival Factor: Israeli Intelligence from World War I to the Present. New York: Putnam, 1981.
10. BROWN, Anthony Cave. Bodyguard of Lies. New York: Harper & Row, 1975.
11. BURANELLI, Vincent, and Nan Buranelli. Spy/Counterspy: An Encyclopedia of Espionage. New York: McGraw-Hill, 1982.
12. CALVOCORESSI, Peter. Top Secret Ultra. New York: Pantheon Books, 1980.
13. CASTRO HIDALGO, Orlando. Spy for Fidel. Miami, Fla.: F. A. Seeman, 1971.
14. CENTRAL INTELLIGENCE AGENCY/MATHTECH, INC. Deception Maxims: Fact and Folklore. Washington, D.C.: CIA, Office of Research and Development, January 1980.
15. CLARK, Ronald William. The Man Who Broke Purple: The Life of the World's Greatest Cryptologist, Colonel William F. Freidman (1st American ed.). Boston: Little, Brown, 1977.
16. CLINE, Marjorie W., ed. Scholar's Guide to Intelligence Literature: Bibliography of the Russell J. Bowen Collection in the Joseph Mark Lauinger Memorial Library, Georgetown University. Frederick, Md.: National Intelligence Study Center, University Publications of America, 1983.
17. CLINE, Ray S. Secrets, Spies, and Scholars: Blueprint of the Essential CIA. Washington, D.C.: Acropolis Books, 1976.
18. COLBY, William Egan, and Peter Forbath. Honorable Men: My Life in the CIA. New York: Simon & Schuster, 1978.
19. CONSTANTINIDES, George C. Intelligence and Espionage: An Analytical Bibliography. Boulder, Colo.: Westview Press, 1983.
20. CORSON, William R. The Armies of Ignorance: The Rise of the American Intelligence Empire. New York: Dial Press/J. Wade, 1977.

376

21. COX, Arthur M. The Myths of National Security: The Peril of Secret Government. Boston: Beacon Press, 1975.

22. CRUICKSHANK, Charles C. The Fourth Arm: Psychological Warfare 1938-1945. London: Davis-Poynter, 1977.

23. DABRINGHAUS, Erhard. Klaus Barbie—The Shocking Story of How the U.S. Used This Nazi War Criminal as an Intelligence Agent: A First-Hand Account. Washington, D.C.: Acropolis Books, 1984.

24. DEACON, Richard. The Israeli Secret Service. London: Hamilton, 1977.

25. DEACON, Richard. Kempei Tai: A History of the Japanese Secret Service (1st American ed.). New York: Beaufort Books, 1983.

26. DEFENSE INTELLIGENCE COLLEGE. Bibliography of Intelligence Literature: A Critical and Annotated Bibliography of Open-Source Intelligence Literature (8th ed.). Washington, D.C.: Defense Intelligence College, 1985.

27. DELMER, Sefton. Black Boomerang: An Autobiography, Volume Two. London: Secker & Warburg, 1962.

28. DENGLER, Dieter. Escape from Laos. New York: Zebra Books, 1979.

29. DE SILVA, Peer. Sub Rosa: The CIA and the Uses of Intelligence. New York: Times Books, 1978.

30. DEVORE, Ronald M. Spies and All That: Intelligence Agencies and Operations—A Bibliography. Los Angeles: California State University, Center for the Study of Armament and Disarmament, 1977.

31. DONNER, Frank J. The Age of Surveillance: The Aims and Methods of America's Political Intelligence System. New York: Knopf (distributed by Random House), 1980.

32. DULLES, Allen W. The Craft of Intelligence. New York: Harper & Row, 1963.

33. DVORNIK, Francis. Origins of Intelligence Services: The Ancient Near East, Persia, Greece, Rome, Byzantium, the Arab Muslim Empires, the Mongul Empire, China, Muscovy. New Brunswick, N.J.: Rutgers University Press, 1974.

34. ENNES, James. Assault on the Liberty: The True Story of the Israeli Attack on an American Intelligence Ship. New York: Random House, 1979.

35. FORD, Corey. A Peculiar Service. Boston: Little, Brown, 1965.

36. GARLINSKI, Josef. The Swiss Corridor: Espionage Networks in Switzerland during World War II. London: J. M. Dent & Sons, 1981.

37. GODSON, Roy, ed. Intelligence Requirements for the 1980's: Analysis and Estimates. Washington, D.C.: National Strategy Information Center (New Brunswick, N.J.), distributed by Transaction Books, 1980.

38. GODSON, Roy, ed. Intelligence Requirements for the 1980's: Clandestine Collection. Washington, D.C.: National Strategy Information Center (New Brunswick, N.J.), distributed by Transaction Books, 1982.

39. GODSON, Roy, ed. Intelligence Requirements for the 1980's: Counterintelligence. Washington, D.C.: National Strategy Information Center (New Brunswick, N.J.), distributed by Transaction Books, 1980.

40. GODSON, Roy, ed. Intelligence Requirements for the 1980's:

Covert Action. Washington, D.C.: National Strategy Information Center (New Brunswick, N.J.), distributed by Transaction Books, 1981.

41. GODSON, Roy, ed. Intelligence Requirements for the 1980's: Elements of Intelligence. rev. ed., Washington, D.C.: National Strategy Information Center (New Brunswick, N.J.), distributed by Transaction Books, 1983.

42. GOULDEN, Joseph C., with Alexander W. Raffio. The Death Merchant: The Rise and Fall of Edwin P. Wilson. New York: Simon & Schuster, 1984.

43. GUEVARA, Che. Guerrilla Warfare (authorized translation). Translated from the Spanish by J. P. Morray, with prefatory note by I. F. Stone. New York: Vintage Books, 1969.

44. GUNSTON, Bill. An Illustrated Guide to Spy Planes and Electronic Warfare Aircraft. New York: Arco Publishing, 1983.

45. HALPERIN, Morton H., et al. The Lawless State: The Crimes of the U.S. Intelligence Agencies. New York: Penquin Books, 1976.

46. HAREL, Isser. The House on Garibaldi Street: The First Full Account of the Capture of Adolf Eichmann. told by the former head of Israel's Secret Service. New York: Viking Press, 1975.

47. HARRIS, William R. Intelligence and National Security: A Bibliography with Selected Annotations. Cambridge, Mass.: Harvard University, Center for International Affairs, 1968.

48. HARTCUP, Guy. Camouflage: A History of Concealment and Deception in War. Newton Abbot, England: David & Charles, 1979.

49. HASWELL, Jock. Spies and Spymasters: A Concise History of Intelligence. London: Thames and Hudson, 1977.

50. HERBERT, Anthony B. The Soldier's Handbook: A Manual for Survival. Englewood. Colo.: Cloverleaf Books, 1979.

51. HOWARTH, Patrick. Undercover: The Men and Women of the Special Operations Executive. London/Boston: Routledge & Kegan Paul, 1980.

52. HOWE, Ellic. The Black Game: British Subversive Operations Against the Germans During the Second World War. London: Michael Joseph, 1982.

53. HUNT, Howard. Give Us This Day. New Rochelle, N.Y: Arlington House, 1973.

54. HUTTON, Clayton. Official Secret: The Remarkable Story of Escape Aids, Their Invention, Production, and the Sequel. New York: Crown Publishers, 1961.

55. JONAS, George. Vengeance: The True Story of an Israeli Counter-Terrorist Team. New York: Simon & Schuster, 1984.

56. JONES, Reginald Victor. The Wizard War: British Scientific Intelligence, 1939-1945. New York: Coward-McCann, 1978.

57. KAHN, David. The Codebreakers: The Story of Secret Writing. New York: Macmillan, 1967.

58. KARAS, Thomas. The New High Ground: Systems and Weapons of Space Age War. New York: Simon & Schuster, 1983.

59. KENNEDY, William V. Intelligence Warfare: Today's Advanced Technology Conflict. New York: Crescent Books, distributed by Crown Books, 1983.

60. KIRKPATRICK, Lyman B. The U.S. Intelligence Community: Foreign Policy and Domestic Activities. New York: Hill and Wang, 1973.

378

61. KLASS, Philip J. Secret Sentries in Space. New York: Random House, 1971.

62. KOOP, Theodore F. Weapon of Silence. Chicago: University of Chicago Press, 1946.

63. LASKA, Vera, ed. Women in the Resistance and in the Holocaust: The Voices of Eyewitnesses, with a foreword by Simon Wiesenthal. Westport, Conn.: Greenwood Press, 1983.

64. LEARY, William M. Perilous Missions: Civil Air Transport and CIA Covert Operations in Asia. University, Ala.: University of Alabama Press, 1984.

65. LE CARON, Henri. Twenty-five Years in the Secret Service: The Recollections of a Spy. London: William Heinemann, 1982.

66. LEWIN, Ronald. Ultra Goes to War: The First Account of World War II's Greatest Secret Based on Official Documents. New York: McGraw-Hill, 1978.

67. LEWIS, David. Sexpionage: The Exploitation of Sex by Soviet Intelligence. New York: Harcourt Brace Jovanovich, 1976.

68. LIBRARY OF CONGRESS, CONGRESSIONAL RESEARCH SERVICE. Soviet Intelligence and Security Services: A Selected Bibliography of Soviet Publications, with Some Additional Titles from Other Sources. Washington, D.C.: Government Printing Office, 1972 and 1975.

69. LORAIN, Pierre. Clandestine Operations: The Arms and Techniques of the Resistance, 1941-1944 (English adaptation by David Kahn). New York: Macmillan, 1983.

70. LOTZ, Wolfgang. The Champagne Spy: Israel's Master Spy Tells His Story. New York: St. Martin's Press, 1972.

71. LOTZ, Wolfgang. A Handbook for Spies. New York: Harper & Row, 1980.

72. LOVELL, Stanley P. Of Spies and Stratagems. Englewood Cliffs, N.J.: Prentice-Hall, 1963.

73. LUNG, Col. Hoang Ngoc. Intelligence. Washington, D.C.: U.S. Army Center of Military History, 1982.

74. MACDONALD, Elizabeth P. Undercover Girl. New York: Macmillan, 1947.

75. MARCHETTI, Victor, and John D. Marks. The CIA and the Cult of Intelligence, introduction by Melvin L. Wulf. New York: Knopf, 1974.

76. MARKS, John D. The Search for the "Manchurian Candidate": The CIA and Mind Control. New York: Times Books, 1979.

77. MARSHALL, Bruce. The White Rabbit, from the story told to Bruce Marshall by F. F. E. Yeo-Thomas. Boston: Houghton Mifflin, 1953.

78. MASHBIR, Sidney Forrester. I Was an American Spy. New York: Vantage Press, 1953.

79. MASSON, Madeleine. Christine: A Search for Christine Granville, G.M., O.B.E., Croix de Guerre. London: Hamilton, 1975.

80. MASTERMAN, J. C. The Double-Cross System. New York: Avon Books, 1972.

81. MEYER, Cord. Facing Reality: From World Federalism to the CIA. New York: Harper & Row, 1980.

82. MEYER, Karl Ernest, and Tad Szulc. The Cuban Invasion: The Chronicle of a Disaster. New York: Praeger Publishers, 1962.

83. MONTAGU, Ewen. The Man Who Never Was. Philadelphia: J.

B. Lippincott, 1954.

84. MR. X, with Bruce E. Henderson and C. C. Cyr. Double Eagle: The Autobiography of a Polish Spy Who Defected to the West. Indianapolis: Bobbs-Merrill, 1979.

85. Operation Zapata: The "Ultrasensitive" Report and Testimony of the Board of Inquiry on the Bay of Pigs. Frederick, Md.: Aletheia Books, University Publications of America, 1981.

86. ORLOV, Alexander. Handbook of Intelligence and Guerrilla Warfare. Ann Arbor: University of Michigan Press (1963).

87. PADDOCK, Alfred H., Jr. U.S. Army Special Warfare—Its Origins: Psychological and Unconventional Warfare, 1941-1952. Washington, D.C.: Fort Lesley J. McNair, National Defense University Press, 1982.

88. PAINE, Lauran. German Military Intelligence in World War II: The Abwehr. New York: Stein and Day, 1984.

89. PAUL, Doris A. The Navajo Code Talkers. Philadelphia: Dorrance & Co., 1973.

90. PERSICO, Joseph E. Piercing the Reich: The Penetration of Nazi Germany by American Secret Agents During World War II. New York: Viking Press, 1979.

91. PHILBY, Kim. My Silent War, with an introduction by Graham Greene. New York: Grove Press, distributed by Dell, 1968.

92. PORETSKY, Elizabeth K. Our Own People: A Memoir of "Ignace Reiss" and His Friends. Ann Arbor: University of Michigan Press, 1970.

93. POWERS, Francis Gary, with Curt Gentry. Operation OVERFLIGHT: The U-2 Spy Pilot Tells His Story for the First Time. New York: Holt, Rinehart & Winston, 1970.

94. PRANGE, Bordon W. Target Tokyo: The Story of the Sorge Spy Ring. New York: McGraw-Hill, 1984.

95. PRINCE, Alfred. Instruments of Darkness. London: William Kimber, 1967.

96. RA'ANAN, Uri, and Robert L. Pfaltzgraff, eds. International Security Dimensions of Space. Hamden, Conn.: Shoe String Press, published as an Archon Book, 1984.

97. RANSOM, Harry Howe. The Intelligence Establishment (rev. and enl. ed.). Cambridge, Mass.: Harvard University Press, 1970.

98. ROBERTSON, Eric. The Japanese File: Japanese Penetration in Southeast Asia. Hong Kong: Heinemann Asia, 1979.

99. ROSITZKE, Harry. The CIA's Secret Operations: Espionage, Counterespionage and Covert Action. Pleasantville, N.Y.: Reader's Digest Press, 1977.

100. ROSITZKE, Harry. The KGB: The Eyes of Russia. Garden City, N.Y.: Doubleday, 1981.

101. The ROTE Kapelle: The CIA's History of Soviet Intelligence and Espionage Networks in Western Europe, 1936-1945. Washington, D.C.: University Publications of America, 1979.

102. ROWAN, Richard W. The Story of the Secret Service. N.Y.: Literary Guild of America, 1937. [Also published as Secret Service: Thirty Three Centuries of Espionage. London: Kimber, 1969.]

103. SAWATSKY, John. Men in the Shadows: The RCMP Security Service. Garden City, N.Y.: Doubleday, 1980.

104. SCHEMMER, Benjamin F. The Raid. New York: Harper & Row, 1976.

105. SETH, Ronald. Encyclopedia of Espionage. London: New English Library, 1972.

106. SHACKLEY, Theodore. The Third Option: An American View of Counterinsurgency Operations. New York: McGraw-Hill, 1981.

107. SHORT, K. R. M., ed., Film and Radio Propaganda in World War II. Knoxville, Tenn.: University of Tennessee Press, 1983.

108. SLATER, Leonard. The Pledge. New York: Simon & Schuster, 1970.

109. SMITH, Bradley F. The Shadow Warriors: OSS and the Origins of the CIA. New York: Basic Books, 1983.

110. SMITH, Myron J. The Secret Wars: A Guide to Sources in English, with an introduction by Lyman B. Kirkpatrick, Jr. Santa Barbara, Calif.: ABC-Clio, 1980-1981.

111. SNEPP, Frank. Decent Interval: An Insider's Account of Saigon's Indecent End. New York: Random House, 1977.

112. STARR, Chester C. Political Intelligence in Classical Greece. Leiden, Holland: E. J. Brill, 1974.

113. STEAD, Philip John. Second Bureau. London: Evans Bros., 1959.

114. STERN, Philip Van Doren. Secret Missions of the Civil War: Firsthand Accounts by Men and Women Who Risked Their Lives in Underground Activities for the North and the South, Woven into Continuous Narrative. Chicago: Rand McNally, 1959.

115. STEVEN, Stewart. The Spymasters of Israel. New York: Macmillan, 1980.

116. STEVENSON, William. A Man Called Intrepid: The Secret War. New York: Harcourt Brace Jovanovich, 1976.

117. SUGNET, Christopher L., and John T. Hickey, with Robert Crispino. Vietnam War Bibliography: Selected from Cornell University's Echols Collection. Lexington, Mass.: Lexington Books, 1983.

118. SUN-TZU. The Art of War. Translated and with an introduction by Samuel B. Griffith, and with a foreword by B. H. Liddel Hart. London/New York: Oxford University Press, 1971 (1977 printing).

119. THEOHARIS, Athan G. Spying on Americans: Political Surveillance from Hoover to the Huston Plan. Philadelphia: Temple University Press, 1978.

120. THOMPSON, James Westfall, and Saul K. Padover. Secret Diplomacy—Espionage and Cryptography, 1500-1815. New York: Ungar, 1965.

121. TINNIN, David B. The Hit Team. Boston: Little, Brown, 1976.

122. TREPPER, Leopold. The Great Game: Memoirs of the Spy Hitler Couldn't Silence. New York: McGraw-Hill, 1977.

123. TROY, Thomas F. Donovan and the CIA: A History of the Establishment of the Central Intelligence Agency. Frederick, Md.: Aletheia Books, 1981 (First published in a limited edition in 1975).

124. TUCHMAN, Barbara W. The Zimmerman Telegram. New York: Viking, 1958.

125. VARNER, Roy D, and Wayne Collier. A Matter of Risk: The Incredible Inside Story of the CIA's Hughes Glomar Explorer Mission to Raise a Russian Submarine. New York: Random House, 1978.

126. WALTERS, Vernon A. Silent Missions. Garden City, N.Y.:

Doubleday, 1978.

127. WAY, Peter. Codes and Ciphers. London: Aldus Books, 1977.

128. WHALEY, Barton. Codeword BARBAROSSA. Cambridge, Mass.: MIT Press, 1973.

129. WILLIS, George. Surreptitious Entry. New York: D. Appleton-Century, 1946.

130. WINTERBOTHAM, Frederick William. The Ultra Secret. London: Weidenfeld and Nicolson, 1974.

131. WISE, David. The American Police State: The Government Against the People. New York: Random House, 1976.

132. WISE, David, and Thomas B. Ross. The Espionage Establishment. New York: Random House, 1967.

133. WOHLSTETTER, Roberta. Pearl Harbor: Warning and Decision. Stanford: Stanford University Press, 1967.

134. WOYTAK, Richard A. On the Border of War and Peace: Polish Intelligence and Diplomacy in 1937-1939 and the Origins of the Ultra Secret. Boulder, Colo.: East European Quarterly (New York) distributed by Columbia University Press, 1979.

135. YARDLEY, Herbert O. The American Black Chamber. London: Faber & Faber, 1931.

Glossary

Abwehr - Intelligence and counterintelligence service of the German General Staff prior to and during most of World War II.

ACDA - Arms Control and Disarmament Agency.

BNE - Board of National Estimates.

CI - counterintelligence.

CIA - Central Intelligence Agency. Also commonly called "the Agency" or "the Company."

CJB - Congressional Justification Book.

COMINT - COMmunications INTelligence. Technical and intelligence information derrived from the intercept of foreign communications signals. See also SIGINT, ELINT.

DCI - Director of Central Intelligence. Created by the National Security Act of 1947, the DCI is also the Director of the Central Intelligence Agency.

DCIA - Deputy Director of the CIA. As the DCI has become more involved with intelligence community activities, he has had a greater role in the daily operations of the CIA.

DDO - Deputy Director for Operations. In this context, a CIA position. Formerly DDP, Deputy Director for Plans.

DIA - Defense Intelligence Agency.

DoD - Department of Defense.

ELINT - ELectronic INTelligence. Technical and intelligence information derrived from the intercept of foreign nonliteral communications. See also COMINT, SIGINT.

EXCOM - EXecutive COMmittee of the National Security Council, formed by President Kennedy during the Cuban Missile Crisis.

FISA - Foreign Intelligence Surveilance Act.

FOIA - Freedom of Information Act.

G-2 - the intelligence division of U.S. Army division and higher staffs. Where these staffs are multiservice, the organization is known as J-2. See also S-2.

GDIP - General Defense Intelligence Program.

GSA - General Services Administration.

HAC - House Appropriations Committee.

HASC - House Armed Services Committee.

HPSCI - House Permanent Select Committee on Intelligence. Permanent successor committee to the Pike Committee.

HRES - House RESolution.

HUMINT -HUMan INTelligence. Intelligence gained from human sources, e.g., defectors, agents, etc.

I&W - Indications and Warning. The branch of intelligence concerned with preventing tactical or strategic surprise.

IC Staff - Intelligence Community Staff.

IRA - intelligence-related activities.

KGB - Komitet Gosudarstvennoye Bezopasnosti, the Committee for State Security. The Soviet secret police. Predecessor organizations were the MGB, the NKGB, the OGPU, the GPU and, immediately after the revolution, the Cheka.

MI5 - the British Security Service.

MI6 - the British Secret Intelligence Service (SIS).

NFIB - National Foreign Intelligence Board. Advises the DCI on the NFIP (see next entry) and NIEs and consists of representatives from the various members of the intelligence community.

NFIP - National Foreign Intelligence Program. The intelligence community budget, overseen by the DCI.

NIE - National Intelligence Estimate. A coordinated document produced by the intelligence community and issued by the DCI with the advice of the NFIB.

NIO - National Intelligence Officer.

NSA - National Security Agency. Produces SIGINT. Also responsible for protecting all government communications.

NTM - National Technical Means. An arms control term referring to the technical means of collecting intelligence to verify arms control agreements.

OKW - Oberkommando der Wehrmacht. German armed forces headquarters during World War II.

ONE - Office of National Estimates. A CIA office that produced NIEs. Abolished in 1973; reconstituted as National Foreign Assessment Center (NFAC) under Turner.

ONI - Office of Naval Intelligence. A World War II organization.

OSI- Office of Special Investigations of the U.S. Air Force.

OSS - Office of Strategic Services. World War II predecessor organization of the CIA.

PFIAB - President's Foreign Intelligence Advisory Board.

PHOTINT - PHOTographic INTelligence.

S-2 - the intelligence division of U.S. Army brigade and battalion-level staffs. See also G-2.

SAS - Special Air Service. A British Army regiment started in World War II, and now used primarily in counter-terrorist and counter-insurgency operations.

SASC - Senate Armed Services Committee.

SD - Sicherheitsdienst. German World War II secret service.

SIGINT - SIGnals INTelligence. A generic term comprising COMINT and ELINT.

SIS - British Secret Intelligence Service. Also known as MI6.

SNIE - Special National Intelligence Estimate. See NIE.

SOE - Special Operations Executive. A British World War II organization charged with controlling various clandestine operations.

SRES - Senate Resolution.

SSCI - Senate Select Committee on Intelligence. Successor permanent organization to the Church Committee.

USIB - United States Intelligence Board. Predecessor organization to NFIB.

ZBB - zero-based budgeting. A budget method introduced by the Carter administration in which every government agency justified its budget from zero (hence the term) every year, as opposed to justifying bugdets as deviations from the previous fiscal year.

About the Editors and Contributors

James D. Austin is currently special assistant to the governor of Texas. He is a political scientist with a strong background in pyschology, and has taught political science and intelligence at the University of Texas at Austin.

David Charters is deputy director of the Center for Conflict Studies at the University of New Brunswick. He received his doctorate in war studies from King's College, University of London. He has taught and published in the field of low-intensity conflict, with emphasis on terrorism, intelligence, and special operations. Dr. Charters is executive editor of the center's journal, Conflict Quarterly, and an editor of the forthcoming The Tangled Web: Deception in East-West Relations.

Donald C. Daniel is an associate professor in the department of national security affairs at the Naval Postgraduate School. He has performed research in the areas of surprise and deception and is coeditor with Katherine Herbig of the book Strategic Military Deception.

R. Joseph DeSutter has a doctorate in international relations from the University of Southern California. His areas of expertise include U.S. national security policy, arms control, verification and compliance policies, and U.S. national space policy. A former associate professor of political science at the U.S. Air Force Academy, he is currently assigned to Headquarters, U.S. Air Force's Arms Control and International Negotiations Division.

William L. Dunn is chief of the SIGINT committee analytic staff of the Intelligence Community Staff. Before coming to the IC Staff, has worked for the Rand Corporation as an economist and lectured at California State College at Los Angeles. From 1983-1984 he attended the Executive Seminar in National and International Affairs at the Department of State.

Morton H. Halperin is director of the Center for National Security Studies. A former assistant secretary of defense, he is also coauthor of The Lawless State: The Crimes of the U.S. Intelligence Agencies.

388

Michael I. Handel has written widely on the subject of intelligence, surprise, diplomacy, and strategy. Among his many works are The Diplomacy of Surprise: Hitler, Nixon, Sadat (Harvard, 1981) and the forthcoming Intelligence and Deception. Educated at the Hebrew University and Harvard University, Dr. Handel is now professor of national security affairs at the U.S. Army War College and editor of a new journal dedicated to the study of intelligence, Intelligence and National Security.

Glenn P. Hastedt is an assistant professor of political science at James Madison University. Among his many articles and chapters are "Teaching About Understanding Intelligence Failures," "The Intelligence Community and American Foreign Policy: the Reagan and Carter Administrations," and "Studying the CIA: an Agenda for Research." He is currently writing a textbook on U.S. foreign policy.

Katherine L. Herbig is an adjunct professor at the Naval Postgraduate School, division of National Security Affairs. A historian by training, she has written a number of articles on deception in military strategy and twentieth century military history. She co-edited Strategic Military Deception with Donald Daniel, and is currently writing Strategic Deception in the Pacific, 1942-1945.

Hans Heymann is a visiting professor at the Defense Intelligence College. An economist by training, he has had wide experience with political economy both in government and for the Rand Corporation. From 1975 to 1983 he served the CIA as the National Intelligence Officer for Political Economy and NIO at Large. After leaving the DIC, he will be a senior research fellow with the Hudson Institute.

Roger Hilsman has a long and distinguished career in government service, beginning with World War II service with Merrill's Marauders and the OSS. During the Kennedy and Johnson administrations, he worked in the Department of State as director of the Bureau of Intelligence and Research (INR) and assistant secretary of state for far eastern affairs. Among his many books are Strategic Intelligence and National Decisions (1956) and The Politics of Governing America (1985). Since leaving government service he has been a professor of government at Columbia University.

Robert Jervis is a professor of political science at Columbia University. He is on the editorial boards of several well-known journals, including the Journal of Strategic Studies and the American Political Science Quarterly. Among his many publications is Perception and Misperception in International Politics.

Loch K. Johnson is an associate professor of political science at the University of Georgia. He was an investigator for the Senate Select Committee on Intelligence Activities in 1975-1976, and a staff director for the house intelligence committee in the following years. Among his many publications dealing with intelligence are "Seven Sins of Strategic Intelligence," "Legislative Reform of Intelligence Policy," and the forthcoming book, A Season of Inquiry: The Senate Intelligence Investigation.

James M. Keagle has a doctorate from Princeton University. He has published articles on U.S. foreign policy and the Eisenhower administration. He is currently an associate professor of political science at the U.S. Air Force Academy and honorarium associate professor, Graduate School of Public Affairs, University of Colorado, Colorado Springs.

Paul Gordon Lauren is a professor of history at the University of Montana, specializing in modern diplomacy and international relations. He has travelled extensively throughout western Europe, performing extensive research in the foreign ministries and archives of Britain, France, and Germany. Among his many publications are Diplomacy: New Approaches in History, Theory, and Policy and Diplomats and Bureaucrats: The First Institutional Responses to Twentieth-Century Diplomacy in France and Germany.

Mark M. Lowenthal is a specialist in national defense with the Congressional Research Service of the Library of Congress, where he is head of the Defense Policy and Arms Control Section. Dr. Lowenthal has a doctorate in history from Harvard University. He is the author of numerous studies and articles on intelligence, arms control verification, defense organization, national security structure, and U.S. planning for World War II. His is also author of a novel, Crispan Magicker.

Alfred C. Maurer is a career signals intelligence officer. His most recent assignment was as assistant professor of political science at the U.S. Air Force Academy where he taught political theory, quantitative methods, and intelligence and politics.

Robert La Liberté Migneault is associate dean of library services at the University of New Mexico and former assistant director of the U.S. Air Force Academy library. Presently he is engaged in research on mercenaries and hopes to produce a book from that effort.

George Pickett currently conducts research on intelligence matters for the Mitre Corporation. From 1976 to 1980, he was a budget and program analyst for the senate intelligence committee. He also worked on net assessment programs for the National Security Council staff and the office of the secretary of defense.

John Prados is a noted writer and researcher in the fields of intelligence and U.S. foreign policy. He is the author of The Soviet Estimate and The Sky Would Fall: Operation Vulture: the U.S. Bombing Mission in Indochina.

Harry Howe Ransom is a professor of political science at Vanderbildt University. Previously he taught at Vassar College, Princeton, Michigan State University, and Harvard, where he was a principal organizer of the Defense Studies Program. He is the author of several books, including The Intelligence Establishment and Can American Democracy Survive Cold War?

Herbert Scoville, Jr., is a former deputy director for research of the CIA and currently president of the Arms Control Association. He was also the assistant director for science and technology with the U.S. Arms Control and Disarmament Agency. He has written widely on the subject of strategic arms, including the recent MX: Prescription for Disaster.

Stafford T. Thomas is an assistant professor of political science at California State University, Chico. He has taught undergraduate courses on intelligence since 1973 and has authored several works on the subject, including The U.S. Intelligence Community. His current research interest is an assessment of intelligence as a field of scholarly inquiry.

Marion D. Tunstall is an assistant professor of political science at the U.S. Air Force Academy. His academic specialties are american government and Latin American politics. Before coming to the Academy, he served as Central American analyst for the U.S. Southern Command. As an analyst and participant in U.S. policymaking for the region, he obtained a unique perspective on the intelligence/policy interface.

Index